The Scattered Court

The Scattered Court

Hindustani Music in Colonial Bengal

RICHARD DAVID WILLIAMS

The University of Chicago Press
Chicago and London

PUBLICATION OF THIS BOOK HAS BEEN AIDED BY A GRANT FROM THE BEVINGTON FUND.

The University of Chicago Press, Chicago 60637
The University of Chicago Press, Ltd., London

Published 2023
Printed in the United States of America

32 31 30 29 28 27 26 25 24 23   1 2 3 4 5

ISBN-13: 978-0-226-82543-4 (cloth)
ISBN-13: 978-0-226-82545-8 (paper)
ISBN-13: 978-0-226-82544-1 (e-book)
DOI: https://doi.org/10.7208/chicago/9780226825441.001.0001

Library of Congress Cataloging-in-Publication Data

Names: Williams, Richard David, author.
Title: The scattered court : Hindustani music in colonial Bengal / Richard David Williams.
Other titles: Chicago studies in ethnomusicology.
Description: Chicago : The University of Chicago Press, 2023. | Series: Chicago studies in ethnomusicology | Includes bibliographical references and index.
Identifiers: LCCN 2022032914 | ISBN 9780226825434 (cloth) | ISBN 9780226825458 (paperback) | ISBN 9780226825441 (ebook)
Subjects: LCSH: Hindustani music—India—Bengal—19th century—History and criticism. | Hindustani music—Social aspects—India—Bengal—History—19th century. | Oudh (Princely State)—Court and courtiers—History—19th century. | Kolkata (India)—Court and courtiers—History—19th century. | Wajid ʻAli Shah, King of Oudh, 1822–1887.
Classification: LCC ML338.4 .W55 2023 | DDC 780.954/14—dc23/eng/20220808
LC record available at https://lccn.loc.gov/2022032914

♾ This paper meets the requirements of ANSI/NISO Z39.48-1992 (Permanence of Paper).

Contents

Note on Transliteration

This book uses written sources in several vernacular north Indian languages, particularly Hindi, Urdu, and Bengali. These can be written across three scripts (*devanāgarī*, *nasta'līq*, and *bāṅglā*), each with its own system of transliteration into the Roman alphabet. To keep things relatively simple, I have adopted the following system.

All proper names are presented without diacritics. Place names are a combination of colonial and indigenous spellings (Dacca, Dhaka) following the predominant form in my sources. All other words from Indian languages are italicized and transliterated with diacritical markings, except for those that are widely used in English scholarship, including nawabi (rather than *nawābī*).

For texts that appear in *devanāgarī* or *bāṅglā* scripts I use the conventional International Alphabet of Sanskrit Transliteration (IAST) system, with some minor modifications. Applying this system to Bengali obscures the actual pronunciation of the living language: one word for "music" might be transliterated as *saṅgīt* but pronounced closer to *shongeet*. However, since my sources speak to a shared musicological discourse, it is important to be able to read the conceptual relationships across languages, which a hypothetical reconstruction of pronunciation might hide. For readers who are unfamiliar with Bengali, I would note that the "short" vowel *a* is usually pronounced closer to the English *o*, and the unmarked *sa* is soft, closer to *sho*. For words in *nasta'līq*, I generally follow the conventions used by John T. Platts.[1]

Introduction

> The Gomtee, the sad daughter of the sacred Ganges, glides meaninglessly by, between the open ruins of Dil Khoosh and the plastered ruins of Chutter Manzil, whose walls now echo to the music of Yankee Doodle and to billiard-cannons and hiccups, as they, before the Mutiny, echoed to the music of tinkling feet of dancing-girls and the notes of the Seetar and the hubbling-bubbling kisses of the hookah.
>
> —SHETTJEE SAHIBJEE, *Vanity Fair*, 1882[1]

> The kingdom is drowned in the salt of the harem:
> His Majesty is going to London.
> In every palace, his ladies are weeping:
> Come to the alley, in the alley the cobbles weep.
>
> —"LUCKNOW *ṬHUMRĪ*" LYRIC, 1870[2]

At first glance, these two very different kinds of text appear to tell the same story. Following the East India Company's annexation of the kingdom of Awadh in 1856, and the Uprising that rippled across the north of the subcontinent in 1857, the British Crown took possession of India, and Indian society and culture were dramatically transformed. Sahibjee's journalistic account, written in English, invited his readers to return to the desecrated city of Lucknow, the former capital of the nawabs of Awadh. There, Sahibjee ruminated nostalgically upon this rupture, and strained to hear some echo of the music so closely associated with the lost court. Similarly, the Hindustani song lyric, marked specifically as a "Lucknow *ṭhumrī*," recalled the very moment of that loss of sovereignty; as the last nawab, Wajid Ali Shah (1822–87), contemplated pleading his case in London, the streets of his city were filled with wailing. In both passages the moment of rupture and loss was captured through sound.

The essay and the song could also be read as marking a crucial turning point in the historical narrative of Hindustani music. In the wake of the weeping and the devastation of palaces described in these texts, the late nineteenth century is commonly understood as an era when musical society broke with its past and began the process of becoming "modern." In north India, with the declining power of aristocratic patrons, music entered a different domain, dominated by a new elite, consisting first and foremost of upper-middle-class Hindu men whose families had prospered in the colonial economy. This transition in patronage cascaded through the performing arts industries and had serious consequences for hereditary professionals, especially Muslim master musicians (*ustāds*) and female dancers and singers.[3] Attitudes to music and musicians changed, and, at the level of intellectuals and musicologists, music became a site of contested cultural values between the colonizer and the colonized, Orientalists and nationalists. New histories of music, systems of notation, formal societies, and approaches to patronage saw the performing arts enter a modern arena of reform and "public" concern.[4]

Nonetheless, these new directions only represent one rather thin layer of the intellectual and social history of Hindustani music in the nineteenth century. The emphasis on middle-class modernity and reform is partly a product of the archive: print provided a platform for colonial elites involved with the "public" life of music to represent their culture self-reflexively, making their own concerns and perspectives appear normative.[5] Because previous scholarship has privileged these authors—who wrote much of the time in English, and often for European readers—a vast trove of musical sources in vernacular languages has been ignored. These unexplored texts suggest a more complex picture of musical culture, and demand that we reconsider how smooth the transition of music from aristocratic patronage into the "modernity" of the colonial public sphere really was.

Histories of colonialism have recently begun to reconsider the transition of local knowledge systems to modernity as multiple and varied. In the history of South Asian Islam, for example, Francis Robinson has stressed how the modern can take many forms, by examining the diversity of engagements with tradition and technology employed by different sets of actors in colonial north India.[6] Similar patterns emerge among Hindi and Sanskrit intellectuals in the nineteenth century, who could deploy the same modern tools for a variety of purposes, from challenging the status quo to upholding long-standing principles.[7] Likewise, when we examine nineteenth-century musical literature, we can trace reformers, modernizers, and neotraditionalists competing in the marketplace alongside other musicologists or songbook writers. Some of these were less radical in their rhetoric, though similarly "modern" in their deployment of print technology and fresh approaches to musical transmission. Reading these different texts together enables a new sense of a social and literary landscape, shaped both by its immediate colonial context and by older vernacular conventions regarding how to represent the musical arts on paper. According to the received narrative, 1857 served as a singular moment of rupture, positioning the "nonmodern" aristocratic *jajmānī-ustād* patronage system as a discarded past. However, alternative sources in Bengali and Urdu used other tropes to tell different stories about the fate of late Mughal music under colonial rule.

In light of these alternative accounts, the opening texts read quite differently. Sahibjee's description of ruined Lucknow belied the fact that Wajid Ali Shah continued to patronize dancing girls, *sitārs*, and so-called "hookah" culture in his exiled court in Calcutta, which flourished for another thirty years after he was deposed (1856–87). Although, when we think of music in the colonial capital we are often drawn to the activities of new Anglophone elites (often referred to as *bhadralok*, the new Bengali gentry), in fact the "past" aristocratic world of the nawab deeply penetrated the musical life of the city, blurring the boundaries between old and new cultures of listening and patronage, and informing the character of what has been thought of as the colonial "modern." The song lyric above was composed in Urdu, but then was published at least twice in Bengali script, and by 1905 had been attributed to Wajid Ali Shah himself.[8] The inclusion of a nawabi lament for 1856 in the publishing enterprises of elite Bengalis does not indicate a sharp rupture in musical culture as much as a more complicated transition.

The Scattered Court presents a new social history of how Hindustani art music and dance responded to the political transition from the Mughal empire to British colonialism. I examine musical culture through a diverse and multilingual archive, primarily using sources in Urdu, Bengali, and Hindi that nuance the complexities of this period, which have so often been framed in terms of cultural rupture and displacement, or economically as "a passage from an archaic, constraining patronage system into the realm of the market."[9] The central chapters focus on the two courts of Wajid Ali Shah: the first in Lucknow, and then his court-in-exile at Matiyaburj, erected in a southern suburb of Calcutta. The book charts the movement of musicians and dancers between these courts, as well as the transregional circulation of intellectual traditions and musical genres, and demonstrates the importance of the exile period for the rise of Calcutta as a celebrated center of Hindustani art music. Establishing the connections between Lucknow in Hindustan and Calcutta in Bengal challenges the notion of distant, regional performance cultures, and underlines the importance of aesthetics and the performing arts to mobile elite societies. Since Lucknow is associated with late Mughal or nawabi society, and Calcutta with colonial modernity, examining the relationship between the two cities sheds light on forms of continuity and transition over the nineteenth century, as artists and their patrons navigated political ruptures and social transformations.

As a case study of continuity and exchange, this book provides an analysis of the court-in-exile of Wajid Ali Shah in Matiyaburj in south Calcutta. The thirty years of his exile were a transformative chapter in the history of Bengali-Hindustani musical connections. My analysis has two broader implications.

First, although in musical circles this court has been remembered as a crucial point of contact between geographical regions and social circles of connoisseurship, the thirty years of exile are little understood, generally appearing as a postscript to more developed studies of Lucknow. The arrival of Wajid Ali Shah gave the culture of Hindustani music that was already present in the British capital a significant impetus.[10] By reconstructing the life of the exiled court at Matiyaburj, it becomes possible to evaluate the nawab's influence on colonial-era musical fashions, and more important, the social interactions between the Awadhi court and Bengali musicians and patrons. These interactions determined the growth of Hindustani music in the colonial capital from 1856 to 1887, paving the way for a new generation of performers, and the central role of the city in commercial recording industries.

Second, by foregrounding the cultural activities of the nawab after 1857, I maintain that we cannot equate the political end of indigenous rule in Awadh with the death of nawabi cultural values and conventions. Most studies of nawabi culture, and of the paradigmatic nawab himself, finish with the Uprising of 1857. Notable exceptions include recent work by Partha Chatterjee, and a meticulous biography by Rosie Llewellyn-Jones.[11] However, neither study explores the cultural connections forged between Wajid Ali and the colonial city. I reexamine the historiography of Awadh throughout this book, since the neglect of the "afterlife" of Lucknow has had damaging consequences for studies of colonial-era culture and society, particularly in the study of its musical life.

The Exiled King and His Scattered Court

Wajid Ali Shah was one of the most colorful and controversial characters of nineteenth-century India. His personality has seeped into popular memory and culture, surfacing in the most imaginative of places: from anecdotes about Lucknow's kebabs to the celebrated films of Satyajit Ray, and more recently as the face of Uttar Pradesh in the sixty-sixth Republic Day parade. He was the last of the nawabs of Awadh (1722–1856), an especially wealthy kingdom in northern India that had gradually devolved from the Mughal Empire. The founder of his dynasty, Sadat Ali Khan Burhan-ul-Mulk (1722–39), an officer from Neshapur in Khorasan, had been appointed subahdar (governor) of the region by the emperor, Muhammad Shah, in 1722. As the structural integrity of the empire began to splinter and break down over the early eighteenth century, Sadat Ali Khan's successors carved out their own autonomous domain, erecting their capitals first in Faizabad (c. 1764–75) and then Lucknow (from 1775). The nawabs formally declared their independence in October

1819, and the East India Company crowned Ghazi al-Din Haidar (1814–27) "king" of Awadh (often spelled in English sources as Oude). Over the late eighteenth and early nineteenth centuries, a variety of Europeans had significant interests in Awadh—ranging from the strategic to the economic and cultural—and, as Rosie Llewellyn-Jones in particular has documented, they cultivated an evolving and mixed relationship with its nawabs and kings.[12] As is well known, the English Company ultimately dethroned Wajid Ali Shah and annexed his kingdom in 1856, after a drawn-out defamation campaign in which, as we will see in chapter 3, ideas about music and dance were strategically weaponized.

In most commentaries on his life and career, Wajid Ali Shah is remembered as a hedonist or a political failure who failed to resist the machinations of the East India Company. These recollections of self-indulgence and weakness are, naturally, largely based on colonial sources, which represented him as an irresponsible ruler in the build-up to annexation and in its aftermath. However, cultural histories tell another story. Wajid Ali is credited with inventing new *rāga*s and developing new genres of song and dance (especially *ṭhumṛī* and Kathak), cultivating a taste for light or "semiclassical" music that has persisted in its popularity to the present day. In circles of musicians and connoisseurs, it is well established that the king's exile to Calcutta established the city's credentials in the arts and was a turning point for classical music across northern India.

The discordance between political histories' emphasis on his humiliation and music histories' celebration of his influence makes Wajid Ali Shah an especially instructive case for rethinking cultural history under colonialism. His exile from Lucknow and thirty years in Calcutta brought two worlds—one nawabi and Hindustani, the other colonial and Bengali—into conversation. Reconstructing the musical life of the exiled court indicates how these categories were constructed by writers and artists invested in ideals of place. Following the Uprising of 1857, Lucknow came to epitomize the ruins of precolonial India, whereas Calcutta was both celebrated as the cosmopolitan seat of empire and burdened by the weight of colonized consciousness. As Calcutta's Bengali intellectuals grappled with this consciousness, the culture of the city was increasingly celebrated in highly localized, regional terms; the multilingual, multicultural flows from outside Bengal that pooled there have received far less attention. Wajid Ali's exiled court was one such pool which irrigated the new cultural forms that clustered together in the city, and distilled Mughal sensibilities into modern social mores.

In both Lucknow and Calcutta, Wajid Ali cultivated highly dramatized courts that blurred the boundaries between fantasy and reality. Music was foundational to the nawab's conception of a magical courtly paradise, one in which he was the enchanting king, surrounded by angelic fairies (*parīs*), and was able to manipulate the emotions and desires of his courtiers. This self-fashioning as the overlord of the fairies was at the heart of a clash of cultures. The British ridiculed Wajid Ali Shah and viewed his fascination with magic and music as proof of his immaturity, delusion, and debauchery. Yet the nawab understood his enchanted court as ideologically sound, heir to an Indo-Persian cultural logic, and in the tradition of the ideal magical king, Solomon. This book examines how these two perspectives came into conflict, and how the world outside the court grappled with that tension.

While Wajid Ali's distinctive personality and innovative approach to music and dance sits at the center of this study, it is also vital to look beyond his own works and court. This book examines the significant contributions of his wives, the musicians who passed in and out of his service, and other patrons who came into his orbit, in order to ground his influence in a more complicated landscape. In particular, my focus on the satellite household of his senior wife, Khas Mahal, in chapter 5 considers courts as societies rather than monolithic entities tied to a specific location or the larger-than-life personality of a male monarch. By tracing the paths of the scattered musicians from Lucknow into Calcutta and rural Bengal, it becomes possible to reflect on how the conventions of precolonial courtly society were extended into new, self-consciously "modern" settings.

Music in History

Within South Asian history, we are increasingly conscious of the need to historicize and nuance the transitions between precolonial and colonial worldviews, and to consider how ideas and social practices changed by first critically examining their longer histories. This book thus begins with developments in the eighteenth century, long before Wajid Ali Shah's exile to Calcutta, in order to chart a landscape of circulating musicians and artistic exchanges between northern India and Bengal, before British colonialism took root. The first chapter reconstructs a longer social history of court music in Bengal, which challenges our modern sense of regional musical cultures and problematizes our notion of the exalted court musician. This excavation of the late Mughal musical hinterland provides a context for Wajid Ali Shah's own movements in a colonial environment and offers a critical framework for future historians of music and empire.

The core practices of what we today call Hindustani music have been actively patronized and performed since at least the sixteenth century across the north and central regions of the subcontinent, from Karachi to Dhaka and from Kathmandu to Hyderabad, mediated through locally inflected assemblages of performing artists, lyricists, theoreticians, patrons, poets, painters, scribes, printers, and moralists, as well as material culture including instruments, texts in multiple languages, and images.[13] Each assemblage was an idiosyncratic interaction between a locality and a cosmopolitan, panregional elite canon, considered to be associated in some way with the region of Hindustan and the aristocratic courts of the Mughal era. Variously described in sources across the languages of India as "exalted" (*a'lā*, *uccāṅga*), a knowledge, science or art (*'ilm*, *hunar*, *śāstra*), or *rāga*-based, this elite music was associated with written theoretical treatises (in Sanskrit, Persian, and north Indian vernaculars); recognized sets of celebrated personalities (the most famous being Tansen); and court cultures in the core territories of Mughal Hindustan, especially Delhi and Lucknow. This music was cosmopolitan and embedded in an idealized mental geography.

These multiple experiences and understandings of elite music have been obscured in the postcolonial era by a normative historiography based on a simplistic chronology of Hindu roots, Muslim mediation, and nationalist revitalization.[14] Charles Capwell has cautioned against teleological histories of music that attempt to itemize the steps toward an inevitable culmination in today's Hindustani "classical."[15] Over the last few decades, revisionist histories have complicated and critiqued such narratives, but these studies often focus on similar groups of reformers and their followers and generally do not go back earlier than the 1870s. The Bengali musicologist Sourindro Mohan Tagore (1840–1914) has gained much exposure in recent studies as a major architect of music's modernity.[16] Yet in his earlier studies of Tagore, Capwell insightfully posited him as a "marginal man," noting that his interventions between music and politics ultimately did not come to dominate the performing arts, and were only briefly influential in their own time. Following Capwell, however, several scholars continued to discuss Tagore, his associates, and similar thinkers as a hegemonic middle-class body of intellectuals and educationists who dominated the prehistory of the "classical" and advocated the reform or revival of music in the interests of public culture.[17] The nationalist dimensions to the middle-class project were particularly underlined by Gerry Farrell, who selected Tagore as a case study precisely because he spoke so directly to the relationship between the West and Indian music.[18]

However, Farrell himself also acknowledged the limited impact of the middle-class public in this period: "in the meantime, the *actual* performance of Indian music was developing and adapting as it would throughout the century, largely impervious to such debates."[19] This observation is especially significant in light of Janaki Bakhle's account of the twentieth-century construction of "classical" music, which is substantially a critique of discourses developed in western India by the Marathi bourgeoisie. Bakhle's narrative suggests a transition in musical leadership from Muslim *ustād*s in the eighteenth century to Maharastrian musicologists by the late nineteenth. However, she also admits in the conclusion to her important monograph that the (modified) culture of the *ustād* continues unabated to this day, still providing the most prestigious education in music, rather than the "modern" academies of Bhatkhande and Paluskar.[20] Bakhle and Farrell's remarking on this frequently noted paradox suggests that we must not take the fin-de-siècle reformers, educationists, and nationalists at their own estimation, but relativize their interests against a larger canvas. Alongside the middle-class sphere that was explicitly communicated and projected as "public," the *ustādī* culture of musical transmission and knowledge continued. The courtly realm of music was not as devastated as the common historiography might suggest; quite apart from anything else, many Bengali reformers trained under *ustād*s from Hindustan and patronized them in their own salons. This *ustādī* culture becomes accessible if we extend Capwell's project further and more deeply into vernacular sources that were not immediately interesting to the British, or to those local actors invested in the "public" role of music.

By beginning in the eighteenth century, this book explores the convergence of Persianate and Bengali musical cultures through the interaction between Hindustani and Bengali musicians and patrons, ultimately leading to a crucially influential period of exchange in the second half of the nineteenth century. I stress how this convergence in Calcutta was extremely significant to the course of late Mughal music as it evolved through the colonial context. Rather than foregrounding colonialism, I integrate it into a study of several strands of late Mughal musical culture as I follow their internal developments across northern and eastern India.

With the exception of chapter 3, which focuses on Lucknow, this book is primarily concerned with Hindustani art music when it was conveyed to or cultivated beyond Hindustan, primarily in rural Bengal and Calcutta. This music entailed performance practices and ensembles which were considered distinct from the local music of eastern India. This book asks how these spatial connotations evolved over the nineteenth century, as the imaginative and ideological power of Hindustan changed in Bengali discourse about music. While Kumkum Chatterjee in particular has stressed the connected history between Mughal Bengal and the Indo-Persianate culture of the imperial heartlands up to the eighteenth century, few histories of the colonial period acknowledge the importance of other regions or different vernacular arenas to Bengali society.[21] This study forms a bridge between Chatterjee's "Provincial Mughal" landscape and the Calcutta-centric geography of colonial Bengal. By introducing music into this history of imagined geographies, it is possible to explore the decline of Mughal political power and the concomitant rise of regionalized Bengali authority through the performing arts.

The predominant musical assemblage in this period was the *meḥfil* (also commonly referred to as *majlis* or *jalsa*). As a starting point, this would entail a vocalist or instrumentalist, or a singing dancer, performing with percussive, melodic, and drone accompaniment for a patron and guests. The *rāga*-based song genres typically associated with this assemblage include *dhrupad*, *k̲h̲ayāl*, *ghazal*, *ṭappa*, and *ṭhumrī*, and a body of gestures and footwork that were later reconfigured as Kathak dance.[22] While these forms have all survived—in one guise or another—to the present day, other varieties proved less successful in the long run. Therefore, I have expanded the remit of late Mughal elite performance in this book to include genres that were prominent at the time but have been subsequently ignored by historical studies, including *naql* comic sketches (chapter 4).

The *meḥfil* was a nuanced social space that allowed patrons to negotiate social conventions among themselves (including expressions of companionship and displays of connoisseurship and self-mastery) and in relation to the performing artists.[23] This book considers how music was used in the cultivation of emotion in different settings, including the nawabi court and the *bhadralok* household. The importance of social relationships and embodied comportment in Mughal governance was explored by Rosalind O'Hanlon and brought into the realms of literature and music by Carla Petievich and Katherine Butler Schofield (formerly Brown).[24] Margrit Pernau and Peter Robb have also emphasized the role of emotions in the history of the colonial period,[25] while a parallel project has investigated the senses as objects of intellectual history and cultural study.[26] However, the potential inherent in music for cultivating sensibilities and forging relationships has yet to be extensively explored in the nineteenth-century context. I contend that appreciating this dimension of musical culture has significant wider implications for social and political history, especially given the ferocity of criticisms leveled at musical connoisseurs under colonialism. At the heart of this book, I read Wajid Ali Shah's Urdu writings on music as a guide to nawabi aesthetics in order to present a more nuanced understanding of elite sensibilities. This presents an alternative perspective on a society that to this day is regularly dismissed as "decadent."

Throughout this book, I refer to Hindustani "musicology" and "music treatises." These are convenient terms for works of music theory, history, and instruction understood collectively in Persian and Urdu sources as *'ilm-i mūsīqī* ("science or knowledge of music") and in Sanskrit-derived language cultures as *saṅgīta śāstra* ("canon of music-dance-drama").[27] By the eighteenth century this was a long-established mode of writing, dating in Sanskrit back to the first millennium CE, and in Persian and the vernaculars to the pre-Mughal period.[28] The mainstream of the eighteenth-century tradition, largely in Persian and high vernaculars, displayed an internal logic and conventions that shaped the abstract dimensions of art music for practicing musicians and nonpracticing connoisseur patrons.

The Sanskrit side of this scholarship has been the most documented so far, though more recently there have been a number of studies of the Persian transmission and redaction of this material, especially up to the seventeenth century.[29] Eighteenth- and nineteenth-century texts have received far less attention, especially the many works written in Hindustani dialects and Bengali.[30] While early twentieth-century music reformers argued that the science of music had been neglected since the classical period and was only restored by their own endeavors, this book gestures to the diversity and proliferation of musical scholarship beyond Sanskrit in the eighteenth and nineteenth centuries, and discusses how the multilingual canon of musical scholarship was transmitted in the colonial era. The prevailing view has represented this transmission as being dependent on the interventions of European Orientalists.[31] However, this can only be said for a very narrow portion of the total musicological literature of this period. Innovative works on Hindustani music have been neglected due to an overreliance on reformist scholarship and English language texts. This has narrowed our vision of the musical landscape to a few interactions with "colonial knowledge," and has flattened our sense of indigenous scholarship and musical creativity.[32]

In terms of social history, musicological literature is problematic when read by itself, since it is often prescriptive, or often gestures back to a nostalgic ideal rather than describing living practice. Therefore, alongside music-technical literature I have considered a wider range of writings in Brajbhasha, Hindi, Urdu and Bengali, including song collections, *rāgamālās*,[33] poetry, memoirs, and autobiographies, as well as English sources, particularly the archives of the colonial government.[34] These texts are drawn into conversation and occasional disagreement with a later but crucially informative body of secondary scholarship that focuses on the biographies of *gharānā* musicians.

Daniel Neuman, James Kippen, and many others have explored the *gharānā* as the primary social organization of professional musicians in north India.[35] It is not wholly clear when *gharānā* became a definitive term for identifying and organizing art musicians. The term appears to have crystallized and become popularized relatively late—perhaps even at the turn of the twentieth century—while the principle of lineages of semihereditary training and shared aesthetic styles is significantly older. Katherine Schofield has reconstructed one especially significant lineage of this kind, that of the imperial court musicians of Delhi, from a range of late Mughal sources, terming this community the *kalāwant birādarī* (brotherhood of artistes).[36] The earliest appearance of *gharānā* in a literary source that I have located so far is from 1863: the *Ghunca-yi Rāg* of Muhammad Mardan Ali Khan, who refers to a *gharānā* in Lucknow led by the dance masters Miyan Abdullah and Pragas.[37] Today, the criteria for *gharānā* status include at least three generations of distinguished musicians beginning with a charismatic founder, a unique and distinct style, and an association with the ancestral home of the core family (*k͟h͟āndān*).[38] To this day, *gharānā* musicians are guardians of expertise, cultural knowledge, and oral histories vital to any study of Hindustani music. However, there are several difficulties with the way in which *gharānā* testimonies have been framed and employed in works of musical scholarship.

First, due to the vociferous writings of reformist musicologists at the turn of the twentieth century, who dismissed their competitors and predecessors as intellectually redundant (and often morally degenerate), it has long been assumed that *gharānā*s were almost entirely oral or illiterate communities. *Gharānā* musicians today are generally sought out as repositories of family lore, yet until very recently the writings of their forefathers and other nineteenth-century musicians have continued to be neglected.[39] Second, while some studies follow Neuman and Kippen in exploring the *gharānā*s' complex configurations of organization, many others are uncritical reference works. These treatments often ignore complex social negotiations in order to present an almost hagiographical streamlined narrative: an uninterrupted series of celebrated, tremendously brilliant, and much-admired men.[40] Third, contrary to the ideological conventions of the *gharānā* today, which stress the exclusive relationship between faithful students (*shāgird*, *śiṣya*) and their teachers (*ustād*, *guru*),[41] in the nineteenth century musicians—hereditary and otherwise—roamed between multiple teachers, adapting styles from multiple places. This disrupts the defined and localized associations of style to one place or family. Finally, and crucially, women are often entirely absent in writings on nineteenth-century *gharānā*s. While the vital role of women to the life of music has been well attended to in works on courtesans, the continuing invisibility of other kinds of performing women in historical scholarship projects late-colonial reformist attitudes toward gender into an earlier period, and misrepresents the place of women in the performing arts.[42]

These caveats aside, lineage is nonetheless vital to the history of Hindustani music. Indeed, as Indrani Chatterjee has persuasively argued in her work on “monastic governmentality,” the social phenomenon of the domestically situated school and community of common thought and practice is deeply entrenched in north Indian culture and intellectual history.[43] In a similar vein to transmission in religious scholastic and spiritual communities, where concepts of authorization (*ijāza*) and affiliation (*bai'a*) are crucial,[44] musical genealogies are not merely details, but are foundational to what I will be calling the networked musical economy of colonial north India; and they continue to be essential for professional musicians today as they situate their individual performances in a longer authorized heritage.

Print and Public

How musicians, music scholars, and music reformers presented their authority is a question of their chosen platform: that is, to whom, through what medium, and by what authority they spoke. Musical scholarship to date has been hampered by a tendency to read the archive of a limited (and usually Anglophone) circle without contextualizing its readership or its relationship to social reality. This has led to an overemphasis on hegemonic voices that flourished under colonial rule, and a stress on reform, “revival,” and innovations. However, as Nile Green has demonstrated for Bombay, intellectual and cultural activities in the colonial period were heterogeneous and multiple, such that it is misleading to focus on a single narrative or set of concerns as propagated by a single faction.[45] Francis Robinson has underlined how the adoption of print technology enabled new forms of authority in what Green calls the “economy” of colonial Islam.[46] Applying these considerations to the musical market, I argue that reformist texts prescribed but did not generally describe large-scale changes in musical society, and that print served as one platform for opinion and knowledge, alongside or rearticulating preexisting arenas of communication and music making, oral and written.

To date, many narratives stress how royal patrons were disenfranchised, and how *ustād*s and *ṭawā'if* lost their roles as the custodians of music as they entered the new public sphere of colonial India. However, this sense of a relentless downward trajectory is challenged at least in part by the continued importance of *gharānā* training and lineage to success in Hindustani music's highly competitive professional layer. The narrative of displacement must be qualified by examining the archive for points of continuity and resistance to change. Rulers with curtailed political powers continued as patrons of musical culture well beyond independence. While some communities of musicians were marginalized in certain social spheres, others adapted and prospered, and went on developing their repertoires into the twentieth and twenty-first centuries.[47] It is more appropriate to see many of these figures, from kings to *nautch* girls, as autonomous or partially detached from a specific "public sphere" dominated by the Western-educated upper-middle classes. While earlier histories accepted this public as the only space of colonial culture, it is now apparent that it was but one arena, prescribed by the interests of its finite, elite membership. It did not represent the broader experience of colonial India.[48]

My approach in this book builds on ground tilled in other branches of cultural history that challenge the intellectual hegemony of narrow publics, and which trace continuities between Mughal and colonial developments. To take but one example that is closely related to music, recent research has indicated alternative spheres within the print markets of north and east India. Anindita Ghosh's study of the publishing industry in Battala indicates that alongside the expansion of *bhadralok* intellectual movements, a trade in cheaper, transient pamphlet literature thrived, sustaining an irreverent alternative culture.[49] Margrit Pernau has suggested that new ventures by the middle-class elites were also heavily indebted to developments outside the common rubric of colonial modernization. Thus, the earliest experiments with the journalistic press in Calcutta, the *Aina-e Sikandar* and the *Sultan ul Akhbar* of the 1830s, were influenced in their choice of material and stylistic conventions by the official *akẖbārāt* (newsletters) of the Mughal emperors.[50] Social reform movements under colonialism likewise drew on earlier enterprises, in cases dating from the eighteenth century.[51] These studies indicate that even projects dear to the middle-class public were not new creations, but might be understood rather as developments of earlier trajectories. My study therefore locates colonial musicology and *bhadralok* initiatives within the larger context of the confluence of Indo-Persianate, Hindustani, and Bengali musical cultures, within the changing society of colonial India.

Conversations beyond Colonialism

There can be no question that performance cultures, like all aspects of Indian society and culture, were directly impacted and redirected by colonialism.[52] The British persecution of female singers and dancers, regulated and abused as "prostitutes," or the legislative controls imposed on itinerant musicians (under the Criminal Tribes Acts between the 1870s and 1890s) are concrete examples of direct colonial interventions in the economy of music. These changes in the governance of society impacted on the social standing of musicians and dancers, but also on the genres and instruments associated with them. To take but one example, when courtesans were denounced as prostitutes, the genres enjoyed in their salons, like *ṭhumrī*, fell from favor in certain quarters, were labeled superficial at best or pornographic at worst, and—eventually—were slowly "redeemed" by a long classicization process, leading to a gradual change in the delivery and formal properties of the songs themselves. Likewise, the accompanying musicians connected to *ṭhumrī*, primarily *tablā* and *sāraṅgī* players, were often regarded as pimps, and also had to negotiate their new notoriety and find ways to reclaim their instruments.[53] Colonial legacies of a different kind can be traced in new musical forms and performance practices, including the Indian appropriation of instruments and forms acquired from European military bands and ensembles—including the harmonium, violin, and clarinet—or creative exchanges and engagements with English classical and popular music.[54] Imported technologies, from commercial printing to wax cylinder and gramophone recording, also impacted the ways in which music was composed, disseminated, and appreciated. All of these processes posed new possibilities for music makers, theorists, and lovers, and presented the custodians and consumers of colonial music culture with choices about what was essential, desirable, or disposable. Edward Said noted that cultures are "structures of both authority and participation, benevolent in what they include, incorporate, and validate, less benevolent in what they exclude and demote."[55] Expanding on this, he argued that nationally defined cultures seek to sway and dominate others. One must ask, however, which actors were most significant to the strategies of incorporation and demotion?

Because the majority of scholars of colonial-era music have prioritized Anglophone writings by Indians, or treatments of "native" music by Orientalist and colonial scholars, colonialism automatically appears to be a dominant determining force in shaping the character of Hindustani music.[56] Hence, for Bob Van der Linden (writing primarily on the early twentieth century), "the imperial encounter partially was also a sound exercise and . . . music is an essential topic for the discussion of processes of (national) identity formation, as well as transnational networks and patterns of cross-cultural communication between colonizer and colonized."[57] From this perspective, Hindustani music was a contested space of negotiation between Europe and India, colonizer and colonized, providing a platform both for hegemonic discourses and for nationalism.[58]

In other fields of cultural history, however, scholars have explored continuities in patronage and creativity beyond the overt rubric of colonialism.[59] In the same way, I suggest, musical culture under colonialism was not dominated by social and political questions—nationalism, social reform, identity politics—to the exclusion of aesthetics, creativity, and taste. When historians of music cast a wider net and examine sources in Hindi, Urdu, and Bengali, it becomes more apparent that significant discourses like "Hindu Music" (i.e., the idea that Hindustani music is ancient, is derived wholesale from Sanskrit thought, is not Muslim in its pure form, and is scientific, notated, and thus controlled under the purview of "colonial knowledge") pertained to but one public arena jostling against several others.[60] We need to reframe the musical conversation. Rather than thinking of a homogenous community of "Indians" negotiating the content and meaning of music with the British, we must also consider internal conversations between different regional cultures and socially defined groups. The situation becomes much clearer when we think of Hindustani, Bengali, late Mughal, and *bhadralok* actors and writers as major conversation partners, and explore these categories not as monolithic or oppositional entities but as a range of cultural possibilities forged in explicit dialogue with one another. Beyond identity politics, negotiation of colonialism, or classicization, taking these different priorities into account sheds light on the nineteenth century as a period of creative dynamism, experimentation, and intimate engagement with treasured musical aesthetics.

Culture between Regions

One approach to reframing the conversation is to consider the significance of precolonial ideas about music and how these persisted or were reimagined in the nineteenth century. Art music was cultivated in aristocratic courts across the Mughal and colonial period, and cultures of music appreciation were transregional and cosmopolitan in nature. Said further observed, "Culture is never just a matter of ownership, of borrowing and lending with absolute debtors and creditors, but rather of appropriations, common experiences, and interdependencies of all kinds among different cultures."[61] While he was referring to the cultures of colonialism, the same rubric may be applied to the internal cultures of South Asia. Rather than homing in on a single location, such as Lucknow or Calcutta, this book explores the connected history of elite musical culture as it moved between regions. This interregional framing underlines the role of circulation and movement in the knowledge systems of the subcontinent,[62] and the need to appreciate the fundamentally multilingual worldview of early-modern intellectuals.[63] The benefit of this approach is that music is not simply provincialized to a single sphere or politically marked terrain: the diffusion of expertise was fundamental to the infrastructure of colonial-era music making.

The interregional and multilingual dimension of this study is especially significant in the context of Bengal. Most studies of the colonial cultures of Bengal concentrate on the Bengali-language account of the region's culture, and often neglect the Persian and Urdu spheres that were so active in the same space. The prevailing historiography posits that following colonial language policies that stripped Persian of its official administrative role (1837) and promoted the vernaculars, heteroglossia in Bengal was replaced by a pride and confidence in an elevated register of Bengali.[64] Sudiptu Kaviraj has remarked upon the social legacy of this shift, noting, "By the time of Bankimchandra or [Rabindranath] Tagore, proficiency in Arabic-Persian language or familiarity with Islamic culture are not required as marks of a cultured Bengali. The Bengali bhadralok elite had decided to give themselves a resolutely Hindu past."[65]

This book explores this process in the Bengali sphere, but also draws upon recent scholarship that has indicated the limits of the Tagorean *bhadralok* arena, with insights from other kinds of popular print and Muslim Bangla. Musical writings, though often classed as "poetry" in archival catalogues, do not follow precisely the same pattern of development in society as do "literary" texts. Bengali writings on *saṅgīta* (musical arts) required reference to a human authority, and due to cultural expectations explored in chapter 1, the associations of this authority with Muslims and musicians from further west (i.e., Hindustan, Awadh, Delhi) were not easily displaced. This suggests that musical culture resisted to some extent the epistemological transition that Bayly has described in terms of precolonial "affective" and colonial "institutional" knowledge.[66] Sound art produced by the body cultivates an embodied knowledge. While I chart textual efforts by Bengalis to assert their intellectual authority in music, ongoing relationships with Hindustan suggest that Kaviraj's observation does not hold for musical culture as a whole, and that the Bengali *bhadralok* did indeed accommodate an appreciation for Islamic culture into their colonial, increasingly provincialized identity.

This is largely in contrast to the distinctive new Bengali musical culture engineered by Rabindranath Tagore, which came to dominate the region's interests in art music, and provided repertoires of symbol and affect that competed with, and partially displaced, the older referents learned from Hindustan. Rabindranath is largely absent from this book for two reasons: first, I am investigating Hindustani music in Bengal, rather than *Rabindrasaṅgīt*; and second, while Rabindranath first lectured on music in April 1881, his thoughts and performance practices were largely consolidated and disseminated in the early twentieth century, especially in the 1930s, which lies beyond the purview of this book.[67]

Court Music beyond the Court

Reflecting on the changes wrought by the aftermath of the Uprising of 1857 and the consolidation of colonial rule, the satirical Urdu poet Akbar Illahabadi (1846–1921) wrote:

> *wah muṯrib aur wah sāz wah gānā badal gayā*
> *nīndeṅ badal gayīṅ wah fasāna badal gayā*
>
> The minstrel and the instrument and the song have changed
> Our dreams have changed, the story has changed.[68]

While this book explores the losses incurred by the annexation of Awadh—the exile of Wajid Ali Shah, the final fall of the Mughal emperor in 1858, and the British looting and destruction of much of Delhi and Lucknow—it also considers how far the political upheaval translated into a cultural rupture.[69] Although the pillage of the principal centers of Hindustani culture was devastating, scholars have questioned the obliteration of the old regime and its total substitution by a colonial, protomodern intelligentsia. Reading Narayani Gupta's study of post-Uprising Delhi indicates that while the physical city was unrecognizable, there were still possibilities for local performance cultures to continue, despite the massacre of artists and patrons and the destruction of their homes and other venues. So much is apparent from Urdu musical treatises, such as the *Sarmāya-yi ʿIshrat* (1874–75), which were written in Delhi after the destruction of the Mughal city yet explicitly invoked the expertise of musicians and connoisseurs living there.[70] From the early 1860s there was a revival in *melā* festivities, and as the city was transformed into a commercial metropolis, "cheap and democratic" entertainment was patronized in the private homes of the *nouveaux pauvres* Muslim aristocrats and of prosperous moneylenders and merchants.[71] This transitional culture lacked the prestige of the Emperor's Fort, but continued with defiant persistence. In Awadh, Mushirul Hasan has identified smaller towns and *qasba*s as the key arenas for culture and music, which with the decline of the Mughal Empire became "the involuntary heirs of the once-powerful Indo-Persian culture, whose gifts they were to pass on in one direction or another."[72] These smaller locales were influential centers of musical patronage even before the Uprising,[73] and other courts such as Rampur, Gwalior, and Bhopal were evidently important channels for late Mughal culture in this period.

Drawing together continuities in the conventions and values of late Mughal and colonial musical cultures, this book contributes toward a growing appreciation of the "post-Mughal."[74] In particular, *The Scattered Court* interrogates a nawabi aesthetic that was informed by, yet departed from, the imperial culture of Delhi; and it analyzes the role of nostalgia in the historiography of these variant cultures. In regard to the latter, I suggest that scholars' reliance upon the "historical" writings of the Urdu journalist Abdul Halim Sharar (1860–1926) is particularly problematic.[75] This builds upon recent studies of nostalgia in Urdu literature, but I also use sources in Bengali and my own reconstruction of Matiyaburj to substantiate my critique of Sharar and his misrepresentations of the Mughal and nawabi past.

Nostalgia gestures to the complexities of the emotional afterlife of the Mughals.[76] As I have argued elsewhere, in the wake of 1857, Urdu poets and connoisseurs of the performing arts formed themselves into emotional communities that continued to relish older art forms, even when public reform campaigns rebranded those arts as social ills.[77] Likewise, this book traces how music lovers continued to intimately engage with the arts in nineteenth-century Calcutta, and how personal encounters with music and musicians from Lucknow allowed Bengali listeners to develop relationships with the nawabi heritage of northern India. To trace these emotional communities and the affective responses elicited by music, we have to consider how ideas about feeling and emotional practices—including the outward display of sensibilities, and understandings of appropriate behaviors and responses—were evolving in colonial India. In particular, listening to music in the salons of Calcutta brought two sets of considerations into conversation: on the one hand, an older, Persianate understanding of embodied listening and ethical homeostasis derived from the Mughal *meḥfil*, and on the other, more recent colonial debates concerning the appropriate comportment of the modern gentleman, be he *ashrāf* or *bhadralok*, and to what degree women should engage with music at all.[78]

By centering my study on a dethroned nawab, his queen, and the musicians in their retinues, I analyze new developments in music in light of continuities with late Mughal values and practices, rather than subscribing to the more established (and nostalgic) narrative of a conclusive end to the ancien régime. My exploration of the "afterlife" of nawabi culture and Mughal listening practices is informed by revisionist approaches to the court as an assemblage of cultural codes as well as a political institution.[79] These codes might outlive the society or economy that originally produced them, and thence be assimilated into new settings. The courtliness of court music was flexible in practice, and could be a question of space, patronage, reputation, relationships, aesthetics, and the imagination. Before the dissemination of gramophone recordings at the very end of the nineteenth century onward, the possibility of emotionally engaging with Hindustani art music was fundamentally a question of access. Today, *gharānedār* musicians perform on stages and albums but invoke the memories of their ancestors as exalted court musicians in princely households. I argue that in the eighteenth century, courts were often fragile sites of patronage that could ill afford musical artistes. However, a networked sphere of musical patronage evolved in the early 1800s, with artists moving between urban centers, the homes of newly moneyed elites, and aristocratic courts.

This form of courtly patronage, broadly defined, did not dissolve in 1857, but flourished through to independence. Indeed, while we conventionally think of the decline of the Mughals as the point of conception for a modern market of classical musicians, in fact, many aristocratic and *zamīndārī* patrons were only seriously diminished as late as the 1950s (e.g., the U. P. Zamindari Abolition and Reforms Act, 1951) or even 1970s (e.g., the abolition of the privy purses in 1971).[80] At the same time, beyond economics, elite cultures of music appreciation enabled emotional communities of musicians and listeners to cultivate the experience of courtly art music without the physical space of the court. Crucially, because music can activate alternative senses of space and time, I suggest that Bengali listeners in colonial Calcutta could project themselves, through listening, into the imaginary of Mughal Delhi or nawabi Lucknow.

Organization of This Book

The Scattered Court examines the views, writings, and activities of Hindustani and Bengali musicians, patrons, and connoisseurs as they explored the aesthetic and social value of music and its role in the advancement of their societies and regional cultures. I begin by charting the social contexts for Hindustani music in Bengal over the eighteenth and early nineteenth centuries, indicating both the prestige north Indian musicians and styles enjoyed in eastern India, and the changing conditions of patronage around 1800. Chapter 1 considers the social history of Bengali court musicians from the late eighteenth to the early nineteenth century. This was a restless period, when the Mughal Empire was faltering and new regional powers—including but not only the British—were rising to prominence. Since certain kingdoms and aristocratic powers could no longer support the arts the way they had done before, musicians began to turn their attention to new clients and patrons, including members of the landed gentry (*zamīndārs*). These patrons adopted the older preference for north Indian art music, so artists engineered their reputations to underline their expertise in transregional repertoire, or to stress how they had studied with bona fide northern, non-Bengali maestros. This chapter also challenges the popular image of the exalted court musician, arguing instead that while musicians often claimed connections to celebrated kings, in reality many of the royal courts had suffered financially in this period and were unable to maintain their patronage of musicians. This accounts for the migration of court musicians from the provincial kingdoms to Calcutta in the early nineteenth century. In chapter 2 I reconstruct networks of music enthusiasts who came together from mixed, socially unfixed backgrounds, from Mughal poets and exiled princes to Bengali merchants and American travelers. Excavating the life of art music in Calcutta, I suggest, reveals how there was a significant demand for musicians from northern India immediately before the migration of Wajid Ali Shah and his musical entourage to the city in 1856.

With a historical context elaborated for the nineteenth-century developments at the center of the book, chapter 3 introduces Wajid Ali Shah. Turning from Bengal to Lucknow in north India, and drawing on a range of English newspapers and government archives, I examine how Wajid Ali Shah came to be seen as a notorious figure and the epitome of the Oriental despot. I demonstrate how his passionate fascination with music and dance was weaponized by the East India Company in the period leading up to the annexation of his kingdom in 1856, and in the wake of the Indian Uprising in 1857. Widespread portrayals of the king as a decadent aesthete—that emphasized his sensuality, his obscene body, and the corrupt musicians he kept as his intimate companions—were galvanized as an excuse for British intervention, but have also influenced how nineteenth-century musical culture is remembered more broadly. Having deconstructed British accounts of Wajid Ali Shah, I examine his own writings in Persian and Urdu—especially his erotic memoir, the *'Ishqnāma* (Book of Love)—and consider how he understood the appreciation of music in terms of the Solomonic ideal of the Islamicate ruler, the political virtues of mastering the emotions and exploring the affective self through music, and his aesthetic preference for the fantastical. This chapter historicizes the now pervasive characterization of nineteenth-century Hindustani music as decadent, and argues that this was a period of nuanced—and highly politicized—engagement with music, the body, and the emotions.

When Wajid Ali Shah was dethroned by the East India Company in 1856, he relocated to Calcutta, where he proposed to challenge the annexation of his kingdom. However, following the violence of the Indian Uprising the following year, it soon became apparent that he would never regain his throne or leave the city again. Known thereafter as the "Ex-King of Oude [Awadh]," Wajid Ali Shah built a new court-in-exile in a southern suburb of Calcutta called Matiyaburj. This court grew substantially over the next thirty years, only to be auctioned off and all but destroyed upon his death in 1887. The British government had grown increasingly frustrated with the ex-king (and his expensive pension), and hoped that the palace would be erased from memory. Instead, the court has survived in musical histories of the city, as a key forum of exchange between musicians from northern India and Bengal. Chapter 4 reconstructs the musical life of Matiyaburj from a range of perspectives—English government agents, Bengali diarists, Urdu journalists—and examines how court musicians navigated the changes wrought by the annexation of Awadh and the demise of the Mughal Empire by locating themselves in the king's liminal and ephemeral music rooms. In particular, I explore Wajid Ali Shah's innovative contributions to art music, especially through his own song collections and music books, and argue that the musicians, dancers, and choreographers at Matiyaburj did not merely exchange repertoires from northern India but developed innovative styles and original forms, from semiclassical genres to sketch comedies. This challenges the popular memory of the court as a monument to a dying Mughal world, by underlining the modernity and creativity of the musical king and the performing artists in his employ. Plotting the afterlife of Lucknow in Calcutta, I examine how north Indian art music connected with the Bengali music lovers I introduced in chapter 1, demonstrating the historical continuities between generations of musicians and patrons, as well as the innovations of artists in the nineteenth century.

Historians of Hindustani music often neglect the contributions of women. In general, courtesans are the only female musicians or dancers from the nineteenth century who have been remembered or studied in any detail. In chapter 5 I propose a more nuanced approach to examining gender in music history, by drawing attention to the extensive music education Wajid Ali Shah devised for female performing artists, but also to the musical contributions of his first wife, Khas Mahal. Although she was forgotten in later accounts, Khas Mahal was a vocal and highly creative figure at Matiyaburj. She wrote volumes of poetry, and worked with the king on song lyrics and musical theater projects. I explore her creative outputs, and consider the life of music in the women's quarters of royal courts, where women like Khas Mahal lived behind purdah. Drawing upon an extensive legal archive, I also reconstruct how the queen emancipated herself from Wajid Ali Shah, achieved financial independence, and acquired her own household in Calcutta, where she could enjoy music on her own terms. This chapter also traces how she came under the influence of a relative, Pyare Saheb, who later became one of India's leading celebrity gramophone recording artists. Pyare Saheb is remembered for his musical career—especially his talent in singing like a woman—but this revisionist history is the first to document his connections to Khas Mahal and Wajid Ali Shah, and to suggest that he became proficient in women's genres through his intimate relations with Khas Mahal's attendant female musicians. This chapter challenges our understanding of women's involvement in the life of music in colonial India, and demonstrates how the private music making of courtly households became entangled with public, commercialized recording industries.

Chapter 6 explores how musicians who had originally come to Calcutta as members of Wajid Ali Shah's court began to fan out across the city, locating patrons among the Bengali urban intelligentsia and injecting the city's relationship with Hindustani music with new energy and expertise. As well as providing a history of court musicians as they moved outside of courtly patronage across the 1860s to 1890s, I also examine musical reformist movements and neotraditionalist scholarly enterprises, especially the circle surrounding the Bengali musicologist S. M. Tagore. I demonstrate how hereditary Muslim professional musicians were in fact deeply entangled in the self-consciously Hindu and modernizing projects of the new, self-proclaimed custodians of classical music. While other histories of this period have focused on these modern initiatives, I examine their schools and societies relative to other spaces and argue that music lovers' homes became more significant sites for communities of musicians than ticketed concerts or proscenium stages. I develop the idea of a networked sphere: of musical households that provided spaces for musicians, their disciples, and their patrons, and which were not wholly private yet also required personal introductions of their participants. I trace these intimate networks through Bengali memoirs from the late nineteenth and early twentieth centuries and explore how the aged court musician from Lucknow or Delhi became a literary trope. I argue that when urbane Bengali music lovers adopted the mantle of patronizing Hindustani art music, they also appropriated the emotions of loss and nostalgia associated with the fall of the Mughal Empire. As I examine the relationships between Muslim musicians and their young Hindu clients-cum-students, I explore how the emotional values of court music were translated for a new, colonial audience.

Wajid Ali Shah is a household name in India today, but he has a highly mixed legacy: while he persists in popular memory as a musical genius and a bridge between courtly Lucknow and colonial Calcutta, he is also condemned as a political failure who lost his crown to the British, and therefore personifies the weaknesses of the Indian ruling classes in the nineteenth century. While these two storylines are repeated across textbooks, films, and novels, his own contributions to musical thought and practice, and the history of the musicians around him, have largely been neglected. This book demonstrates how the two narratives—artiste and despot—are deeply entangled, and how their partiality has limited the ways in which we think about the history of Hindustani music. By tracing how Wajid Ali Shah forged a musical connection between disparate regions of the subcontinent, I stress how much of the musical archive from this period has been discarded and forgotten. I explore how Matiyaburj became an innovative and deeply influential forum, but also how it spoke to a longer history of transregional movement and conversations about music, tapping into a shared appreciation for music and sound in both emotional and political life. When Bengali music lovers wept over songs from Lucknow at the end of the nineteenth century, their tears can be traced back to the affective stylings of Wajid Ali Shah, but also to a longer history of Bengali engagement with the sound worlds and art music of Mughal north India. Against this entangled history, colonialism emerges as a driving force behind certain pressures and priorities, but also as one consideration among many others that emerged in Bengali, Persian, Urdu, and Hindi sources on the nature of music over this period. This book challenges the existing historiography of Hindustani music and Indian culture under colonialism by arguing that our focus on Anglophone sources and modernizing impulses has directed us away from the aesthetic subtleties, historical continuities, and emotional dimensions of nineteenth-century music.

1

Courts in Crisis: Listening to Art Music in Mughal Bengal

saṅgīta śāstrera kathā, atyanta bistāra
nānākalpe nānāmata, nānā parakāra
eka kalpe chaẏa rāga, triṅgśata rāgiṇī
nāma rūpa beśabhūṣā, bali saba bāṇī

The sayings of musicology cover a great range:
so many systems, so many opinions, so many methods.
In the one system, six *rāgas*, thirty *rāgiṇīs*,
their names, forms, and attributes—I shall describe them all![1]

In 1891, Raja Kamal Krishna Simha of Susang Durgapur (in present day Greater Mymensingh, on the border of Bangladesh and Assam) was deeply troubled by the state of Bengali language and literature. Urged to act by what he saw as an insidious decline in Bengali taste and refinement, he published a collection of poems by his great-grandfather, Maharaja Rajasimha (b. 1745), as a reminder of the way things used to be.[2] At the center of his selection was a *rāgamālā*: a "garland" (*mālā*) of poetic verses that described the iconographic features and affective associations of the *rāga*s, as outlined in works of canonical musicology (*saṅgīta śāstra*). *Rāgamālā* poetry had blossomed in north Indian vernaculars from the sixteenth century onward, appearing in chapters of musicological treatises or as inscriptions over miniature paintings, depicting *rāga*s and *rāgini*s as lovers, sages, acrobats, and gods.[3] This particular example had a complicated provenance. Sometime in the late eighteenth century, Kamal Krishna's great-grandfather had purchased a set of *rāga* paintings from a salesman from Delhi. These paintings were of a standard only seen in the homes of the *shāhzāde* ("sons of kings," aristocrats), and Rajasimha was so enamored with them that he wrote Bengali verses (in *devanāgarī* script) to accompany each image. For Kamal Krishna, this fusion of Mughal miniature painting with Bengali poetry was the height of civilization. However, he lamented, times were changing. Gradually, the paintings themselves had become damaged, and when his father took them back to upper India to have them repaired, he could not find any artists in the old cultural centers like

Banaras who could help; the traditional skills were gone for good. To Kamal Krishna, his great-grandfather's *Rāgamālā* represented a lost chapter of Bengal's engagement with elite Hindustani culture.

This lament by an eastern Bengali *zamīndār* over the demise of Mughal arts gestures to a longer history of engagement between north Indian and Bengali society: one that was especially resonant with regard to music. Rajasimha's taking inspiration from a north Indian musical source to compose his own verses in Bengali was part of a longer tradition of transregional culture, and but one instant in a larger set of conversations on aesthetics. While some of these conversations paved the way for nineteenth-century developments in Bengali musicology and Hindustani music more generally, others were forgotten or ignored by the mainstream.[4]

What had elite Hindustani musical aesthetics, as captured in *rāgamālā* paintings and poems, meant to Bengali collectors and writers like Rajasimha? How did cultural ideas and practices circulate between regions in the Mughal period? What had changed over the generations, and why did men like Kamal Krishna look back with nostalgia and regret? Examining a variety of Bengali music enthusiasts and patrons gestures to a landscape of complex engagements with north Indian musical aesthetics and Mughal listening practices. A common theme, however, was that for a variety of social reasons, aesthetes, scholars, and aristocrats in eastern India routinely looked westward to upper India, and cultivated real or imagined relationships with Hindustan through music.

The significant geographies cultivated in Bengal over the eighteenth century continued to reverberate through the colonial period, but their full implications have largely been muted in modern histories, where Bengali culture often appears cordoned off, self-contained, and exceptional. Andrew Sartori has examined how the idea of "Bengali culture" has emerged relatively recently and has largely been entangled with the works of a relatively small and elite community that flourished in colonial Calcutta. This idea of a regional, discrete culture was revised and reified in the nineteenth century, via early experiments with liberalism and the more conservative "culturalism" of the 1880s onward. The national prominence of Calcutta as capital of British India and the international reputation of Rabindranath Tagore propelled the intellectual prestige of the region, while the hinterland of colonial rule cultivated an "anxious pessimism" concerning identity, ethics, and society. The cultural legacy of this period continued in the Bengali arts of the twentieth century, which Sartori has characterized in terms of a "cosmopolitan humanism" troubled by the aesthetic and ethical vacuity of the materialist trappings of modernity.[5]

Looking back to the Mughal period, the shifting meanings of "Bengali" at any time poses a problem for a longer cultural history. Sartori's analysis of culturalism, for example, was underpinned by very specific definitions:

> Used without qualifiers, the term Bengalis refers not, it turns out on closer inspection, to the inhabitants of Bengal generally (including the Muslim peasants or the low-caste laborers who numerically predominated), but rather to the Bengali *bhadralok*—the respectable classes that spanned the range of social positions from lowly clerks and village priests through intermediate tenure holders and professionals to magnates and quasi-aristocrats like the Tagores; who, broadly speaking, combined high Hindu caste with nonmanual employment; and who were responsible for the production of new political, ethical, and literary forms that would overwhelmingly define the self-conception of the region in the colonial and post-colonial eras.[6]

This qualification enabled Sartori to discuss Bengali culture through the celebrated names of the so-called Bengali Renaissance, including Rammohun Roy, Dwarkanath Tagore, and Bankimchandra Chatterjee. However, outside of his study, interpreting "Bengali" in this way limits the field of culture to the elites of colonial Calcutta, engaging neither with the alternative, non-*bhadralok* publics of the city, nor with centers outside the metropolis.[7] By rooting this definition in the soil of Young Bengal, there is a danger that figures like Rammohun Roy emerge from a tabula rasa, rather than from the intellectual ferment of late Mughal, Indo-Persianate society. A legacy of this nineteenth-century historiography, then, is the assumption of Bengali exceptionalism: the achievements of *bhadralok* intellectuals can appear divorced from their past, from other neighboring regions, and from other language cultures.

Lesser-known authors, like Kamal Krishna, gesture to alternative understandings of Bengali culture, while longer histories of scholars engaging with music, like Kamal Krishna's ancestor, shed light on transregional cultural connections before Calcutta became Bengal's center of gravity. Before the nineteenth century, art music in Bengal was conceptualized and practiced within a relational geography that connected eastern musicians and listeners to northern India and Mughal Hindustan in particular. This geography was cultivated through discourses—as seen in conversations on music theory and the lyrical arts—and practices, as embodied in mobile musicians and dancers. These artists and courtly service providers traveled a landscape plotted with intersecting pilgrimage circuits and Mughal bureaucratic networks, extending from Bengal and Bihar to Awadh, Agra, Delhi, and on to the Rajput kingdoms in the west. Examining the routes of migrating musicians and

FIGURE 1.1. Birth in a palace, Murshidabad, c. 1760–70. The David Collection, Copenhagen, D 28/1994. Photograph by Pernille Klemp.

how they were remembered in Bengal retrieves the conduits of sound in this geography, and indicates how when Bengalis engaged with art music they positioned themselves in a relationship to other regions.

This chapter considers the ways in which regional courts in western Bengal patronized Hindustani music, the decline of the smaller rulers, and the survival of merchants and other parties that rode the tides of economic change. Following the trajectory of those musicians who performed in these courtly spaces as they migrated to Calcutta, I consider the city's relationship to other cultural centers in north India, and its ascent as a key forum for a transregional musical society.

Sonic Conventions in Courtly Spaces

A woman is giving birth in a princely court in eighteenth-century Bengal. She lies in her chamber, surrounded by seven attendants and midwives, in one section of the *zanānā*, clearly demarcated by a wall and *parda* (figure 1.1).[8] Sitting patiently beside her bed are two female musicians: one has tucked her *tambūrā* against her shoulder, the other rests her hands over her drum (*ḍholak*), waiting to play in celebration of a safe delivery. Beyond the curtain and down a passage in the hall of audience, the lord of the house waits for word of his wife and child. Everyone on this side is also in a suspended state of anticipation: the sweets are untouched, and the only sign of activity is from the astrologers, who are busy calculating the child's horoscope. Behind them is a troupe of male musicians: one resting his arms over his *tablā*, another waiting to take the cover off his *tambūrā*. Three dancing girls—the only women permitted in this male space—are also sitting, waiting for a signal to start their performance. They all seem composed and restrained, compared to the hubbub coming from outside: another dancing troupe has arrived on the doorstep and is being shooed away by the stewards; a group of ascetics are rolling in the street; and an impatient *naubat* ensemble is ready to start up on their drums and *shehnāī* to announce the birth, but is being told by one of the household servants to hold off a little longer.

In this "noisy" image from mid-century Murshidabad, sound defines the different spaces of the palatial compound, and demarcates them from the world outside. The musicians indicate different connotations by virtue of their gender, choice of instruments (there are three varieties of drum depicted here, each with a different social meaning), and their proximity or distance from the lord. Beyond this, all the actors are qualified by the level of noise they are making: the composure and self-restraint within the court contrasts against the people in the street, whose raucousness indicates a lower social class, and who have to be disciplined by the stewards hanging from the palace porches.

Sonic practices—from orchestrating particular musicians and specific instruments to cultivating appropriately refined listening practices—were understood as a technology of courtliness that could color a space with desirable social connotations and emotional overtones. The aural imaginary of this Bengali painting directly resonates with the coding of sound in Mughal north India, where musical and noisy birthing scenes were often depicted by artists working for the imperial court.[9] Poets were also well aware of the significance of sound in representing particular spaces. In the narrative poem *Vidyā-Sundara* (c. 1752), the Bengali poet Bharatcandra Ray described his hero's approach to the city of Burdwan, highlighting his impression of sound rather than spectacle:[10]

caudike saharapanā
dvāre caudikī koto janā
murucā buruja śilāmaya

kāmāner guṛaguṛi
banduker duṛaduṛi
samukhe pradhāna gaṛa haya

bāje śiṅgā kāḍā ḍhola
naubata jhāñjher rola
śaṅkha ghaṇṭā bāje ghaṛi ghaṛi

tīra guli śanaśani
gajaghaṇṭa ṭhanaṭhani
jhaḍa bahe aśba daṛabaṛi

ḍhālī khele uḍāpāke
ghana hāna hāna hāṅke
rāybeṅśe lophe rāybāṅśa

mallagaṇa mālasāṭe
phuṭi hena māṭi phāṭe
dūre haite śunite tarāsa

The city spreads in all directions:
How many watchmen at the gates!
Guards upon the stone bastions!

The rumble of cannon,
The rattle of rifles:
The principal fortress is before him.

The *shehnāī*, *kāḍā* and *ḍhol* are sounded,
The cry of the *naubat* and *jhāñjha*,
The conch and bell sound hour by hour.[11]

The whistle of arrows,
The tinkle of the elephant's bell,
The scuttle of a storm of running horses;

The shield bearers launch themselves into action
Striking deep as they shout out;
The staff fighters catch them with their quarterstaffs.

Wrestlers slap themselves,
With blows like the earth cracking open.
Hearing this from afar, he was terrified.

Bharatcandra's description of the soundscape of Burdwan is especially delightful because of its onomatopoeic qualities (e.g., "rumble": *kāmāner guṛaguṛi*) but also because he wanted his audience's ears to zoom in on Burdwan, beginning with long-distance, far-reaching sounds—the cannon and rifles—to midrange "soundmarks" like the temple conch, and then settling on intimately terrifying noises (the elephant bell, the slaps of the wrestlers).[12] Bharatcandra also evoked the sounds of the court, identifying the musical ensembles around the king:[13]

> *rabāb*, *tamburā*, *vīṇā* and *mṛdaṅg* are played
> *naṭ*s and *kalāwant*s sing songs and put on many entertainments
>
> the *bhānḍ*s perform their sketches, the dancers dance and sing
> the heralds sing, "Salaam!," proclaim, "Salaam!"

These musicians, dancers, and acrobats (*naṭs*) were staples in the performance cultures of Hindustan. The *rabāb*, *vīṇā*, and master artistes (*kalāwants*) in particular point to the most highly esteemed sounds of the Mughal court. In the Bengali poem they appear alongside the other key personnel of a raja's palace, including poets, civil servants, and judges (*kāji*; i.e., *qāẓī*), and overtly Persianate auditory markers ("Salaam!").

Under the Mughals, the leading political families of Bengal were not ethnically Bengali, but imperial servants of West Asian or Hindustani descent. Their courts promoted the same elite music as the *meḥfil*s of upper India.[14] This was not merely a matter of taste, but was informed by political considerations. Though Mughal rule was first established in Bengal with the battle of Tukaroi in 1575, the administration only became settled under *subahdār* Islam Khan (1608–13).[15] With the move of the regional capital from Rajmahal to Dacca in 1612, the court culture of the *subahdār* was envisaged to flow seamlessly from Agra and Delhi.[16] Passing between these imperial nodes were circulating streams of tribute (*peshkash*) and specialized court servants, particularly eunuchs and musicians.[17] During the office of Islam Khan, an official from Agra visited to procure courtesans and musicians from the provincial court.[18] Musicians were also imported into Bengal from Hindustan and Bihar. As governor of Bengal, Shah Shuja (1616–71) brought Mishir Khan *ḍhāḍhī* and Guna Khan *kalāwant* with him around 1650.[19]

The *Bahāristān-i-Ghaybī* (1632) provides an insight into the significance of Hindustani music in the peripheries of Mughal space. The author, Mirza Nathan (Ala-ud-din Isfahani), was a Persian nobleman and Mughal officer who documented his imperial service in Bengal and Assam, describing the treacherous climate and perils he had to endure. Such adversities were overcome through the strategic extension of upper Indian cultures into this new terrain. Mirza Nathan stressed how, though he could no longer enjoy physical proximity to the emperor, he minimized the emotional distance by dreaming of him, and by wearing his portrait as an emblem in his headgear.[20] Within

Mirza Nathan's party were a number of *kalāwants* who served as emissaries and, through their performances, as vehicles of Mughal civilization.[21]

Music from the Mughal heartlands also had a martial, colonizing dimension, especially through the triumphal boom of the *naubat*: "At the happiness of such a great victory, the age began to play the music of joy and pleasure. The sound of the trumpet of pleasure arose and the sound of the clarion of good tidings reached its pitch."[22] Late Mughal texts attest to the persistent symbolic resonance of Hindustani music. Ghulam Hussain Salim's history of Bengal (1786) echoes Mirza Nathan's notion of the "music of victory" (especially *naqqara* or kettledrums) as celebrating success, but also serving as a weapon in its own right: music manifested the sonic presence of the general, striking fear in his enemies.[23] This history also recounts the legend of Kalapahar the miracle worker, whose drum acted like a sonic missile that could shatter Hindu *murtis* (temple images inhabited by deities).[24] Aside from the civilizing and awesome power of music itself, the *Riyāẓ-us-Salāṭīn* also indicates the currency of musical instruments, which were valued as precious commodities and were gifted by local rulers (Tipura, Kuch Behar, and Assam) to Murshid Quli Khan, and then on to the imperial center.[25]

Ascribing to the court culture of north India was a mechanism of self-transformation: theories of sovereignty were fused with discourses of morality and etiquette (*ā<u>kh</u>lāq* and *ādāb*), and offered the participant entry into an elite, cosmopolitan association of nobles defined through their service to the emperor.[26] In the case of Bengal, the patronage of Hindustani culture translated local magnates into actors in a cross-regional network. Kumkum Chatterjee has suggested that it was precisely because Bengal lay "somewhat outside the circuits of mainstream elite/courtly culture" that the cosmopolitanism inherent in Mughal culture was so effective.[27]

Musical Migrations to Murshidabad

At the beginning of the eighteenth century, the Mughal emperor Aurangzeb Alamgir sent Murshid Quli Khan to Bengal to initiate a series of reforms (c. 1700–27) which increased the region's revenues by almost a fifth.[28] Murshid Quli Khan proved to be more ambitious than the emperor had supposed, and from 1717 he laid the foundations for his own kingdom. The capital named after him became a new cultural center in the eastern reaches of the empire.[29] Although Murshidabad was styled as an autonomous space, the new nawabs were keen to emphasize their participation in transregional elite culture. Painting at Murshidabad developed a distinctive style (though short-lived, c. 1750–70) that harked back to Mughal aesthetics and drew on the expertise of artists in Delhi, but also cultivated an idiosyncratic cold palate, austere arrangement of figures, and naturalistic landscapes.[30] A similar transition may have occurred in music and dance, though this is harder to confirm without a record of the sounds themselves.

According to the *Aḥwāl-i-Mahābat Jang* (c. 1764), Nawab Alivardi Khan (r. 1740–56) deployed military bands, instructing the kettledrums to be played "in a manner contrary to custom" to confuse the enemy.[31] In terms of art music, according to another chronicle, he "did not shew much inclination for such accomplishments, as dancing and singing, or for an intimate society with women . . . [yet] understood arts, was fond of exquisite performances, and never failed to shew his regard to the artistes."[32] This passage indicates the responsibility of rulers to be *au fait* with elite music, and to patronize the sense of society generated by the *meḥfil*, regardless of their personal disposition.

Alivardi's brother, Haji Ahmed (d. 1748) was remembered as being more invested in music, but the chronicles represent this as a vice, suggesting that he neglected his duties to surround himself with "shameless (low) people and all the dancers of Patna." Patna was a central node in the Hindustan-Bengal circuit for musicians. Haji Ahmed's son, Shahamat Jang, the naib nazim of Dhaka, was the most significant patron in the family over the 1740s and early 1750s. Following Alivardi's victory at Katwa in 1745, Shahamat "assembled every kind of instrument of pleasure, [and] wishing to increase them, sent large sums to Delhi and summoned dancers from that city."[33] Bringing Hindustani musicians and dancers into Bengal was extremely valuable for the cultivation of Murshidabad and Dhaka's reputation, and the circulation of performing artists was preserved in painting and literature.

In one painting from this period (c. 1748), Shahamat presides over a *meḥfil* accompanied by his adopted son, Ikram-ud-daula (d. 1753), along with his wife's favorite and rumored lover, Husain Quli Khan, and other notables, including Rupchand from the Jagat Seth banking dynasty.[34] Shahamat and his guests are depicted attending a nighttime concert: four courtesans and six male musicians are named and represented to the same scale as the dignitaries, indicating their social value, if not status.

Some of the musicians invited by Shahamat Jang (naib nazim of Dhaka, d. 1755) settled in Bengal, according to a late eighteenth-century *tazkira* (biographical anthology), the *Ḥayy al-Arwāḥ* (c. 1785–88).[35] The author, Ziauddin, wrote this while serving Muhammad Quli Khan "Mushtaq" of Patna, son of the *dārogha* (chief-of-staff) of Nawab Haibat Jang, *subahdār* of Patna (1778–85).[36] This commemorative text documented the movement of *kalāwant*s and *qawwāl*s into eastern India, some of whom passed through Bengal as they circulated across a network of patrons, including a *qawwāl* from Lahore named Jamil, who relocated from Lucknow to Patna (Azimabad), then Bengal, and then returned to Lucknow.[37] Others settled for the longer term. Ziauddin's own patron, Muhammad Quli Khan, had studied with a musician and *marsiyakhwān* in Murshidabad named Mirza Zohour Ali, who had moved there when his own master and uncle, Alivardi Khan, had been summoned from Delhi to Bengal by Shahamat Jang.[38]

Ziauddin's primary focus was the "scattering" (*tafriqa*) of Delhi's musical community following the invasions of Nadir Shah (1739) and Ahmed Shah Abdali (1750s), when Bengal's distance from the imperial capital became very attractive. Ziauddin refers to several musicians who migrated over this period, including the *qawwāl* Sharif Khan (who later settled near Patna and married his daughter into local *qawwāl* families); a nobleman known as Mirza Ashraf, who composed and performed *dhrupad*, having studied with Hutam Khan *kalāwant*; and the three sons of Sheikh Abdul Aziz. The eldest, Mahyar Khan, a *marsiyakhwān* and *khayāl* singer, found employment under the Bengali administration, and ultimately passed away in Birbhum. There is no further information about his brother Shams al-Din; but the third son, Moazam Khan, was a *marsiyakhwān* and *sitār* player at the court of Nawab Mubarakuddaulah (r. 1770–93).[39]

The best-known figure from this Hindustan-Bihar-Bengal circuit was Munni Begum, wife of Nawab Mir Jafar (r. 1757–60 and 1763–65). Born in Balkunda village near Sikandra (Agra), Munni Begum was sold to one Bisu, a slave girl belonging to Sammen Ali Khan. Bisu taught her dancing for five years in Delhi, where she became famous. Word of her troupe spread to Bengal, where Nawab Shahamat Jang summoned them to perform at the wedding of his adopted son, Ikramuddaulah, for a fee of ten thousand rupees in 1746. The troupe then settled in Murshidabad, and Mir Jafar took Munni and Babbu (another dancer and the daughter of Sammen Ali Khan) into his harem.[40] Munni Begum came to have a highly influential political career, and patronized her own cultural investments in Murshidabad, including the five-domed Chowk Mosque.[41]

The paintings of Shahamat's music parties in particular indicate a desire to commemorate the appearance of celebrity musicians at a particular court, to fix their cultural cache beyond their actual presence. This underlines the importance of artists and service providers in defining culturally refined spaces. Crucially, the Murshidabad court was an eager customer for authentic Dihlawi style, as discussed by Walt Hakala in the context of glossaries commissioned by the nawabs to keep them up to speed with the idioms and poetry of the Mughal heartlands. While Ziauddin's musical *taẕkira* celebrated the movement of professionals, Insha was more cynical:

> You should know that during the time of Sirāj al-Daulah [r. 1756–57], some few *manṣab-dār*s and several actors (*naqqāl*), who are called *bhāṇḍ* ["jester," "buffoon," "strolling player"], two or three singers and courtesans (*kasbīyāṅ*), one or two dancing boys (*bhagete*), two or three bakers (*nān-bā'ī*), ten or twelve elegy-reciters (*marśiyah ḳhẉāṅ*), one or two greengrocers (*kunjṛe*) and grain-parchers (*bharbūṅje*) seeking profit arrived in Murshidābād from Shāhjahānābād, for which reason in that era even a chickpea roaster would not proceed towards Murshidābād from Delhi without [the promise of] ten thousand rupees.[42]

Although the administrative policies of the nawabs of Murshidabad suggested devolution and separatism, their musical investments indicate an ongoing commitment to upper Indian elite aesthetics, and a desire to minimalize the cultural distance between courts. The expenditure of the provincial Mughal courts on music was a means to recreate the imperial aesthetic in the margins of empire, and to keep abreast of fashions in the Hindustani center.

Tuning into North India: the Bengali Courts at Burdwan and Nadia

In the early stages of Mughal rule in Bengal, imperial officers, *mansabdār*s from the west, had overseen a large number of small, controlled *zamīndār*s (landed gentry), who in turn regulated lesser landholders who ran the cultivators themselves. In times of difficulty, strength came from the relationships between the *mansabdār*s and the larger *zamīndār*s in the administration, and their connections to powerful businessmen. The more powerful *zamīndār*s had profited first from the collapse of the Bengal Sultanate (1204–1575), when Hindu kings took the role of middlemen in maritime trade to Europe and West Asia. New Mughal policies of commercialization saw the rise of new, primarily Hindu, elites.[43] Under the revenue reforms of Murshid Quli Khan, the many *zamīndārī*s were consolidated into a smaller number of larger properties, particularly Burdwan, Dinajpur, Nadia, and Natore, closely followed by Birbhum and Bishnupur.[44] Although their territories paled in comparison to the kingdoms of Hindustan, the *zamīndār*s of Bengal were nonetheless influential patrons of the arts.[45] The administrative strength and concomitant cultural prestige of this elite regional ruling class increased following the death of Aurangzeb in 1707, declining piecemeal only in the late eighteenth century. Because these *zamīndār*s enjoyed a similar economic or political status, there was an extra incentive to distinguish themselves and compete through cultural elevation, including through the curated patronage of court music.

Musical memories of Burdwan often point back to the career of the singer and lyricist Raghunath Ray (1750–1836), the *dewān* (manager) of the *zamīndār* Tejascandra (1770–1832).[46] Tejascandra had specially invited *ustād*s from Delhi and Lucknow to train Raghunath; he became a specialist in *ḳhayāl* and innovatively began composing his own lyrics for the genre in Bengali.[47] How he came to be remembered gestures to larger considerations in nineteenth-century musical culture. According to one short biography from 1889, Raghunath was from a line of *raṛhi* Brahmans that had traditionally served the lords of Burdwan.[48] Legend has it that his ancestor, Brajkishor Ray, had shown remarkable loyalty by successfully negotiating his master, Raja Kirticandra, out of debtor's prison at Murshidabad. However, in the process of negotiations, Nawab Sirajuddaulah (r. 1756–57) had Brajkishor punitively circumcised. Although the raja gave his family tenure in the *dewānī* administration as compensation, the circumcision effected Brajkishor's loss of caste, and he was forced to abandon his Brahmanical training. All of this provided the background for Raghunath's training in Sanskrit, as his ancestral right; in Persian, as the medium of his business; and his musical instruction by the Muslim *ustād*s.

The rest of Raghunath's biography relates an anecdote about his encounter with a dancing girl. This unnamed but apparently highly celebrated performer had come to Calcutta from Delhi, but had failed to find a worthy patron there, and so had begun sailing the waterways of Bengal. As her boat moored in Burdwan, Raghunath was performing his ablutions in the Ganga, and she complained to him: "In the whole of Bangladesh I have not found even one listener worthy of my music!" Raghunath arranged for her to be invited to perform at Burdwan, but after performing several pieces she was left wondering whether anyone present was suitably attuned (*marmmajña*) in music to appreciate her talents. So she subtly mixed her *rāgini*s into the performance. Without saying a word, Raghunath raised a finger. The anecdote concludes by saying that the *baiji* salaamed him and declared that he alone was *marmmajña* in Bangladesh. Raghunath's biographer concluded, "To this day many famous singers cannot master the music he composed."

There are several layers to this biographical sketch. Raghunath's Brahmanical credentials were highlighted, and while the fallen status of his family perhaps excused his interaction with baijis and Muslim *kalāwant*s, his personal piety was underlined to compensate. Interestingly for a late nineteenth-century telling, the *baiji* courtesan was identified as a connoisseur and discerning (albeit haughty) judge, and her claims about Bengali ignorance in music go uncontested, since the biographer is keen to stress that Raghunath was exceptional. That said, Raghunath's gentle authority affirmed the reputation of Burdwan as the refuge of civilization in Bengal.

Despite his popularity, Raghunath did not initiate a line of *ḵẖayāl* singers in Bengal, and his son and grandson seem only to have continued his administrative functions.[49] In the court of Tejaschandra's adopted son, Mahtabchandra (r. 1832–79),[50] there were another two Bengali *ḵẖayāl* singers from nearby Bishnupur: Kanailal and his brother Madhavalal Cakravarti, who are said to have studied with a musician remembered simply as "Senior Muhammad" of Bundelkhand.[51] However, these brothers do not seem to have had any lasting influence either. Their example alongside Raghunath's story indicates the ongoing connections between Burdwan's court musicians and *ustād*s from upper India, though in the case of *ḵẖayāl* the long-term effects were limited.[52] Indeed, that Raghunath's legacy was curtailed and the Bengali *ḵẖayāl* vocalists did not establish their own lineages indicates a continued preference among patrons for musicians from Hindustan, a choice informed by regional prestige rather than artistry. In other words, while Burdwan patronized cosmopolitan, transregional pedagogy and localized innovations in sung genres, such developments were short-lived due to the desire to have bona fide north Indian *ustād*s in one's court, however talented their pupils.

The most celebrated patron of the arts in rural Bengal was Raja Krishnachandra Ray (b. 1710, r. 1728–82) of Krishnanagar (Nadia).[53] The royal family of Nadia claimed descent from Bhattanarayana, the foremost of the five Brahmans imported from Kanauj by King Adisura to "purify" Bengal. Against this heritage, the region cultivated a reputation for learning and students assembled there from across the subcontinent.[54] Krishnachandra was remembered as being "fond of music, and patronized musicians and *kláwaths* [*kalāwant*s] of the Upper Provinces. He delighted in *dhrupads* and *kheáls* [*ḵẖayāl*s], and was a great connoisseur in matters regarding the *rágs* and *ráginis* regulating oriental music."[55] In the description of Krishnachandra's court by his favored poet Bharatcandra Ray (1712–60), we hear:

> The *kalāwant* singer Visram Khan and the rest,
> The discerning *mṛdaṅg* player performs, like a celestial musician (*kinnara*).
> In the court the *premier danseur* is Sher [or Shekh] Mamud,
> Mohan Khoshalcandra is an expert.[56]

Elsewhere, Bharatcandra referred to a gifted singer, Nilmani Dinusai, to whom the poet handed over certain compositions for performance.[57] At present this poem is the only known source to identify these musicians,[58] though since they would not have performed in isolation, one can envisage larger ensembles of accompanying musicians from both upper India and Bengal.

Krishnachandra's grandson, Isvarachandra (r. 1782–88?), though less celebrated than his forefather, is also remembered for his patronage: "He built a beautiful villa called *Sriban*, situated in a romantic spot at a distance of two miles from the Rájbárí. It was at one time the seat of luxury and resonant with music."[59] Isvarachandra's son Girishchandra (r. 1802–41?) invited two *dhrupad* artists from Delhi, Hasnu Khan and Dilwar Khan (sons of Kayem Khan) to his court, and a *qawwāl* named Miyan Miran.[60]

The Delhi *ustād*s taught the three sons of a court pandit (Kaliprasad Cakravarti): Krishnaprasad, Bishnucandra (c. 1804–1900), and Dayarama Cakravarti.[61] Bishnucandra became an exponent of *dhrupad* and *k͟hayāl* and studied with another *ustād* named Rahim Khan, possibly in Calcutta, since the latter was living there for the last four months of his life at the invitation of Rammohun Roy, who had wanted to study Persian songs from him.[62] Bishnucandra then forged a connection with Rammohun Roy, who invited him (and Krishnaprasad, though he died prematurely) to develop the music of the Brahmo Samaj from 1830. Bishnucandra's ongoing career lay in Calcutta, where he disseminated his style of *dhrupad* and became the *acārya* of the Jorasanko Tagores.[63] While little is known about Bishnucandra beyond this outline, his career encapsulates a significant stream of development in Bengali music. Like Raghunath Ray before him, he was from a courtly Brahman family who studied with Muslim *ustād*s imported from Hindustan. He took his experience and status (as hailing from the regional epicenter of learning) with him to Calcutta, and was engaged in a neospiritualizing musical project. Finally, he entrenched his career teaching *dhrupad* to the urban Hindu elite. This pattern of behavior would be followed by many Brahman musicians across the nineteenth century.

We also find references from the early decades of the century of Bengali nobles studying music from upper Indians themselves, and Bengali musicians becoming teaching authorities in Hindustani genres. Man Khan came from the west (potentially from Gwalior) and in 1806 settled in Chuncura (Chinsura), where he taught the local magnate, Ramacandra Sil (the *dewān* of the Palmer Company) *dhrupad* and *k͟hayāl*. He retired and died there, and his tomb was erected to the west of Sil's residence. Ramacandra Sil also frequented the court at Murshidabad, where he became acquainted with the court musician Bara Miyan and would bring him to Chuncura for his instruction. In time, Ramacandra himself was invited to sing at the court of Krishnanagar, and took on several students of his own.[64] At Krishnanagar, Girishchandra's successor Sirishchandra (1799–1837) was himself a singer, as well as a patron of musicians.[65] Two Bengali singers at his court, Madhavchandra Mukhopadhyay and Maheshchandra Khajanchi, went on to teach a later *dewān* of Krishnanagar, Kartikeyacandra Ray (1820–85), who took up Raghunath Ray's mantle as the leading exponent of Bengali *k̲h̲ayāl*.[66]

While many courts continued to patronize musicians, others had only a nominal influence due to social changes at the end of the eighteenth century. Nadia was less fortunate and underwent serious financial pressures, resulting in the royal lands being farmed out in 1771, and *taluka* grants then sold in 1776.[67] When Bishop Heber visited Nadia in 1824, he met with a descendant of Krishnacandra, then living in one room of a ruined palace.[68] However, Bengali musicians with familial ties to these courts strategically maintained the legendary reputations of the regional courts as prestigious centers of the arts while they developed their careers elsewhere. This is especially pronounced in the music history of Bishnupur.

Bishnupur: Patronage between Kings and Merchants

The nearby Malla kingdom of Bishnupur enjoyed its own era of cultural efflorescence between the sixteenth and eighteenth centuries.[69] Today, Bishnupur is famous for its characteristic terracotta temples that idiosyncratically distill stylistic motifs and architectural influences from Buddhist, Jain, Oriya, and Mughal prototypes. The friezes that cover the facades of the temples bring together a host of figures drawn from both religious texts and everyday life. Monuments from the seventeenth century are emblazoned with female and male musicians and dancers with bent legs and outstretched arms, while acrobats appear entwined around the pilaster brackets.[70] In the early nineteenth century, the mercantile Bose family of Bosepara commissioned a small *nabaratna*[71] edifice near the town's margins (figure 1.2).[72] The terracotta decoration on this temple suggests an evolving aesthetic, depicting across tiny panels horsemen, soldiers, a nobleman clutching his hookah, and an array of dancers. While the uppermost friezes of the temple represent the conventional local style of curvaceous women dancing to the rhythms provided by long drums, the decorations around the shrine's foundation display finely detailed, round-faced men and women in late Mughal dress, playing on instruments associated with Hindustani music ensembles. In one vignette, a woman plays the *tablā* with a man on the *sāraṅgī*, while nearby another musician plays the violin. This violin was symptomatic of a wider change in the decoration of provincial temples, with European objects and costumes appearing on other sites from the same era.[73] In the past, these temples bore testimony to the Malla kings' political standing, casting them as the peers of Mughals and

FIGURE 1.2. Sridhar Temple, Bishnupur, and detail of base frieze depicting musicians and dancers. Photograph by the author.

Hindu kingdoms alike. However, by the nineteenth century, these kings were often impoverished and temples were increasingly patronized by merchants who decorated them with Hindustani musicians, camels, and Europeans.

Today, these monuments are celebrated as expressions of a wholly local aesthetic, yet the placement of these terracotta Hindustani musicians gestures

FIGURE 1.2. (*cont.*)

to the circulation of north Indian culture in the heart of what is often called "provincial" Bengal. How does the Bose family's temple gesture to a larger shift in the late eighteenth century from courtly to mercantile patronage? Rather than thinking in terms of a sea change from aristocratic patrons to new mercantile elites, it is more helpful to first reconsider what we mean by "courtly." Courtliness was not the essential property of political elites, but rather a designation of cultural space and an invocation of a prestigious ideal: a "court" could be produced by commissioning works and making specific claims about them. In post-Independence India, many musicians' family histories speak of lineages of "court musicians," and there is often an assumed historiography which positions the "courtly" against "modern." Destabilizing the category of the court at the turn of the nineteenth century therefore raises new possibilities for the history of art music. On the one hand, a courtly patron did not have to be a king or ruler, and we should expand our purview to consider merchants and religious patrons under this category. On the other, a royal "court" was not necessarily a site of luxuriant wealth and generous patronage, even if it offered a prestigious "label" for musicians seeking more stable employers.

The distinctive culture that developed in early-modern Bishnupur exemplified the confluence of distinct cultural streams in provincial Bengal, specifically the flows of upper Indian court culture and *vaiṣṇavism*. While the court (*darbārī*) musicians of Bishnupur branded themselves as immersed in this confluence, the nature of their patronage deserves qualification. The relationship between the musicians of Bishnupur and their rajas has always been taken for granted. Indeed, Chhaya Chatterjee problematically binds the two lineages together, claiming that the history of the *gharānā* goes back to the seventh century.[74] However, both the *gharānā* and the royal family have contested origins.

According to one narrative, the Malla kings were indigenous to the area, and ruled with the blessing of the goddess Chandi. Another suggests that Adi Malla was the abandoned child of a Rajput prince, whose royal credentials were fortunately recognized by a cobra, an elephant, and a Brahman who arranged for him to be crowned. It has also been suggested that the Mallas were descended from the local low-caste (or untouchable) Bagdi tribe, and employed mythology and rituals to conceal their less-than-exalted roots.[75] To mitigate this uncertain heritage, the Mallas augmented their status from the seventeenth century by emphasizing their relationships to other regions: these connections were political (Mughal), ethnic (Rajput), and religious (*vaiṣṇava*). The Rajput connection, already apparent in some of the origin myths, was cultivated in the eighteenth century through the patronage of paintings which "can hardly be distinguished from contemporary Rajasthani paintings."[76] From Raghunath (r. 1626–56) onward, the kings added "Singha" to their names, forged marriage alliances with "other" Kshatriya power-brokers, and later claimed a Sisodia princess for an ancestress. It is probable that the Bishnupur rajas aspired to a similar relationship to the Mughals as their Rajasthani "cousins." They also capitalized upon their credentials as *vaiṣṇava* kings on the pilgrimage road between Vrindavan and Puri. A "hidden" (*gupta*) Vrindavan was mapped onto the Bengali terrain, employing new structures and institutions to project the kingdom into Krishna's realm.[77] In the nineteenth century, members of the royal family spoke a combination of Bangla and Hindustani, as a continuing gesture to their cosmopolitanism and north Indian heritage.[78] These "strategic traditions" and appropriations of Hindustani culture are indicative of a larger policy of legitimization of rule through culture, "an attempt to elevate their social standing, probably to set themselves apart from their subjects and their own past."[79]

In the period following Murshid Quli Khan's reforms, Bishnupur was a prosperous kingdom. Due to the concentration of idiosyncratic terracotta temples in the region, European visitors considered Bishnupur to be an enclave of ancient Hindu government.[80] Thus, although the kingdom was profiting from the Mughal administration, it was mistaken for a space outside Muslim influence. By extension, it is widely believed that Raghunath (II) Singha Dev (r. 1702–12) was a pious king who patronized musicians to flaunt his rejection of Aurangzeb Alamgir's policies.[81] This tradition was built upon a popular misconception surrounding Aurangzeb's attitude to music,[82] but it should also be noted that Raghunath II was a Mughal loyalist. Raghunath joined forces with Nawab Ibrahim Khan of Dacca against Shova Singh, the *zamīndār* of Chetuwa-Baroda (Midnapur), who had rebelled against Mughal authority and killed Ram Krishna, the raja of Burdwan.[83] It is reasonable, therefore, to suppose that the raja was not asserting his own vitriolic local identity in his support of music, and was very conscious of his connections to Mughal society.[84]

According to the Raghunath legend, Bahadur Khan (a descendent of Tansen through the line of Bilas Khan) came to Bishnupur accompanied by Pir Bux, a *mṛdaṅg* player. Raghunath II sheltered the musicians and made Bahadur Khan his court musician on a monthly salary of five hundred rupees.[85] Bahadur Khan went on to teach the "Delhi style" of vocal (chiefly *dhrupad*) and instrumental music (being an expert *rabāb* player) to local disciples, including Gadadhar Chakraborty and Ramsankar Bhattacharya. Gadadhar became the next court musician, and established what came to be known as the Bishnupur *gharānā*, followed by Ramsankar. Proponents of this account point to a *dhrupad* text, said to have been composed by Bahadur Khan himself, which explicitly eulogizes Raghunath as his patron.[86] However, this tradition has been called into question by a number of scholars who suggest that neither Bahadur Khan or Gadadhar Chakraborty ever existed.[87] One problem is chronological: Dilipkumar Mukhopadhyay and Charles Capwell identified two descendants of Tansen named Bahadur, but neither was active in the reign of Raghunath II. The *dhrupad* text at the heart of the story has a dubious provenance, having been published only in 1893. This leaves Ramsankar Bhattacharya (c. 1761–1853) as the earliest identifiable musician of the lineage that ultimately became the Bishnupur *gharānā*.

Amal Das Sharma has noted that stylistically the *gharānā* does not suggest Seniya influence. Bishnupuri *dhrupad* is distinctively simple, with a milder use of *alamkār* and *gamak*, and an idiosyncratic rendering of *rāga*.[88] Rather than looking outside Bishnupur for a figure like Bahadur Khan, the local *vaiṣṇava* temple performance culture might provide a more convincing context for the stylistic development of the kingdom's musicians. Under the auspices of Sri Nivas Acarya, *kīrtan* had been cultivated there from the end of the sixteenth century, and received royal patronage until the 1780s or later.[89] Oral traditions of musicians' families suggest that a number of influential eighteenth-century *kīrtana* exponents were based in Bishnupur. Significantly, the locally preferred *prabandha-gīti* style of *kīrtan* is very close to *dhrupad* in its musical structure.[90]

At present, few examples from the vast literary output of Bishnupur have been made available for scholarly analysis.[91] However, one text, the *Madanmohanabandanā* ("Salutation to Madanmohan," c. 1784), by a local poet named

Jayakrishna Das, gives an impression of the town and its sacral traditions. While he makes no mention of *dhrupad* per se, Jayakrishna Das referred to *saṃkīrtan*, including to the king of Bishnupur himself enthusiastically playing the *khol* drum. The text was composed when the local deity Madanmohan had been removed to Calcutta to the house of Gokul Chandra Mitra (below); it concludes with a petition to the god to come back to Bishnupur, and depicts the sounds that would await him upon his return:

> In an instant, Lord, you disrupted the forum of your love:
> Without you, the door to your blessed temple has been shut.
> There are no Rāsa or Holi festivities, no more pilgrims come,
> Has Gokul Mitra ensnared you with love in Calcutta that much?
> That day when we hear Madanmohan is crossing the Ganges,
> Bishnupur's people will perform *nāma saṃkīrtan*,
> That day when you mercifully come and sit on your own throne,
> The king of this country will come to your house, the cannon will fire on the ghats.
> The king and his subjects will hail you with every word,
> Such that everyone's mind will cling to your feet.[92]

Written when Ramsankar would have been in his twenties, the sonic practices evoked in this passage gesture to the convergence of court and temple, with festivals and cannon fire alike celebrating the presence of the god, and the devotional attitude of the king in his assumption of an active role in the *kīrtan* recitals.[93]

As Capwell has already suggested, against this context of highly developed *kīrtan* it seems likely that tales of "upcountry" connoisseurs sharing their knowledge with disciples from select families in Bishnupur were strategically propagated in order to demarcate the nascent "*gharānā*" from their local competitors. This is not to say that no one from north India ever visited Bishnupur and shared their knowledge. However, it seems most likely that Ramshankar, or rather his disciples, may have stressed a connection to the world outside Bengal to enhance their prestige in the patronage market, offering *both* local *vaiṣṇava* genres and cosmopolitan, north Indian art music.

It is extremely significant that Ramsankar was born in the 1760s. Bishnupur had entered the eighteenth century as a prosperous and largely autonomous tributary of Murshidabad. However, a period of hardship began from mid-century, with Maratha raids, famine (most notably in 1770), and pressure from the expanding Burdwan *zamīndāri* to the north of Bishnupur.[94] Subject to financial losses and persistent revenue demands from the East India Company, the *zamīndārs* of the oldest families were becoming impoverished. Moreover, the royal family was exhausting itself through the 1760s and 1770s

FIGURE 1.3. The first generations of the Bishnupur *gharānā*.

in a war of succession fought between the grandsons of Gopal Singha (r. 1712–48), Chaitanya Singha Dev (r. 1748–1801) and Damodar Singha Dev. This was a destructive and expensive dispute, and Chaitanya was forced to mortgage the primary *murtī* of Bishnupur, Madanmohan, to Gokul Chandra Mitra, a salt merchant in Calcutta. By 1775, Chaitanya was in debtors' prison.[95] Even without the war of succession, Bishnupur was going through a turbulent period. From the summer of 1789, Bishnupur was plundered for an entire year until the peasantry finally turned on their marauders and slaughtered them.[96] In the 1790s, each year signaled a defaulted revenue payment, and portions of the kingdom were auctioned off to cover outstanding debts.[97] The local authority of established landholders was beginning to deteriorate and, significantly for music, the loss of collection rights also meant a decline in patronage.[98] Half of the Bishnupuri *zamīndārī* was sold in auction to neighboring Burdwan in June 1791. In 1820 the Burdwan collector reported on this area (now part of the "Jungle Mahals" district) and commented on the "distressing" condition of the ruined building complexes (figure 1.3) and the "mud cottages" in which the royal family now lived.[99]

However, Ramsankar Bhattacharya's career supposedly flourished in this same period, and he became the first in the series of musicians who claimed the court of Bishnupur as their illustrious heritage. Yet calling him a "court musician" would be slightly misleading, since for much of his working life the *rājbāri* (palace) was a ruin, and its kings too poor to stay out of prison, let alone patronize the high arts. Putting aside the problematic origin story of Mughal *ustād*s, we can say that the rise of the Bishnupur lineage began not with the court but with its demise. The value of a court lay in its name and connotations rather than its material reality.

The decline of Bishnupur gestures to a neglected chapter in the history of colonial-era patronage. Rather than narrating the smooth transition of "court musicians" from princely patrons in the provinces to the *bhadralok* of Calcutta, we must consider an intermediate phase. While the immediate royal family suffered financially, there were still pockets of patronage available. One of the sons of Chaitanya Singha, Nimai Singha, raised funds to establish a *zamīndārī* at Kuchiakole. He is remembered as being charitable and educated: he knew Sanskrit, and wrote a *Rāgamālā* (now lost).[100] During the Uprising of 1857, the regional power magnate seems to have been one Ray Gadadhar Chandra Banerjee, who pacified local soldiers with a feast and music until a detachment from Calcutta secured the situation. He had accumulated a fortune from indigo farming and the purchase of local *zamīndārī*s, and lived in Ajodhya, six miles northwest of Bishnupur. In 1866 he inherited many of the distributive responsibilities of the kings, including temple building, feeding of Brahmans, and care for famine victims.[101] The aforementioned temple constructed by the Bose family of Bosepara also points to the increasing significance of the local gentry. It seems likely that this local network of mercantile and business-oriented families, and those members of the landed gentry who were able to adapt to a turbulent economy, provided some degree of patronage to the musicians of Bishnupur, including Ramsankar Bhattacharya.

Alongside the master narrative of the Bishnupur court musicians' migration to Calcutta, many anecdotes from individual careers survive, allowing us an insight into where high art musicians could turn during this period (figure 1.4). Ramsankar's own family was originally from Qasimpur village, Natore in Rajshahi, but he was born in Bishnupur. Amal Das Sharma records that his father was a priest to the royal household and that Ramsankar was the first musician in the family. Of his five children, at least two were musicians: Madhav Bhattacharya (a *vīṇā* player), and Ramkeshav Bhattacharya (c. 1809–50).[102] Ramkeshav was a vocalist and *esrāj* player, and successfully secured patronage outside of Bishnupur as a teacher to Ashutosh Deb ("Satubabu" 1805–56), an influential patron and lyricist in Calcutta.[103]

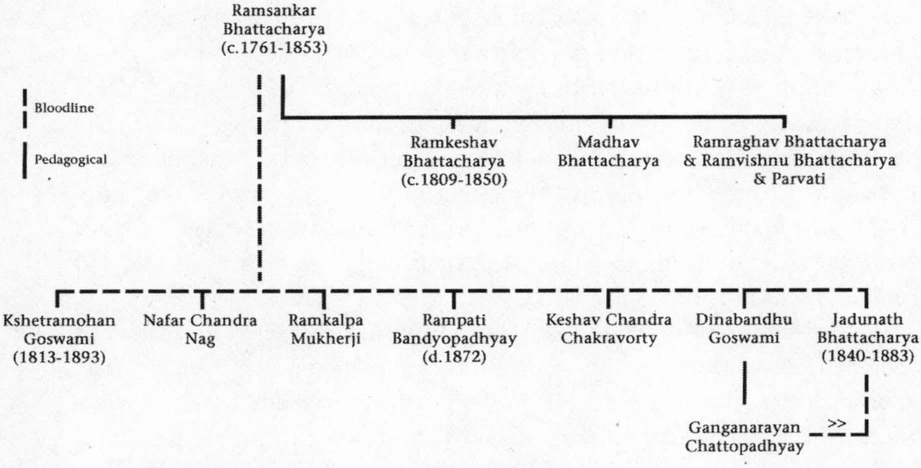

FIGURE 1.4. The first generations of the Bishnupur *gharānā*.

The majority of Ramsankar's disciples remained local, though Calcutta became increasingly significant for the next generation. Anantalal Bandyopadhyay (1832–96) seems to have stayed in Bishnupur. Later in his lifetime, when the music school was operational, he was considered a venerable music professor (*saṅgītācārya*), and was known to have composed his own *dhrupad* lyrics in Bengali and Brajbhasha. It is unclear who supported him financially, but mercantile families in the area were his most likely patrons.[104] His clearest influence lies with his disciples, including the famous Radhika Prasad Goswami,[105] and his three sons: Ramprasanna Bandyopadhyay (1870–1928), Gopeshwar Bandyopdhyay (1880–1963), and Surendranath Bandyopadhyay.

A similar career path was followed by Dinabandu Goswami, who also remained in Bishnupur and taught Radhika Prasad Goswami. Dinabandu's son Ganganarayan Chattopadhyay (c. 1806–74) migrated to Calcutta aged seventeen, and also studied in north India, specializing in the *khaṇḍār bānī* style of *dhrupad*.[106]

Ramapati Bandyopadhyay (d. 1872) was born locally, in Chandrakona village, Midnapur. He studied *dhrupad* with Ramsankar,[107] but also with masters from Hindustan. He was the court musician of Burdwan, and was employed further afield by the Raja of Mayurbhanj (now in Orissa). He developed a different style from that associated with the other Bishnupur musicians, and compiled an anthology (*Mul Saṅgītadarśa*, "The Root of Musical Insight," 1862) of traditional songs and lyrics in Bangla translation, along with his own compositions and those of his wife, Karunamoyee Devi (d. 1890).[108]

These three principal disciples of Ramsankar established the core of the Bishnupur atelier, in that they disseminated the local style of *dhrupad* to a body of disciples and sons. None of them could have relied upon the royal court; they were dependent on now forgotten local business or landholding families. Only Ramapati was working for rajas, but at two courts rather than one, and not at Bishnupur.

The two most celebrated disciples of Ramsankar actually had a very slight connection to him. Jadunath Bhattacharya ("Jadu Bhatta," 1840–83) only studied briefly with Ramsankar as a child, when Ramsankar was around ninety years old. He was also local to Bishnupur, being born to a poor family in Bankura, but at age fifteen he moved to Calcutta, where he studied the *khāṇḍār bānī* style with Ganganarayan Chattopadhyay. Like Ganganarayan, he later travelled widely in north India, including Delhi, Gwalior, and Jaipur, before returning to Calcutta. He found employment at the provincial courts of Panchakot (close to Bishnupur), and Tripura,[109] before later turning to Calcutta: first the court of Wajid Ali Shah, and then Jorasanko, where he taught Rabindranath and Jyotirindranath Tagore.[110]

Kshetramohan Goswami (1813–93) was perhaps the most influential of the Bishnupur circle, since he became the leading house musician and teacher of the Pathuriaghat Tagores and was at the forefront of many of S. M. Tagore's projects (see chapter 6). Little is known of his early career, when he began his education with Ramsankar, and in later times we hear mention only of his training with Lakshmi Narayan of Banaras. He was originally from the same village as Ramapati, but their styles became very different. Kshetramohan's later success helped to shape the royal, courtly narrative, since his patron Tagore encouraged the view that in its day Bishnupur was the "Delhi of Bengal," with Ramsankar as "one of the most distinguished musicians" there.[111] Perhaps when Kshetramohan was established in Calcutta and consorting with musicians from Hindustan's most celebrated *gharānā*s (and courts), he encouraged the rebranding of his hometown as a local prestigious center of the arts. Tagore's cultivation of this idea—followed by his establishment of a music academy in Bishnupur in 1883, the Bishnupur Sangeet Vidyalaya, as a "continuation" of a royal tradition of music[112]—indicates how the nineteenth century saw various attempts to refashion the musical relationship between Bengal and Hindustan: in this instance, translating a ruined court vying for local prestige through cosmopolitan claims into another Delhi.

From this outline of the early generations of the Bishnupur *gharānā* we can garner several insights into musical patronage at the beginning of the nineteenth century. This was an intermediate period; the time of royal patronage was effectively over in Bishnupur, and may have had no bearing on these generations at all. At the same time, Bishnupuri musicians were not yet established in Calcutta, as they would be by the 1860s. These musicians were from local, poor, and often nonmusical families, though many of them began their musical training in childhood. Calcutta was becoming an important collective of patrons (such as Ashutosh Deb), but clearly other provincial centers continued to provide support for musicians. These included gentry close to Bishnupur, such as Panchakot and Burdwan, and famous centers such as Murshidabad, but also places further afield, like Mayurbhanj and Tripura. Of course, many of the *zamīndār*s and mercantile families who survived the economic changes of the late eighteenth century went on to build houses in Calcutta, and this made the city an increasingly sound option for musicians seeking sponsors. It is also apparent that early in the nineteenth century Bengali musicians were traveling to the major centers of Hindustan (and then Rajasthan) to study with north Indian masters. They then returned and developed their own distinctive repertoires that cannot necessarily be conflated into a single, characteristically "Bishnupuri" style. Nonetheless, these musicians are thought of as a *gharānā*, with a distinctive approach to *dhrupad*. The origin myth of Bahadur Khan training Bengalis in the high art music of the Delhi court provided a prestigious, distant background for a parochial school, but also encouraged the view that Bishnupur musicians were rendering elite Hindustani music with local Bengali flavors.

Conclusion

Before the rise of Calcutta, Mughal households, the nawabs of Murshidabad, and regional courts drew north Indian performing arts into conversation with Bengali audiences and musicians. In particular, from the late eighteenth century onward, aristocratic patrons contracted Muslim *ustād*s to teach their Brahman administrators and other personnel who were attached to their households. Facets of *vaiṣṇava* performance culture, especially *kīrtan*, became allied with north Indian courtly repertoires, especially *dhrupad*. Traces of these transregional exchanges and brief experiments, including innovations in Bengali *k͟hayāl*, indicate the diverse spread of currents of Hindustani music circulating through Bengal. Although this sphere was part of a larger, transregional musical network, it appears that these courtly patrons attempted to find a balance between a shared elite culture and a local flavor. This localization is most visible in the distinctive painting style that developed at Murshidabad and the "Banglafication" of Rajput artistic conventions in the Hindu courts. This might suggest that the sound worlds of Bengal were also adapted for local audiences.

At the same time, listeners across these courts appeared to consistently rank music masters from northern India above the local talent. *Ustāds* continued to be summoned from the Mughal heartlands, and local families of musicians were keen to stress that their lineages had been imported into the region. The careers of the Bishnupur musicians, in particular, highlight two significant problems for reconstructions of musical society in this period. First, the prestige question continued to cast its shadow long into the nineteenth century; throughout the *gharānā* biographies are unsubstantiated references to musicians or their family members studying with anonymous Hindustani *ustād*s in exalted courtly settings. While we should not dismiss all of these accounts as strategic or fabricated traditions, it is also possible that, like Ramsankar Bhattacarya before them, these musicians were not as cosmopolitan in their training as they would have their audiences believe. Second, to be employed as a "court musician" clearly entailed a broad range of economic opportunities. A court was more than a palace, but it signified a particular set of connotations—Bishnupur could be framed as Malla, *vaiṣṇava*, or Rajput, and as being in conversation with the Mughals—as well as signifying prestige in a more abstract sense. This may account for musicians' ongoing affiliation with increasingly depressed and impoverished kingdoms.

These two considerations help to explain why the arrival of Wajid Ali Shah in Calcutta in the 1850s was such a milestone in the history of Hindustani-Bengali musical dialogue. His court was home to a very large retinue of Hindustani *ustād*s who easily satisfied the demand among Bengali patrons and Brahman musicians-in-training for prestigious upcountry artists. It was also a far wealthier and more celebrated court than the often precarious *zamīndārī*s of Bengal, and thus offered unrivaled opportunities for career advancement as well as musical exchange. In the next chapter, we turn to Calcutta, to consider the kinds of patronage available to musicians there in the early nineteenth century, before the nawab's arrival.

2

The Musical Ascent of Calcutta

What possibilities did Calcutta hold for musicians like Kshetramohan Goswami or Jadunath Bhattacharya? Did turning to the city for patronage imply a natural progression from "courtly" sponsors, or were urban patrons different? Before the mid-nineteenth century, the city did not represent a single center of musical activity, and it seems that there was no local style of Hindustani music that could be considered distinctive to Calcutta. While most studies of early Calcutta's performance cultures focus on the development of regional music traditions rather than those which were considered Hindustani,[1] it is important to consider the enthusiasm felt in the city for transregional, north Indian genres and styles.

Like other eighteenth-century Bengali courts and cities, Calcutta attracted artists and professionals traveling through the Mughal networks; but this port city also benefited from the larger possibilities of maritime trade. The northwest of the city was especially mixed, home to merchants from Persian, Arab, Parsi, Armenian, Jewish, Greek, and Gujarati backgrounds.[2] These trading communities offered cultural patronage and established many religious and philanthropic institutions, including the Grand (later Naquda) Mosque. Elite Islamicate cultures were pervasive across the city, since Muslim aristocrats, including the nawab of Chitpore and the descendants of Tipu Sultan, did not congregate in any single area. Although Persian was replaced by vernaculars in administrations overseen by the British from 1837, its elevated status and mainstream currency could not be eradicated immediately. While the pervasive presence of Persianate culture has been occluded by Calcutta's later self-fashioning through an emphasis on Bengali language and literature, we must remember that when the poet Ghalib visited Calcutta in 1828 he could conduct all his daily business in Persian, from technical debates on poetry to negotiation of his debts. Since the introduction of Rammohan Roy's *Mir'āt-ul-Ak̲h̲bār*, the first Persian language newspaper in northern India, the intellectual climate and scope of general knowledge Ghalib found in Calcutta surpassed that available to him in Delhi.[3] Persian poetry continued to be cultivated over the century in Calcutta as well as in Murshidabad and Dhaka, and the government opened an Anglo-Persian department at Madrasa Aliyah in 1854.[4] It is highly likely that music was patronized in Muslim households alongside Persian poetry, though this aspect of Calcutta's heritage has received little attention thus far.

With the decline of both Murshidabad and the smaller Hindu courts in the late eighteenth century, the rural landed gentry who had successfully navigated the changing sociopolitical landscape of colonial Bengal were building urban mansions. In Calcutta they joined ranks with a new aristocratic class, consolidating a substantial body of patrons.[5] In this environment the parlor or *baiṭhak* provided new spaces for established Hindustani performance repertoires, alongside innovative and, increasingly, Bengali musical forms. Texts like the *Ārāīsh-i-Meḥfil* ("Ornament of the Assembly," 1808), a description of India and its customs prepared by Sher Ali Afsos (1735–1809), offer brief glimpses into the world of the *baiṭhak*. Afsos had originally been employed in Delhi, then migrated to Murshidabad before coming to Calcutta, where he found employment at Fort William. While the text was nominally based on a significantly older work in Persian, the *Ḵẖulāṣat-ut-tawārīḵẖ* (1696) of Sujan Rai Batalvi,[6] Afsos included descriptions of contemporary Bengal, foregrounding the lavish festivities of Durga Puja in Calcutta. In his vignettes, north Indian and Bengali homes celebrated by employing troupes of mimics, dancing boys and girls (*bhāṇḍ, bhagat, kaṅchanī*), who Afsos identified as staple elements of elite entertainments in Calcutta.[7] This was the same patronage culture of the Bengali courts, in a new setting.

This chapter explores how the conceptual dimensions of Hindustani art music were discussed in early-nineteenth-century Calcutta, and considers those Bengali individuals who first curated ideas inherited from Sanskrit and Persian sources and then redirected them for new audiences. I then identify the elite circles that became invested in patronizing north Indian music, how they interacted with the city's public performance culture, and how some of these music lovers began to study performance practice themselves, inaugurating an age in which elite performers would gradually become increasingly influential in musical society.

Multilingual Conversations about Music

Ten years after Afsos, another professional scribe associated with Fort William College, named Radhamohan Sen Das, prepared a comprehensive musicological treatise in Bengali verse, the *Saṅgītataraṅga* ("Wave of Music").[8] While early-modern Bengali intellectuals had written before on the theoretical and poetic principles of *rāga* and *tāla*, Radhamohan's work was a departure: he positioned himself explicitly as a translator and interpreter of a scholarly tradition as cultivated and preserved in Sanskrit, Persian, and Brajbhasha. The *Saṅgītataraṅga* was the first book-length study of music to be printed in an Indian language, laying the foundations for colonial-era musicology. Naturally, it was especially influential in Bengal; and Bengali works on music, especially scholastic theoretical works and songbooks, proliferated across the nineteenth century.[9] The *Saṅgītataraṅga's* first edition in 1818 was a substantial work of 276 pages and included six illustrations; 288 copies were pre-ordered, including by at least six Europeans.[10] The work enjoyed two further editions over the following century (1849, 1903), supplemented by the publications of Radhamohan's separate song collections, which were ultimately collated with his music treatise.[11]

Radhamohan was less interested in presenting a revolutionary perspective on sound and music than providing his European and Bengali readers with a solid grasp of an elite, nuanced tradition of writing about music. Under the Mughals, elite men were expected to aspire toward the status of recognized connoisseur (*rasika*), and they patronized or personally composed works on the technical lore and aesthetics behind elite art music (*saṅgīta śāstra* or *'ilm-i mūsīqī*).[12] Writing in the first decades of the nineteenth century, Radhamohan was part of a transitional generation that tasked itself with navigating the possibilities of a nascent urban culture and providing the necessary tools to preserve and transmit the values of the past. In 1817, only a year before the publication of the *Saṅgītataraṅga*, the Fort William scholar Lallu Lal (1763–1825) presented his own treatment of music as the final section of the *Sabhā Vilās*.[13] This was a cursory Hindi digest of the Brajbhasha *rāgamālā* tradition which had flourished in the seventeenth and eighteenth centuries. Radhamohan was more ambitious and covered the minutiae of musicological theory, beginning with the *śāstric* (canonical, scholastic) conception of the foundations of sound.

Radhamohan explained to his readers that music (*saṅgīta*) and vocal music (*gāna*) had a complex relationship to *nāda*, the essence of sound before its interpretation as music. *Nāda* existed in the silence of the great void, manifesting as the one *śabda* (sound and the kernel of utterance) inherent in the sacred syllable (*praṇava*) and the *nāda-bindu* (a focus of divine sonic energy, the seed of reality).[14] The syllable resonates from the great void (*mahā-śunẏa*) through the five sequential elements: sky (*śunẏa*), wind (or ether/breath, *vāẏu*) fire (*tej*), water (*jal*), and earth (*kṣiti*). Following the principles of Ayurveda, these elements correspond to the five *guṇas*—sound, touch, form, taste, and smell—sound being the quality of the sky. Following the conventions of *saṅgīta śāstra*, Radhamohan guided his readers through the seven notes that issue from *nāda*, the alignment of these notes with the channels of the yogic body, and their association with sounds from the animal world. From there, he continued to consider the division of sound into different melodic structures (*grāma, rāga, murcchanā* etc.). Sometimes his descriptions were technical and obscure, but in other cases he used human behavior as an explanatory metaphor for theoretical points, such as the differences between scale degrees and microtones (*sur* and *śruti* [here spelled *śorat*]):

> The conduct of man is not hidden away
> But womenfolk remain screened from view.
> Therefore, these popular practices are the system of behavior by which
> *Sur* and *śorat* correspond with one another.
> The *surs* are men, they go here and there, far into the distance;
> *Śorat* are women, they remain in the inner quarters,
> They do not frequent the outside, for this reason:
> Who knows what would happen if anyone else saw them?
> For this reason, *śorats* remember themselves,
> They always stay inside, abandoning the world outside.
> That is to say, the *sur* is expressed with forms,
> And the beauty of *śorat* is seen through tiny forms.
> The *śorat* always accompanies the *sur*,
> Such that, before all else, it is in the underlying layer.

Radhamohan relayed the established *śāstric* mode for understanding the metaphysics of sound and the mechanics of music with a personal touch, and his own distinctive interpretative framework. Over the course of its three editions, the *Saṅgītataraṅga* achieved Radhamohan's aim of planting the culture of Hindustani music and connoisseurship in Bengali soil, and his digest of Sanskrit and Persian sources enabled later Bengali writers to hold forth on *saṅgīta śāstra*.

Jagannath Prasad Basu Mallik drew upon the *Saṅgītataraṅga* in his own writings twenty years later: first in his long entry for *mūsīqī* in his dictionary, the *Śabdakalpataraṅginī* ("River of Conceived Words," 1838) and then in a work dedicated to music, the *Saṅgītarasamādhurī* ("The Sweetness of Musical Emotion," 1844). As I have discussed elsewhere, Jagannath Prasad reoriented Radhamohan's material, denigrating the accomplishment of Muslim musicians and intellectuals and pushing the musical prestige of the region of Bengal to the foreground.[15] While Radhamohan positioned himself as a translator of a multilingual tradition that was meditated through Persian scholarship, Jagannath Prasad propounded that *saṅgīta śāstra* was a gift from

God given to the Hindu nation alone (*Hindujātītei*), and sidelined Muslim involvement:

> The Yavans were hardly trivial and of almost the same value as the Hindus; as a result, in Arab-stan, Farsi-stan and such places to this day they take the slightest blessing from the Hindu teachers, yet propel their vanity with Persian *rāga*s only, and advance nothing else. By conducting investigations, one will know that at some time those (*rāga*s) were from this land.[16]

Jagannath Prasad's introduction discredited the involvement of Muslim musicians in Hindustani musical knowledge, rendering the field exclusively a Hindu *śāstra*, and the Muslim a "Yavan" (barbarian, foreigner). In itself, this text is a very early instance of the now familiar trend of making Hindustani music Hindu.[17]

Culturally Mixed, Socially Unfixed Music Lovers

Little is known about Jagannath Prasad, but it is possible to reconstruct his larger social circle. In 1849 he gave a copy of the *Saṅgītarasamādhurī* to an American visitor, Charles Eliot Norton (1827–1908), who would later become professor of art history at Harvard University. This exchange merits proper discussion, since it sheds light on foreign engagements with Hindustani music in this period and adds to our sense of the indirect influence of the West in Indian musicology, putting the contributions of better-known Orientalists, particularly William Jones (1746–94), into a larger context.

Over his two-year visit to the subcontinent (1849–50), while working for a trading company from Boston, Norton became deeply interested in Indian society. While he was not unusual in studying Hindustani or frequenting the collections of the Asiatic Society, he was especially keen to experience local culture. He was reluctant to socialize with "unedifying" Anglo-Indians, and actively sought out the "infinitely more curious circle" of elite Indians in Calcutta, but was disappointed when they entertained him in the European style. This was apparently the case when he called on Ashutosh Deb, who, he discovered, proudly displayed a full-length portrait of Washington at home.[18] Norton infiltrated Calcutta's literary circles and made contact with Rajender Dutt (1818–89) and his uncle, Durgacharan (d. 1852), Maharaja Apurva Krishna Bahadur (d. 1867, the "poet-laureate of Delhi"),[19] and Ghulam Muhammad (1795–1872, son of Tipu Sultan), as well as Jagannath Prasad Basu Mallik. Norton said of his contacts in Calcutta, "We are now warm friends, the more so as they see that I am interested in the Hindus and desirous to see all that I can of their characteristic customs and habits."[20]

This social circle was one of the most prestigious in 1840s Calcutta, but examining its members gestures to the kind of culturally mixed and socially unfixed characters who took an active interest in Hindustani music in this period. Ghulam Muhammad was a prince in exile; following the removal of Tipu Sultan's family to Calcutta in 1806, his eleven brothers had all either died from sickness or in prison, or had committed suicide.[21] Ghulam Muhammad successfully negotiated financial security for his family, deploying his pension to create a vast estate in the city, and he worked hard to preserve the nobility of his family. A little earlier he had published an account of his forefathers in Persian,[22] and ten years later he would travel to London to discuss the conditions of his family with Queen Victoria (1859).[23] His family erected a house dedicated to musical assemblies, known variously as the *nautch ghar* or *kothi* of Tollygunge;[24] engaging with music as a patron was one way to reassert the aristocratic privilege of the royal family, even in the context of colonial exile and personal tragedy.

Apurva Krishna Bahadur was in a more secure position financially, but struggled in his attempts to carve out a form of bicultural preeminence satisfactory to both European and Mughal arbiters of taste. When Norton met him, he was "a man of about forty, well looking, and graceful in his manners;—he is not, however, one of the most elegant of the Hindus and his expression is sensual."[25] Apurva Krishna was the scion of the celebrity Kayastha dynasty of Shobabazar, the grandson of Nabakrishna, Lord Clive's *bania*, who had assisted in negotiating the grant of the *diwānī* of Bengal, Bihar, and Orissa to the East India Company. The family was extremely well connected: Nabakrishna's son, Maharaja Rajkrishna, studied Persian with "the first Qazi of the British Empire," Sirajuddin 'Ali Khan.[26] Rajkrishna held lavish celebrations to mark Durga Puja, and commissioned his Urdu teacher, Mirza Jan, to write eulogies about them.[27] Patronizing the performing arts was yet again a way of articulating one's "soft power" in colonial Calcutta, and later accounts recalled that "among the distinguishing traits in the Raja's character, might be observed, a great love of music and dancing. He frequently beguiled his tardy hours so employed."[28] Apurva Krishna documented his audiences with, and honors from, European royals, including Prince Waldemar of Prussia when he was visiting in Calcutta, and William III of the Netherlands, to whom Apurva Krishna sent a signed copy of his *The History of the Conquerors of Hind* (1848). He was proudest of two titles: member of the Hamburg Academy and poet-laureate of the Mughal emperor. These achievements did not endear him to local society, however. A review of his *History* in *The Friend of India* commented on "how much amusement the Raja has afforded both the Native and European community, by his insatiable vanity, and by the folly of bedecking himself with the title of Poet Laureat." It sardonically narrated how he had extracted the title from a visiting, unwitting Mughal prince, Firoze Shah, "who never fails to express his astonishment at the ingratitude of mankind."[29] Norton took a similar view of Apurva Krishna, writing that he was "not much respected by the better and more intelligent Hindus. He does not write his own poetry, but employs Moonshees, who compose for him the works which he published under his own name. He likes notoriety, and is as fond of appendages to his name."[30] It is tempting to view Rajkrishna and Apurva Krishna's personal investments in music as another form of cultural capital. They both enjoyed hosting parties for social networking and being seen to support elite art music and Mughal literary tastes, while also fashioning themselves as the partners and peers of European aristocrats.

Norton was closest to Rajender Dutt, the great-grandson of Akrur Dutt (1722–1809). By the 1830s the Dutts were considered one of the more prominent families in the city, focused around Mallanga and Dinabhanga. The house of Dutt amplified its public profile by playing host to extensive Durga Puja festivities, musical and dramatic performances—including productions of *Nala-Damayantī*—and additional celebrations for European visitors.[31] Norton's letters from this period suggest that the Dutts viewed their patronage of the festivities as one of the demands of their social rank, necessary for preserving their caste status by demonstrating their commitment to Hindu practices through the arts, but that they were not themselves personally invested in the "folly" and "superstition" of religion.[32]

Norton's descriptions of the sounds of the Puja were very much his own, but they also suggest how the Dutts framed and explained the celebrations to him. Although they oversaw parades in the street and nautches in their homestead, these had quite distinct sonic and social connotations. Norton described how "the Hindus take their images of the goddess Durga, and parading them through the streets with the most horrid noise of drums, cymbals, and buffalo horns, carry them down to the bank of the river, and drown them." For Norton, this was not a refined art form but a disquieting superstition, "the noise of the discordant music and the shrill cries of the natives."[33] Horns shorn from beasts and clanging cymbals, culminating in the drowning of a goddess—a particularly violent choice of words—defined Norton's experience. To him, this was humanity pulling itself away from civilization.

By contrast, Norton could turn from the streets to the genteel environment of his friends' houses, and then penetrate deeper inside to a very different kind of musical culture. His account of the production of *Nala-Damayantī* underlines his appreciation of stillness as a mark of respectable audiences:

> The music was more various and pleasing than I had supposed from the accounts of Hindu music that I had read. The drums and the stringed instruments were sometimes discordant, and sometimes, as happens in our orchestras, they were played so loud as to require an exertion of voice on the part of the singer, which destroyed any delicacy or sweetness of tone. The female parts are all played by boys, and one of them had an exceedingly fine voice, soft, full and sweet. The strongest voices, however, are soon overstrained and worn out, for the performances are mercilessly and to a stranger wearisomely long. This evening, for instance, the play was going on from seven till half-past twelve, and as during this month, which is the great season for festivals and entertainments among the Hindus, the troupe is engaged for almost every evening, the labour and fatigue of the principal performers is excessive. During the remainder of the year they are, however, engaged only rarely. A great exercise of the memory is also required from the actors, for the music is learned entirely by ear, without written notes, and the words of the parts are committed in the same way, that is, without being learned from a printed text. The troupe which we saw, which is considered in every way one of the best in Calcutta, are able to perform five or six different pieces, and this is thought to be an unusually large variety. There was no attempt at scenery the other night, and I am told that shifting scenes are never used. The dresses were showy, and there was some conformity in them to the represented positions and characters. . . . The only mark of applause among the audience was the occasional throwing of some rupees tied in the corner of a handkerchief at the feet of the actors, and this was only done by the family or the guests in the verandah. It was only by their stillness and attention that the crowd below showed their approbation, except indeed during the acting of two men who played the parts of clowns, and on the appearance out of a small basket of a remarkable dwarf, when there was universal laughter and something approaching to a stamp of admiration. The Hindu, whose highest idea of happiness is inaction, can hardly understand that state of excitement which finds vent in a Western audience in a whirlwind of applause.[34]

Calcutta's dramatic arts were transformed in the latter half of the nineteenth century with the establishment of professional theaters, and this description from 1849 offers a glimpse into an earlier period of seasonal troupes of singer-actors. Norton was evidently conscious of there being a market for performing artists, in which this particular ensemble was recognized as a superior option. The choice of drama, *Nala-Damayantī*, was already well known to European audiences too, especially after the publication of the Sanskrit text by Henry Hart Milman in 1835. Bengali *nāṭak* versions of the story proliferated in later decades, an early instance being a dramatization by Abhayananda

Bandyopadhyay (1859). Again, Norton observantly noted that the troupe were not following a printed text.

Norton's friends also smuggled him into a nautch reserved for a distinguished Indian audience (including the grandsons of Tipu Sultan), in which the star performer was a woman called Hira, "the most distinguished singer."[35] Rajender disguised Norton and three other European interlopers in Mughal muslin dress, and gave Norton the alias "Nondolal Shan" for the evening. To Norton, this nautch brought him into the inner realm of his companions. In the streets, they were bound by considerations of caste to show their pious enthusiasm for the violent, cacophonous rituals; but at home they could cast convention aside, and subversively bring their American friend into a refined gathering. Norton underlined the restrained movements of the elite musicians, who only made a gesture at dancing before sitting down for the rest of the performance (perhaps to begin seated *abhinaya*):

> In this upper room was the most distinguished of the nautch girls performing before the umeers. The slow dancing or rather gliding movement is very little cared for, it has little grace, and after commencing with it for a few moments the girl sits down on the floor to sing. This girl, whose name is Hera [Hira], is the most celebrated of all for her voice. It is low, but as far as I could judge not a complete contralto. The accompaniment of stringed instruments is entirely ad libitum, and is constantly, I think, in one key, and not very loud. Still, as the singer and the musicians have no concert you often hear discords . . . To a stranger the music is quite uninteresting, but I have no doubt it would become less so the more you heard, particularly if you knew anything of the science, for it is cultivated as a science, of Hindu music.[36]

Though Norton did not enjoy the performance, he acknowledged his own unfamiliarity with the music and was evidently aware of the intellectual foundations of the Indian "science" behind the entertainment. It was presumably in the context of these observations that Jagannath Prasad gave him a copy of his *Saṅgītarasamādhurī*. Jagannath Prasad does not appear in Norton's letters, but he is recorded in an inscription in that same copy. However, it is unclear how much progress Norton made of the work himself: he left India in 1850 and donated it to the library at Harvard on 24 February 1851.

If Norton had hoped to acquire a better understanding of Indian music from this work, he would have been disappointed. The *Saṅgītarasamādhurī* is first and foremost an anthology of Bengali song lyrics, as the subtitle suggests ("A book of collated music on various subjects relating to the *rasa*s of devotion, love and others"). Indeed, James Long recorded the work as a collection of popular love songs.[37] The work was prefaced by a ten-page prose introduction on music theory: this was intended to be instructional, but was densely theological and uninformative. Jagannath Prasad posited music as a Hindu *śāstra*, reflecting the emanation of the divine lord, Jagdisvar: when the connoisseur or gnostic (*marmmabodhe*, "informed in one's soul/heart") studies them, he is "drowned in the shoreless ocean of the aforementioned forms of *śāstra*."[38] The introduction briefly explores *rāga* and lists further principles without defining any of them: "Later in the systems of music theory there is *tān, mūrcchanālaṅkāra, ālāpcāri, bādi, bibādi, anubādi, sambādi, ṭhāṭ, gṛha, barjjita, tivr, kamal*. . . ."[39] Jagannath Prasad included names of genres and instruments, including the violin and guitar, and indexed standard themes in treatises, such as the dance of Parvati in relation to the creation of *tāla*; the varieties, vices and virtues of singers; and the appropriate times for *rāgas*—without explaining anything in detail. The work only served to reinforce the perceived unintelligibility of musical discourse rather than shed light on it. Had Norton made a study of this work, he would no doubt have been none the wiser about Hindustani music, though his sense of the science's complexity would have been confirmed.

Jagannath Prasad's extended circle was highly elite, but also mixed and unfixed: comprised of nouveau riche Hindu *bania* dynasts, exiled Muslim princes, and Western travelers. I suggest that they were "socially unfixed," in the sense that these men were certainly not unestablished, but were all invested in defining and articulating their privilege in a liminal society, one in which Mughal-era vocabularies of social prestige no longer functioned as they had a generation earlier, and where the Indian gentry's relationship with Europeans was being negotiated. In this context, Norton experienced sounds differently according to the social class of the musicians, dancers, participants in parades, and audiences he heard. This social differentiation was marked in the volume and qualities of music, its materiality (animal horns versus muslin gowns), and its indexing in bodies ranging from riotousness to stillness. Within the elite realm, Norton heard a drama staged for a privileged society, and a courtesan singer reserved for the most select audience. I suggest that Europeans were generally excluded from the courtesan's *jalsa* because they risked violating the protocol of poised, refined listening. Norton perceived the significance of etiquette and embodied listening in this elite space, and could identify (but not interpret) the consensus of connoisseurship: Hira was a "dancing girl" who barely danced, performing her reputation as a recognized singer by sitting down to sing early in her recital. The audience knew how to reward performers politely and quietly, but crucially, it also silently intimated its knowledge of the science behind the music. This culture of connoisseurship gave integrity to the cultural assertions of these unfixed patrons by tapping into the Mughal-era culture of informed patronage. In this setting, Jagannath Prasad provided his social circle with reference works on musicology which did not actually shed substantive light on the practice of music, but gave his readers the technical terms and vocabulary needed to "pass" as authentically *marmmabodhe*.

Sound and Satire

While Jagannath Prasad wrote with the understanding that his readers were patrons of music, elite Bengalis were also practicing musical performance and composition themselves. Just as Raghunath Ray had drawn on his Hindustani training to engineer a Bengali form of *k̲h̲ayāl* in Burdwan, the new setting for *baiṭhak* music in Calcutta informed several innovations. The soiree format consisted of a *dhrubapada* program, with innovative *ṭappa* and *ṭap-khayāl* forms.[40] *Ṭappa* became particularly popular in Bengal, partly due to the contributions of Ramnidhi Guptu ("Nidhu Babu," 1741–1839), a resident of Kumartuli. He had been educated in Sanskrit, Persian, and English, and between 1776 and 1794 was employed as a clerk working for the Collectorate in Chhapra, Bihar. There he studied *ṭappa* with an *ustād*, and spent his retirement adapting the form into Bengali from his house at Sutanuti.[41] He published an anthology of Bangla *ṭappa*s, *Gītaratna* ("The Jewels of Song," 1837), and the genre was adopted by contemporary artists such as Kalidas Chattopadhyay ("Kali Mirza," c. 1750–1820).[42] Ashutosh Deb, who was identified earlier as a disciple of the Bishnupur musicians, was also a *ṭappa* composer, indicating the genre's penetration of the highest social circles.[43] The pioneers of such developments were not from lineages of musicians, but were clerks and *dewān*s who took up music as an amateur interest, and then later published their own compositions and were engaged to perform. Their careers intersected with actors from the rest of Bengal, including the Brahman students of Hindustani *ustād*s in rural courts.

In their own time, these gentleman lyricists and singers enjoyed a mixed reception. Music carried different social connotations depending on whether it was treated an intellectual discipline or as a practice: under the Mughals, elite men were encouraged to critically enjoy and consume music, but not to perform it themselves (see chapter 3). Music could be considered a luxury service: musicians were service providers, and automatically of a social status lower than that of their patrons and customers. As in today's culture of elite wristwatches or cars, the gentleman music enthusiast was expected to be a knowledgeable collector—knowledgeable about the technical specifics and how to distinguish the desirable from the garish—but was not expected to personally roll up his sleeves and get his hands dirty. However, attitudes about the nature of musical work were changing across northern India in the nineteenth century.[44] Mid-century writers and critics in Calcutta observed these changes in social expectations and sonic connotations, and playfully commented on the ambiguities around the new figure of the amateur gentleman musician.

Over time, Bengali authors developed a literary tradition of listing the names of musicians, students, and patrons, and recounting specific gatherings of celebrity artists. An early instance of this literature is one nuanced text, *Samāj-Kucitra* ("The Evils of Our Society," 1865), by an anonymous author who wrote under the pen name "Nisacar" (literally "Nocturnal Creature," though translated on the cover as "A Midnight Traveller"). This text has much in common with other works of Bengali satirical-sketch (*naksā*) literature;[45] Nisacar's Calcutta was the city of playboy *babus* and it reverberated with a soundscape of excess, music being treated in the same breath as intoxicants: "*tānpurā*, *sāraṅgī*, flute, *bīna*, and *mṛdaṅg* play unremittingly. 'Spirits,' hashish, and ganja do the rounds non-stop." *Samāj-Kucitra* abounds with irony and parody, but also inventories Hindustani musicians and their Bengali students:

> Sigh! Such is the misfortune of Bengal's musicology (*saṅgita śāstra*)! Such charming and admired musical knowledge has been forsaken in this land. Long ago, many superior *kalāwants* descended in the western quarter. The *babus* of Calcutta know their names, so that modern troupes remember them, and some ancient name gets invoked for a day. Tansen, Gopal Nayak, Bayju Baura, Amir Khusrau, Hasnu Khan, Shah-Saheb, (Bahurupa) Daksni Bai, Bara Miyan, Chota Miyan, (Rahim Baksh), Nikki Bai, Brindavan Das, Firoz Khan (*rabābī*) etc. are foremost among them. In our neighborhood, the resident of Chunchura [Chinsurah] Babu Ramacandra Shil, Babu Ramakanai Mukhopadhyay, Babu Ganganarayan Chattopadhyay, Hatkhola's Babu Radhikaprasad Datta, Bhawanipur's Babu Tolanath Chaudhuri, Srirampur's Babu Ramdas Goswami, Gharisha's Babu Candranath Gupta, etc. have studied instrumental music to the highest degree. Among those who are alive, Esadaulah, Amir Khan, Rasul Baksh, Hardar Baksh, Murad Ali Khan, Ramapati Bayu, Bishnu Bayu etc., are the ones who preserve the dignity of Bengal's knowledge of music today.[46]

Hiding behind his pen name, Nisacar slides between mock oratory and precise documentary; most of his jibes were dependent on his readers being familiar with the personalities he name-dropped. Referencing the passage of master musicians from Hindustan gestures to those who came from Lucknow. Nisacar drew ironic parallels between a glorious past and an underwhelming present: the living *kalāwant*s are confused with the giants of yore, beginning with Tansen. The first names on the list are canonical figures, who were enumerated as *nāyak*s (paradigmatic master musicians) in music treatises. However, since Nisacar begins by lamenting Bengalis' spurious grasp of musicology, his inclusion of these names suggests that certain *babu*s had done *a little* reading and were clumsily displaying their erudition by casually associating legendary artists with today's musicians. The list flows from Tansen to Firoz Khan ("Adarang," a celebrated eighteenth-century Delhi *kalāwant*), but also drops out of the *kalāwant* canon to include figures like Nikki Bai (fl. 1810s–20s), one of Calcutta's celebrity *baiji* singers. The reconfigured pantheon of great artists is then followed by a list of specific patrons in Calcutta and Bengal, and Nisacar both names and locates them in the geography of the cultured city. Finally, Nisacar reveals that these patrons have themselves become musicians, having studied with Hindustani *ustād*s who have recently arrived from Awadh. This passage therefore gestures to the relocation of Wajid Ali Shah's court from Lucknow to Calcutta, and suggests how developments in the first half of the nineteenth century readied a new Bengali elite for the mass influx of north Indian elite musicians.

Conclusion

The early nineteenth century is well established as a key period in the development of Calcutta's distinctive urban culture. In terms of music and dance, historians have gravitated toward popular entertainments, street music, and the soundscapes of the city's sex industry. In a separate vein, we also know that European communities had cultivated a Western art music scene in Calcutta from very early in the city's history.[47] North Indian music is often neglected by comparison, falling between the interests of Bengali cultural history and studies on colonial society. Nonetheless, Hindustani art music had a significant role in the cultural life of the city in this period, and appealed to the highly mixed, multilingual, and multicultural society that called Calcutta home. Music in the city was varied, and the urban soundscape was fragmented on the basis of class and access. As Charles Norton found out, the festive music making of the street felt worlds apart from the intimate gatherings supported by elite patrons and music enthusiasts. The patron class was itself very diverse, made up of factions and cliques of upwardly mobile businessmen alongside aristocrats who had fallen on hard times or had been deposed and exiled by the British. In this culturally mixed, socially unfixed arena—made up of Bengalis, north Indians, and Muslim nobles from other parts of the subcontinent—deep engagement with music and dance was a meaningful way to assert one's rank and nobility. The long-established Mughal ideals of comportment and connoisseurship, as performed and perfected in the musical *meḥfil*, resonated for this community, whatever their personal fortunes.

Against this background, Bengali intellectuals developed new attitudes and approaches to musical culture. On the one hand, scholars like Radhamohan Sen Das prepared accessible resources for deepening one's appreciation of cosmopolitan musical theory, while others, like Jagannath Prasad, began the work of claiming music as the property of Bengali Hindus. Whatever their ideological position, the city's music enthusiasts benefited from the possibilities of print and the burgeoning book trade, which provided modern tools for aspiring connoisseurs. As Nisacar's satirical commentary indicates, the expansion of musical knowledge led to new conversations—and jokes—about how people were fashioning themselves as aesthetes. Crucially, the excitement of urban music enthusiasts extended to performing the music for themselves, and from the early nineteenth century patrons increasingly began to study with *ustāds* and to sing or play publicly themselves.

As the musicians from families of service providers attached to the older Bengali courts migrated to Calcutta, they became attached to these households and social networks. However, this landscape of musical patronage, learning, and taste was dramatically transformed from 1856 onward with the arrival of Wajid Ali Shah and another musical society, which he had been cultivating in Lucknow.

3

Rethinking Nawabi Decadence

In her study of nineteenth-century Urdu literature, Carla Petievich introduced her readers to Lucknow in the following terms:[1]

> Lucknow bears a fascinating, fairy-tale reputation as a centre of Indo-Muslim culture. The paradox of its place in history is quite intriguing: it is acclaimed as the quintessential symbol of what Muslim culture in India achieved, yet is simultaneously denounced today for the societal immorality, waste and decadence of its past.

The last nawab of Lucknow, Wajid Ali Shah (1822–87), in many ways became the embodiment of these themes, and was condemned by British commentators as a decadent despot, entirely cut off from reality. This notion of decadence has permeated subsequent histories of late premodern elite culture, and even musical genres and styles associated with Wajid Ali, including *ghazal* and *ṭhumrī*.[2] Over the last decades, studies of Urdu poetry have indicated how value judgements based on social issues have shaped literary considerations, projecting the topos of decadence into the realm of aesthetics.[3] In this chapter I extend this argument to music, and question the origins and implications of the rhetoric of decadence in the interpretation of nawabi society. British representations argued that Wajid Ali was indulgent by European standards, but also guilty of violating "native" sensibilities. Since later nineteenth-century *ashrāfī* newspaper editors and journalists took up the theme of decadence in their own writings, it would be inaccurate to characterize this rhetoric as a wholly British intervention in colonial systems of propriety.[4] Sensibilities concerning music in the life of public figures and concomitant moral questions related to luxury and decadence were in fact undergoing revision in both European and Indian arenas in this same period.

Just when the moral value of music was undergoing transformation, Wajid Ali was exiled for the last thirty years of his life. The expectations and obligations of a dethroned king were uncertain: as seen over the following chapters, the nawab struggled against both the British government and his own family to retain certain prerogatives, while other actors felt empowered by his changed circumstances to criticize his lifestyle and personal investments. Following the annexation of Awadh in 1856, Wajid Ali had left Lucknow for Calcutta with a view to sail to England to plead his case for unfair deposition. He set out with three hundred retainers, five to six wives, and an English businessman named Brandon to serve as his liaison in the British-held territories.[5] When he finally arrived he was taken ill and chose to remain in Bengal, while his mother, Janab-e-Alia, and brother, Mirza Sikander Hashmat, went to Europe in his stead.[6] However, their petition was thwarted by events back in India: the Sepoy Mutiny initiated the Uprising of 1857, and Wajid Ali was confined to Fort William. When he was finally released in 1859, he returned to his family in their new properties to the south of Calcutta, at Matiyaburj, also known as Garden Reach or Muchikhola.[7]

Over the next thirty years, the Europeans of this suburb filtered away and the palace complex grew, surrounded by an expanding settlement of migrants from Awadh. The court at Matiyaburj became a point of contact between late Mughal Hindustani culture and colonial Bengali society, and it sheds light on how artists and intellectuals from the nawabi regime navigated the changes wrought by the events of 1857 onward. Before turning to the music at Matiyaburj, however, it is first necessary to disentangle the moral claims made of the court, and to reassess the relationship between music and decadence in nawabi culture.

Commentators on the musical practices of Matiyaburj wrote in multiple languages—English, Persian, Hindustani, Bengali—and from very different standpoints. This presents a challenge to any reconstruction of the music in the court, since the exiled nawab and his new palace were extremely contentious topics. Reflecting on his strained relationships with the government of Bengal and his apparently eccentric behavior, European accounts of Wajid Ali projected Orientalist anxieties and condemnations onto his personality and, notably, his body. Matiyaburj itself was problematic for British commentators. As a court-in-exile, it wielded no political influence, but was expensive, noisy, and growing: the palace thus seemed to exemplify notions of the Oriental court as a decadent waste of resources divorced from reality. Music was emblematic of these criticisms, since Wajid Ali's apparent addiction to music and his keeping company with musicians and dancing girls were often drawn out in condemnations of his character.

Here I locate Wajid Ali within a debate about the role of music in political culture, and indicate how this larger discourse framed the terms of his representation. I will first discuss how the British media (primarily newspapers, published journals, and travelogues) represented the nawab in exile. Then, using Wajid Ali's own writings as a guide, I will propose an alternative interpretation of his behavior and love of music, shaped by the nawabi distillation of late Mughal cultural conventions, rather than British sensibilities.

"A Picturesque and Almost Legendary Personage"

In 1862, the Bengali satirist Kaliprasanna Sinha made a critical record of the festivities and gossip of Calcutta in a series of sketches, *Hutom Pýaṅcār Naksā*.[8] There he recalled the excitement in the city surrounding the arrival of Wajid Ali Shah:

> The Badshah of Lucknow took centrestage. News spread that he'd taken up residence in Muchikhola, and would be leaving for England soon. Some reported, "He's garishly dressed. His feet are reddened with lac-dye." Some said, "He's lean and lanky, and very handsome. He looks just like a celestial damsel." Others said, "He's pot-bellied, and has a hog-like neck. The only good thing about him is that he can sing well." Some interrupted, "Oh that's rubbish. We were in the same steamer when he crossed the river. He's dark-complexioned, lean, and wears glasses. He looks just like a *maulvi*." The city brimmed with excitement when the Badshah settled in Muchikhola after being released from internment.[9]

Sinha incorporated these musings over Calcutta's latest celebrity resident as a reflection of the ephemeral and insubstantial quality of urban popular culture. Here, public speculation about the nawab was but one episode in a series of fashionable subjects: the diverse opinions about his appearance expressed how superficially the denizens of Calcutta were interested in the man himself. Nonetheless, the speculative ideal of the nawab spoke to the frivolous essence of Sinha's satirized city. Music, dance, and sex featured prominently in this world, and the arrival of the nawab drew these strands together into a single, complex public personality. As the king of Lucknow, Wajid Ali Shah held an extremely significant political position, yet this did not register in the account of his arrival; this was partly a testament to the loss of autonomy the nawabs had experienced over the course of the dynasty's interactions with the British, but also a reflection of the colorful, contentious celebrity that overshadowed his political career. Speculation revolved around the Badshah's body, dress, and decorations. His profile here was somatic rather than political, yet the detailed descriptions of his skin and weight were conflicting, leaving the overall impression confused and sexually ambiguous: the lac-dye and the "damsel" stature sat uncomfortably with the pot-bellied, dark caricature. This tension between fascination and confusion was a persistent aspect of the public conception of Wajid Ali, and the disagreements over his real nature suggest that the idea of the nawab resisted easy categorization or satisfactory judgements.

The initial excitement that surrounded Wajid Ali's arrival in Calcutta was not to last. The ex-king was a marginal figure in the public life of the city, and featured little in the city's Bengali-, English-, and even Urdu-language newspapers.[10] When he died in 1887, *Amrita Bazar Patrika* printed an article titled "Wajid Ali Shah and the Annexation of Oude," which was largely a reprint of an earlier article from 1882 on the misconduct of the British following 1856, and provided no discussion of the king's thirty years in Calcutta.[11] *The Times of India* provided a more reflective piece, and commented:

> The death of the late King of Oudh deprives Calcutta of a picturesque and almost legendary personage. Perhaps the inhabitants themselves seldom thought of the king as he lived in mimic state in the narrow limits of his compound walls at Garden Reach with 7,000 followers, all ruled, within his petty jurisdiction, with true Oriental despotism. . . . Latterly he was a prisoner only because he declined to go outside his domains. . . . Just as he never drove into Calcutta, so he never revealed himself to his visitors.[12]

This image of a reclusive despot was an oversimplification. In fact, the grounds of the palace compound were thrown open to the public once a year, in a period extended to three days in 1875 to mark the visit of Prince Edward. On such occasions the site filled with curious visitors from the city.[13] Audiences with British notables at Matiyaburj were reported by the press across northern India. When Wajid Ali met with the viceroy in December 1868, the occasion was featured in Lahore's newspapers, along with descriptions of the king's vast menagerie and aviary.[14] Wajid Ali himself was similarly curious about Calcutta and is recalled in one Bengali gentleman's memoir as smoking a hookah in his barouche, watching the immersion processions of the Durga Puja.[15] Nonetheless, Wajid Ali was rarely physically present in journalistic or travelogue accounts of the palace at Garden Reach; his dangerous, debauched specter haunted the background, behind the curtains of his private quarters.

The king's trips into Calcutta were strategically discreet events. Indeed, the British stipulated that they should be conducted without "unnecessary ceremony." In June 1882 the monarch asked to take a railway trip to Hughli (a journey time of approximately four hours), since he had never traveled by train before. Arrangements were finalized two months later for a special train from the East India Railway Company to transport him with the agent of the government. The final permission from Shimla somewhat overcautiously reminded the agent that Wajid Ali was not to use this trip as an opportunity to proceed back to Awadh.[16] Members of the royal family could only leave Calcutta having secured permission from the government of Bengal, and senior individuals were barred from entering Lucknow. However, within Calcutta the queens and princes of Lucknow set up houses and business enterprises (see chapter 5), though certain transactions required additional paperwork, including certificates of naturalization.[17]

Gatherings involving music and dance were the primary basis for Wajid Ali's interactions with his neighbors. Wajid Ali had never habitually invited Europeans to his musical festivities, even in Lucknow, and this accounts to some extent for the British sense of his isolationism.[18] Although only a select few witnessed the musical spectacles at Matiyaburj, the sound that carried over the palace walls intimidated and aggravated the inhabitants of this previously European suburb.[19] In March 1861, Wajid Ali's neighbors issued a series of complaints to the magistrate of 24 Parganas when they found they could not sleep for the constant din of gunfire, masonry, fireworks, and "music and tomtoming, which prevail often throughout the night within the private residence of the Ex-King and his relations."[20] These continued into the following year, with additional concerns over "noisy processions on the high road and such other amusements as can be declared to be a public nuisance."[21]

"A Mad Debauchee"

Though Wajid Ali was no longer a serious political player, to the British he came to personify the Muslim ancien régime: neglectful of public duty, and excessive in personal indulgence.[22] In the colonial public of English language and reform-oriented vernacular opinion, it was desirable to relegate this eccentric figure to inactive obscurity. British writers tended to condemn the character of Wajid Ali in passing, as illustrative of the broader theme of Oriental despotism. Travelogue descriptions of Calcutta often included a description of his palace compound as the writers sailed past on their approach to the city. These accounts were generally very similar in content, drawing together extravagance and financial mismanagement, near-childlike irresponsibility, and musical dissonance.

In two near-contemporary accounts, one by Frederick F. Wyman (1866) and another by Charles Wentworth Dilke (1866–67), the palace itself was symptomatic of despotic ruin. Dilke briefly described Matiyaburj as "gaudy and architecturally hideous, but from its vast size almost imposing: it was the palace of the dethroned King of Oude, the place where, it is said, are carried on deeds become impossible in Lucknow."[23] That this edifice was "almost imposing" underlined Dilke's premise that the impotent court was a shadow of real power: his piece expressed his frustration that although the king was no longer a genuine political consideration, the British government was continuing to accommodate his wicked behavior. Wyman provided a more extensive description of the palace from the river, noting its painted villas, garden enclosures, kiosks, and dovecotes. Yet this too was colored by a political sentiment, employing metaphors of decay:

> A purposeless kind of outer verandah, some hundred yards long, of the suburban tea-garden order of architecture, is seen perched on the top of a newly-erected river wall . . . only, like the throne of the Moguls, it has an irreparable fissure in it, from top to bottom; and the verandah has in consequence received an awkward twist, foreboding a not remote descent into the dirty stream beneath.[24]

Thus even a new palace was read as a ruin. Indeed, Wyman's description presented a strongly illusionary dimension to "this shadow of a native court,"[25] with hyperbolic royal titles and gleaming solar discs, and dignitaries lounging "above the reeking mud, as if they really enjoyed it."[26]

For Dilke the farcical quality of the court was an insult to the rationalism of British governance: "Whatever income is allowed to native princes they always spend the double. The experience of the Dutch in Java and our own in India is uniform in this respect. . . . Native princes supported by European Governments run recklessly into debt."[27] This characterization of Asian rulers as whimsical and ill-disciplined spoke to a larger discourse of the childish nature of the colonized, which affirmed the vocation of the civilizing European as the instrument of historical progress.[28] Native rulers who continued to operate under the auspices of British rule were public figures without public prerogatives; hence, their spending of government funds on private pursuits seemed abhorrent to writers like Dilke. Financial frivolity was a quantifiable index of the incompetence of the colonized. The financial was readily coupled with other notions of profligacy: "It is not the king's extravagance alone, however, that is complained of. Always notorious for debauchery, he has now become infamous for his vices. One of his wives was arrested while I was in Calcutta for purchasing girls for the harem, but the king himself escaped."[29] Likewise, Wyman described how "the peaceful charm of the spot in years gone by, its quiet placid beauty and air of utter repose, are replaced by the harsh discordance of native tom-tom and drum."[30] The king's pursuit of women (implicitly for his musical and sexual entertainment)[31] and his pollution of the formerly European Garden Reach with sound and spectacle created the image of Matiyaburj as a cancerous pocket of "riot, licentiousness, and extravagance"[32] at the margins of the colonial capital. Dilke himself was concerned that Wajid Ali was influencing the local population of Bengali gentlemen through "the spread of careless sensuality,"[33] highlighting both the ongoing threat of the deposed monarch and the moral susceptibility of Indians in general.

A decade after the annexation and the Uprising, Wajid Ali was presented in an article defending the actions of Lord Dalhousie and the subsequent conduct of the British in India. Here, the king was "an effeminate tyrant" and a "mad debauchee," while the British had annexed his kingdom to "free a peaceful and industrious people from the yoke of the licentious tyrant, who was ruining their estate and corrupting their morals."[34] While the impression was one of ineptitude and contagious debauchery,[35] it was also made clear that British influence had restrained that contagion by relegating the king to "comfortable obscurity."[36] Wajid Ali was likened to the Bengal tiger in his menagerie, contained yet still "pacing up and down in all his majesty."[37]

However, other British accounts of Wajid Ali were not as hostile. In the period around the visit of the prince of Wales to India in 1875–76, Matiyaburj received renewed attention, including an extended description in the travelogue of J. Drew Gay (1877). While this account was haunted by the memory of the "butcheries" of 1857 and perpetuated the trope of rightful confinement, here the palace itself was considered beautiful, surrounded by "lovely" gardens, ornamented with "surpassingly beautiful" pigeons. Of the king himself, the writer judged that "he should have been a gentleman of moderate means residing somewhere in the South of England; his skill and his patience would have astonished his rivals; he would have gained prizes everywhere, and everybody would have united to praise him. He was unfortunately a King, and all his excellencies are forgotten in the one fact that he was a Royal failure."[38] This seemingly sympathetic portrayal nonetheless drew on the same ideological framework as the more negative accounts. In European society, his love of beauty, encapsulated here in architecture and pigeons, would be virtues in the private realm, but excessive and unwelcome attributes of a public figure, especially a king. This accommodation of Wajid Ali's personality was removed from the horrors of 1857 by two decades; in another ten years, a visitor to Calcutta had nothing ill to say of the king, and merely included him "among the many native noblemen and gentlemen" of the city, alongside the fiercely loyalist and respectable Tagores of Pathuriaghat.[39]

The Tagores were extremely well-regarded patrons and connoisseurs of music (see chapter 6), and their being named in the same breath as Wajid Ali points to the complexities of British views on "native" music. Incessant drumming and whiling away the hours with dancing girls could be taken as evidence of debauchery and hedonistic neglect of state affairs, but this was rather a question of application rather than a vice essential to the musical arts. The British emphasis on public service (in opposition to private pleasure) cast Wajid Ali's interests in a negative light, since his position as a king entailed expectations and obligations his behavior did not satisfy. Aside from this division of the private and public spheres of action and responsibility, gender anxiety also colored how the British viewed the king's musical pursuits.

"Immersed in Ease and Luxury"

Such obligations were informed both by European attitudes to proper governance, liberalism, and the morality of consumption,[40] and by developing Orientalist expectations of the qualities of an Eastern despot. English responses to Indian courtly culture were not static, and this field of interaction has a complex history.[41] These encounters were influenced by a shifting debate in English society concerning the place of the arts and luxury in civil society. Since notions of private pleasure and overindulgence were alienated and characterized as a specifically "Asiatic luxury,"[42] over the eighteenth century Wajid Ali had unknowingly been drawn into a longer discourse that was colored both by economics and gender.[43] David Hume had reexamined luxury and argued for its moral neutrality: put to good use, it could inspire the elevation of the senses and stimulate economic growth.[44] While English civic humanism had conventionally drawn on the model of the classical Republic, idealizing the masculine warrior as its guardian, Clery and Head have noted a mid-century turn toward both the feminine and the refined. Progress in civilization could be indexed by "a positive feminization," measured in terms of civility rather than strength.[45] However, by the mid-nineteenth century the tide had turned in British discourse: luxury had become an object of moral criticism, and the sphere of consumption made private—that is, separate from the domain of public production and labor. Against this new framework, Sassatelli notes, consumption took on "ambiguous connotations": at best, private vice (a love of music) could become a public virtue (sponsorship of a musical industry); at worst, the pursuit of pleasure was a passion that needed to be reformed into a rational, capitalist, or self-improving project.[46] Thus, when colonial officials charged the nawabs of Lucknow with decadence and immorality, their criticisms were framed by a contemporary attitude that had only recently been renegotiated in British society.

On a more immediate level, the British had harbored grave concerns about the political influence of musicians in Wajid Ali's retinue from the very beginning of his reign. In March 1847 the nawab had sanctioned the destruction of several Hindu temples associated with a caste of jewelers, after he heard a spurious rumor that one among them, named Chhote Lal, had ritually sacrificed a Brahman child. At the same time, one of Wajid Ali's favorites, Mir Mahdi, sent a hired thug named Farzand Ali to destroy several Shaiva temples and private properties in Haidarganj.[47] After making enquiries, the British discovered that Mir Mahdi was a drummer from a dancing girl troupe who had risen up in the royal court. He had coveted land at Haidarganj and had ordered the demolitions there without the nawab's consent. Reprimanded by the British, Wajid Ali put Mir Mahdi under temporary house arrest, but this did little to assuage British concerns. Over the next nine years of his reign, Wajid Ali was routinely criticized for keeping company with musicians, "a body of low intriguing men, players on Native Instruments and Women. . . . He has given himself up to all sorts of excesses allowing the first mentioned parties to carry every species of intrigue and entirely neglect all care, or thought of the government of his kingdom."[48] Richmond, the resident in Lucknow early in the nawab's reign, had warned of "the unlimited control" of "the dancing and singing men."[49]

Against the background of gendered discourses of luxury, pleasure, and public morality, Wajid Ali became the embodiment of self-indulgent impropriety. During a cholera epidemic in Lucknow in August 1851, it was reported in the *Calcutta Englishman*:

> The King is as usual "immersed in ease and luxury," as the natives express it, knowing and seeing little of his unhappy country. He employs his time in a way suited to a mind so little as his decidedly is. Like most oriental princes he deems indolence the height of blessing. His time is principally spent in the Zenana, and in his Purrisian, or garden of angels, represented by lightly habited women, in listening to music, looking at nautches, dancing himself at times, a thing abominated by Mahomedans, and in composing poetry and Hindoostanee airs.[50]

Rather than dealing with the needs of the public in a time of crisis, Wajid Ali was represented as pursuing his private pleasures and musical entertainments. These pursuits were overtly effeminizing:

> Though no great favourite of Europeans he shocks the rigid faithful and the severe moralists by publicly setting at defiance all the rules of native etiquette,

> and thus makes himself contemptible in the eyes of all. He drives out with rings in his ears, false locks hanging down his cheeks, and with that horror to all good Musselmans—a shaven chin.[51]

Following the annexation, this article was used as a source for an extended piece, "Oude, as a Kingdom," which considered the region's architecture, culture, and recently dethroned ex-king.[52] Foreshadowing the Bengali rumors, this article focused on his physical appearance, which though handsome was described as "coxcombical and effeminate," especially due to his "long black women's locks" and "smooth chin—quite an abhorrence to religious Mahommedans."[53] The article developed a sophisticated narrative to explain the king's self-indulgence, stating that his father had been intimidated by early signs of his talents and had debilitated him purposively by confining his upbringing to the *zanānā*, where he was "imbued" with feminine "whims, follies, and vices . . . frivolous pursuits." The dangerous result was the narrow intellect and sensuality of a *zanānā* woman yoked unnaturally to the body and responsibilities of a male ruler. This judgement extended to Wajid Ali's accomplishments:

> His most intellectual employment was the effusion of rhythmical rhapsodies, in which the faintest semblance of an idea is smothered in the most mellifluous Oordoo. Like his brother mock-potentate of Delhi, the ex-King of Oude is considered a very tolerable poet as far as fluency of words and choice of expression are concerned; but both monarchs are equally deficient in thought and feeling.[54]

This femininity condemned the kings to an inferior intellectual capability and a superficiality in their achievements. While rhapsodies were invoked as evidence of the king's weakness, it was music rather than composition that was especially provocative:

> Not content with poetic fame, he would display his skill on the sitar to an applauding throng of fiddlers, singers, eunuchs, "mendici, mimi, balatrones, hoc genus omne." Degrading as was even this in the eyes of a Musulman, it was not the lowest depth to which the Majesty of Oude descended. Dressed in female attire, Wajid Ali Shah entered into rivalry with Nautch girls; or trifled in his garden amid swarms of beautiful women draped in transparent gauze, with wings fastened to their shoulders, in humble imitation of the female angels of the Mahommedan paradise. Nothing was deemed too silly or impertinent that furnished an excuse for neglecting public business.[55]

This characterization employed three strands of critique. The first was gendered: the king was not only neglecting his public duties by enjoying the nautch, but was himself in "rivalry" with the dancing girls, suggesting that he took them as his peers.[56] A second strand invoked European traditions: citing a Latin phrase from the *Satirae* (I.2) of Horace projected Sleeman's recent damning report of the court of Awadh as being full of "singers, eunuchs and females"[57] into the classical tradition of musical debauchery. The original passage discussed "a troupe of mourners for the dead singer Tigellius, dredged from the seamy underside of Roman society: prostitutes, drug pushers, beggars, mime-artists and clowns."[58] This cast lamented the musician's demise, claiming that he was a generous patron, though in reality he was a spendthrift and debauchee. Tigellius's death served as an opportunity to reflect on extravagance by conflating impolite society, immorality, and the arts. By gesturing to a comparison with Wajid Ali, the nawab was rendered a mock potentate, unphilanthropic toward society, a hero to its lowest characters. Finally, the argument invoked Islamic notions of propriety, suggesting that the king was violating three taboos in the Muslim tradition: performing on a musical instrument, dressing as a woman, and recreating paradise with his harem.

These various criticisms of Wajid Ali Shah drew on reports of activities in Lucknow and Matiyaburj that can be corroborated elsewhere. Though claims that he himself danced and dressed as a woman are less authentic, his love of music, dancing, fanciful sartorial practices, and recreations of paradise were accurate representations of life in his court. However, these facets of his character have been used in a colonizing, frequently apologetic discourse, employing a hermeneutic shaped by Orientalism and post-Enlightenment notions of decadence and public responsibility. My analysis of these criticisms has sought to reconstruct the discursive and historical foundations of the colonizer's view of Wajid Ali's love of music. I will now consider how the attitude of the colonized differed in this regard, drawing on considerations inherited from late Mughal conventions, rather than those of English civil humanism. Before turning to the music and dance patronized in Matiyaburj (chapter 4), I will return to Lucknow to discuss the foundations of Wajid Ali's musical development, and the nawabi cultural connotations to his love of music.

"I Made People Cry as They Laughed and Laugh as They Cried"

While Indian rulers who followed the Mughal paradigm of self-governance were expected to show an informed but restrained interest in music,[59] Wajid Ali Shah was unusually enthusiastic and expert in his appreciation. It is said that as a child he would tap his feet during his lessons, and his irritated tutor, Imdad Husain Khan, slapped him with such force that one of his ears was permanently damaged.[60] Wajid Ali was indeed hard of hearing, and British residents occasionally had to repeat themselves when talking to him.[61] Nonetheless, he undertook extensive training in music from his adolescence, and became a celebrated patron and teacher in his own right. His connoisseurship was widely recognized by complimentary and hostile commentators alike. In this section I will consider how his engagement with musical aesthetics deepened after his succession in 1847.

As a prince, Wajid Ali interacted with various kinds of musical professionals: his first interactions would have been with palace employees, including *k̲h̲awāṣṣ* attendants in the *zanānā* and singers who performed for his father, but in time he began exploring the city's courtesan salons, where he met both expert *ṯawā'if* and male musicians. In the *'Ishqnāma* ("Book of Love," c. 1848, his memoir up to the age of twenty-six), Wajid Ali described his emotional connections to the arts.[62] Music could cheer and reanimate him, yet when he felt disturbed or dispirited he would discontinue *meḥfil*s, and it would be up to his companions to arrange a gathering and break the hold of his melancholia.[63] The king was almost wary of the influence music held over him: though it might cheer him, it could also potentially overpower him. When he first met Waziran the *ṯawā'if*, "upon her singing and dancing tears from my eyes had become fixed in my pupils, until at last I was left in a stupefied state [*be-k̲h̲ẉudī ke 'ālam meṅ*] and unable to contain myself [*mujhmeṅ ẓabṯ kī ṯāqat na rahī*]."[64]

The nawab described a variety of emotional states stemming from music, romantic trysts, and poetry: even periods of melancholia were opportunities to explore the fundamental components and contours of emotional perception. His evident love of music and appreciation of its restorative effects would suggest that his avoidance of *meḥfil*s in times of sadness was a preparation of sorts. He would distance himself from music to deepen his grief, in order to enhance his elation when his spirits were finally uplifted.

Propelled by his interests in the manipulation of the inner life through musical affect, Wajid Ali cultivated a retinue of musicians in Lucknow in order to guide his training as a performer and technician of the emotions. He studied broadly, encompassing vocal, instrumental, and percussion music within his *ta'līm* (training). He studied *dhrupad* from a *rabāb* player of the Delhi *kalāwant birādarī*, Pyar Khan,[65] and forged a connection with his family, particularly the branch related to his brother, Basat Khan (c. 1800–c. 1887).[66] The king also began teaching *dhrupad* to his own disciples, including Mir Gauhar Ali.[67] Qutub Ali Khan, a native of Bareilly (his family claimed descent from Raja Jagat Dev)[68] and himself a disciple of Pyar Khan, trained the king in the *sitār* (figure 3.1). Qutub Ali Khan was a celebrated poet and musician in Lucknow, and his Purab and Masitkhani *gat* compositions

FIGURE 3.1. Wajid Ali Shah learns *sitār* with Qutub Ali Khan, as depicted in the *ʿIshqnāma* (Lucknow, India: 1849–50). Royal Collection Trust / © Her Majesty Queen Elizabeth II, 2015.

are still available through oral and written transmissions.[69] Wajid Ali described how he appointed Qutub Ali Khan as his *ustād* "to put an end to my woes," and in time became so accomplished in the art that "the attendants of *meḥfil*s were astonished. I made people cry as they laughed and laugh as they cried. Pyar Khan used to praise me and would begin to reel when he heard my sitar."[70] Evidently Wajid Ali understood music not simply as a therapy for his own emotions, but as a potent technology that could be deployed over others (notably affecting even the *kalāwant* Pyar Khan). In the early stages of his training, the king relished opportunities to surprise and overwhelm the unsuspecting attendees of *meḥfil*s, as on one occasion when he played the *sitār* from behind a curtain: "That I should possess such knowledge was unexpected, and it was felt throughout the cosmos all around, up to the moon and stars."[71]

Another musician from the Lucknow period who featured prominently in the *'Ishqnāma* was Chote Khan, a *tablā* player from Shahjahanabad who arrived at the court in his mid-thirties. Wajid Ali was very close to him and gave him the title *Bahār-i-meḥfil* ("Glory of the Assembly"), and upon his accession to the throne renamed him Anisuddaula.[72] The king noted that he was very attractive and intelligent, and was a favorite of the ladies in court. Wajid Ali was conscious of this, and included anecdotes in the *'Ishqnāma* that explicitly declared that he was more attractive than Chote Khan. Despite their rivalry, the two became close companions, and their relationship is illustrative of the king's unconventional attitudes.

According to Sharar, Chote Khan took training in vocal music from Pyar Khan, though he did not excel in it.[73] It is perhaps surprising that a *tablā* player would acquire this *ta'līm* from a musician of the Delhi *kalāwant birāderī*, since it is generally assumed that a strict distinction is maintained between vocalists and accompanists.[74] Fertilization between these fields was rarely acknowledged openly—none of the percussionists in *Ma'dan al-mūsīqī* (c. 1858),[75] for example, are known to have sung—though in reality there was some precedent.[76] Though Sharar did not denounce Pyar Khan's training of Chote Khan, his stressing that the latter never became proficient in singing was perhaps a reaffirmation of the status quo.

Wajid Ali's facilitation of this training gestures to the king's larger concern with the power in exchange and processes that allowed a person to appropriate another's faculties. This is a recurring theme in the *'Ishqnāma*, in which the king would consciously perform a character and thereby incorporate into his own essence the associated qualities of that role. At times this was an overtly dramatic process, as when he was so moved by his own verses that he tore his clothes and "became" a yogi (see below). On other occasions, appropriating qualities could be a more intimate, immediate experience. In one episode, Wajid Ali and Chote Khan visited the house of a beautiful woman living in Golaganj. The king conspired with the *tablā* expert to seduce her:

> She applied attar to my clothes and made a *pān birri* and presented it to me. I surreptitiously concealed myself, like a knavish street dealer, and took out that *pān* that I had pressed to my mouth and gave it to Chote Khan. He took out another *pān* from his betel-box and gave it to me, and I put that one in my mouth. Straight after this I asked for a *bāyāṅ* (left-handed) drum and began to play. Along with this I began to intone my own finely-balanced *ghazal* in Jhinjhoti *rāg*. Ecstasy from my music took this mocking mistress by surprise, and she lost her grasp of her mind and senses. At last she clasped my hand and began to declare her love, but I did not exploit her burning. In that house there was a cat called Pearl, and I began to play with her instead.[77]

This apparently minor detail, whereby Wajid Ali substituted his betel for Chote Khan's own and suddenly became especially proficient in drumming and seduction, suggests that the king was playing a trick informed by a theory of consubstantive incorporation, whereby the ingestion of a food substance given by a handsome drummer could invest the king with his attributes. This sharing through substance echoes Mughal understandings of fabric (especially the conveyance of authority from the emperor through the *k͟hullat* robe),[78] and Indic understandings of food as a mediator (particularly in the context of *prasād*). However, these practices were informed by a hegemonic understanding of the direction of transference: the superior agent (be they a god or emperor) condescended to share essential qualities with a grateful inferior. Therefore, though Wajid Ali's sense of musical ability and pedagogy was informed by established understandings of the physical incorporation of attributes, his manipulation broke with the conventions that preserved the integrity of such exchanges: by allowing *tablā* players to study singing from the line of Tansen, and by ingesting the qualities of a drummer in his royal body, Wajid Ali was courting controversy.

The controversial undertones to Wajid Ali's musical ventures became more explicit as he drew closer to a family of musicians from Rampur. In 1843 he met two sisters, Aman and Amaman, who had previously been in the employ of a *raīs* noble of Farrukhabad. These singers were extraordinarily influential in the king's musical development, as he explained that he only began composing *ṭhumrī*s after listening to them perform.[79] They were joined by their father, Nathu Khan; his brother, Ghulam Nabi; a cousin, Ghuman Jan; and Ghulam Haider, the brother of their mother, Majju. The king accompanied their performances on the *sitār* and sang with Nathu's students. In time, Wajid Ali boasted that he came to surpass the *ustād* in skill.[80]

However, it was the sisters' brother, Ghulam Raza, who developed the most significant ties to the king. When he first arrived in Lucknow he was around twenty-six years old, and was notably attractive and strong. Wajid Ali made him his confidante and ordered for him to be with him at all times.[81] In the illustrations that accompany the text of the Royal Library '*Ishqnāma* (1849–50),[82] Ghulam Raza is a recurring figure and is represented as bearing a strong physical resemblance to the king's image. This reflected how Wajid Ali saw himself as the paradigm of male beauty, as seen in his comparing himself to Chote Khan: Ghulam Raza's resemblance to Wajid Ali identifies them as a pair of handsome ideals. However, the likeness also reflects their personal intimacy. Several illustrations represent Wajid Ali consorting with the musicians, including one folio that depicts the dance of Sarfaraz Mahal, a major love interest of the king in the narrative (figure 3.2). As she dances, Wajid Ali accompanies her on the *tablā*, while Ghulam Raza and members of his family stand alongside him, two playing *sāraṅgīs*. That the king chose to present himself as a rank-and-file musician is further emphasized by the negative space across from the huddle of musicians, where a regally fashioned chair bearing the insignia of Awadh is left empty. Whereas convention demanded that the king be presented sitting in that chair as the patron, enjoyer, and connoisseur of the musical entertainment, this work situated Wajid Ali on the other side of a socially imperative line, representing the king as a technician of the musical arts.

Certain musicians, including Ghulam Raza and Qutub Ali Khan, converted to Shi'a Islam, and took on new names.[83] For their services, Qutub Ali was renamed Qutubuddaula and made judge of Kacheri Sultani,[84] while Ghulam Raza (Raziuddaula) was given command of a platoon. From 1849 onward the British in Lucknow invoked these appointments as evidence of Wajid Ali's mismanagement of state affairs, and they formed part of the official rationale for annexation in 1856.[85] However, the influence of Ghulam Raza in the affairs of Lucknow was brought to a premature end when it was reported that he was having an affair with Sarfaraz Mahal. He was banished in 1850 and is thought to have returned to Rampur. Several other core musicians went into exile in the same year, including Nathu Khan, and Qutub Ali Khan who settled in Rampur at the court of Yusuf Ali Khan.[86] While this episode marked a personal loss for Wajid Ali and was taken up in the political discourse of British officials, its impression on the musical legacy of the Lucknow court was less severe, since the performance culture developed there continued apace and ultimately survived the king's own exile too.

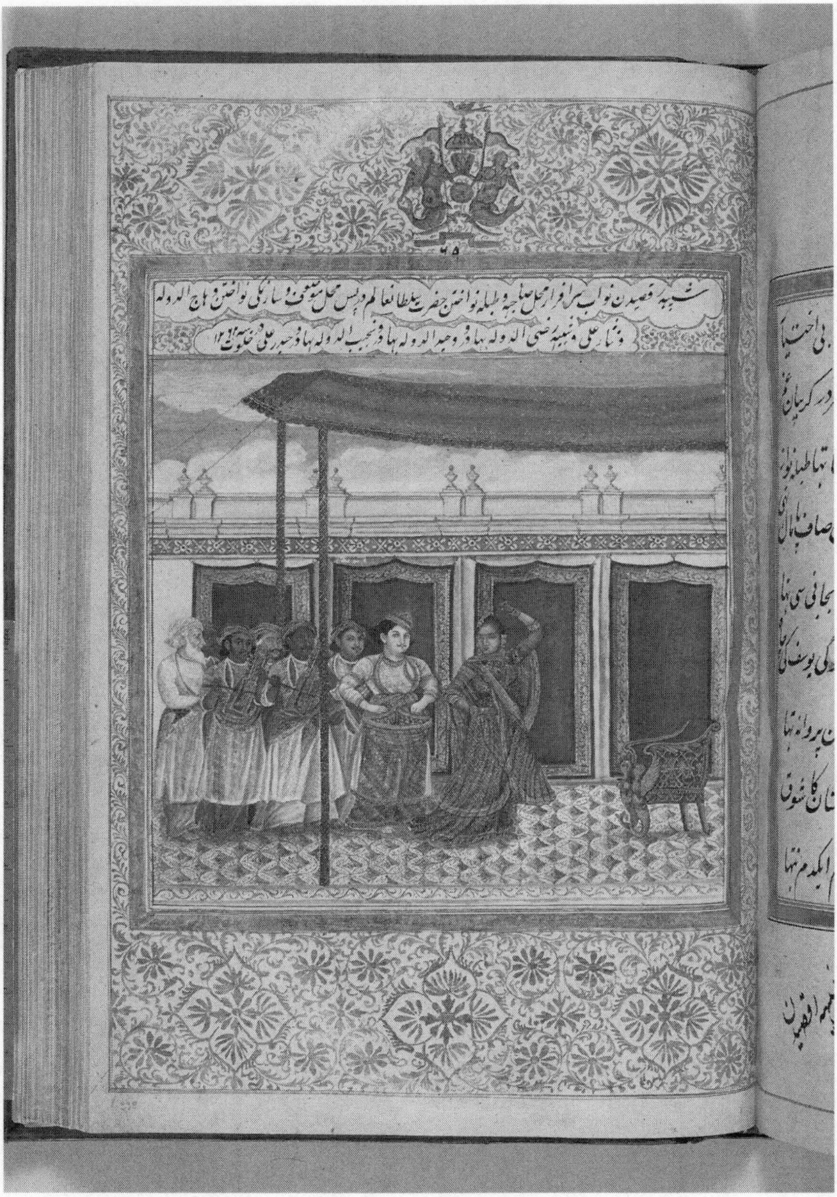

FIGURE 3.2. Wajid Ali Shah accompanies the dance of Sarfaraz Mahal, as depicted in the *'Ishqnāma* (Lucknow, India: 1849–50). Royal Collection Trust / © Her Majesty Queen Elizabeth II, 2015.

Patrons and Performers

Wajid Ali's early engagements with musical performance in Lucknow were contentious in several respects. His writings, authorized pictorial representations, and choice of companions gesture to a mode of behavior that would have seemed highly inappropriate according to certain Indian systems of protocol: his intimate connections to low-status men, including his open admission of taking their substantial attributes into his own person; his performing alongside musicians as a musician; and finally his unusually close engagement with women. Here I will discuss why these aspects may have been problematic, and the apologia Wajid Ali himself formulated in anticipation of criticism.

An important manual of etiquette from the high Mughal period, the British Library *Mīrzānāma* (c. 1660), gave detailed prescriptions for the elite *mīrzā*'s proper intellectual study of musical science (*'ilm*). While his study should entail theoretical principles such as *āhang* (consonance) and *maqām* (Persianate modes), as well as the art of singing, he should avoid singing himself outside the circle of his closest peers. Singing in the *meḥfil* was to be left to professional musicians (*mughanniyān*), since it could lead the *mīrzā* down an undignified path: "Singing can lead to dancing, and that necessarily to other disgraceful and ignominious actions."[87] Knowledge of music was one limb of the *mīrzā*'s cultural education, and the patron's ability to correct any mistakes by his musicians was indicative of his cultural refinement:[88] that he could become knowledgeable to a professional degree without actually performing music only enhanced his sophistication.

Wajid Ali's writings were consistent with this value system, since he underlined how he surpassed professional musicians in his understanding of music and was able to correct them.[89] This seventeenth-century valorization of unapplied knowledge continued even into the early twentieth century, when Sharar defended Wajid Ali in these very terms. Sharar insisted that the nawab never disgraced himself by dancing, yet

> by watching dance in abundance and being a music *ustād*, he acquired so much knowledge of the modes of dance that when a dancing girl made a mistake in a dance, he would raise both hands while sitting on his bed and say, "Not like that!" He was truly proficient in singing. Even though he had a bad voice, he understood the principles of music so well that he even "caught the ears" of very great singers. Through the ages in Hindustan several emperors are said to have been excellent music *ustāds*. But I do not believe that any one among them acquired a knowledge as exalted as that acquired by Wajid Ali Shah.[90]

Sharar's highlighting the nawab's knowledge and intellectual stature was apologetic in its rationale, and only dimly reflected Wajid Ali's self-representation. While the nawab certainly celebrated his own understanding and theoretical proficiency, he was also keen to represent his practicing singing and instrumental music.

While the British were critical of these activities and maintained that they were abhorrent to a native understanding, was this an accurate understanding of elite Indian sensibilities around 1850? On the basis of seventeenth-century *mīrzānāma*s, Wajid Ali was courting controversy. According to Katherine Schofield, "the prohibition on the *mīrzā* performing music in public is the most universally agreed injunction in the Indo-Persian literature."[91] That said, Schofield has also suggested that the prescriptive *mīrzānāma*s represented a reaction to a culture where elite men were in reality transgressing the more conservative codes of elite masculinity and musical propriety.[92] The wider body of evidence indicates that singing was an acceptable practice for elite men, subject to repertoire and context. Idul Singh, a Rajput prince from Kharagpur whose father had voluntarily converted to Islam, was celebrated as a singer of *k̲h̲ayāl* and *tarānā* in the *Rāg Darpan* (1666).[93] In this case, the prince sang for a Sufi *majlis*, and performed genres associated with the *qawwāl*s, hereditary shrine singers, which legitimized his participation in music as a form of spiritual practice. Other examples from this period suggest that the sharp definition between patron-connoisseur and public performer was not as impermeable or consistent as the prescriptive literature would suggest.[94]

By the nineteenth century it was not always problematic for elite men to perform music. Commenting on musical culture in the immediate period around 1857, Karam Imam noted that "Raja Shibnath Singh of Rewa, Maharaj Uditnarain Singh of Benaras, Raja Rattan Singh of Charkhari, Nawab Ahmad Ali Khan of Rampur and Sultan-e-alam Badshah of Lucknow are great patrons of music. In fact they all sing to some extent."[95] Although Wajid Ali received special attention, evidently the phenomenon of a singing ruler was acceptable in itself. Likewise, S. M. Tagore noted the proficiency of rulers in Bihar, including Maharaja Sir Lachmiswar Singh of Darbhanga and Maharaja Newal Kisor of Betia.[96] Thus, when colonially sanctioned rulers and new urban elites, such as members of Calcutta's *bhadralok*, took up musical instruction and performance (see chapter 2), this was not a break from the conventions of the late Mughal elites, but rather a continuance of sanctioned behavior.

This is not to say that the British invented Indian reservations about the propriety of music when it came to the ruling classes. However, these reservations were more nuanced and varied than European sources suggest. For example, in the second half of the nineteenth century it was unclear whether elite men should be condemned if they danced. In public debates over this question, it was assumed that "Indian tradition" did not sanction rulers dancing, but that this tradition, like so many others, could be reexamined in light of colonial attitudes. In 1871 an article from the Lahore-based newspaper *Akẖbār-i-Anjuman-i-Punjāb* asked "how far it is proper for the Natives of India to imitate the manners and customs of the English, French, Germans, or Turks,"[97] with a specific view to the recent rise in ballroom-style dancing among chiefs and princes. The author suggested that a dancing prince was akin to other forms of Western accommodation, such as the abandonment of female seclusion: it called for discussion, lest an aspect of indigenous morality be compromised. He argued that "from time immemorial" dance had been "exclusively confined to women as an accomplishment most becoming the fair sex, so that not only is it held extremely reprehensible for men of the highest classes to dance, but even very few of those of the lower classes have adopted the practice . . . but simply in order to obtain their subsistence by means of it." This hesitation over the preservation of public masculinity was very much in keeping with the spirit of the earlier *mīrzānāmas*. However, other newspaper editors had argued in favor of dancing, on the basis that Krishna was known for his own enchanting dance.[98] This did not convince the writer from Lahore, who saw Krishna's behavior as indicative of a class question: this was an "exceptional case," not because Krishna was a god, but because he had been adopted by socially inferior cowherds, and as such "ought not to be adduced as an example in justification of the practice." Clearly not everyone was so conservative. The article's editor caustically remarked how the maharaja of Jaipur had recently danced in the presence of the British viceroy, and how the maharaja of Vizianagram "displayed his skill in the art in a recent festive assembly, as if by so doing he had gained the empyrean of civilization, and trampled superstition under foot. Well done, indeed!"[99]

That this particular critic raised the class question in relation to Krishna's dance is telling: indeed, this article was a component in a larger project within these newspapers to reify the emergent values of an upwardly mobile *sharīf* (genteel Muslim) society, by condemning aspects of both aristocratic and working-class cultures.[100] Before this society became more prominent and vocal in the later nineteenth century (especially after 1857), they were already critical of the musical interests of the contemporary elites. In 1838, Montgomery Martin noted that "in the country, few men are guilty of the indecency of singing or performing on musical instruments; but in Patna and Gaya many wealthy people indulge themselves."[101] Following 1857, the urban aristocrats associated with the Mughal or nawabi regimes lost their foothold, and in the course of their ascendancy the upwardly mobile classes condemned the old elites and their musical culture. Therefore, contrary to British accounts of a single condemnatory "native opinion," there was a class-specific variety to attitudes toward the propriety of elite performance, which was undergoing extensive reformulation at the time in line with the social changes wrought by the consolidation of colonial rule.

However, Wajid Ali was not attempting to appeal to the middle classes. Beyond their purview, within the cultural milieu of nawabi society, the king legitimized his musical passions by appealing to several distinct conceptual frameworks: his cultivation of erudite companionship, the desire to externalize the inner world of torment, the legacy of earlier Indian royal patrons, and the imaginary of a magical court.

Courtly Intimacy

In texts and paintings associated with Wajid Ali Shah, music is always grounded in the intimate social setting of the *meḥfil* or the larger *melā*. Engaging many participants, from boon companions to larger circles of the aristocracy, musical gatherings were sanctioned opportunities for consolidating relationships with and around the person of the king. This was directly inherited from the Mughal notion of the *meḥfil* as "an ideal venue in which Mughal men could display to their most intimate male companions their command of Indo-Persian codes of masculinity in dress, comportment, conduct, and knowledge."[102] Wajid Ali's interests in music were shared by a number of close companions, including his friend, vizier, and ultimately father-in-law, Ali Naqi Khan. They had first met in the house of Waziran the courtesan, and over time Ali Naqi took on more responsibilities in court, including the arrangement of the garden at Huzur Bagh. His accomplishments in such ventures impressed the king, who promoted his career, which continued long into the Matiyaburj years.[103]

Music parties were also important for poetic networking. Musicians like Qutub Ali Khan were well regarded for their poetry, and poets in Wajid Ali's retinue would sit with him in his *meḥfils*. The nawab made a point of identifying poets recognized from his Lucknow and Calcutta mushairas as his intimate companions in *Banī* ("Bride," 1877), a treatise written at Matiyaburj.[104] Though the work is primarily interested in music, one substantial section is in effect a poetic *tazkira*, offering both sample verses and short biographies of writers arranged alphabetically by their pen names (*takhalluṣ*).[105]

These miniature sketches of his friendships indicate how Wajid Ali used musical and poetic spaces as opportunities to strengthen the ties of intimacy that held the nawabi court together. While critics of the nawab emphasized the unprecedented influence of the likes of Ghulam Raza, who as a *ḍom* was considered a social upstart, other prominent figures in the nawab's personal life were drawn from established lineages in the Awadhi civil service.[106] One of the most emotionally significant companions in the Lucknow years was Muzaffar Ali Khan (Tadbiruddaula), whose father and grandfather had been in royal service, and who was himself an official for the state prisons and the high court. He was also a poet, writing under the *taḵẖalluṣ* Āsīr ("Bound"), and "for a period of ten to fifteen years this person remained my intimate-companion (*hampiyāla aur hamnawāla*), and there was not a gathering (*ṣŏḥbat*) or mushaira in which we were not together. Indeed, I needed but express the slightest kindness and he would profess his affection and count himself among my lovers. . . . He was so firmly in my good graces that he was in my attendance night and day."[107] In the context of the nawabi political system, gatherings for music and poetry were not diversions from governance, but provided a platform for the forging of human ties, which were the warp and weft of the court and state.[108]

Wajid Ali was strikingly overt in this passage, since he described Muzaffar as "a lover (*'āshiq*) in my service." Regardless of whether his primary sense was physical or emotional, the nawab was evidently comfortable positioning himself as the object of the other man's desire. Muzaffar was older than Wajid Ali, and in such a relationship it would be conventional for the younger partner to be the passive beloved (*ma'shūq*). This positioning was ambiguous. On the one hand, passive erotic behavior was considered emasculating and stigmatized in Indo-Persian culture, at least at the level of discourse concerning the comportment of elite men.[109] It would therefore be disabling for any man, let alone a king, to admit assuming a passive role in a relationship, by recording the attentions of his older lover. However, Muzaffar did not have authority in their friendship, since Wajid Ali underlined that he was a lover in service. According to traditions fostered by Urdu literary conventions, the beloved held emotional power over the lover, whereas the lover was rendered senseless by his infatuation and longing for the beloved, despite being "active."[110] To the south, Dakani rulers were identified as the objects of desire in their own lyrics, as well as in the works of their peers.[111] Wajid Ali explicitly aligned himself with this culture (see below), and stressed his own desirability in the *'Ishqnāma*. In this passage from *Banī*, the relationship is recalled through literary suggestions that invoke a combination of Mughal and Dakani tropes. Having outlined the extent of their friendship in Lucknow, Wajid Ali revealed that "when the comportment of the heavens changed, that is, the Sultanate met its end" and he went to Calcutta, Muzaffar abandoned him and ultimately transferred his allegiance to Rampur. Wajid Ali criticized him for his formal disloyalty, since the nawab was "his rightful patron," and simultaneously lamented their bitter separation, which by then had lasted twenty years. The account of their relationship therefore serves as a foil for the nawab's reflections on the poor treatment he had received over his lifetime, conflating his despondency in political exile with his personal grievances. In this sense, the passage confirms the personal dimension to nawabi politics, and gestures to the vulnerability of the nawab as the object of both desire and betrayal.

Introspection and Projection

This vulnerability was a central topos in the culture of Wajid Ali's court. Writing about musical encounters, studying the process of musical affect on the listener's homeostasis, and having relationships forged in musical gatherings all served as opportunities for the nawab to explore himself as lover and beloved, agent and victim of seductions, betrayals, grief and moments of rapture. The abundance of references to personal response, and the components of emotion, reflect Wajid Ali's enduring fascination with sentience. Themes that were familiar in literature were enacted on and through the king's body—a form of connoisseurship through participation.

The most pronounced example of this was the king's idiosyncratic exposure of his left breast and nipple, which began to appear in a number of his portraits in Lucknow, and continued much later in life (figure 3.3).[112] In these images the king is represented as dressed in an *angarkhā*, a fitted tunic characterized by a round or triangular "window" (*khiṛkī*) over the chest, with a square panel (*parda* or, less commonly, *kiwāṛī*) inserted behind the missing portion of the yoke. The *angarkhā* demands a relatively complex cut (it has been suggested that it was originally designed as a cavalry costume); the curved window was framed with binding on the bias that resulted in a mismatch between the window and the straight borders of the panel.[113] The square panel would not necessarily cover the entire circular section, especially given the curve of the chest. This left a segment of skin exposed, and it became customary to wear a vest under the *parda*. Wajid Ali was an early proponent of abandoning the vest, leaving bare a skewed portion of exposed chest and a nipple.[114] It has been suggested that removing the undergarment was a practical response to the hot weather, or considered erotic in courtly circles.[115] However, this is not wholly satisfactory: in a portrait of Wajid Ali alongside reproduced images of the other rulers in his lineage, he alone is

FIGURE 3.3. Wajid Ali Shah, as depicted in a portrait in Sibtainabad Imambarah, Kolkata. Photography by Eric Parker.

represented with an exposed nipple.[116] As far as any fashion gestures to a wider cultural context, the cleavage of the *angarkhā* can similarly be justified by the symbolism of nawabi aesthetics.

A clue to the *angarkhā* presents itself in the *tazkira* in *Banī*. Wajid Ali cited a verse by Shaikh Imam Bakhsh "Nāsiḳh" (1776–1838), considered by some to be the founder of the "Lucknow school" of poetry; according to the

Urdu literary critic Muhammad Husain Azad, he was "revered by his whole age, and everyone thought it an honor to be his pupil."[117] Nāsiḳh was a prolific poet, so it is striking that Wajid Ali only noted one sample verse:[118]

> *merā sīna hai mashriq āftāb-i dāgh-i hijrān kā*
> *ṭulū'-e ṣubaḥ-i maḥshar cāk hai mere girībān kā*
>
> My chest is the dawning sun of this separation's calamity
> In the assembly of morning's rising my collar is rent.

The word translated here as "collar," *girībān*, refers to the opening or breast of a garment, and therefore gestures to the heart and bosom, and the inner world of experience.[119] A collar that is rent open (*cāk*) is conventionally evocative of introspective affliction and sadness.[120] For Wajid Ali and his like-minded contemporaries, the exposure of the nipple and the bosom was a sartorial realization of a literary trope. This verse in particular underlined the public exposure of internal suffering: the opening of the *angarkhā* was an ornamented form of the collar torn in the lover's anxiety and pain, laid bare (quite literally) for the world to see and admire. Here, the virtuous or at least fashionable qualities were sensitivity, vulnerability, and a willingness to externalize one's tormented soul for public scrutiny. That Wajid Ali ascribed value to these concepts informs our sense of his writings on, and personal engagements with, musical performance: music was instrumental to his larger investment in the articulation of emotion as a virtue for public consumption.

Historical Precedent

The *'Ishqnāma* was Wajid Ali's most explicit exposition on emotion and the senses. His plight as a lover (both psychologically and physically, since the narrative ends with his contraction of gonorrhea) is explored through a catalogue of romances, friendships, and betrayals. However, the narrative also serves as a history of the development of the nawab's formulation of a musical conservatoire for women, including his recruitment of the singers and dancers he called *parī*s (fairies or angels), and their male *ustād*s.[121] By his own admission and the witness of contemporaries, Wajid Ali became preoccupied by the "House of Fairies" (*parīḵẖāna*), and perhaps suspected that he might come under criticism for investing himself so completely in its creation. Aside from the opportunities the *parīḵẖāna* presented for his own aesthetic and emotional stimulation, the nawab put forward an additional apologia within the text of the *'Ishqnāma*, stipulating that he was judiciously following a model set by earlier Indian rulers:

> In accordance with ancient histories, every emperor prepared training in every accomplishment for those people admitted under his purview, and managed them thoroughly to bring them up to the level of perfection; and among such emperors, Muhammad Shah, the emperor of Delhi, and Ibrahim Adil Shah, the sultan of Bijapur, and other earlier sultans had beautiful and elegant women given an education in the arts of music and considered them by the term *gā'in* [singers].
>
> Accordingly, I also followed this pattern, and prepared the musical arts for fairy-faced women with brows bright like Venus: whose glances are signals for the spirit's passion, a torch to the darkness. The ribbons in their braids are serpents. Their eyebrows are poisonous scorpions, poised to sting. When they begin to sing the sound appears like David's miracle,[122] and the soul comes out from the body and becomes restless [or powerless]. If they are adorned with dance costumes, then those who worship fire prostrate and fall down overwhelmed. People are dazzled when they see their glittering costumes and beautiful ornaments. When they dance, the planet Venus flings away her orbit and struts over with compliments so she might learn this magical, ornamental skill. When they lift their skirts, the peacock follows them obediently.[123]

Wajid Ali legitimated his active role in the cultivation of the arts (rather than a purely instrumental form of patronage) through historical precedent, suggesting that his interests in musical women were not excessive, but were in accordance with the expectations of a ruler. His specific identifications with Muhammad Shah (r. 1719–48) and Ibrahim Adil Shah (r. 1580–1627) were appropriate, since both rulers were remembered as patrons, composers, and performers in their own right.[124] Though it is unknown whether Muhammad Shah taught anyone music himself, Ibrahim Adil Shah seems to have taken an active interest in musical pedagogy, and claimed Saraswati, the Hindu goddess of music and learning, as his mother.[125] In Ibrahim Adil Shah, Wajid Ali had a clear precedent of a Shi'a Indian monarch, singer, instrumentalist, and writer of music treatises.

This apologia also asserted the excellence of Wajid Ali's activities by their fruits. The review of the ladies of the *parīḵẖāna* was further embellished through an allusion to a Qur'anic affirmation of sound art as worship, but also by several references to the effect of music in the body, on the senses, and in the wider astrological sphere. The text therefore drives the reader away from a carnal or purely sexual reading, suggesting that the cultivation of these women, and the technical interaction between music and the inner sentient life, is an admirable and profound activity for a ruler, as expertly executed by Wajid Ali Shah: "When I gave the order for the perfection of this art, only a little later the fairy-faced ones acquired such proficiency in both [music and dance] that if those *ustād*s in this art like Tansen and Baiju Bawra were still here, even they would consider themselves inferior by comparison."[126]

Fantasy

Subscribing to a precedent set by earlier rulers was perhaps the safest rhetorical strategy at Wajid Ali's disposal. However, a less conventional explanation for his behavior was perhaps more pertinent to the music in his court. The nawab was fascinated by the supernatural and magical, and musical performances provided a foundation on which to build his own fantastical court. Despite drawing on various tropes from Indo-Islamic cultural history, these practices seemed quite alien and abhorrent to the British in Lucknow.

During the Lucknow years, Wajid Ali put on a series of entertainments at the Qaisarbagh ("Caesar's Garden"), primarily for a select audience of members of the court. The British of Lucknow were never invited,[127] though accounts of the festivities from 1851 are recorded in the recollections of the nawab's uncle, Iqtidaruddaula.[128] These recollections are of particular interest since they discuss Wajid Ali's innovation in musical theater, the *rahas* (see chapter 4). The plots and texts of these performances were based largely on his earlier writings (c. 1837–42), especially his *masnavī*s (romantic narrative poems) including *Daryā-yi Ta'ashshuq* ("The River of Love"), *Afsāna-yi 'Ishq* ("Love Story"), and *Bahār-i Ulfat* ("The Spring of Affection").[129] The first of these was played out in 1851 through the many gardens of the Qaisarbagh and occasionally at different spaces in the city; the others followed over the next two years.[130] According to Iqtidaruddaula, the *rahas* was staged in fourteen episodes spread over one month and ten days, and employed a number of temporary set designs, from forts to deserts, and ornate costumes.[131] This *rahas* related the love story of Ghazalah and Mahru, leading the audience through an idealized court setting in which royalty and courtiers were placed alongside dervishes, demons, and fairies. As already intimated by the earlier account of the *parīḵẖāna*, the performing women of the court assumed dazzling qualities through their training. In the context of the courtly imaginary developed in Lucknow, these women were not merely fairies (*parī*s) by name, but had all the conventional attributes associated with supernatural beings. Llwellyn-Jones notes how the drama seamlessly coalesced the real and the imaginary, and how "it emphasised the semi-magical qualities of Wajid Ali Shah, a man who had the power to create another kingdom within his own kingdom."[132] Entertainment and dramatic spectacle aside, the *rahas* thus projected a nexus between magic, beauty, and Wajid Ali's personal charisma. This conflation of themes real and imagined became a hallmark of performances in Lucknow, as the king enacted his life and works (including a dramatization of the *'Ishqnāma* in October 1851) on a magical scale.

The king had a profound interest in jinns, and several anecdotes from the Lucknow years indicate their being a consideration in his life outside of performance.[133] Again, this was consistent with earlier notions of royalty and the arts: in the Qur'an the archetypal sovereign Solomon was given power over jinns.[134] This appealed to the Mughal emperors Jahangir and Shah Jahan, who identified with an "allegorical construction" that combined the connotations of Majnun, Orpheus, David, and Solomon.[135] Solomon "had long been represented in Persianate painting as a sovereign on his throne surrounded by his pacified animal subjects and his servants, the winged angels and spirits (*parīs*) and subjugated demons (*dīvs*)."[136] The poet Nizami had established Majnun as a Solomon-like figure and called him *shāh-i jahān*, "King of the World"—a trope taken up by Emperor Shah Jahan, who had a Florentine *pietra dura* tablet image of Orpheus set into the back wall of his throne. Wajid Ali appealed to David's miracle and identified with Majnun's inner turmoil, and by surrounding himself with magical beings under his own musical direction, he too appropriated the Solomonic ideal. These associations were made explicit by a portrait (figure 3.4) of Wajid Ali as Sri *rāg* in the music treatise *Ghunca-yi Rāg* (1863): he appears flanked by *parīs*, borne aloft by *dīvs*, and is called "Sultan of the World, Wajid Ali Shah, Solomon of Awadh."[137] The same series of drawings presented three ladies of Qaisarbagh, perhaps *parīs*, in a depiction of Basant *rāgini*.[138] These illustrations, prepared while the nawab was in Calcutta, suggest how Wajid Ali understood the magical authority of music over all creatures, and its potential to evoke both Qur'anic ideals and the culture of the Mughal emperors. While Shah Jahan drew upon the visual image of Orpheus to invoke these associations, Wajid Ali used his individual musical prowess and patronage to translate his court into the fantastical domain of the Islamicate Solomon.

The Lucknow courtly imaginary also engaged royal elements drawn from Hindu religious traditions (figure 3.5). The most overt connection was to the paradigm of regal splendor, riches, and musical accomplishment: the court of the god Indra. Allusions to this heavenly court were cemented in the popular imagination due to the commercial success of the Parsi theatrical production *Indar Sabha*, which is heavily associated with Wajid Ali (see chapter 4). Wajid Ali also appropriated the romanticized attributes of a majestic, explicitly yogic figure in his identification with Majnun. In the years 1853 to 1855, a public *melā* took place in the Qaisarbagh courtyard during the Hindu month of Sawan, often referred to as the Yogi Melā.[139] In the *'Ishqnāma*, Wajid Ali described how he once sat under a banana tree in the Hazratbagh garden to

FIGURE 3.4. Wajid Ali Shah as Sri *rāg*. Lithograph print, 1863, in Khan, *Ghunca-yi Rāg*.

FIGURE 3.5. Musical theatre in the Lucknow court, as depicted in the *'Ishqnāma* (Lucknow, India: 1849–50). Royal Collection Trust / © Her Majesty Queen Elizabeth II, 2015.

read his own poetic compositions. As he read, he became so impassioned that he tore off his clothes until he stood in his loincloth, the very image of the heroic lover-turned-fakir Majnun.[140] As his female companions came out to join him in the garden, they smeared themselves with ashes like Hindu ascetics, and musicians came out to join the improvised festival. Two courtiers held peacock fans in his honor, and toward evening the party settled by the stream to watch fireworks.

This celebration became a formal *melā* in future years, and all the invitees were requested to arrive dressed in saffron, to continue the ascetic theme. Adorned with ashes from burnt pearls, Wajid Ali would hide himself in an artificial mountain until he was "discovered" by two of his ladies, which then prompted a celebration involving music, cannon fire, and fireworks.[141] The festival became legendary in the lore of Lucknow: an alternative explanation for the *melā*'s theme claimed that upon Wajid Ali's birth his horoscope had declared that he was destined for the life of an ascetic, rather than that of a king. Therefore, to appease the forces of fate, he would always celebrate his birth by dressing as a yogi. However, there are no contemporary sources for this explanation, which seems to address his status as a ruler from a post-1857 perspective. The tale is decidedly less sensual than his own account in the *'Ishqnāma*, as though to diminish the common criticism of his oversexed decadence, while the claim that he was never meant to be a ruler also neatly absolved him of responsibility in the annexation.

The Royal Fair of Qaisarbagh was taken to Matiyaburj, where all celebrants were strictly instructed to dress as glamorized yogis and yoginis. In 1869, the newspaper *Nusseem Jounpore* printed an account of the *melā* under the heading "Jashn Sulateen" (The Sultan's Festival), noting that Wajid Ali had "passed orders that all who attended the fair, whether men, women, or prostitutes, should appear in red clothing. The fair was held in the Royal Gardens, and some ten thousand persons of both sexes and all classes, were present."[142] The article also referred to an inscription over the doorway to the fair: "If there is a Paradise on earth, It is this, it is this, it is this!" If this is an authentic witness, then the inclusion of the verse at Matiyaburj gestures to an ongoing affiliation with the now desolated Mughal court,[143] and also the declaration of the court as a heavenly, fantastical realm. It appears that by making such claims, Wajid Ali wished to create a living realization of a magical court within his own grounds. This playful performance of fantasy drew on the visual and ideological registers of the Mughal court, colored by local Awadhi and Hindu connotations. By cultivating his fairy attendants in the likeness of the *apsarās* (celestial musical nymphs) from the court of the divine king Indra, and training them proficiently in musical knowledge for performances of magical romances, Wajid Ali brought his idealized realm into reality.

Conclusion

While this chapter has focused on the particulars of Wajid Ali Shah and Lucknow, decadence is a pervasive and often unchallenged theme in the historiography of late premodern India, informing basic assumptions about the nawabs themselves and the musical or artistic cultures under their purview. With the accounts of Wajid Ali placed in context, it is apparent that British views of king and court were shaped by discourses that yoked together decadence, misgovernment, and music. This combination was itself a recent development in British thought when it was transplanted to India. In the process, the pursuit of luxury and pleasure was denigrated as an Oriental vice, and projected onto Wajid Ali. In the course of annexation and its public defense in the late nineteenth century, decadence served as an apologia for British "intervention," legitimating the East India Company's actions as a response to neglectful rule. Though such arguments invoked "native" conventions, suggesting that Wajid Ali was also offending Indian sensibilities, this did little justice to the variety and shifting basis of value judgements in north Indian society at that time.

Scholars of the "decadent phenomenon" in Italy, France, and England in the late nineteenth century have sought new ways to nuance the connotations of decadence as an immoral and degenerate sensibility. Walter Binni and Richard Drake have proposed a set of distinctions that help separate the moral and aesthetic character of decadence. One reading of decadence ("la decadenza") is as a foil for the values of whoever uses the term: it is a moralistic judgement that can be applied to whatever is being rejected. A separate concept is decadentism ("il decadentismo"), a movement in art and literature, which Drake views as "the beginning of the modern cultural idiom, stressing pure musicality as the supreme good in art as opposed to the more traditional didactic and entertaining functions of art."[144] This is seen as a transformation of European romanticism, a step beyond a third concept, the intermediary "decadent romanticism," which was more overtly sexualized and mystical than the work of the earlier Romantics. This tripartite distinction is rooted in the particularities of European decadence, but it nonetheless provides a helpful framework for reconsidering "decadence" in nawabi culture.

Examining Wajid Ali Shah's own writings on music indicates a set of priorities consciously drawn from late Mughal aesthetics, though reformulated in innovative and therefore sometimes controversial directions. When we turn to Urdu and Persian works drawn from the nawabi court itself, the relevance of decadence or conspicuous consumption is diminished. Instead, the nawab's ruminations on music indicate an original endeavor to harness, manipulate, and express emotion; to embody literary tropes; and to create a fantastical realm that was nonetheless conversant with historical precedents of connoisseur kings. Though to British commentators the outward expressions of this culture were suggestive of whimsy and excess, from an insider's perspective they indicated highly aestheticized attempts to assume control over the self and the magic of the court, at a time when the real political power of the nawab was at its most vulnerable.

4
Music at Matiyaburj

He spends his days in his menagerie, and in drawing, painting, and writing poetry. His songs are said to be excellent, according to native taste, and some which are called after his name—"Huzrut-Ki-Thoongree"—are sung, I am told, by dancing girls all over Calcutta, Benares, and many other of the principal towns of India. . . . His Ex-Majesty's evenings are spent among musicians and dancing girls. One of his four principal houses (all of which are furnished "in great style") is selected for the day, and there he passes the night—Calcutta meanwhile as ignorant of his pleasures and he of its as if he were still in Oude. . . . The King maintains a little town, providing the élite of it with choice amusement, and the whole town with amusement of some sort, in addition to providing them with the means of living. The little camp is, in its way, royal—as Eastern peoples understand royalty.

—"A RETIRED KING," *New York Times*, 11 November 1874

The achievements of exile are permanently undermined by the loss of something left behind forever.

—EDWARD SAID[1]

The annexation of Awadh in 1856, followed by the Uprising across north India, brought an end to nawabi rule and definitively transformed the lives of Wajid Ali Shah, his family, and his companions. However, this was not the end of nawabi or even Lakhnavi culture, which continued in other centers, particularly Rampur, and for thirty years flourished in Calcutta, in Wajid Ali's court-in-exile at Matiyaburj. Though in moments of anger the nawab said that he looked "upon his house as a gaol and his garden as a wilderness,"[2] he was nonetheless able to continue his experiments with musical theory and performance. While most cultural studies of nawabi Lucknow finish in 1856 and represent Matiyaburj as an afterthought or ghost of its predecessor, the nawab himself compared his achievements there to a new and fresh rose.[3] In terms of music, the court deserves its own study in two respects: first as a site of novelty and variety, and second as a forum that drew together Hindustani *ustāds* and Bengali patrons and disciples. The forum facilitated the transfusion of upper Indian musical practices through the arteries of elite Calcutta and beyond. This chapter is concerned with the first of these concerns, and will present an analysis of the forgotten music of Matiyaburj.

Since his death in 1887, Wajid Ali has attracted literary and scholarly attention in several languages. To a large extent, the popular memory of the nawab has been shaped by historical fiction, most notably Satyajit Ray's film *Śatrañj Ke Khilāṛī* ("The Chess Players," 1977), itself based on the Hindi and Urdu short story of the same name by Premchand.[4] In his adaptation, Satyajit Ray developed the character of the nawab and focused on his artistic patronage and sensitivity as redeeming qualities.[5] Other fictional accounts of the nawab (in Hindi, Urdu, French, and thence translated into other European languages) similarly evoke the colorful court life of Lucknow, and situate Wajid Ali as a tragic or eccentric figure.[6] Popular histories written in Bengali have a similar focus, furnished with greater historical detail; they are distinct from the novels, though, in that they generally acknowledge the existence of Matiyaburj.[7]

The neglect of Matiyaburj outside of Bengali literature gestures to the conceptual importance of Lucknow in the imagination of Urdu writers and historians after 1857, who privileged Wajid Ali's Lucknow career in their biographies and literary histories.[8] Even works which consider the nawab's post-1856 writings in depth nonetheless situate them anachronistically against the Qaisarbagh palace rather than the Matiyaburj court. While twentieth-century writers with the requisite language facility drew upon a variety of older Urdu sources, many cultural studies of the nawabi courts privilege just one: the series of essays collected under the title "The Last Example of Eastern Civilization in Hindustan" by Abdul Halim Sharar (1860–1926).[9] Sharar has had an enormous historiographical influence, and is invoked as a contemporary witness in a broad sweep of studies on literature, the performing arts, architecture, gastronomy, and many other aspects of cultural history. This is partly because his account of nineteenth-century culture is extremely comprehensive and detailed, but also because his work has been made available in English translation. While this translation has proved invaluable for scholars, until very recently there has been little critical engagement with Sharar's particular frame of reference.[10] This criticism has underlined the significance of nostalgia in Sharar's writings, which colored his "ethnographic" detailing of nawabi society. Here I will extend this analysis to Sharar's depiction of the musical life of Wajid Ali's court, by drawing upon a larger range of available sources that present a very different image of the ex-king.

In her recent biography of the nawab, Rosie Llewellyn-Jones unpacked the insights into Wajid Ali's personal life that might be gleaned from the colonial archive. Particularly enlightening is the correspondence of the British administrators closest to the nawab, the "Agents of the Governor General with the King of Oudh." One of these, Charles Herbert, was extremely sympathetic to Wajid Ali: an informal sketch of the nawab taken from life and drawn by Herbert's own hand gestures to a level of familiarity beyond that enjoyed by most

European visitors.[11] Yet Herbert himself informed his superiors that he felt ignorant about real life behind the walls of Garden Reach, as the British were not invited to experience the inner life of the court.[12] As a result, the colonial archive overemphasizes the nawab's apparent isolation.[13]

When one reads Wajid Ali's own commentaries on music at Matiyaburj alongside Bengali reminiscences of the nawab, another side of his character comes into view. This chapter will begin with an introduction to the court in Calcutta and the financial investment in musicians there, which was on a scale unprecedented in Bengal. I will then discuss the historiography of the court and argue that Sharar's writings, which have become foundational to cultural studies of the nawabi period, are both problematic and inaccurate. I will then suggest an alternative view of Matiyaburj, with a focus on the nawab's work on vocal music, dance, and musical theater. Finally, I will consider the larger social implications of Matiyaburj, reflecting particularly on the women who were instrumental in performing Wajid Ali's creations, and the Shiʿa scholars who were working elsewhere in the court, with opera, dancing, and processions sounding in the background.

Music and the Menagerie

When Wajid Ali arrived in Calcutta on 13 May 1856, he did not know that he would remain there for the rest of his life.[14] The next three years remained uncertain: in that time his mother and brother journeyed to London to plead for his restoration in Awadh; Lucknow was devastated by the Uprising and Siege, during which the Qaisarbagh Palace was looted and largely destroyed; and one of his divorced wives, Hazrat Mahal, became a figurehead in the resistance against the British.[15] Wajid Ali spent much of this time imprisoned in Fort William, and when he was released on 9 July 1859 to his new home in Garden Reach, his world had changed.[16] Many refugees from Awadh had already begun to settle around the royal houses, and that same month many wives and courtiers also arrived.[17] By 1866 the palace complex had grown from three to at least fifteen core properties, surrounded by an expanding community of migrants and court dependents.[18] Indeed, the court was in a constant state of repair or development, suffering setbacks such as a fire in 1860 and two cyclones in 1864 and 1867;[19] but it also grew to accommodate the nawab's demand for "a very large number of mirrors, chandeliers, marble and stone statues, pillars, vases, and other ornamental furniture."[20]

As noted in chapter 3, the British took a dim view of the court and Matiyaburj became "unfortunately notorious" for crime.[21] Although administrators in Calcutta disapproved of Wajid Ali's lifestyle, they were nonetheless compelled to finance it. Upon the annexation, the government agreed to provide him with a fixed annual income of 1,200,000 rupees to cover the expenses of his family and household. Over the next thirty years the nawab insisted that this was inadequate, and he fought against further interference in his domestic affairs. While certain agents, particularly Herbert, were sympathetic to his position, others were not—especially Mowbray Thomson, who called him "senseless, querulous, and rambling. . . . His weakness of mind borders on insanity."[22] Whatever their individual stances, however, the administrators felt it necessary to maintain a certain standard of living for the nawab: "Any suggestion that the richest princely house in India had been deliberately impoverished by the government could have had dangerous consequences in a country so recently emerging from the Uprising."[23] Although Wajid Ali often felt his hands tied economically, to musicians he must have seemed especially affluent, particularly in comparison to the other aristocratic families of old Bengal. Matiyaburj was a well-endowed source of musical patronage for Lakhnavi musicians, but also for other artists who, as seen in chapter 2, were beginning to settle in Calcutta.

Despite British attempts to curtail his expenditure, it soon became apparent that Wajid Ali was spending beyond his means and working up a long list of creditors. Much of the correspondence from the government of Bengal regarding Matiyaburj is concerned with the king's extravagance, which was creating difficulties inside Garden Reach and beyond.[24] When pushed to make cuts, Wajid Ali targeted the stipends of his relations, reducing allowances, or in one case proposing to divorce twenty-seven of his oldest *mut'a* wives all at once.[25] The government was extremely conscious that, since it was responsible for the king's stipend, it would ultimately take responsibility for his creditors upon his death, and set up a series of interventions. Herbert drew up a report on the finances of Matiyaburj on 11 September 1866.[26] Apart from the extensive and ever-increasing royal family, the palace was home to 2,225 employees and 717 soldiers. All in all, the establishment cost 52,490 rupees, 4 annas per month—26,830 rupees, 12 annas constituting the overall pay of all the palace staff, from eunuchs to retained musicians. At this early stage in the exiled court's career, the king's debts had risen to somewhere between 7,000,000 and 7,500,000 rupees.

Two of the most serious expenses were the king's menagerie and his musical entertainments. Wajid Ali was exceptionally proud of the former, and resented the government's suggestion to redistribute his funds from the animals to his family: "I am therefore attached to it with a degree of fondness which far exceeds that [which] I entertain towards my sons, daughters, etc."[27] This was an endless drain on the monarch's stipend. Every month, 500 rupees went to the purchase of new fish; 1,193 rupees, 10 annas on "country" animals; 2,334 rupees, 8 annas on foreign animals; and 855 rupees, 6 annas, 5 paisas on new pigeons. One member of the household, Ryhan ud-Daulah, was responsible for several running accounts, including the foreign animals. He was also allocated 248 rupees, 10 annas, 9 paisas per month specifically for gold ornaments "for the dancing girls." The dancing girls' wardrobe was catered for with an additional budget of 2,877 rupees, 14 annas, 6 paisas per month.[28] The British paid particular attention to the menagerie, because the gardens and enclosures were visible to them and occasionally posed serious problems—as in 1879, when a tigress escaped Matiyaburj and mauled a German gardener in the Botanical Gardens.[29] Behind closed doors and drawn curtains, however, Wajid Ali was spending a similar amount on a constantly updated wardrobe of costumes and jewelry for his performers. These were not meager sums, especially at a time when Wajid Ali was proposing to limit the income of his eldest living son, Faridun Kudr Mirza Mahomed, to a mere 90 rupees a month.[30] These official figures were probably also extremely conservative. Six months later, Mowbray Thomson reported that Wajid Ali was becoming even more extravagant, and had spent 40,000 rupees on new birds and animals in the last two months alone.

In Herbert's report on Matiyaburj's finances (1866), musicians and singers are listed alongside other categories of employee. In her study of musical patronage at the court of Baroda, Bakhle compared the status of musicians to wrestlers, and saw them as part of the household's human apparatus, rather than as exalted artists in residence.[31] Herbert provided the total number of staff of each category, and their collective income per month, so it is possible to provide the mean wage of individuals. There were twenty-four male and five female musicians and singers registered as receiving a monthly income: on average, a salary of 19 rupees each. This was a base salary, supplemented through gifts after performances, making the actual income of musicians much higher than this estimate.[32] The base alone was a very respectable salary relative to that of other servants: the keepers of the king's beloved pigeons averaged 8.5 each, tailors 10, poets and reciters 13, and eunuchs 14. Therefore musicians, before gifts, were highly valued employees, ranking just under clerks, who were paid 20. Apart from these musicians were the separate categories of *naubat* players (twenty-two men paid 13 rupees each), and an "English band" of twenty-five men who, curiously, were paid most of all, averaging 28 rupees each.[33] Aside from the "house musicians," visiting or invited musicians would perform on an ad hoc basis, and were rewarded as occasions demanded.

We are able to compare these "official" figures to Wajid Ali's own estimates prepared ten years later: he counted 145 musicians in his court, on a total salary of 3,261 rupees—that is, an average of 22.5 rupees each. More expensive were the 216 female artists in his training schemes (nearly all of whom would have been *mut'a* wives), on varied salaries accumulating to 8,598 rupees per month, averaging 40 rupees each.[34] Additional gifting and income aside, the average for *ustāds* is extremely close to the British figures. However, the government did not take note of Wajid Ali's investment in female performers, presumably because they were paid out of another allowance for his family rather than one for servants and other dependents. Another significant disparity lay in the number of musicians involved: the British were evidently unaware of the scale of the nawab's collective of performing artists.

Swan Song of Awadh?

As already noted, many studies of nawabi society have relied heavily upon the essays of Abdul Halim Sharar. While these writings are extremely rich, they are particularly problematic on the subjects of Matiyaburj and musical culture. Ostensibly writing about Lucknow, Sharar himself had never seen the pre-1857 court that interested him most. He had spent a portion of his adolescence in Matiyaburj from 1869 to 1879; and his maternal grandfather Munshi Qamaruddin, had held an appointment in the administration between 1877 and 1879.[35] Sharar went on to become an extremely prolific author and journalist, his works including fifteen popular histories and twenty-eight historical novels.[36] Though Sharar himself never personally saw what he termed the "Lucknow of Old" (*Guzashta Lakhna'ū*), his essays harked back to the lost world of Islamicate Hindustan. The Calcutta court was mentioned sparingly, and only as a clone of Lucknow:

> From the time of the King's arrival in Calcutta, a second Lucknow had arisen in its neighbourhood. The real Lucknow had ended and was replaced by Matiya Burj. . . . No one thought he was in Bengal.[37]

By claiming that for thirty years the culture of Lucknow had been impeccably preserved, Sharar crafted a romantic ideal of an authentic nawabi world, uncompromised by colonial modernity until its dissolution upon the death of the king.

Sharar characterized Lucknow as the apex of civilization in a bygone age. Etiquette and social graces came from royal courts; these alone were refined and cultured (*muhazzab aur shā'ista*).[38] C. M. Naim has suggested that Sharar's notion of "culture" (*tamaddun*) was influenced by a social discourse developed by Arabic writers, including Mohammad Halim Ansari on Jurji Zaidan: *tamaddun* was evolutionary, advancing from barbarity to civilization, only to deteriorate if dominated by another culture or political power. Rather than viewing colonialism as the conquest of an inferior civilization by its superior, Zaidan and Sharar understood the loss of dominion to mark the advent of cultural decline.[39] Lucknow was the successor and better of Delhi, and the highest attainment of Indian *tamaddun*: "All refined men from other regions now follow the ways of the citizens of Lucknow."[40] Following the loss of dominion in Awadh, according to Sharar's model, Lakhnavi culture could not advance further at Matiyaburj, but could only stagnate before its ultimate dissolution.

Sharar's notion of a conclusive end to the development of Lakhnavi culture was particular to his work, and was not shared by other cultural commentators, who suggested that certain nawabi customs and practices had continued into the twentieth century.[41] Sharar neglected the persistence and evolution of the "old world" at Matiyaburj and among the *ta'alluqadārs* of Awadh—landed elites who became increasingly prominent after 1857—for rhetorical and stylistic reasons: "Nostalgia becomes truly enjoyable to the nostalgic only when he manages somehow to convince himself that the 'golden' past was totally lost and for good."[42] Nostalgia was increasingly popular in Urdu literature in the early twentieth century, and Sharar had to euthanize nawabi culture in order to make it more appealing and tragic to his readers.[43]

Although Sharar was personally acquainted only with Matiyaburj, his essays spoke of Lucknow, making only sporadic references to the court-in-exile.[44] For example, on the subject of Persian literature:

> Without a knowledge of Persian our sentiments cannot be correctly expressed nor can we correctly achieve polished conversation. Of the few people who lived in Matiya Burj, Calcutta, with the ill-fated last King of Avadh there was not a single educated person who did not know Persian. The language of the secretariat was Persian and there were hundreds of Hindus and Muslims who wrote Persian poetry. Even women composed Persian verses and every child could make himself understood in the language.[45]

Matiyaburj was indeed a center for Persian poets. However, even this anecdote was less concerned with a historical reality than with a particular rhetoric. By chronicling the nawabi world, Sharar was commemorating its loss; and thus he implied that Persian literary culture had truly ended, while claiming that this world had cultivated the fundamentals of authentic Indianness. Indians, Hindu and Muslim alike, could not express themselves without Persian, yet Persian had disappeared along with the nawabs. Matiyaburj was seen as an enclave for a small party of refugees from a dying civilization. Sharar did not see it as a court with material concerns and an evolving culture, in conversation with its new Bengali surroundings.

A brief glance at the poets of Matiyaburj indicates that while there were continuities in Lucknow's mushaira culture, the nawab's retinue in Calcutta was very different. While the impact of the trauma of 1857 on the Urdu poetic imagination is receiving increasing recognition today,[46] the annexation and the Uprising also brought about very worldly changes to the life of court poets.[47] While several poets did follow the nawab to Calcutta (including Sayyid Muhammad Husain "Sami," Sayyid Sarafraz Husain "Mukhlis," Ganga Prasad Bahadur "Badr," Gopal Singh Bahadur "Thaqib," and Fatehuddaulah "Barq"),[48] many migrated instead to join the nawab of Rampur.[49] New poets emerged over the Matiyaburj years, including one Sadiq Ali Khan, the grandson of the renowned poet Khwaja Atish, who customarily sent his *ghazal* compositions to the nawab for constructive criticism.[50] Once he had settled in Calcutta, Wajid Ali was joined by other poets who were already based in Bengal, including Sayyid Fath Ali "Waysi" (1816–86), a Sufi originally from Chittagong, who had studied in Murshidabad before joining Matiyaburj as a secretary. His *diwan* (179 *ghazal*s and 23 *qaṣīda*s) was published posthumously in 1898, and his grave at Maniktalla is now venerated as a shrine.[51]

Similarly, Sharar foregrounded musicians from the Lucknow years, such as Ghulam Raza and Qutub Ali Khan, and a set of significant musicians associated with the Delhi *kalāwant birāderī*: Pyar Khan, Jafar Khan, Haidar Khan, and Basat Khan.[52] Sharar did not include the names of musicians active in Matiyaburj from the late 1870s to 1887, whom he may have actually heard, such as Murad Ali Khan, Taj Khan, and Ali Bakhsh (see chapter 6). This in itself is evidence of Sharar's misrepresentation of the stagnation of music after its evolutionary climax in Lucknow. Since Sharar related Pyar Khan and his family to the older trajectory of Hindustani *tamaddun*, going back to Tansen and Delhi, the demise of music at Lucknow was the demise of Hindustani music as a whole. However, this is also a reflection of his choice of informant on musical culture, Asadullah "Kaukab" Khan (c. 1850–1915).[53] Sharar and Kaukab were ideally suited collaborators, since they shared a similar experience of Lakhnavi culture. Kaukab had also known Matiyaburj fleetingly as a child: his father, Niamatullah Khan, was attached to the court in the late 1860s, but then proceeded in the early 1870s to Kathmandu, where he trained Kaukab and his older brother Karamatullah Khan (1848–1933). Kaukab was a highly educated Urdu litterateur in his own right, and was preparing a treatment of music, the *Jauhar-i Mūsīqī*, though he died before he could arrange for its publication. Like Sharar, Kaukab drew on the memories of his predecessors to fashion a memory of nawabi musical culture. Also like Sharar, he distilled this memory through his contemporary misgivings about the position of Muslim civilization in early-twentieth-century India, and by what he considered to be the decline of culture. Here I will consider Kaukab's claims about Wajid Ali and court music, and assess their contribution to Sharar's vision for the legacy of Matiyaburj.

Dilettante or Expert?

Sharar quoted at length from a letter in which Kaukab detailed musical life under the nawabs. Kaukab's overall argument was that music had flourished in the court *in spite of* Wajid Ali, who had limited its potential by focusing on tawdry styles and forms.[54] His letter began by declaring that Wajid Ali had conferred titles upon the less able musicians, to the neglect of experts. Yet shortly after this, Kaukab contradicted himself: "Whilst little interest was taken in pure classical music, expert musicians were much esteemed at the royal court." Kaukab added that the nawab "had been taught the science of music by Basit Khan and had a very good understanding of it. Being highly talented, the king had evolved new raginis to his own liking."[55] Kaukab was thus torn between two images of the king: as a superficial dilettante who did not recognize true artistry; and as an expert and innovator trained by Niamatullah Khan's own *ustād*, and thus a *guru-bhāī* of Kaukab's father.

Kaukab disapproved of Wajid Ali's innovations and was frustrated that a connoisseur so highly trained in aesthetic theory should make an informed decision to support seemingly tawdry music:

> Wajid Ali Shah was a master at the art and possessed the knowledge of an expert but he cannot escape the criticism that it was his conventional and cheap tastes that made the music of Lucknow frivolous and easily understandable by all. In accordance with popular tastes even the most discriminating singers omitted difficult techniques and based their music on light, simple, and attractive tunes which could be appreciated by everyone.[56]

Clearly a different critic might view this characterization—music as enjoyable and accessible—as a positive development. Kaukab was harsher in his own manuscript treatise. He charged Wajid Ali with neglecting musical knowledge, arguing that no reliable books on the art were written in his reign, nor any study of earlier works, specifying the *Uṣūl al-Naghmāt-i Āṣafī* (1793), the *Toḥfat al-Hind* (c. 1675), and the *Shams al-Aṣwāt* (1698) as examples of discarded scholarship.[57] This criticism is evidence of Kaukab's serious underestimation of Wajid Ali's intellectual accomplishments.

Wajid Ali Shah himself composed and published at least five works on music. The first of these, *Ṣaut al-Mubārak* ("Voice of the Blessed") was written in Persian in Lucknow, 1852–53. Wajid Ali's introduction expressed his frustration with the existing literature on music: he had consulted several texts, including the *Uṣūl al-Naghmāt-i Āṣafī* , the *Kh̲ulāṣat al-ʿAish-i ʿĀlam Shāhī* (1798), and the *Saṅgītadarpaṇa* (c. 1600).[58] The first of these was named for its patron and Wajid Ali's predecessor Nawab Asafuddaulah (r. 1775–97), so it would have been surprising if Wajid Ali had ignored it entirely. In Wajid Ali's digest he eliminated sections of music theory he thought redundant, preserving a chapter on *sur*,[59] another on rhythm,[60] a brief discussion of instruments, and three larger and wholly unprecedented chapters on dance (*raqṣ*), anecdotal stories (*naql*), and musical theater (*rahas*). It was not that Wajid Ali was unread, as Kaukab suggested, but rather that he considered earlier scholarship inadequate:

> From my childhood, I have felt attracted to music, but I did not acquire even a glimpse of its countenance. Those who are knowledgeable in this art are miserly and unambitious. . . . Finally, I acquired this art, enchained to discipline and through mental struggle, and this book [*Ṣaut al-Mubārak*] was written with the view to extending it to others.[61]

Kaukab may not have approved of Wajid Ali's approach, but it was inaccurate to accuse the nawab of neglecting his studies.

Wajid Ali was both well-read and prolific. By 1877 he had written forty-six works, rising perhaps to one hundred before his death ten years later.[62] There are no known copies of many of his compositions, due to two great calamities to the royal estate, the first in 1857 and the second in the auctioning of Matiyaburj thirty years later.[63] The libraries of Lucknow were looted during the Uprising, and many volumes were burned.[64] Wajid Ali was personally aggrieved by this loss, and composed a verse on "the pillage of vile men":

> *ek ḥasrat ṭaur par bhī bhar mūsī rah gayī*
> *āīsā kuch dēkhā ki ānkhōn kō tamnnā rah gayī*
>
> The rat filled itself up, even in a state of grief:
> Seeing such things, the eyes retained their longing.[65]

This did not dissuade him from continuing his literary pursuits in Matiyaburj, where he installed a printing press. He published several new works, chiefly in Urdu, on music: two song anthologies, *Nāju* ("Delicate Woman," 1868)[66] and *Dulhan* ("Bride," 1873);[67] a larger work named *Banī* ("Bride," 1877); and then *Chanchal Nāzanīn* ("Trembling Mistress," 1879).[68] *Banī* echoes *Ṣaut al-Mubārak*, with treatments of *sur* and *tāla*, but these are relatively brief from a theoretical perspective: the primary interest of the work is to document the musical activities of the Matiyaburj court, especially lyrical compositions, directions and plots for performances, and a detailed commentary on the musical education of Wajid Ali's court women.

Max Katz's analysis of Kaukab's own treatment of music, the *Jauhar-i Mūsīqī*, indicates a similar intention to organize and clarify Hindustani music theory.[69] However, Kaukab was writing in the early twentieth century, from a very different social position. In particular, his work was a statement of Muslim *ustādī* scholarship. His brother Karamatullah had attempted to share his own book, the *Isrār-i Karāmat urf Naghmāt-i Nia'mat* ("The Secrets of Miracles [or of Karamatullah]; or, The Melodies of Beneficence [or of Niamatullah]," 1908) with the Hindu reformer V. N. Bhatkhande. Bhatkhande dismissed this work and its author, an "ignorant and obstinate" hereditary musician.[70] Kaukab's work was essentially a rejoinder, pointing out the Islamic roots of Hindustani music theory and history, but also the depths of his own knowledge of the intricacies of older Persian and Sanskrit texts. This was very different, then, from Wajid Ali's approach; the nawab took it for granted that there was a substantial corpus of Indo-Persianate learning at his disposal, but was frustrated by what he saw as arcane redundancies. In particular, the nawab desired a textual formulation for dance and musical theater that had not been provided in earlier works. In other words, Wajid Ali and Kaukab were conversant with the same epistemological tradition, but the nawab was an innovator while Kaukab was a curator.

The influence of Wajid Ali's theoretical writings cannot be qualified without further studies of subsequent treatises, noting where the nawab was adopted or disregarded. Walker has begun this work in her analysis of prescriptions for dance *gats* (steps)[71] in five works: *Ṣaut al-Mubārak* (1852–53) and *Banī* (1877) by Wajid Ali, and, written in the interval between them, the *Ma'dan al-mūsīqī* ("The Mine of Music," c. 1858, first published 1925),[72] the *Ghunca-yi Rāg* ("Garland of *Rāgas*," 1862–63), and the *Sarmāya-yi 'Ishrat* ("The Value of Pleasure," 1875).[73] The fourteen *gats* in *Ṣaut* have not been identified in any earlier treatise, and it is assumed that Wajid Ali was the first to document if not personally develop them. These were duplicated in the *Ma'dan* (framed by an additional seven) and the *Ghunca* (under alternative names). Walker found that *Sarmāya* had a different combination of *gats*: some with similar names to those in *Ṣaut*, but with different descriptions. Intriguingly, Wajid Ali's last work, *Banī*, has twenty-one *gats* which do not follow his earlier fourteen prescriptions in *Ṣaut*, and are closer to *Sarmāya*.[74] There are several implications to be drawn from Walker's analysis, but in the current context I will underline three. First, textual prescriptions of dance *gats* were not part of Mughal musicology prior to Wajid Ali's intervention,[75] but were immediately taken up as a standard subject by later musicologists. Second, Wajid Ali was seen as an authority; when Karam Imam developed the *Ma'dan* he turned to both the well-established *Toḥfat al-Hind* and the writings of the nawab, whom he considered expert.[76] Third, it is apparent from the discrepancies between Wajid Ali's own works that in the twenty-five years between them, his thought was evolving, and he was in dialogue with other connoisseurs (in this case Sadiq Ali Khan, the author of *Sarmāya*). Contrary to Sharar and Kaukab, Wajid Ali was not an ignoramus wholly rejected by "authentic" musicologists. Nor did his cultivation of new directions in music cease abruptly in 1856.

Tearful Bride or Majestic Elephant?

Kaukab suggested that the nawab's musical creations "became popular with the masses with the result that music was cheapened. . . . Matters got to the state that if by chance someone listened to pure classical music,[77] he could not appreciate it nor take any interest in it. In fact he often disliked it."[78] According to Kaukab, more elevated forms of music (exemplified by the figure Pyar Khan) were actively curtailed: "This music had no place in the court and was not appreciated."[79] Kaukab thus drew a contrast between Pyar Khan's music and the "light, simple, and attractive tunes" favored by the nawab: that is, *ṭhumrī* and *ghazal* rather than *dhrupad*. The distinction continues to this day: *ṭhumrī* and *ghazal* are considered "semiclassical" and "lighter"[80] vocal genres than *dhrupad* and *k͟hayāl*, and have a deeply entrenched association with Wajid Ali, to the extent that he is often mistakenly believed to be the creator of *ṭhumrī*.[81]

The personal connection between the nawab, *ṭhumrī*, and his exile was further cemented in the popular imagination by a famous *bandiś*, sung in *rāga* Bhairavi, "*Bābula morā naihara chūto jāya*":

> Father, my maternal home is being left behind.
> Four water-carriers together lift up my palanquin;
> what's mine, what's not, it's all being left behind.
>
> Father, my maternal home is being left behind.
> When my palanquin arrived, oh, on my doorstep;
> what's mine, what's not, it's all left behind.[82]

The song became especially famous after its performance by Kundanlal Saigal in the film *Street Singer* (1938), and has received much critical (and literary)[83] attention since. Between them, Shukla, Manuel, Du Perron, and Katz have outlined five modes of the lyric's interpretation: as a bride on her wedding day, as departure from this mortal coil, as the lament of Wajid Ali Shah in the moment of annexation, as an expression of a collective memory of nawabi Lucknow, and as the embodied memory of the *gharānā* of Kaukab Khan's own family.[84] However, I have been unable to identify documentary evidence of this song prior to 1925, despite having searched through three of Wajid Ali's own collections of lyrics.[85] Given the nawab's predilection for publishing his many compositions, it seems unlikely that he would have chosen to omit the one lyric that became his most famous song, though of course this is inadequate grounds for dismissing the witness of oral history and popular memory altogether.[86] What can be said is that the two primary associations between Wajid Ali and *ṭhumrī* are from the early twentieth-century: a lyric loosely identified with the nawab, and the letter of Kaukab Khan.

However, Kaukab may not have been the most accurate informant. Aside from his disregard of Wajid Ali's theoretical writings, he evidently did not know about, or chose to ignore, the full range of the nawab's compositions. In his testimonial, he identified Wajid Ali by the *taḵẖalluṣ* "Kadar Piyā."[87] In fact Wajid Ali did not use this name, and consistently wrote as Aḵẖtar, Aḵẖtar Piyā, or Akhtar. Kaukab was evidently unfamiliar with the writings he condemned as "cheap."[88] Otherwise, he would have noted the scope of genres that interested Wajid Ali.

Nāju (compiled 1868) is an anthology of the nawab's lyrics along with those by his senior queen and *nikāḥ* wife, Khas Mahal, who composed extensively under the *taḵẖalluṣ* ʿĀlam (see chapter 5). In his introduction, Wajid Ali noted that though he normally wrote as Aḵẖtar, he used an alternative (and he thought better suited) spelling, Akhtar, for lyrics in Sanskrit, Hindavi, or Brajbhasha.[89] The compositions are arranged around fifteen genres: songs of praise, *dhrupad*, *sādrā*, *sargam*, *caturaṅga*, *horī*, *ḵẖayāl*, *tarānā*, *paṭa*, *ṭhumrī*, *cācar*, *sāvan*, *dādrā*, *ṭhekā*, and *dohrā*. This collection merits a thorough literary analysis on its own terms, but here I will just make two observations pertinent to the current discussion.

First, as one might expect, *ṭhumrī* features prominently, with 117 compositions. However, Wajid Ali was not the principal lyricist. He gave his *taḵẖalluṣ* to thirty-one *ṭhumrī*s here (further identified as coming "from the author," *min muṣannif*). Five *ṭhumrī*s belong to five additional writers,[90] while the majority—eighty-one lyrics—are by Khas Mahal. Since each genre section is subdivided by *rāgini*, it is also clear that Khas Mahal wrote for a larger range of *rāgini*s; many subdivisions contain only her lyrics. When Wajid Ali wrote a *ṭhumrī* for a *rāgini*, such as Khamach, he placed his lyrics first. His take precedence before those of Khas Mahal in each section, but are drowned out by the number of her compositions. Wajid Ali's *ṭhumrī*s predominate in the section dedicated not to a *rāgini* but to *rahas*.[91] That the queen wrote more than twice as many *ṭhumrī* lyrics than the nawab indicates that his fame as the pioneer of the genre demands further qualification—as does the importance of women other than courtesans to musical history.

Second, while some of the genre chapters are quite thin, *dhrupad* is very well represented with sixty-seven lyrics, of which twenty-four are by Wajid Ali himself, thirty-five by Khas Mahal, one by both in collaboration,[92] and one each by Nayak Bakhsu, Nayak Gopal, Nayak Biju, Tansen, and Pyar Khan. The appearance of Pyar Khan is especially striking, given that Kaukab claimed that Pyar was unappreciated.[93] In their *dhrupads*, the royal couple used innovative language to explore traditional subjects. Khas Mahal, for instance, wrote several lyrics to the god Rama (king of Ayodhya, thus of special relevance to the royal family of Awadh) which fused registers of Hindu imagery with local Islamicate references: "Raja Rama, flawless Hindu Lord and Sultan!"[94] Wajid Ali wrote a *dhrupad* in his own honor, set in *rāgini* Sultani, his own invention (*ījād-i muṣannif*). When sung in *cautāl*, the song was apparently intended as a declaration of his creative genius and majesty:

Āstāī:
ʿālam-panāh shāh Ākhtar sulṯān-i ʿālam ṭhīk kahāyo

Āntarā:
jin tujhe sulṯān
jāno sar bhed tīr vahi
māno gaj turang inʿām pāyo

Rightly called Protector of the Universe, Shah, Akhtar, Sultan of the Universe!
He who is "Sultan" to you is
Like multitudes of arrows from one bow
Like receiving honors of elephants and horses.[95]

The imagery suggests the abundance of the king's titles and qualities, which though many in number are consistently strong and powerful, like the martial animals. The effect would have been extended through the lengthy *dhrupad* performance, particularly in a *rāga* overtly associated with royalty. Wajid Ali's experimentation with *dhrupad* and his compositions on the subject of his own majesty are in contrast to the popular image of the effeminate nawab, famous for a *ṭhumrī* in which he took on the persona of a tearful bride.

Aside from the lyric collections, there is extensive evidence of *dhrupad* at Matiyaburj. Wajid Ali continued the musical instruction of court women from Lucknow's *parīḵẖāna* in Calcutta, organized into "assemblies" (*jalsa*). Many of these women were associated with his novel musical theatricals, but several others were given training in established genres, including *dhrupad*. Wajid Ali noted that the women of the *Choṭī Jalsa* (Small Assembly) were dismally untalented, but nonetheless he deigned to teach them a few of his own *dhrupad* compositions.[96] Given that today *dhrupad* is considered an extremely complex and primarily masculine art form, this in itself seems extraordinary.[97] While this *jalsa* was a disappointment, Wajid Ali delightedly reported that other assemblies, such as the *Nūr Manzil* (House of Light), were extremely skilled (*krtiyaṅ*) in *dhrupad*, and made their audiences weep with pleasure.[98] These women required instruction, and many of the male musicians in court specialized in *dhrupad*, including Hindustani *ustād*s and their Bengali disciples who recognized Matiyaburj as a center of traditional training as well as innovative entertainments.

Before turning to these modes of training and innovation, what can now be said of Kaukab's characterization of Matiyaburj? His major observations were evidently misleading: Wajid Ali did not neglect musicological literature or "elevated" genres such as *dhrupad*, but rather wrote, published, and taught his own contributions to these fields in his personal music school. While he certainly enjoyed *ṭhumrī*, particularly in its connection to musical theater (*rahas*), this was hardly his only investment, and his wife composed far more lyrics than he. Kaukab thus presented a one-dimensional vision of the nawab, but also crafted the musical legacy of Matiyaburj to suit the demands he faced as a professional *ustād* in the early twentieth century. By lamenting Wajid Ali's "cheapening" forays into music, and simultaneously extolling the virtues of the "neglected" Pyar and Basat Khan, he positioned himself as a serious player in a moment of revival. The Khan brothers were a kernel of elevated culture submerged in the muddied waters of the nawab's musical experiments. As the son of Basat's disciple, Kaukab presented himself as the custodian of a "superior kind" (*a'lā qism*) of music.

"Do You Know That Calcutta House?"

Despite Kaukab's criticisms, Sharar had to position Wajid Ali at the turning point in the trajectory of Hindustani culture, when "the lamp which was about to be extinguished flared up for the last time."[99] Hence, Wajid Ali oversaw the efflorescence of music, but only for a brief moment, and only in Lucknow. The "real" Lucknow ended with the annexation, followed by the desolation of 1857: Matiyaburj was an undead memorial to that world, so convincingly cloned that no one thought Wajid Ali was in Bengal—at least according to the nostalgic vision of *Guẓashta Lakhna'ū*.

In one of Sharar's lesser-known works, *Jān-i 'Ālam*, he dealt with Matiyaburj on its own terms. There he revealed that among the dance teachers in court there was one specifically employed to train the *jalsa* women in *jhumur*, and another in *khemṭā*. Sharar had to explain *khemṭā* to his Hindustani readers as "a particular kind of dance of Bengal, in which beautiful women whirl around and shake their hips in various styles. In Calcutta it is very fashionable."[100] Indeed, both kinds of dance were characterized in Bengali satires as the staple entertainment of the hedonistic urban gentleman or *babu*: *jhumur* and *khemṭā* were erotically charged local dances, named after their particular rhythms.[101]

The *khemṭā* was performed not only by women at Matiyaburj, but by troupes of Bengali *bhānḍ*s. The *bhānḍ*s (often called "mimics" in English sources) were singers, dancers, and comic actors who assumed different guises to present farcical and satirical sketches.[102] Wajid Ali included a number of these sketches in *Banī*. Following his prescriptions, the *bhānḍ* would impersonate a Bengali water carrier, sweeper, milkmaid, and *khemṭāvālī*:

> He takes the form of a *khemṭivālī* [sic]—that is, tying up the sari, and decorating himself with all the Bengali ornaments—and says, "Bengali *khemṭivālī* dance like this." His companions say, "Like what?" Then the following is danced with *laya* and sung with *sur*:
>
> Āstāi:
>
> | | |
> |---|---|
> | *aur jatanā shohite na re* | I cannot bear this pain any longer |
> | *ami eki abalā tā kalo nārī* | I am a helpless and uncomely woman |
>
> Āntarā:
>
> | | |
> |---|---|
> | *ekalo ghuri ekalo ki ami* | I roam alone, I remain alone |
> | *shankule shunno dekhi ami* | Everything I see is hollow |
> | *eki he huppo ki banacarī* | The only thing is to become a hermit.[103] |

Wajid Ali's inclusion of this genre, prescribing the costumes, dialogue, and Bangla songs, is illuminating on several fronts. First, it reveals a deep interest in local Bengali entertainments, rather than exclusively preserving an untarnished Lakhnavi culture. Wajid Ali was interested not just in the elite artists of Calcutta, but in the repertoires of *bhānḍ*s and *khemṭāvālī*s: varieties of entertainer that, though popular, often had low social status in the city. Kaliprasanna Sinha's satirical sketches represented the *khemṭāvālī* in particular as a sexual object rather than a genuine artiste. In *Banī* her dance was an orchestrated performance, and even the satirical imitation by the *bhānḍ*s was detailed with precision. Wajid Ali thus provided a formal study of popular comic performances from the 1870s, on subjects relating to the working classes. This gestures to his unusually comprehensive approach to the arts, his meticulous attention to detail, and his pedantic attitude toward collecting.[104] His interest in popular entertainments was an extension of his experiments in musical theater in Lucknow, supplemented by his experiences of their Bengali equivalents.

The lyric prescribed for this performance was composed at least nine years before *Banī*, since it was first published in *Nāju*, where it is identified as one of Khas Mahal's *dādrā* compositions.[105] Indeed, there are several similar verses that play with phrases borrowed from Calcutta. While the Persian headings to these *dādrā*s declare them to be "of Bengali language" (*dar zabān-i bangla*), it is more accurate to consider the majority of them "Banglafied" Hindustani, rather than Bengali proper. Wajid Ali and Khas Mahal shifted between dialects and languages in very short pieces, teasing their listeners with different sounds and levels of intelligibility.

āmīṅ tumheṅ bāḍo bhālobāshī
bhaiyo parbash gorī le prān more[106]

I love you very much,
I have been overwhelmed, that fair one took my soul.

Here the Bangla element is minimal. It is the first line or *āstāī*, though even here Wajid Ali has awkwardly used the Hindustani *tumheṅ* rather than the Bangla *tomāy*.[107] With the *antarā* in the second line, where the interest of the lyric lies, the song slips into unaffected Brajbhasha.

In other examples, the slide between languages is playfully explicit:

āsho bosho nā bolo Bangalin, merī jān
ānkhen terī rasa rasīlī bhauen caṛhī kamān[108]

[In Bengali] Come, sit, but do not speak Bengali, [in Hindustani] my dear,
Your eyes flow wet and passionate, drawing (open) like a bow.

Again, in this verse by Khas Mahal the *antarā* carries the prevailing image of the song and favors Hindustani dialects to Bengali, which is relegated to a secondary position. The irrelevance of the *āstāī* to the *antarā* is a recurring feature: even when both are in Bengali, the primary rationale of the first line is to identify the local, leaving the weight of poetic content to the almost independent second clause:

tumi kālkotā bāṛī ceno
āmī tomhār mayā cunnī, pāgal hoye phirte ceno.[109]

Do you know that Calcutta house?
I knew your mystique, and am wandering in madness.

These flirtations with Bengali provide a sense of Wajid Ali's environment without compromising his customary aesthetics. Du Perron has argued that *ṭhumrī* lyrics conflate dialects in order to set them apart as a poetic communication, separate from the living languages of worldly exchange.[110] "Banglafication" would have seemed a natural embellishment for the character of *dādrā* then, but it also clearly imbued the verses with a local flavor and a sensitivity to "old" Lucknow's new surroundings. Although we cannot be certain how Wajid Ali's Bengali visitors would have responded to these songs, it seems that his Banglafied lyrics were not especially popular. This is not particularly surprising; as already noted, even the simple phrase "I love you very much" is corrupted with Hindustani. Bengali musicologists and compilers of songs included a number of Wajid Ali's compositions in their anthologies. His works appear transliterated in the Bengali script, alongside those of Bengali lyricists; and this indicates that for this circle of musical publishers and readers, Matiyaburj was considered part of Bengal's musical heritage as early as 1870.[111] However, all of Wajid Ali's transliterated songs in these compilations are from his Urdu compositions. "Lucknow *Ṭhumrī*" had been appropriated by Bengali musicology, but his Banglafied *dādrā*s had been left behind.

While Wajid Ali and Khas Mahal were considering how to spell Bengali words in *nasta'līq*, Bengalis from Calcutta and beyond were finding ways into the court in order to study "upcountry" music from Hindustani *ustād*s. While the colonial officers who had access to the court noted that the nawab dealt only with tradesmen and businessmen from Awadh,[112] if they had been invited to the *meḥfil*s in court they would have seen several Bengali musicians and music enthusiasts. This aspect of exchange at Matiyaburj had a more significant legacy than the Banglafication of *dādrā* or the Bengali *bhāṇḍ*s: a network of patrons, *ustād*s, and students branching out of the exiled court and its satellite households (see chapter 6).

Dhrupad was crucial to the foundations of this forum. It will be recalled from chapter 2 that by the end of the eighteenth century, singers associated with Bishnupur were developing a reputation in the new courts and households of Bengal for a distinctive style of *dhrupad*. One of these singers, Jadunath Bhattacharya ("Jadu Bhatta"), is associated with Matiyaburj. Chatterjee suggests that he was introduced to Wajid Ali by Rupchand Mukhopadhyay, the officer appointed to deliver the government pension.[113] One of Jadunath's disciples, Bamacaran (Shiromani) Bhattacharji, also made several connections at Matiyaburj and studied singing with Ali Bakhsh, Taj Khan, and Sajjad Muhammad Khan. One of Bamacaran's biographers, Dilipkumar Mukhopadhyay, reconstructed his impression of the court when his then *ustād*, Ali Bakhsh, consented to take him into the *darbār* proper in 1884:

> At first he was astonished, seeing four people tuning their *tānpurā*s together. No one had come to listen to them at that moment, and the soiree (*āsar*) had not yet begun. Nonetheless, the four were sitting, playing a melody on their *tānpurā*s. The melody's constant drone was rising up against a slow rhythm. Not only *tānpurā*s. A *tablā* player was sitting with an enormous left-hand

> drum. He was only playing the left-hand *bols*, and he did not play any *ṭhekās*. And there was no *tablā* in his right hand. He went on playing an almost constant melody, only with the enormous left-hand drum. He perfectly matched the slow rhythm of the *tānpurās*!
>
> With the noise of the drum the humming drone of the four *tānpurās* produced a saturated sound.
>
> Bamacaran asked Ali Bakhsh, "There is no one else in this soiree. But they are playing their *tānpurās*, and he is keeping up a tune on the drum. Why?"
>
> The *darbārī ustād* Ali Bakhsh explained, "Nawab Wajid Ali Shah arranged it like this in his *darbār*. This is always the *rīyāz* (repeated practice). The Nawab wishes the soiree to remain filled with sound at all times. . . . The Nawab cannot rest without melody."[114]

We cannot accept this passage as an unmediated primary source on Matiyaburj, though Mukhopadhyay's work was consistently well researched, drawing on substantial oral and written histories. But the text serves as a further reminder of the adoption of the court in the Bengali imagination as the heritage of Calcutta rather than Lucknow. This was made possible through the activities of Bengali singers such as Bamacaran, Aghorenath Cakrabarti (1852–1915), and Pramathanath Banerji (1868–1956), and the *ustāds* who engaged them in training.

Many of these relationships developed outside the *darbār* proper, including in the satellite households of Matiyaburj (see chapter 5) or in the palaces of Calcutta's Bengali elites. Although Wajid Ali acquired a reputation as a recluse, there are various reports of his visiting government officials and the magnates of north Calcutta,[115] including Pasupati Basu, who invited him to his house in Bagbazar to watch the Bengali drama *Victory of the Pandavas* (c. 1878–86?).[116] Through such connections, Wajid Ali developed an interest in specifically Bengali styles of music and dance, which perhaps filtered through into his *bhāṇḍ* prescriptions. Generally, however, Wajid Ali played host rather than venturing out of his own domain. It is said that the noted musicologist Sourindro Mohan Tagore brought one of his household musicians, Kaliprasanna Bandyopadhyay,[117] with him to Matiyaburj. Kaliprasanna specialized in an unusual instrument, the *nyastaraṅga*, and it is extremely plausible that Wajid Ali would have taken an interest in it, given his enthusiasm for innovation. Tagore himself was evidently influenced by many of the nawab's initiatives in music, and implemented them in his own institutions (see chapter 6).

It is alleged that during the preparations for Holi in 1867, Wajid Ali invited Tagore to an evening's entertainment. The program included *dhrupads* performed by Bengali musicians employed at the court, Jadu Bhatta and Aghorenath Chakrabarti, along with the *esrāj* player Syamlal Goswami. The story goes that the king himself performed a short *k̲h̲ayāl* (*Jab chor̤ cale lakhnaū nagarī*), and then, wearing a *peshvāz*, sang and danced to a composition in *rāga* Kamod (*Nīr bharan kaise jāūṅ sakhī rī*).[118] Thus far, I have not found confirmation of this story in any contemporary sources, and certain elements have been contested, including the very notion that Wajid Ali ever danced.[119] Nonetheless, these various stories suggest an alternative understanding to that promulgated by Sharar, of a more accessible, selectively open Matiyaburj, which engaged the inhabitants of Calcutta.

While Kaukab claimed that Wajid Ali's tastes were "conventional and cheap," it is important to note that to a large extent the nawab was unconventional in his own time, and defined what became conventional and popular in his wake. His major interventions in both *Ṣaut* and *Banī* were three expansions of performance culture: dance (*raqṣ*), sketches (*naql*), and musical theater (*rahas*).

Raqṣ

Wajid Ali was extremely interested in the technicalities of dance, and oversaw its instruction. When he prescribed *gat*s in *Banī*, he explained that they were the postures used in his court, and that he had described them so that others might re-create them.[120] Beyond the detailing of *gat*s, however, Wajid Ali did not discuss the larger social or performance context of dance. While his vocabulary of postures was developed to accompany singing, it is likely that they were intended primarily as a component of the *rahas*, which received far greater attention in his works than did dance for its own sake.

This is not apparent from Sharar's account, which has since been taken as the authoritative source for the nawab's relationship to dance. Sharar did not name his source, but it is extremely likely that his information came directly from Binda Din Kathak, who was seventy-seven years old at the time of writing. Other than atypically general comments on dance from a global perspective, the entire section of Sharar's text consists only of praise for Binda Din and a detailed history of his family.[121] Sharar related how communities of *kathaks*, Brahman dancers and instructors based in the temples of Ayodhya and Banaras, were attracted to the royal courts, particularly Lucknow:

> From the time of Muhammad Ali Shah until Wajid Ali Shah's reign, Durga Prashad and Thakur Prashad, the sons of Parkash Ji, were famous. It is said that Durga Prashad taught Wajid Ali Shah to dance. Later the two sons of Durga Prashad, Kalka and Binda Din, became renowned and nearly everyone acknowledged that no one in the whole of India could rival either of them at dancing.[122]

However, none of this history can be corroborated from Wajid Ali's own writings; while he named many musicians and dancers in his court, there is no mention of Durga Prasad.[123] Moreover, Karam Imam (c. 1859) recorded that Durga had died young, which would contradict the idea that he had had a successful career with Wajid Ali and established his own sons in court.[124] Walker's study of the nautch and the prehistory of Kathak dance indicates that Sharar's views—including his genealogy of dance, and his distinction between the repertoires of men and women—were not representative of nineteenth-century dance culture, and that his claims about the family of Binda Din cannot be taken as authoritative.[125]

There is evidence from the *Ghunca-yi Rāg* (1863) of a community of expert dance *ustād*s in Lucknow called *kathaks*; however, the text does not appear to associate them directly with the royal court. The author, Muhammad Mardan Ali Khan, states that the *gharānā* (term used in the text) of Abdullah and Pragas (Prakas?) had been famous for a long time. He admits that not every disciple of "an *ustād* or *kathak*" will be able to dance as well as their teacher (such that "their spectators fall into ecstasy"); nonetheless, after studying with them "it is certain that your feet will be prepared to match/keep up with the *pakhāvaj* and *paran* tempo."[126] In his discussion of styles, Mardan Ali noted that the long-established "dance of the *rāsdhārī* has been neglected, even in the dances of the King of Awadh, but the miraculous result is that the *kathak*s teach their discourse (*kalma*)."[127] Mardan Ali then outlined four forms of *bhāv* (expression through dance): *sabhā*, *ārtha*, *āṅg*, and *nīn*. In Lucknow, he wrote, the *kathak*s and *ṭawā'if* specialized in the last of these. This text is the most detailed evidence from a nineteenth-century record of an organized body (*gharānā*) of dance professionals called *kathak*s interacting with the court culture of Lucknow,[128] though even here Mardan Ali only suggests proximity, rather than Wajid Ali's actual recruitment of a *kathak* as his personal tutor in dance.

Indeed, opinions differ over whether Wajid Ali ever danced himself. Although in the above passage Sharar stated that the nawab studied dance, elsewhere he furiously denied this.[129] Although Kaukab was critical of Wajid Ali, he also leaped to his defense in this debate:

> Others may think that these movements are senseless and absurd, but the person who makes them cannot help doing so. His limbs start moving on the impulse of lai [rhythm]. When Wajid Ali Shah acted in this manner, people would say he is dancing, but in actual fact Wajid Ali Shah had never danced at any time. He was more affected by rhythm than the musicians themselves. I have heard from reliable court singers who were his companions that even when asleep, the King's big toes used to move rhythmically because of the

> influence of lai. *Nirat*, which is to depict inner feeling through bodily movements, is also an important part of the science of music. Important speakers and lecturers practice this and no one ever criticizes them, whilst the same habit was criticized in Wajid Ali Shah.[130]

Kaukab's apologetic approach attempted to push apart the connotations of different Hindustani words that nonspecialists might conflate under the general rubric of "dance." Rather than thinking of *nāch* (the origin of the Anglo-Indian term *nautch*), Kaukab suggested a scientific term, *nirat*. *Nirat* means gesticulation or pantomime, but comes from the Sanskrit *nṛtya* (and the root *nṛt*), itself signifying dance (a dancer may be called a *nirt-kār*, or *nartak*).[131] Indo-Persian musicology conventionally differentiated between abstract dance (*nṛtta*), expressive dance (*nṛtya*), and dance that acts out scenarios (*nāṭya*). In isolation, *nirat* is an embodied expression of meaning, but in practice Kaukab's claim that it was distinct from *nāch* feels somewhat forced. The most plausible conclusion is that Kaukab was expressing a difference between *nāch* and *nirat* based on context rather than content. He claimed that Wajid Ali never performed gestures before an audience as entertainment, which would qualify as *nāch*. The same gestures performed in consultation with "scientists" of music, in discussion of dance theory, or in instruction was not *nāch*, but *nirat*.

This is similar to the position of Karam Imam, who claimed that Wajid Ali did indeed dance, but in a specific context:

> Nawab Ahmad Khan, *ra'īs* of Rampur and . . . the Sultan of Lucknow are great authorities (discerning judges, *muḥaqqiq*) and patrons (or appreciators, *qadrdān*) of this science of music (*'ilm-i mūsīqī*), and to some extent practice it themselves (*kisī qadr k̲h̲ud bhī karte*). Besides this, the Badshah himself used to execute a praiseworthy dance (*mamdūḥ nāch ko k̲h̲ud aisā karte the*) such that he was unique in his time, and this activity (*kārk̲h̲āna*) continues in Calcutta.[132]

Later, Imam called Wajid Ali a "model" or "exemplary" (*namūna*) in singing and dancing.[133] It was only here that Imam used the verb "to dance" (*nāchna*). In the larger quotation he was less direct, and put the "praiseworthy" dance in the context of an *'ilm* or productive activity (*kārk̲h̲āna*). Both authors leave an impression of Wajid Ali's discernment and expertise, rather than his personal performance of a nautch routine.

Wajid Ali envisaged his *gats* to be applied to vocal recitals, but also saw them as a building block in other kinds of performance. It appears that in Matiyaburj the performers were usually women—almost without exception, *mut'a* wives of the king, arranged into *jalsas* of around twenty women each.[134] Every *jalsa* had overlapping courses of training, sometimes purely in different vocal genres, while others staged the *naql*s and *rahas* pieces. Each *jalsa* had a set of male music and dance instructors. For dance, the leading *ustād* was Qayam Khan (called *raqqāṣ*, a dancer),[135] who oversaw the Radha Manzil *jalsa*, training them particularly for the *naql* and *rahas*.[136] Wajid Ali called him his own disciple; given that Qayam was responsible for bringing the king's inventions to life on stage, it is unsurprising that Wajid Ali trained him personally. The Radha Manzil was one of the oldest *jalsa*s, having been established around 1863, and was the most proficient in *rahas*. Qayam also taught the highly accomplished Nur Manzil, which did not perform *rahas* but was trained in vocal genres; his presence indicates that the *mutʿa* wives were expected to dance while singing.[137] Another disciple, Qalandar Bakhsh *raqqāṣ*, oversaw dancing for several of the younger *jalsa*s, including the Sharadah Manzil (c. 1870), and the Sultan Khana (below).[138] All these *jalsa*s were established during the Matiyaburj years, rather than continuing seamlessly from Lucknow, and it is unclear how long the *raqqāṣ* instructors had been in the service of the nawab. Besides Qayam and Qalandar, there were four further dancers known to have served in Matiyaburj, all disciples of the king and denoted *raqqāṣ*: Muhammad Hussain, Ghulam Abbas, and prior to 1877 Haidar Ali and Bishnu (Vishnu?).[139]

Wajid Ali also taught dance himself. In *Banī*, he admitted to this with stylistic humility (referring to "my sorry self," *naḥīf k̲h̲ud*), but then made it clear to his readers that he was a prodigy:

> Now, *mashallah*, [the ladies] are becoming informed and precise in *laya* and *sur*. Making them dance and sing, to express *ārthabhāv*, to take little steps [? lit. broken/fragmentary feet], to dance the *gats*; everything is dependent on me [*sab mujhse mutaʿalliq hai*]. No musician [*sāzanda*], player [*nivāzanda*] singer [*mughannī*], or dancer [*raqqāṣ*] had even the slightest grasp, and apart from me, the writer, there was no one else. I had the musicians play whatever my heart desired. After the second or third month, at the snap of a finger they could sing *dhrupad, caturang, trivat, tarānā, dhamāl, rupak, tivrā, cautāl, dhima, titāl, kabīr kī chab, barm kaphi, solfā, k̲h̲ata chab tāl, chāchar, ghazal, ādha k̲h̲ayāl,* and *ṭhumrī*, and perform on the *tamburā*, but even without the *tamburā* they could sing on the basis of the notes [produced by] their own throats. . . .[140]

Wajid Ali's confidence in his own accomplishments is attested elsewhere, and it is clear that he often challenged professional musicians.[141] There are at least two instances of his offending musicians at Matiyaburj by his unappreciative behavior, and it is possible that the reason so many of his musicians were his own disciples was because independent *ustād*s felt humiliated or antagonized in court.[142]

Dogs and Dandies in *Naql*

It is apparent from the descriptions of the *jalsas*' training routines that the dance *gats* could be deployed in *naqls*. *Naql*, meaning a story or anecdote, was a genre that particularly interested Wajid Ali; in its performed context in Matiyaburj, we might translate the term as "sketch comedy," or envisage something similar to vaudeville.[143] In the fourth section of *Banī*, the nawab compiled a series of short sequences: these included prose stories, sometimes with lyrics and stage directions ("He takes a crumpled handkerchief rag in his right hand. . . . Then this is sung. . . .").[144] The early *naqls* include descriptions of working-class Bengali occupations, with songs drawn from the king's earlier song anthologies in mixed registers. It is unclear precisely who performed these pieces. The *mutʿa* ladies in their *jalsas* performed at least some of them, such as the *naql* of the water carrier, milkmaid, and *khemṭavālī*.[145] Llewellyn-Jones has suggested that the nawab had a predilection for working-class women, and it appears that he enjoyed watching his wives singing his lyrics while costumed as a romanticized version of the urban poor. While it is possible that some of these pieces were also performed by a "conventional" *bhānḍ* troupe, that the wives of the nawab were performing these roles was extremely unconventional, and many of them complained about these enforced theatricals.

Other *naqls* are more difficult to envisage as performed sketches. For example, the "Tale of the *Ustād* and His Pupil" relates how an unscrupulous boy fed his *ustād* some *khir*, concealing from him that a dog had put its slobbering mouth into the pot while it was cooking. The comedy is based on what the reader (or audience) knows and what the *ustād* does not, since the boy and his mother conspire to hide the ruined *khir* with silver-leaf and pistachio nuts. It could be that such stories were intended only for reading (which would make this chapter a kind of scrapbook, or *naql-bahī*). One *naql* is actually a biographical *taẕkira* of poets known to the nawab,[146] which may never have been performed. Alternatively, these comic tales may have been intended for some kind of "slapstick" staging.

Several *naqls* involve a dog, and it is likely that some of the performers would have acted as dogs in the sketches:

Naql sixty-three: of the barking of the dogs of the *bhānḍ*, singer, and *nāyak*.

The *bhānḍ*'s dog barks like this:
Dūt ḥaq shādī ʿaf ʿaf! [Messenger—true—joy! Arf Arf!]

The singer's dog barks like this, in words [*ālfāẕ*], in the *ālāp*, and in every *rāga*:

Rīn na ta tanā na nom ta ʿaf nom nana ta ʿaf tā nā nom tana tūm ʿaf ʿaf ʿaf!

The *nāyak*'s bitch barks like this: she lies flat on her back, shakes her four hands and feet, and says:

tūm paisā na do, kūṛī na do, yoṅ hi muft mere pās rah jāo, ʿaf ʿaf ʿaf ʿāāʿa ʿāāʿa ʿāāʿa [Don't give me money! Don't give me that shit! Stay with me free of charge! Arf arf ow wow wow!][147]

This *naql* combines wordplay and physical comedy, and seems more suited to performance than to being read. The *bhānḍ* troupe would have begun with their "dog baying fairly straightforwardly (the three words in the "bark" are obscure). The singer's "dog" effectively sang a *nom tom ālāp* or *tarānā*, interspersed with barking sounds. In the third stage the "dog" is explicitly replaced by a "bitch." The word *nāyak* is extremely multivalent, and affords the *naql* several possibilities. It can mean a romantic hero (implying that the "bitch" is the archetypal heroine, or *nāyikā*), but in this context the primary sense is that of a musician, conductor, or troupe leader.[148] Nineteenth-century critics of debauched musical culture associated the *nāyak*s with pimps, and their accompanying dancing girls with prostitutes.[149] This sense informs the behavior of the "bitch," who is represented as a prostitute literally baying for sex, indifferent to money.

The next *naql* is similarly graphic, and also plays with *nāyak*s, dogs, and lustful women:

> While doing her housework and preparing her pots for lunch, the degenerate whore [*naucī*] of a *nāyak* fell asleep right beside the hearth, fantasizing about her lover. She was not in control of herself and muttered things, making noises and enjoying herself. But she was afraid of the *nāyak jī*, and couldn't even look him in the face. For this reason, her lover had not met with her. He came into her thoughts as she was sleeping. A marketplace pariah dog that had already licked the pots began to sniff around her mouth too, and her hand, which lay over her ears. She began to speak in her sleep. She said, "Ah! Today you've come with your turban dangling loose!" Unobserved, the dog clawed her. Feeling his nails against her hand, she said, "Ah! Today you have come with a plectrum on each of your ten fingers!" The dog turned around, lifted a leg, and urinated in her mouth. She burbled for a moment, stood up and said, "Wow, wow, wow! So you haven't come; you just abandon me to the dogs!'[150]

The inclusion of these *naql*s in a work ostensibly on the theory and practice of court music is thought-provoking for several reasons. First, while apologists for Wajid Ali have represented him as an elevated aesthete, it is apparent that he also enjoyed and composed scenes demanding explicit innuendo and animal impersonation. Second, Wajid Ali was obviously aware of, and untroubled by, stereotypical associations between musicians and prostitution, and played with the scandalous potential of these connotations in his own work. Finally, if this *naql* was indeed intended for the royal *jalsa* ladies rather than a professional *bhāṇḍ* troupe, then the culture at Matiyaburj must have seemed shockingly liberal.

Music itself was the subject of several *naql*s, including one in which the performers acted out images or associations of different *rāga*s, like a comedic and embodied *rāgamālā* series.[151] In another, Wajid Ali played with the character of an eccentric and demanding patron-cum-instructor, perhaps in parody of himself. This *naql* is the tale of Jahangir Beg the *nakṭī*: literally meaning "nose-clipped," this word conveyed the sense of a shameless rogue, and here Wajid Ali used the feminine form for a male character, underlining his transgressive personality. Jahangir Beg is also called a *bāṅkī* (another feminine form), a "crooked" dandy or maverick. He enters the *naql* with a white band tied around his (implicitly clipped) nose, wearing an *angarkhā* without a "skirt" portion, and brandishing a shield and fencing stick. As he arrives, a *raqqāṣ* is dancing, and in his excitement Jahangir Beg asks him to dance some more. He then ties a sash around his arm and unexpectedly thrashes the other spectators. He spontaneously begins to sell tobacco:

> And he called out, saying, "Strong tobacco!" and set off from the *meḥfil*. Then his companions asked, "Khan Saheb, why did you not keep a skirt on your *angarkhā*?" Cracking a joke and cracking his stick, wounding the head of the questioner, he said: "Ho! So that no one will make a claim of me [there being no 'skirt-grasper'] in the assembly." Then he asked, "What is that tied to your arm?" Then dealing the questioner a blow from his stick, he said: "This is my armour/armlet [*jaushan*]." Then he said to the musicians and singers, "When my finger points up, you should all reach up; when my finger points down, you should all drop down." Seven or eight times he made them drop and sit like this, and kept cracking jokes, and one by one struck blows with his stick on everyone's head. Then he asked, "What are you all singing?" They said, "Heed my plea, do not stay at home like this, my love!" He said, "Villain! You have the audacity to drive me out of my home?!" Joining their hands, they pleaded, "We did not say this to you! It is only a song lyric!" Then he dealt a blow with his stick upon all their heads again and again, and the singers sang this lyric:

Āstāī:
Heed my plea, do not stay at home like this, my love!

Āntarā:
My mother-in-law and sisters-in-law cotton on to everything! Once and for all, be gone from this *meḥfil*![152]

This eccentric behavior would have been superficially comedic in performance, but on a deeper level the *naql* spoke to a subculture of individualistic comportment that became especially fashionable in nineteenth-century Delhi and Lucknow among men known variously as *bāṅke* or *waẓʿdārī* (mannered, stylized).[153] According to Naim's analysis of these figures, their social interactions took *adab* (deportment and courtesy) to its extreme, making simple requests a lifelong obligation, and prizing steadfastness. This often led to affected habits, including taking casual remarks very literally.

Against this background, the figure of Jahangir Beg may have appealed to Wajid Ali in several respects. The description of his conducting dancers with his finger echoes anecdotes of the nawab's own finger-wagging during performances.[154] The *nakṭī* is also a highly theatrical character, pointing out his ornaments which could be taken as either virile or decorative (*jaushan*), and customizing his *angarkhā*, in an echo perhaps to Wajid Ali's conscious exposure of his breast (see chapter 3).[155] While his behavior might seem ridiculous to the uninitiated, Jahangir Beg also displays noble qualities, including self-respect (*k̲h̲uddārī*) and readiness for a challenge (*mustaʿiddī*), unhesitatingly calling the musicians "Villain!" (*buṛcod*). While he is a figure of fun in contrast to the muted, suffering singers, the *nakṭī* also plays with possibilities afforded to him by a literal identification with the lyrics he hears, becoming the offended lover spoken to in the song. The song performed at the end of the sketch is on a conventional subject: clandestine love. Yet the lyric also uses the word *meḥfil*, disrupting the distinction between the female persona in the song and the audience members in the *meḥfil* where the song is sung. The specific wording of the lyric allowed Wajid Ali to design a complex moment between imagination and reality: his *meḥfil* audience in Matiyaburj would watch Jahangir Beg disrupt another orchestrated *meḥfil* ensemble, in which a song is sung about yet another *meḥfil*. This *naql* thus resonated with Wajid Ali's performances in Lucknow, which blurred the distinction between romantic narratives and reality, especially in the staging of the *rahas*.

Rahas

The *rahas* was perhaps Wajid Ali's most precious and considered literary creation, and there are already several studies of its development in Lucknow.[156] Signifying "mystery" or "entertainment," by 1884 the word *rahas* was also widely understood as referring to "a kind of ballet or theatric representation of Krishn and the Gopīs (a similar entertainment was invented by Wajīd 'Ali Shāh of Lakhnau and given in his court)."[157] Rizvi argued that the King's *rahas*, *Rādha Kanhaiya kā Qiṣṣa* (1843), was the first drama in Urdu. This in turn provided inspiration for Syed Agha Hasan Amanat (1815–59), whose *Indar*

Sabha (completed 1853, premiered 1854) was the first Urdu drama for the popular stage (rather than a court entertainment for an elite audience).[158] Wajid Ali was proud of his innovation, calling it "a unique, celebrated domain in the art of music."[159] The courtly *rahas* was musical theater with a substantial dance portion. Wajid Ali's story sees Krishna lose his flute; he appeases Radha with songs and dances, they dance together, and then Krishna undertakes a journey to recover his instrument.[160] After this venture, Wajid Ali rewrote his *masnavī* compositions for *rahas* staging, and by 1877 he had formalized thirty-six *rahas* plots in *Banī*.[161]

It seems that Wajid Ali began coordinating the *rahas* at Matiyaburj from about 1864.[162] Several authors, following Sharar, have suggested that Wajid Ali saw something of Krishna in himself, and even played the role of Kanhaiya in his *Qiṣṣā*.[163] V. Prem Kumari has rejected this tradition, however, and points to the description of the Lucknow *rahas* by the king's uncle, Iqtidaruddaula, which suggests that Kanhaiya was played by Mahrukh Pari, while Wajid Ali sat and watched.[164] Sinh suggests that the king made a cameo appearance as a general in a performance of *Daryā-yi Taʿashshuq*.[165] For the Matiyaburj period, it certainly appears that Wajid Ali saw himself as a director and producer rather than the principal actor of the *rahas* series. Future studies of the texts and performances of the *rahas* will be able to shed light on the kinds of identification and association cultivated in the genre. For example, the demon in the *Qiṣṣā*, Ifrit, was dressed in a black European suit, complete with gloves and stockings.[166]

Since many *jalsa* troupes were dedicated to rehearsals for the *rahas*, and were taught by a large entourage of musicians and dancers with different specialties, it is clear that these operas constituted a serious investment. The actresses were required to study diverse skills, including percussion from the *tablā* player Khwaja Bakhsh, and oration from the poet Mahtabuddaulah "Darakhshan."[167] However, the women themselves were not as enthusiastic as Wajid Ali about their groundbreaking training in music, and their struggle with the king provides a nuanced perspective on the interaction between the gendered politics of the body, performance cultures, and class-specific notions of respectability.

Music and *Mutʿa*

Wajid Ali had been interested in instructing women in music and singing since his regency, and the *jalsa-khānā* was an evolution of the *parīk͟hāna* (House of Fairies) in Lucknow. Sharar suggested that aside from his *mutʿa* wives, Wajid Ali did not enjoy the entertainments of other women, particularly courtesans.[168] It is apparent from the *ʿIshqnāma* that this had not always been the case, as the prince had visited and had relationships with *ṯawāʾif* in

Lucknow. However, as Wajid Ali's palace women and wives grew in number, it seems unlikely that he also listened to *ṯawā'if* entertainers unless he had married them first. It was not that he had become prudish in his old age, as Sharar suggested;[169] he was comfortable with members of his court watching his *mut'a* wives sing sexually explicit songs and potentially act in comedies involving urinating dogs. However, he was uncomfortable with women musicians performing music he had not personally developed, or performing for other men in his absence—so *ṯawā'if* were no longer desirable. That Wajid Ali became more insistent upon regulating the behavior, performance, and bodies of the women in his court may also reflect his political situation after the annexation. As he became increasingly dictatorial, many of the *mut'a* protested and broke his rules. When he tried to discipline them, the wives turned to the British government. Acts of rebellion, and appeals to the colonial regime that had usurped the nawab, were painful reminders of Wajid Ali's political impotence, and his response was to become more despotic over the women in his domain.

Historians of colonial-era culture have demonstrated that as Indian elites lost their political autonomy, they became increasingly authoritarian over their private, domestic, or spiritual realm, particularly in the sphere of women's culture and education.[170] Late nineteenth-century *ashrāf* men were especially conscious of safeguarding the virtue of their womenfolk, which could be contaminated by sitting next to a *ṯawā'if* in a train carriage, or compromised by their singing "lewd" songs at family festivals.[171] That similar concerns emerged in Wajid Ali's court indicates two additional dimensions. First, that a nawab was also drawn into tight regulation of women demonstrates that such developments were not the preserve of the "new elites."[172] Wajid Ali saw his own form of regulation as a continuation of the schooling of women begun in Lucknow, so we might see the advancement of colonialism as providing extra psychosocial pressure to an earlier development. Second, the nawab's priorities were different from those of the *ashraf*. In certain strands of "progressive" thought, women could enter the public domain (through education, women's journals, etc.), but only in a sanitized and respectable cultural space. For Wajid Ali, women were to be confined to a domestic space, but were expected to study forms of music and dance that the *sharīf* would consider inappropriate for married women. The *jalsa* women themselves felt these tensions: the *mut'a* wife was in a liminal position between a *pardanishīn* queen and a public entertainer, and the expectations and obligations of her role were unclear.

By 1877, twenty-two *jalsa*s were receiving musical training at Matiyaburj.[173] Aside from the four aforementioned *raqqāṣ* instructors employed that year, the *jalsa* ladies were taught and accompanied by fifteen *kalāwant* singers,[174] one male *khemṭā* instructor, two *pakhāvaj* players, twenty-three *tablā* players, forty-six *sāraṅgī* players, twenty-two *manjīra* players, one *nīnivāz*, one juggler, two *ḍholak* players, one *sursiṅgār* player, a nineteen-person *naqqāra* ensemble, and six *meḥfil* attendants.[175] Aside from singing and *arthabhāv*, the ladies also received tuition from poets, and had instruction in the arts of conversation (*muhāwara*) and writing (*mashq*).[176] To take one *jalsa*, Wajid Ali personally taught the twenty-four women of the *Baṛa Jalsa*, the ladies of Sultan Khana, and had them trained by two of the best *mughannī* in court, Ali Bakhsh Khan and Taj Khan; two poets; Qalandar Bakhsh *raqqāṣ*; and several *ustād*s expert in *tāla* (who also trained up the ladies' *pakhāvaj* accompanist, Nishar Ali Khan).[177] The description of the *jalsa* indicates that the rehearsals and performances attracted many spectators and enthusiasts, as well as visiting connoisseurs who then added to the ladies' training. Despite this investment in their education, Wajid Ali complained that "this company of women is dimwitted and deficient in understanding, and only decorate and adore themselves. God the Cherisher of the world made them incapable of any kind of work. Out of the twenty-four names, only three or four are competent and attentive."[178]

To improve standards, Wajid Ali developed a rule book for his *mut'a* wives, the *Qānūn-i Āḵẖtarī* (Laws of Akhtar).[179] Eight rules enforced an attitude of modesty: the women should avoid looking at or coming into physical proximity with anyone other than the king. A further six rules directed these same points to the nawab's servants. Evidently, Wajid Ali was concerned that musical training, with all the necessary interactions with other men, and the sudden promotion of women to royal wives had led to compromises in the basic principles of *zanāna* culture. A final twenty rules were assigned to the conduct of three *jalsa*s in particular: Sultan Khana, Jawahar Manzil, and Khas Manzil. Here, Wajid Ali dictated how the women should perfume themselves, beautify their nails, dress (specifying kinds of nose piercing and size of heel), and converse with him (forbidding undue laughter). He also disallowed them from wandering without his permission or absenting themselves from their music lessons. In class they should listen attentively to their instructors and not eat too much *pān*, since this would ruin their teeth and damage their voices.

The need to stipulate these rules indicates the complexities of the hybrid demands made of the *jalsa* women as wives and performing artists. Many of them were not prepared for either role: Wajid Ali increasingly *mut'a*-married any women he encountered in court, including his domestic servants, many of whom must have felt bewildered by suddenly taking up a demanding schedule of rigorous musical training. Their confusion was compounded by the apparent tension between their rise in status as royal wives, their ironic new titles (a sweeping woman was named Musafa Begam, "the Lady Purifier"),[180] and their having to take part in occasionally obscene entertainments. They were expected to be modest wives and *khemṭāvālīs* all at once.

Major Herbert had clear orders from 1860 that the British were not to interfere in the private affairs of the nawab. This had to be reasserted constantly, as outsiders and family members alike asked the agent to "manage" the monarch. Several of the queens and *mut'a* wives attempted to escape Matiyaburj, and the British government initiated several long conversations over the treatment of former wives. However, drawing up a code of standard practice proved to be complicated: the women had rights as entertainers, and other rights as royal wives. One woman left the court in 1861 and made a claim for her jewelry; it was then clarified that when women entered the king's service they were clothed and given ornaments, but this was a loan, and the women had no rights over the property once they left the court.[181] The *mut'a* were from different social ranks, both in the world outside and according to the internal hierarchies of the court. Mashuk Mahal was paid four hundred rupees a month (though in Lucknow, when she was younger, this had been three thousand a month)[182] and left Wajid Ali with a pension of one thousand. However, Musammat Wala Begam was considered "lower-order," and was paid only forty-eight a month. The nawab accused Musammat Wala Begam of taking a different lover every night, yet she remained under his protection, while other lower caste wives could readily be dismissed with cash payments.[183] Read alongside the *Qānūn-i Āḵẖtarī*, it is apparent that the scale and unprecedented nature of the *jalsa-ḵẖāna* posed social and material difficulties for the women involved and the administrators alike: the performing *mut'a* occupied a new, uncertain position in court. While the *Qānūn* was an attempt to settle these confusions and implement Wajid Ali's authority, the government archive gestures to the ongoing negotiation and rejection of the nawab's system, as women escaped their taskmaster and sought reimbursement for his demands.

The ambiguities around the position of the *mut'a* continued to have repercussions after Wajid Ali died in 1887. In early 1889, one of the managers of the estate at Matiyaburj, a Bengali named Babu Monmotho Nath Mukherjee, filed a report of "immorality." Some of the *mut'a* wives had left the court and were setting up their own properties in Mecchua Bazar, near Battala. One Sahiba Begum had remained at Matiyaburj but was joined by her lover, Gauhar Ali, and his friends, who were treating the property like a brothel. Several *mut'a* ladies were spotted visiting the races "with the doors of their conveyances open like public women and in the company of male attendants sitting side by side with them."[184] The babu argued that these women were unfaithful to the memory of the king, and should be stripped of their pensions. W. H. Grimley, collector of 24 Parganas and superintendent of political pensions, supplemented this report with his own findings about women who had left Matiyaburj or had taken a "favored lover," and a group of forty-one women who remained at Matiyaburj but had taken up sex work in Calcutta by night to supplement their pensions (between fifteen and eighteen rupees): "They are said to receive visits indiscriminately in order to add their income from young men of pleasure, to whom the fact of their having been members of the King's harem lends a peculiar charm to the intimacy."[185] The babu recommended that the government impose routine surveillance, "personal enquiry at night," evidence from a midwife, and medical examinations. In other words, he thought the *mut'a* widows should be treated as prostitutes, in accordance with the practices of the Contagious Diseases Act (1868), officially repealed just one year earlier.[186] Grimley did not instigate any of these recommendations, but advised that the notorious Sahiba Begum should lose her pension. The other *mut'a* would be warned that flagrant misconduct would cost them their pensions, but they were permitted to remarry without forfeiting them. A memorandum on this case concluded that it would be unreasonable to suppose that "in the situation now occupied by these ladies there should not be some at least with a tendency to stray from the strict path of virtue."

It should be noted that other *mut'a* women left happier traces in the archive. For example, a "wonderful Punjabi dancer" who was known as Rashk Mahal during her marriage to the nawab was celebrated in the *Tazkirat-ul-Ḵẖavātīn* (1900) as his "true companion" to the last, as well as for her beauty, charm, and poetry. Writing with the *taḵẖalluṣ* "Begam," she was a noted *rekhtī* poet, though in her later life also wrote various kinds of *mardana* poetry.[187]

The *jalsa* women were one of Wajid Ali's proudest achievements: a school of female artists trained in a variety of genres and musical forms by elite *ustāds*, staging the nawab's own innovative productions. However, this experiment occurred at the same time as the nawab's political disempowerment, resulting in his tightening grip over the women he supervised, and against the background of a larger reexamination of the place of performing women in polite society. The women who survived Wajid Ali therefore found themselves in an extremely difficult position. They were royal widows, and were expected to behave as honorable *pardanishīn* women, but they had to do so on very small pensions, without affluent families to support them. Some took on lovers, enjoyed their minor celebrity as nawabi consorts, and potentially used their musical training to become *ṭawā'if* in Calcutta; this is extremely probable, but it cannot be traced in the colonial archive, which did not differentiate between different kinds of "public women" in this period.[188] Though more elusive than *jalsa* names and *naql* scripts, these human stories provide a sense of the social reality of the musical culture at Matiyaburj.

A Shiʿa Monarch

While this chapter has focused on performance genres and repertoires that were essentially secular, Wajid Ali also invested in sound-art practices that did not share the same social and theological connotations as *mūsīqī*.[189] Many apologists for Wajid Ali note that despite his love of music and women, he was a pious Shiʿa and never missed his prayers or drank alcohol.[190] His many relationships were all codified through *mutʿa* contracts, and he evidently saw no contradiction between religiosity and music.

One of the few instances in which Sharar acknowledged that Matiyaburj had more to offer than Lucknow was related to Wajid Ali's Shiʿa observances:

> The ceremony, pomp and circumstance with which the King's Muharram procession was invested probably could never have been equalled in Lucknow even in the days of his rule. . . . In Calcutta 1000s of people, even the British, came to Matiya Burj as pilgrims.[191]

Customarily, Wajid Ali spent forty thousand rupees on Muharram processions.[192] The nawab also erected several buildings for the mourning rites, including the Sibtainabad Imambarah (1864) that would house his grave.[193] He also wrote a corpus of *marsiyā* texts,[194] and took an active and informed interest in his Shiʿa heritage, commissioning and writing his own works of religious history.[195] The only instance of his interacting with Calcutta's Urdu newspapers that I have identified was an article from 1881 on the spirit of Muharram.[196]

Wajid Ali kept a number of *marjaʿ* (scholars) with him in Matiyaburj,[197] and consulted with the *mujtahid*s (senior clergy) of Calcutta and Lucknow on points of jurisprudence. In the 1870s he asked if the adopted children of his wives should be considered as *shāhzāde* and successors—doubtless to prevent his pension from being siphoned off by his growing family. The mufti of Calcutta, Muhammad Ali (titled Qa'imatuddin, "Firm in the Faith," by the nawab), said the children would not be recognized as his inheritors through an *istifah* declaration; but a leading *mujtahid* from Lucknow, Abul Hassan (1844–95; titled Malaz-ul-ʿUlama, or "Asylum of the *ʿulamā*") decreed the opposite, beginning a lengthy argument over the next decade.[198] The nawab also supported Abul Hassan's older brother Sayyid Muhammad Husain (1851–1907), whom he called Bahr-ul-'Ulum, "Ocean of Knowledge."[199] The same Sayyid Muhammad went on to write a tract condemning music in the celebration of the birth of the Prophet.[200] He made no mention of the nawab, and there is no evidence that the two had any disagreement over music in other contexts. On the contrary, Wajid Ali gave Sayyid Muhammad and his brother titles and recognition for their learning. In chapter 3 I indicated how Wajid Ali understood music as a mechanism to assert control over his inner life and to affect his environment. At Matiyaburj, music and sound art were not only a means to entertain, or to reproduce his lost kingdom;[201] sound was also a means to worship, and to hold together the migrant Awadhi community through the shared practices of Shi'a ritual.

Wajid Ali died aged sixty-five, a little before two in the morning on 21 September 1887, two days into Muharram.[202] He was interred in his Imambarah, where more than two thousand people were fed on the third day. Although the king's funeral was kept to a tight budget of two thousand rupees (his family had requested eleven to twelve thousand), the government did not curb the costs of the rest of the Muharram festival so as not to upset "Muhammadan feeling."[203] Over the next few years, government officials determined how to manage the eight to nine thousand people who were dependent upon the court for their livelihoods, many of whom requested to return to Lucknow. As the court was disassembled and its properties auctioned to pay off Wajid Ali's enormous debts, Matiyaburj all but disappeared.[204] The most lasting legacies of the court were perhaps the continuation to this day of a Shi'a community in the neighborhood, focused around the nawab's tomb and Imambarah; and, in the shorter term, the musicians and singers who had already forged relationships with Bengali patrons and disciples, whom I will explore over the next few chapters.

Conclusion

This chapter began with a newspaper report from 1874 that offered a glimpse into the "mimic court" of a "Retired King." While the reporter made light of the pomp of a powerless court, his account was unwitting testament to a curious tension at the heart of Matiyaburj as a musical center. On the one hand, the king seemed insular and isolationist, and apparently unaware of the world outside in Calcutta. He found comfort in continuing his experiments with performance genres begun in Lucknow, and kept a firm grip over his family, especially when they resisted him. Yet the journalist also recognized that the nawab was interacting with the city's elites, and that his compositions were being sung across India. The king was disseminating his printed works, occasionally writing for the city's newspapers, organizing fairs and Muharram processions, annually opening his grounds to the public, building imambarahs and mosques, and taking an interest in new enterprises such as the railway, gas lamps, and zoological gardens. It would surely be inaccurate to accuse him of being a recluse.[205]

However, this idea of his isolationism was perpetuated both by European journalists and officials—who, it is true, were not granted access to the king's entertainments—and by Sharar, many years after the dissolution of Matiyaburj. Sharar had an agenda in his portrayal of the "end" of Lakhnavi culture: making Matiyaburj a static, short-lived monument to the past. The musical dimensions of the court were further colored by the priorities of Sharar's informants, Kaukab Khan and Binda Din, who prescribed a memory of the nawabi world that would increase the prestige of their families and the music and dance in which they excelled.

My reconstruction of the performance practices of Matiyaburj challenges several prevailing assumptions in cultural history. Wajid Ali did not simply curate a Lakhnavi aesthetic, but evolved new innovations based on his Bengali environment. Though he advanced developing forms, including *ṭhumrī* and *rahas*, he did not neglect earlier scholarship or other genres, as seen in his particular interests in *dhrupad*. In dance, Wajid Ali innovated theories and practices, teaching dance along with at least six dance instructors—all his own disciples, and almost all Muslim. He envisaged dance as a supplement to vocal performance, but also as an ingredient of *naql* and *rahas*, both of which were extremely novel and occasionally risqué genres. Taken together, the nawab's work at Matiyaburj indicates a breadth of interests and skills far beyond Kaukab's characterization, a period of evolution and development that cannot be seen as pertaining to an "old" or "lost" culture, and an active interest in the creative possibilities of engaging with Calcutta society. This study therefore gestures to a much more nuanced interaction between nawabi and colonial cultural regimes and epistemes: it demands that pre-1856 elite culture should be seen neither as a monolithic entity nor as one that was lost or displaced by the new indigenous elites that flourished under colonial rule. I will explore this premise further in chapter 6, through the interactions between Hindustani *ustād*s and *bhadralok* connoisseurs—but first I will turn to Khas Mahal, the senior queen and composition partner of the nawab, in order to further nuance the relationship of the court to musical culture.

5

Songs from behind the Curtain

One of the subtle but long-lasting effects of colonialism in north India was a gradual shift in the way musicians were represented. From across the Mughal period, we have detailed portraits of men and women—singers, instrumentalists, and dancers—appearing as accomplished artists attached to royal courts. By the end of the nineteenth century, however, male musicians were increasingly represented as the celebrities of a modern music industry, appearing together at conferences, or separately as recording artists. At the same time, musicians increasingly identified themselves as representatives of *gharānā*s—semihereditary lineages of musicians who cultivate characteristic techniques and musical styles. While *gharānā* musicians did take on female disciples who became professional musicians in their own right, this was largely a twentieth-century development: the rhetoric and imagery of the *gharānā* ultimately revolved around genealogies of charismatic male *ustād*s, leaving a sense that Hindustani music was primarily a man's domain.

A major exception to the rule was the courtesan. Alongside the archive of male *gharānādār* musicians, we have abundant collections of images of dancing girls, *baiji*s, and *ṯawā'if*, who are increasingly recognized as significant artists and musicians. The two spheres of music making—that of the male *ustād* and that of the courtesan—intersected: *ustād*s taught *ṯawā'if*, and courtesans were known to provide accommodation for *gharānā* musicians and host their concerts as they toured the subcontinent.[1] Likewise, both figures were frequently denounced and forced off stage by certain reformist circles, who declared them equally immoral and corrupting.[2]

The problem with this historiography is that it creates an artificial sense of two spheres of music making: one patriarchal and respectable (though occasionally condescending to teach women), the other feminine and potentially reprehensible (since courtesans were not expected to marry, and thus remained outside mainstream society). The implication is that until the twentieth century—which saw the rise of middle-class female musicians—a woman who engaged with music must have been a courtesan, or attached to her salon. Music lovers know that this is a gross generalization, yet the gendering and differentiating of two musical spheres provided a useful way for artists to protect themselves against stigma. *Ustād*s could downplay their connections with *ṯawā'if*, and female classical singers could emphasize their *gharānā* credentials to avoid speculations about their virtue.

However, this gendered binary disintegrates when we examine sources from the nineteenth century. For one thing, we are now increasingly aware of "male courtesans."[3] But it is also apparent from Persian chronicles, Urdu ethnographies, and English caste directories that there were various communities of female musicians, many of whom were clearly distinguished from courtesans and had the same social expectations as other married women. Women such as *gauharīn*s and *mīrāsīn*s were household rather than salon musicians, and primarily performed for female patrons in the *zanāna* or *harem*.[4] While these varieties of performer frequently appear in miniature paintings, it is more difficult to trace them in the colonial archive; they provided an important domestic service, but did not attract the same kind of stigma or prestige as courtesans. Likewise, because they were associated with the segregated world of the respectable *pardanishīn* lady, who lived behind the "curtain" (*parda*), there was additional incentive not to discuss them openly. Nonetheless, their presence gestures to a well-established world of music making by women for their female connoisseur patrons.

Since women's culture was scrutinized and sanitized by male reformers, women who loved and patronized music have also been muted in the historical record.[5] It is possible to trace the increasing reticence felt toward women and the arts in various domains, including in Urdu poetry. In 1864, Muhammad Fasihuddin "Ranj" of Meerut (1836–85) published an anthology (*taẕkira*) of female poets, the *Bahāristān-i-Nāz* ("Springtime Garden of Coquetry," republished in 1869 and 1882). While many of the poets in this collection were *ṯawā'if*, other women were from aristocratic or *pardanishīn* backgrounds, but were nonetheless identified as accomplished composers:

> '*Iṣmatī* [Chaste] was her *taḵẖalluṣ* (pen name); her name was Nawab Jahan Ada Begam. This *shāhzādī* (princess) was unique, with her own distinctive discernment (*ṣāḥib-i firāsat*) and language (*ṣāḥib-i zabān*) in the art of poetry (*fann-i shĕ'r*).[6]

Decades later, Ranj inspired Maulvi Abdul Bari to compile a similar anthology, *Taẕkirat-ul-Ḵẖavātīn* ("Anthology of Ladies," c. 1930). Bari also included women from *pardanishīn* backgrounds—again, listing them alongside courtesan poets ordered alphabetically by *taḵẖalluṣ* (pen name). But he explicitly noted that he did not want to reveal their identities:

> *Ṭāhirah* [Chaste]: this is her name and her *taḵẖalluṣ*. She is a highly respectable lady [*'iffat-ma'āb ḵẖātūn*]. She is a poet of the current time. But she has never produced a work, like a *guldasta* or *risala*, etc. Even I only have permission to print one or two verses. Although I know more than this, I am not at liberty to write it.
>
> . . .
>
> *Kāmil* [Accomplished]: is the *taḵẖalluṣ* of a living, youthful, educated Sunni Muslim *pardanishīn* lady, who presented her own work for this *taẕkira*, and specifically enjoined that her name and residence and so on should be concealed. Therefore, I do not wish to make people suspicious [*bad-gumān*] toward her by writing down her name or residence, or giving the details of her birth.[7]

Bari's editorial style, especially the suggestion that he had more information he would not disclose, maintains the idea of a curtain: there is more to see, but not everyone has access. The poet Kāmil evidently knew he was preparing to write the anthology, and volunteered her own work, on the basis that only her pen name would enter circulation. These literary identities thus allowed women to detach their social or private personas from the consumption of their poems, and to engage safely with readerships through print.

Like poetry, musical accomplishments were similarly risqué for "respectable" women. Here too, however, some men made a point of publicly celebrating women in their circles who were deeply invested in the arts. In 1863, a year before Ranj's *taẕkira*, Babu Sivaprasad (1823–95) challenged these mores in a brief account of his grandmother:

> Many people say that now in this age women's literacy has disappeared from India and many also say that this caste [*jāti*], that is, women, are not even capable of reading and writing. Those who desire to have them read and write might toil away, but absolutely nothing would come of it. Some also think that the woman who would learn to read and write would necessarily be corrupted and go down a wicked path, and as many forget accounts of women from earlier times they think that the acquisition of learning would not stick in the mind of a woman. The Creator made them only for housework and home making.
>
> For this reason, I endeavored to have published the book *Premratna*, composed by my grandmother Bibi Ratna Kuvar. She was a great scholar of Sanskrit, and an expert in the six *śāstras*. She also knew Persian to the extent

> that when she heard my father reciting the *masnavi* of Maulana Rumi or the *Dīvān-e-Shams-e Tabrīzī* she grasped the entire meaning. She was extremely accomplished in singing and playing music and she knew the treatments of both Unani and Hindustani medicine. She was accomplished in yogic practice and self-restraint [*yam-niyam*] and had the disposition of sages or ascetics. Even at seventy years of age and in a state of ill health it was like she was in the prime of her youth, and her eyes were bright like a child's. She was my grandmother, so I am modest about her extensive reputation in writing, but the pious and learned folk of those days who know of her are present in Kashi and even today remember her virtues.[8]

Sivaprasad was a leading figure in the fashioning of modern Hindi, and took an active interest in developing women's education. He designed a textbook for girls, the *Vāmāmanrañjana* (1859).[9] In this sense, he was holding up Bibi Ratna Kuvar (c. 1777–1842) as a precedent and example to be followed. Indeed, Sivaprasad told George Grierson, "The best part of the little knowledge I may be credited with, I acquired from her." He also revealed that besides the *Premratna*, his grandmother composed many *pad* lyrics, which she personally wrote down in a manuscript book: "She was a good musician, and wrote a beautiful hand."[10] While Bibi Ratna Kuvar may have been exceptionally erudite and creative, this is ultimately hard to judge, given the scarcity of men who, like Sivaprasad, were interested in publishing musical verses by women in their families.

In the world of Lucknow and Matiyaburj, Khas Mahal, the most senior wife of Wajid Ali Shah, was a leading light in composition and musical patronage in her own right. While the queen is often noted for her interests in music and poetry, her agency is typically subsumed as a mere detail of her husband's career. This does poor justice to her own expertise, especially in vocal music. Her prestigious family background afforded her one of the best educations possible for women of her generation.[11] In her adult life, Khas Mahal's marriage to the connoisseur nawab fostered her own interests in musical performance. In later years, her separation from Wajid Ali forced her to draw upon her own family resources, constructing her own miniature court-in-exile, which brought her a degree of independence. Her household at Sarurbagh in Matiyaburj is especially worthy of study due to its connection to Pyare Saheb, one of India's very first gramophone celebrities.

This chapter has three sections. First, I will discuss the relationship between the nawab and the queen, and the role of music in their domestic disputes. Second, I will explore the neglected but important role of serving and attendant women in the musical life of a *pardanīshin* household. And finally, I will present a revisionist biography of Pyare Saheb, underlining his entangled career in Sarurbagh and the fundamental role of Khas Mahal and her attendants in his musical development.

The relationship between Pyare Saheb and Khas Mahal's family casts light on several unexplored facets of the transition from the music of private ensembles to public, commercial music industries. In particular, it highlights the role of women in the cultivation of public musical artists, including the musical labor of domestic servants and personal attendants from families in which music was not necessarily a livelihood. My reconstruction of Sarurbagh is a contribution toward the restoration of such women to the history of Hindustani music, by underlining the role of respectable women as patrons, and providing a case study of lower-status female musicians in a royal household, who were influential in the lives of elite men.[12] Using musical and legal archives to excavate the court of Khas Mahal provides an insight into the influence of the royal *zanāna*, as it was constructed in conversation with the court of the nawab and the offices of the British government, and reconceived as a private and domestic space.[13]

Relationships between elite men and female attendants were extremely common in the courts, and several notable musicians claimed descent from royal fathers and musical mothers. Bhaya Saheb Ganpat Rao (1852–1920), a widely known singer and harmonium player who wrote *ṭhumrī*s under the *chāp* "Sukhar Piyā," was the son of the maharaja of Gwalior and a resident *ṭawā'if*, Chandrabhaga Bai, who was the first to teach Bhaya Saheb *dhrupad* and *k̲h̲ayāl*.[14] His case is unusual in that his mother's expertise was acknowledged and became an openly admitted part of his biography. Here I will argue that a similar situation accounts for Pyare Saheb's own musical abilities, and to some extent explains his distinctive style of performance. Reconstructing a new biography for this celebrity, of the time before he found fame and fortune in the twentieth century, sheds light on the importance of musically adept women in his career, but also on his unexpected provenance, which is quite at odds with the received popular notion of his background.

Before turning to the rise of Pyare Saheb, however, I will discuss Khas Mahal's relationship to Wajid Ali Shah. Their shared history indicates the options available to elite women patrons and the role of music in enacting royal identities, but also how the British, and their ideologies, became pawns in the internal disputes of the royal family.

"His Majesty's Pigeons, and Vultures, and Wives"

Khas Mahal was the shorthand name for Malka Mukhaddara Uzma Nawab Badshah Mahal Saheba, who married Wajid Ali in Lucknow in 1837, when

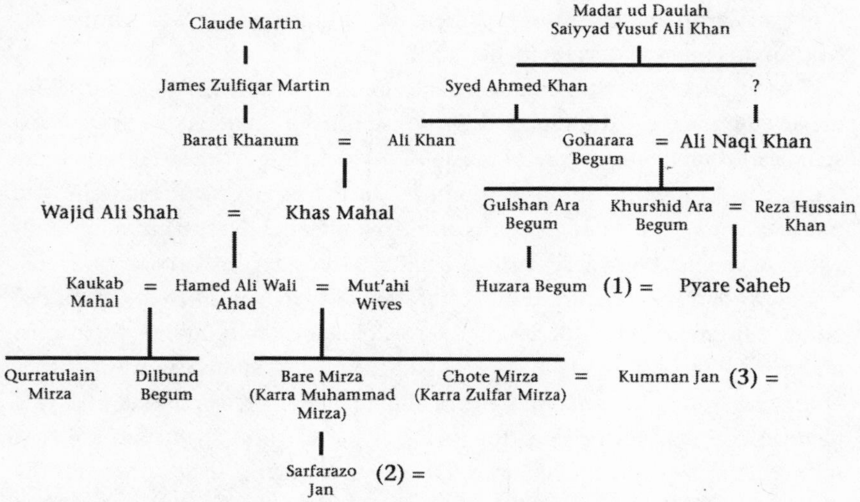

FIGURE 5.1. The shared genealogy of Khas Mahal and Pyare Saheb, simplified

the prince was fifteen years old.[15] Khas Mahal was his senior by perhaps five to seven years, though her precise date of birth is unknown.[16] When the marriage was first proposed, both Wajid Ali and his father were delighted by the prospect of an alliance with her prestigious and wealthy family (figure 5.1). The mother of Khas Mahal, Barati Khanum (alias Nawab Dulhan Begum), was connected to Claude Martin (1735–1800), the famous native of Lyon who made his fortunes with the East India Company and became the richest European in India of that time.[17] According to Khas Mahal, Barati Khanum's father was James Zulfiqar Martin (d. 1835); he had been born to an alcoholic Georgian father and an Indian mother, but Claude Martin had purchased him when he was around eight years old, and then adopted him with his Indian mistress, Boulone. James Zulfiqar was baptized in Calcutta and educated there, and eventually had an Indian family of his own. Khas Mahal related this history to claim descent from Claude Martin.[18] Khas Mahal's father, Nawab Ali Khan, was the son of Saiyyid Ahmad Ali Khan and the grandson of Madaruddaulah Saiyyid Yusuf Ali Khan of Delhi.[19] Nawab Ali Khan was also the cousin of Wajid Ali Shah's confidante and chief minister, Ali Naqi Khan, who had married Nawab Ali Khan's sister, Gohar Ara Begum. This connection would prove extremely significant in later years, since Gohar Ara was the maternal grandmother of Pyare Saheb.

Despite the initial enthusiasm for the match, Khas Mahal's marriage to Wajid Ali was unsettled even before the wedding was finalized. In his own memoir of that time, Wajid Ali described how a relation from each family died just as the *māṅjhā* (pre-wedding festivities) were underway. The wedding was postponed for two months, according to custom, during which Wajid Ali, ever the tragically romantic hero, refused to take off his festal garments, allowing them to become filthy with time.[20] In due course, the wedding resumed; but the royal couple's relationship was never wholly harmonious, and husband and wife battled each other over the course of their marriage with passive-aggressive demands, sanctions, and complaints to the British agent. Relations initially soured when Khas Mahal complained to Wajid Ali's father, Amjad Ali Shah, that the prince had taken on one Moti Khanum as his personal attendant. Amjad Ali had the attendant turned out of his son's retinue, leaving Wajid Ali feeling aggrieved and betrayed by his new wife. In a gesture of reconciliation, Khas Mahal turned a blind eye as the prince collected a host of women for the *parīḵẖāna*, and even began to help in the recruitment process.[21] Wajid Ali approved of this, but went too far when he appointed Khas Mahal *dārogha* (custodian) of the *parīḵẖāna*; she was so insulted that the appointment was quickly transferred to the eunuch Muhammad Hussain Ali.[22]

Following the accession of Wajid Ali in 1847, Khas Mahal's family life in Lucknow continued to be difficult. Her mother-in-law, Janab-e-Alia, fought a war of attrition against her, since she suspected that the young queen would plot with her uncle, Ali Naqi Khan, to overthrow Wajid Ali and accelerate the accession of her son.[23] Khas Mahal had four children: Nausherwan Qadr, who was born deaf and suffered from epilepsy;[24] Javid Ali Khan, who was appointed heir apparent in his stead, but died of smallpox in 1849; Hamid Ali Wali Bahadur; and one daughter, Nawab Murtaza Begum Sahiba.[25] Upon the annexation, Khas Mahal departed from Lucknow with Hamid Ali Wali, but left Nausherwan behind to be cared for in her house at Chowluckkha, unable to anticipate that he would be killed during the Uprising.[26] While Wajid Ali was imprisoned in Fort William, Khas Mahal wrote extensively to the British authorities, insisting that the king was innocent.[27] The correspondence of this period reveals how a precedent was set for the duration of their marriage: a triangle of suspicion was forged, fueled by retainers with their own agendas. Wajid Ali believed Khas Mahal's efforts on his behalf were merely a front for her taking control of his finances. Likewise, Khas Mahal was being influenced by two attendants, Zulfiqaruddaulah and Munshi Safdar, to believe that Wajid Ali was indifferent to her financial hardship as she managed the nascent court-in-exile in his absence. At the same time, the British agent, Charles Herbert, was trying to navigate these conflicting claims, and was skeptical about the queen's claims of hardship when she was maintaining outwardly large and extravagant households.[28]

Once Wajid Ali was freed in 1859, he resumed control of the construction of Matiyaburj. In 1861, Khas Mahal fell out with her only surviving son, Hamid Ali, when their servants had an angry disagreement and the prince left Garden Reach to take up residence at Cossipore. Gradually her relationship with Wajid Ali deteriorated further, and the two contested each other's authority through courtly privileges and correspondence with the British. In June 1864, when Khas Mahal wrote directly to the viceroy and governor-general, Sir J. L. M. Lawrence, to itemize her complaints against her husband, she employed three rhetorical strategies.[29]

First, Khas Mahal appealed to Muslim tradition and courtly protocol, suggesting that these were recognized by the British government, who had a duty to protect them from any infringements. She was certain that her superior rank, as Wajid Ali's equal marriage partner and mother of his eldest son, had been undermined by his servants, who had prevented her from seeing him for the last twelve months, and by the king's constant addition of low-class *mut'a* wives to his harem. Further, Khas Mahal's exalted position was dependent on court rituals, and any changes in her customary privileges had devastating potential. Signifiers such as the presentation of arms and the sounding of the *naubat* for her had been discontinued, and "on occasions of festivals the King is so unmindful of my rank and circumstance, that he commands my presence in the houses of his females, and is angry if I do not comply." She decried how, even as she wrote, her traditional patronage of *majālis* during Muharram was being countermanded; while other Begums continued as before, her own relatives were barred from attending her mourning assemblies. It is striking that festal rites are so prevalent in Khas Mahal's appeal to the viceroy; she wrote with the expectation that the British would appreciate the gravity of symbolic and ritual neglect. The *majālis* in particular were a vital component in the enactment of an authentic queen's station. Apart from its theological content, the *majālis* were a legitimate alternative to musical performance during Muharram.[30] While other festivities were celebrated with dancing and *jalsa*s, during Muharram it became customary to employ either *ṯawā'if*s or male *marṣiyaḵẖwān*s in mixed gatherings, and "respectable" female reciters in gatherings for women to melodically recite the lyrics of *marsiyā*s.[31] The patronage of the *majālis* was both internally oriented, in that it was the queen's privilege appropriate to the Shiʿa character of the royal family, and public, as a pious enjoyment "to which all the Faithful are admitted without distinction."[32] For Khas Mahal, the suppression of her *majālis* was an affront to her personal reputation, but it also gestured to the improper penetration of Wajid Ali's influence into the exclusively female assemblies that were dependent upon Khas Mahal's beneficence.

Having deployed Islamic tradition in her defense, Khas Mahal also invoked her rights as a British subject. She prefaced her demands for a portion of Wajid Ali's pension and greater freedom with an appeal to the colonial burden of social responsibility: "To crown my wrongs, I am confined a close prisoner in my house and my liberty as a British subject interfered with. . . . [I] hope that I may be dealt with in the chivalrous spirit with which English gentlemen treat the prayers of helpless, deeply-injured, and oppressed women."[33] Remarkably, the wife of an Indian ruler tactically played the hand dealt her by the annexation: since the British had declared her husband to be an Oriental despot, then it followed that the British had a moral responsibility to assist her.

Khas Mahal's strategic use of the rhetoric of both tradition and reform prefaced her third mode of attack as an informant and scaremonger on the financial front. Conscious of the government's concerns over Wajid Ali's pension and increasing debts, she confirmed in writing their every fear over expenditure at Matiyaburj, identifying her rivals, the king's retainers and *mut'a* wives, as the crux of the problem:

> The King is adding daily to the number of his wives; they must, each and all be maintained, some of them indeed, in rather an expensive manner; then they have great rejoicings whenever they have children, which is pretty often, and on festival days, and the expense falls on the Royal Treasury.[34]

Khas Mahal identified herself as a champion of restraint against the exploitative retainers, who had apparently told the king that she was keeping back a secret treasury from him. Her response was unambiguous: "Even if I had, should it go for the payment of thousands of Rupees for His Majesty's pigeons, and vultures, and wives?"

Despite her arguments, Khas Mahal was unsuccessful with her petitions for years to come, since the British authorities were reluctant to become more deeply embroiled in the family's affairs.[35] When Khas Mahal asked for a separate allowance of her own (5 June 1869), the government refused—partly because she already had private properties on file, but also because Khas Mahal "was known to be in the keeping of Mr Goodall, the attorney, as she is now, so it is said, living with her paramour and physician Mahomed Muhsee."[36] It was the view of the government that "the separate allowances prayed for would, if sanctioned, only have the effect of inducing the ladies to live lives inconsistent with those of purdah women." Therefore, these government officials had taken it upon themselves to regulate and preserve the dignity of the Royal ladies. While Khas Mahal had asked the viceroy to do so, pleading that the expectations of her rank were being neglected by her cruel husband, she had not anticipated that the British would formulate their own sense of the obligations of a queen in response, and use their sense of endangered tradition to curtail her financial freedoms.

From Khas Mahal's entry into the royal family to her dialogue with the British in Calcutta, the limits of her freedom were contested in three related spheres. Her mother-in-law was concerned by Khas Mahal's loyalty to her own prestigious family rather than the interests of the nawabi dynasty, especially since she held an influential position in court as the niece of the chief minister of Awadh. Wajid Ali himself fought with Khas Mahal on the matter of her financial freedom, insisting that her resources should be at his disposal. The British were reluctant to assist the queen, because they feared her economic independence would facilitate a life of immorality that went against their expectations of her dignified status.

Music played a complicated role in this situation. Honorific sonic signifiers such as the *naubat* and the *majālis* were core issues in the couple's conflicts. However, the evidence from the political and financial archive contrasts with Wajid Ali's musical writings, which suggest a consistent partnership with Khas Mahal in music making and a shared desire to experiment with language and form. Wajid Ali noted that Khas Mahal took an active role in costume design for the *parīk̲h̲āna*.[37] As already discussed in chapter 4, both writers composed *dādrā*s using Bengali idioms, and studied the performance practices of the Bengali *khemṭāvālī* for inspiration. Wajid Ali was evidently impressed by Khas Mahal's efforts, since he published her composition "Aur jatanā shohite na re" in both *Nāju* (1868) and *Banī* (1877). Apart from her "Banglafied" works, Khas Mahal's Hindustani lyrics outnumbered the king's own in *Nāju* and *Dulhan* (1873). Under Khas Mahal's *tak̲h̲alluṣ* of ʿĀlam (World), these selections bear witness to the range of her interests in music. Apart from "light" genres such as *ṭhumrī*, *dādrā*, and *ghazal*, Khas Mahal also wrote substantial numbers of *dhrupad*s and *sādharā*s.[38]

Khas Mahal's *dhrupad*s are primarily invocations to Hindu deities with their customary epithets, indicating her appreciation of the literary conventions of the genre and of Brajbhasha, including *devavaṅdana* (salutations to the god). She employed fairly typical names for the deities, rather than making obscure allusions to their deeds or qualities, and the emphasis in the verses clearly lies with their sound quality. In one instance Khas Mahal arranges the lyric to underline its alliterative and assonant properties:

> *rāga* Tilak Kāmod, *tāla* Rāman:
>
> *bigano-harana bidhi bināyaka nāyaka*
> *ēka danta lambodhare dharanī dharī*
> *Ganapata Guru Ganesa.*[39]

He who eliminates obstacles, the Remover, the Lord!
Single-tusked, pot-bellied one! Support of the earth!
Ganapati, Guru, Ganesa!

In this *āstāī*, the interplay between recurring consonants, especially *ba*, *ha*, *d(h)a*, and *ga*, lends itself to an elaborative exposition in performance, while the artillery of short syllables in the final three names of the god invite a forceful articulation, demarcating the space between this verse and the *antarā* that followed.

Elsewhere, a *sādharā* uses a dedication to Devi as a foil for musical terms, which would presumably have structured displays of technique during performance:

[Megh, Jhaptāla:]
Āstāī
dēbī prashād dījie, āpne janan koṅ
tan raṅg ḍar jota, sur samanda.

Antarā
jota sivāī urvī āwarave
sapta sur tīn grām pāvan jagata.[40]

Devi, give your blessings to your devotees,
Your colored body is a light against fear, an ocean of notes.

Light of Siva, possessor of the earth,
Taking the world with seven notes and three octaves.

Without any record of this text's performance, it is impossible to know for certain what meaning Khas Mahal intended. The second line of the *āstāī* in particular affords several possibilities: the "ocean of notes" (which can also read "ocean of gods") already employs *sur*, the most fundamental of musical terms. But if the singer extended the vowels in *tan* to *tān*, and *ḍar* to *ḍār*, as the Hindi editor Yogesh Pravin suggested in his transliteration, then the line might sound (rather than read), "The *tān* (sung embellishment) unites a line (or branch) of colors, an ocean of notes." This alternative rendering was a possibility open to the singer in the moment of performance, though not to the reader on the page. The explicit evocation of *tān*, adjacent to the sense of arrangement and abundance of sound, seems to be an invitation for the actual performance of embellishments within the structure of the lyric. In his transcription, Pravin also read *āwarave* as *avarohī*, another musicological term indicating a descent of the scale. If we accept this reading as a possibility, at least in the context of oral performance, then Khas Mahal was naming multiple musical devices, perhaps as a way to propel their execution or incorporation into the *sādharā*, while maintaining the original premise of goddess-praise (*devī praśāsti*). It is also possible to see these cascading evocations from the universal Devi to the particular Parvati (the consort of Siva; indeed, his "light"), and then declaring Siva to be the "possessor of the earth" (*urvī āwarave*) as a subtle gesture to Khas Mahal herself. As royal consort and partner-in-composition to Wajid Ali, himself commonly known as "life of the world" (*Jān-e-ʿālam*) and prone to dressing as an ascetic (as in Yogi Mela), she may have flattered herself with an implicit identification with the goddess.[41]

Other *sādharā*s are both overtly Muslim and Shiʿa in tone, though they deploy expressions associated with Hindu soteriological themes. One such lyric shifts between registers seamlessly:

> [Megh, Jhaptāla:]
> Āstāī
> *prathama parwardagāra uttama arsa para raco*
> *jaga tārana koṅ apane murata panja-tana ko avatāra*
>
> Antarā
> *hazrat rasūl makbūl Allah ko piyāro*
> *ʿAli Wāli Haidar Karār.*[42]
>
> First the Cherisher created the highest heaven;
> To cross to the world, his form descended to The Five.[43]
>
> His Excellency the Prophet was pleasing, and loved Allah
> and Ali, the Governor, the Lion, the Great.

On the one hand, the verse uses titles and theological terms (such as "The Five") that are distinctively Shiʿa. On the other, these concepts are positioned in an Indic framework that is expressed both subtly through a Sanskritic lexicon (*prathama*, *uttama*), and overtly through the reference to descent or divine manifestation (*avatāra*), itself the cornerstone of *vaiṣṇava* theology.[44] While north Indian literature provided a long precedent for such forms of combined mixed-register expression, Khas Mahal clearly had a broad knowledge of literary and theological devices to execute such balanced and concise lyrics. While her language is rich, it remains accessible and grounds itself in common devotional terms, such as titles of the imam, rather than obscure references.

Although we cannot authentically reconstruct the performances of these texts, it is clear that Khas Mahal's works were intended as musically informed lyrics rather than poems for recitation alone. Apart from the prescriptions of *tāla* and *rāga* across genres, in *Nāju* we find three *sargams* by the queen (none by Wajid Ali himself) and two *taranās*.[45] Since these verses consist purely of notes and *bols* (nonlexical syllables), they have no literary merit in themselves, so evidently Khas Mahal wrote with musical performance in mind. Khas Mahal was included in anthologies of poetesses as both a writer and musician: the *Tazkirat-ul-Khavātīn* (c. 1900) even suggests that she was a respected *sitār* player.[46]

Khas Mahal independently published other compositions that once comprised an entire *Diwān-i-'Ālam*,[47] which is thought to have contained a number of *rekhtīs*.[48] Her *Masnavī-i-'Ālam* (1866)[49] was a substantial work, and in the latter portions of this narrative poem she incorporated long portions dedicated to *ghazal* and *ṭhumrī*.[50] She worked primarily in Hindustani dialects, especially Brajbhasha and Avadhi, but although her contemporaries did not believe she had a sophisticated knowledge of Persian proper, her Urdu register suggests that she possessed an easy familiarity with Persian poetry.[51] It was through such interests, and thus at the level of connoisseur and musician, that Khas Mahal's relationship with Wajid Ali was strongest.

However, Khas Mahal's interests in music proved to be a disadvantage in certain contexts. Following her death, several aspects of her personality were discussed at length in the Calcutta High Court, in the course of a lawsuit brought by her descendants against Pyare Saheb. It is striking that while Khas Mahal's skill as a published poet was often advanced as evidence of her intelligence, her interests in music were downplayed and muted in court: the association was always negative. Repeatedly, witnesses from her household were asked if Khas Mahal "was a lady given to pleasure as musical parties were daily held before her."[52] The witnesses themselves answered ambiguously, and were evidently ill at ease with the absolute identification of music and unseemly pleasure. Instead they replied with neutral observations: that she held musical parties every day except Thursdays,[53] and would have female servants sing before her, but that this implied nothing about her character, since these were "habits as usual with the Raises [nobles]."[54] This recalls the earlier concerns expressed by government officials that Khas Mahal would be inclined to a life of inappropriate pleasures if given too much freedom. Therefore, it appears that in her negotiations with her husband and the Bengal government, her interests in music were a mixed blessing, since they brought her closer to Wajid Ali, but also opened her up to the same criticisms of decadence and excessive pleasure that had been brought against him.

Khas Mahal's bid for freedom was ultimately successful: she purchased government securities and obtained her own household set apart from the royal apartments of Matiyaburj in 1880.[55] However, the tensions with Wajid Ali continued unabated. Despite her household operating "at a considerable distance from the King's premises," in August 1882 Wajid Ali requested permission from the government to set up his own guards over her house and possessions, which he claimed as his own.[56] In October that same year, their grandson, Mirza Kura Muhammad, also applied to the British for permission to take charge of Khas Mahal's affairs. He claimed that in her old age the queen had become physically and mentally weak, and that she did not realize her servants and ayahs were stealing articles from the inner and outer apartments, and that male employees stayed in the inner rooms overnight, heedless of the infringement of *parda*.[57] Wajid Ali also appealed to the government's earlier hesitations about the propriety of Khas Mahal's living arrangements, reporting that she had filled her house with bad company and lovers. (Since the queen was now in her seventies, the British unimaginatively thought her beyond the age of illicit affairs.)[58] Thus, even when Khas Mahal had gained her independence, her male relatives and servants continued to challenge her freedom to retain "custodianship" over her household. This contestation suggests that the successful establishment of Khas Mahal's property at Sarurbagh was a statement of the queen's ability to administer her own affairs with her own private resources. The activities of the new household echoed those of a royal court without privileging a male space or mixed assembly, as would be necessary in an actively political forum. The documentation relating to Sarurbagh therefore illuminates the place of domestic, private music, and musical women, in courtly households.

Attendants at Sarurbagh

In the management of her own affairs, Khas Mahal was inescapably reliant on male attendants to mediate her dealings with the outside world, including her banking arrangements. Her primary representative, as Pyare Saheb would later become, was authorized to sign receipts on her behalf. That said, lawyers and financial advisors were conducted into Sarurbagh, where Khas Mahal would hold *darbār* and conduct her own business from behind *parda*.[59] From this threshold to the house behind the *darbār*, the life and rites of the household were facilitated by an entourage of eunuchs, servants, and female attendants (*k͟hawāṣṣ*, occasionally *muṣāḥiba*, "companion"). *K͟hawāṣṣ* was a broad term encompassing a range of responsibilities, including musical diversion, and *k͟hawāṣṣ* women held different levels of social status. Indeed, the dignity of these ladies-in-waiting varied according to setting, and their symbolic value was occasionally dissonant with their actual privileges.[60] A close analysis of what their position entailed sheds further light on the category of domestic female musicians in a period when the respectability of diverse varieties of female performer was being renegotiated in colonial society.[61]

To the outside world, the *k̲h̲awāṣṣ* was an extension of the public presence of her mistress. As such, she was expected to conduct herself as *pardanishīn*, and she required her own maids or boys to prepare *parda* for her in mixed company.[62] Apart from her functional role within her lady's household, the *k̲h̲awāṣṣ* also served a quasidiplomatic function, since she could be gifted between royal households.[63] Thus, at least five of Khas Mahal's *k̲h̲awāṣṣ* women were presented to her by Nawab Kalbe Ali Khan of Rampur (r. 1865–87), another famous connoisseur of music: Nourozi Jan, Bhullun, Nazirjan, Wazirijan, and Masiri.[64] Secluded from public exposure and familiar with multiple courts, the *k̲h̲awāṣṣ* bore the outward trappings of a lady of dignity.

Yet within the royal household these women were generally of low status, and on the same footing as other servants. Though many were trained as singers, it seems from the trial of Pyare Saheb that generally the *k̲h̲awāṣṣ* were illiterate, and musical aptitude did not afford women the same prestige as literary skill. The appointment of a *k̲h̲awāṣṣ* had the quality of a commercial transaction between her family or patron and her new mistress; typically this took place when she was around nine years old. Admission during childhood allowed the *k̲h̲awāṣṣ* to be molded to the preferences of her mistress; she would receive a monthly salary (in the case of Khas Mahal's women, six rupees) and stay with her new mistress until her death. There was some scope for upward social mobility, and some *k̲h̲awāṣṣ* women married well and developed blood connections to the royal court. One attendant, Abbasi Begum, was an attendant of Khas Mahal in Lucknow and later in Calcutta, and maintained correspondence with her when they were occasionally separated; she had also entered service when she was a child, since her mother and grandmother had been royal attendants before her.[65]

The *k̲h̲awāṣṣ* ladies provided Khas Mahal with company, conversation, and musical diversions over the course of her day. From six to nine in the morning she would read the Qur'an, followed by her morning meal and smoke between nine and twelve, then after her prayers she would sleep until four p.m., when she would play cards and dice for two hours, pray, and then hold musical parties from six to eleven p.m. In the event of a festival, marriage, or birth of a child in the family, these would be extended into lengthy soirees or *jalsa*s, and would continue until four the next morning.[66] Every eighth day, Khas Mahal would bathe and change her dress and ornaments, and her many precious stones and jeweled items were rotated on this basis. She wore her jewelry at all hours, even while she slept, a practice she continued even after she was widowed.[67] After her death, items from her wardrobe were extensively catalogued, including a tin box full of "theatrical clothing," which may indicate that Khas Mahal patronized entertainments similar to the *rahas* or *naql*.[68] The programs of her daily musical parties went unrecorded, though certain *k͟hawāṣṣ* women would sing before her, and visitors noted the many musical instruments in her house.[69] An auction of her possessions on 10 September 1895 included a violin, a *sāraṅgī*, two *sitār*s, and a damaged pair of *tablā*s.[70]

Festivals interrupted the routines of the household, but also established Khas Mahal's credentials within her extended family. When family events such as weddings were lavishly celebrated with *jalsa*s (which entailed a nautch and other music), this was understood as a gift from the queen to her relatives, and a signifier of her status as the elder of the family.[71] Music also affirmed relationships with the household staff and retinue. The *k͟hawāṣṣ* Dilbund Begum recalled how on Eids and other festivals the servants would give *naẕr*s to Khas Mahal: "Her attendants (Mosahebs) sometimes recited poems in her praise. Musicians sing in her presense [*sic*]. Gardeners presented Boquets [*sic*]. Inferior servants Salams only."[72] Therefore, the patronage of music at Sarurbagh was not merely a reflection of the queen's personal interests in the arts, but a continuation of Mughal codes of incorporation, though confined here to the maintenance of a house and extended family.

The *k͟hawāṣṣ* women were lifelong members of the household, and owing to their role in music making, they were associated with intimate gatherings in the court and may have been considered more sexually available than other kinds of serving women. Certainly Pyare Saheb had sexual relationships with several of these women, at least two of whom were known to be singers from Khas Mahal's retinue. *K͟hawāṣṣ* women could have informal relations with members of the royal family, but were not guaranteed protection or safekeeping. The *k͟hawāṣṣ* Nourozi Jan had a relationship with Chote Mirza, a grandson of Khas Mahal, and bore him a daughter, Mahbub Jan. By this time, Pyare Saheb was resident at Sarurbagh, and when he discovered their affair he beat her; at the time it was suggested that he was also having relations with her. When Chote Mirza heard that Nourozi Jan had been beaten, he quarreled with Pyare Saheb and the two noblemen became estranged. Nonetheless, Nourozi Jan was not assimilated into Chote Mirza's house, but shortly after the birth of her daughter she contracted a *nikāḥ* marriage to Khas Mahal's coachman. A few years later she bore a son, named Ali Bukhsh, and in due course both children went to live in the house of another relation of Khas Mahal, adjacent to Pyare Saheb's new compound.[73] Despite the apparent dignity of being a royal *k͟hawāṣṣ*, such women held a liminal position of intimacy with elite men and women, while they and their children were shared between related households as servants and dependents.

The significance of *k͟hawāṣṣ* women to musical culture has been neglected partly because they only performed in elite private spaces, and so left little trace in the archive, and also because their relationships with elite men largely went unrecorded. Before the rise of widespread middle-class musical practices, upper-class elite "amateur" men were already forging reputations for themselves as musical celebrities. Men like Pyare Saheb and Ganpat Rao were not associated with *gharānās*, but obtained instruction because they were personally interested in music and had access through their elite families to *gharānedār* and other professional musicians—including expert *k̲h̲awāṣṣ* women. Turning now to the details of Pyare Saheb's career at Sarurbagh, I will argue that this amateur-turned-celebrity owed much of his later success to the musical culture developed in Khas Mahal's satellite household.

Pyare Saheb "of Matiyaburj"

As Hindustani music entered "the age of mechanical reproduction"[74] in the first years of the twentieth century,[75] a number of subsidiary industries sprang up in response to the new celebrity culture, as documented by Shweta Sachdeva Jha. As part of the "new" commodification of music, collectible cards with the images and names of recording artists, the majority of them *t̲awā'if*, were mass-produced and widely circulated.[76] In one set, collected by an unknown Bengali gentleman, a series of famous *baiji*s is punctuated by the occasional male face. One of these is labeled in Urdu as "Pyare Ṣaheb, Calcutta" (figure 5.2).[77] Once Pyare Saheb became established as a household name across the subcontinent, he was always branded as hailing from Calcutta. When he performed at the Amravati Ganesh Theatre in the Bombay Presidency in 1924, he was advertised as "Pyare Saheb of Calcutta King of Indian Singers Famous for Gramophone Records," while another announcement declared, "The celebrated Musician needs no introduction."[78] This particular card collector annotated the photographs, translating the name printed in Urdu with an identification in handwritten Bengali. Pyare Saheb's annotation reads "Matiyaburj," rather than the printed "Calcutta." While the particulars of the singer's origins were known locally, the details subsequently became obscured and forgotten.

Today, Pyare Saheb is rightfully counted among the likes of Gauhar Jan, Zohra Bai, Lalchand Boral, and Maujuddin Khan as one of India's first great recording artists.[79] His voice was recorded on wax cylinders for Dwarkin and Son and H. Bose in 1901, and then by William Conrad Gaisberg (1878–1918) on his tour for the Gramophone and Typewriter, Ltd., in 1906–7. At that time, Pyare Saheb was the "staff artist" of Sir Jatindra Mohan Tagore, the brother and partner-in-patronage of S. M. Tagore (see chapter 6).[80] Fifty recordings by Pyare Saheb appear in Kinnear's listings from Gramophone Company

FIGURE 5.2. Pyare Saheb, collectible card. Parimal Ray Collection, Centre for Studies in Social Sciences, Calcutta.

records, mostly from 1913 or 1916—though, as noted in the Bombay advertisements, he was still a renowned and active singer a decade later.[81] His repertoire was largely dominated by *ṭhumrī* and *ghazal*, though in the changing context of recorded music, with new time restraints and the marketability of popular styles, there was some fluidity between these genres in Pyare Saheb's performances. Above all, Pyare Saheb is remembered for his experiments. His recordings are particularly distinctive due to his singing in falsetto—a quality shared by a select number of contemporary male recording artists, including Anant Nath Bose.[82] He created new possibilities in form by borrowing aspects from different genres: thus his rendition of the *ghazal* "Yār kī koi k͟habar" ("Any news of my love") challenges the listener by articulating a song in a very slow tempo against the typically fast rhythm of the accompanying *tablā*.[83] According to Ashok Ranade, this prepared the foundation for the sung *ghazal*'s turn from prosody-obedient recitation to a more *ṭhumrī*-orientated, evocative style. Therefore, apart from his setting a significant precedent for male recording artists, Pyare Saheb was striking for two reasons: his use of a female-coded voice; and his choice of a "feminine" repertoire, prioritizing *ṭhumrī*, *dādrā*, *ghazal*, and *rāga*s such as *jhinjhoṭī*.

Pyare Saheb's background before he rose to fame is little known and was never discussed widely. In popular culture there is a persistent confusion about his origins, since some argue that he was a descendant of the emperor Shah Alam II, while others claim he was one of Wajid Ali's sons. The general impression is that he was part of the musical retinue at Matiyaburj, having migrated from Lucknow, though this is complicated by an assertion that prior to Calcutta he lived in Banaras, near Shivala, where he was a great patron and host of musicians in his own right.[84] However, this narrative is largely an imagined biography, projecting his success and fortune in the twentieth century into the celebrity's "prehistory." The reality was less illustrious.

Pyare Saheb (Nuzhatuddaula Abbas Hussain Khan) was born in Lucknow c. 1854–55, and was related to the royal family of Awadh through his maternal grandfather, Ali Naqi Khan, the chief minister and Khas Mahal's uncle.[85] He spent much of his childhood in Matiyaburj, in Ali Naqi Khan's house, and then left Calcutta for Rampur around 1873 with his father, Reza Hussain Khan, a government *wasikadār* (pensioner) and employee of the nawab of Rampur. Reza Hussain Khan settled in Rohilkhand, but Pyare Saheb's mother, Khurshid Ara Begum, who was mentally ill, remained in Calcutta with her natal family. Pyare Saheb returned to Bengal two years later, though there are two conflicting accounts of how this came about. According to his own version of events, he began to live with his mother again, but a domestic feud soon erupted between his wife and first cousin, Huzarara Begum, and his mother-in-law and aunt, Gulshan Ara Begum. The feud seems to have begun when Gulshan Ara Begum refused to pay off Pyare Saheb's rising debts.[86] Pyare Saheb's uncle, Inayatuddaulah, recommended that he leave to ease the pressure in their family home, so Pyare Saheb began to lodge with his cousin: Khas Mahal. This account formed part of Pyare Saheb's self-defense in a court case at the end of the century: strategically, he represented his decision to live with Khas Mahal as a family affair, an inconsequential matter, which could be neither threatening nor exploitative in its effects.

Pyare Saheb's narrative was in response to an alternative version, supplied by a number of family and household members of Khas Mahal, who recalled his agitated arrival at Khas Mahal's doorstep at Sarurbagh in the middle of the night, following a journey from Kanpur.[87] According to this version, he had fallen heavily into debt and his creditors had executed decrees against him.[88] He arrived at Khas Mahal's gate at two in the morning; but since it was the month of Ramzan, she was due to wake early in preparation for the day's fast, and he was assigned a room a few hours later. He met with Khas Mahal in the *darbār* at nine a.m. and petitioned to enter her service, initially on a salary of one hundred rupees per month (Pyare Saheb denied that he was on this salary, in keeping with his familial version of events).[89] Weary and sick from his journey, he asked for Khas Mahal's superintendent (*karinda*) and doctor, Hakim Muhammad Masih, to treat him.[90]

Hakim Masih had been in Khas Mahal's service for almost twenty-nine years and, according to certain rumors, had been her lover; however, the queen lost her faith in him and took him to court in 1881 for two hundred thousand rupees.[91] Pyare Saheb proved to be instrumental in her winning the case, and thereafter he rose in her estimation, becoming her principal employee and legal and political representative.[92] Khas Mahal became increasingly dependent on him and followed his advice in every matter, rewarding his service with gifts and jewelry. Since they were related, *parda* conventions permitted him to be visibly present before Khas Mahal, and he had access to her inner apartment. He took his meals with her, and was permitted to make use of her four carriages and six horses.[93] Gradually he persuaded her to dismiss other attendants who were not well disposed toward him, and had two of his own attendants appointed her *ām-mukẖtiyār*s (general agents).[94] However, his rise to power was not entirely smooth, and for the first five years of his residence in Sarurbagh he declared insolvency. His creditors opposed his application, so he fled to Rampur but was arrested there. Khas Mahal interceded and paid off all the decrees against Pyare Saheb, whereupon he returned to Calcutta to make his fortunes in her household.[95]

Perhaps it is telling that out of Ali Naqi Khan's many relatives in Calcutta, Pyare Saheb turned to Khas Mahal. It seems likely that just as he was laden with debts, Khas Mahal simply seemed a good prospect, being one of the most financially secure figures at Matiyaburj—indeed, in a stronger situation than the king himself. At that time she was setting up her independent household, and was therefore in need of a reliable confidant to take care of her affairs.[96] Once he was settled at Sarurbagh, Pyare Saheb encouraged hostilities between Khas Mahal and Wajid Ali, which fueled the queen's bid for freedom and thus increased her dependence on her new confidant. The security of Khas Mahal's finances was fundamental to maintaining her freedom. Pyare Saheb played this anxiety to his advantage, siphoning off her possessions to various repositories of his own arrangement (including French bank accounts), on the pretext of the king's machinations, or even the threat of a Russian invasion.[97]

Following the death of Wajid Ali, Khas Mahal became the undisputed head of the family, and Pyare Saheb's increasing influence over her became a threat to her grandchildren. Pyare had his daughter, Badshah Ara Begum, betrothed (*maṅgnī*) to Prince Qurratulain Mirza ("Nanhe Mirza"), the son of Hamid Ali. However, Qurratulain called off the engagement in 1888 when he married the daughter of the nawab of Murshidabad. This deeply offended Pyare Saheb, who then insisted that henceforth the prince would have to get permission from him to visit his own grandmother.[98]

Just as Wajid Ali had prevented Khas Mahal from patronizing the *majālis* in the course of their separation, likewise Pyare Saheb used musical events to articulate his rising influence over the queen. According to her family, Khas Mahal planned to host nautches for the marriage of Chote Mirza, a son of Hamed Ali Wali by a *mut'a* wife. However, this was the same Chote Mirza who had fallen out with Pyare Saheb over the *k̲h̲awāṣṣ* Nourozi Jan, and Pyare Saheb intervened. At his insistence, the *jalsa*s were not on the scale Khas Mahal had originally intended, and she was left feeling extremely dejected (*ranj*). Finally, when dancing girls were employed to perform for the wedding party, Pyare Saheb declined to attend. After the marriage, Chote Mirza visited Khas Mahal at Sarurbagh and insisted that she reclaim all the possessions she had given out to Pyare Saheb. When Khas Mahal refused, they fell out, and Chote Mirza left Sarurbagh for good.[99]

Pyare Saheb's greatest crime against the family occurred around the time of Khas Mahal's death. The queen suffered from gout, paralysis, and recurring heart palpitations from 1891, and her health seriously began to deteriorate in 1893. She died on 1 April 1894.[100] The following month, Pyare Saheb presented a petition to the administrator general that claimed the dying queen had disinherited her principal grandchildren, Qurratulain and his sister Dilbund Begum.[101] The siblings took Pyare Saheb to court in March 1897 to assert the legitimacy of their claims as heirs. In the course of their litigation, Khas Mahal's relatives claimed that they had not been told of Khas Mahal's death for an hour and a half, during which time Pyare Saheb had taken away sixty thousand rupees worth of government currency notes, and forty thousand *ashrafīs* (gold coins).[102] This ugly lawsuit laid bare to public scrutiny every aspect of Khas Mahal's household and family, but ultimately Qurratulain and Dilbund Begum were recognized as authentic heirs to Khas Mahal and Wajid Ali in a High Court judgment of 9 July 1900.[103] Having attempted to secure his financial well-being through his connection to Khas Mahal, Pyare Saheb was now left with very poor prospects and a reputation akin to that of a confidence trickster. At that moment, it must have appeared that his prosperity at Sarurbagh was but a slim interlude in a life burdened with debt.

The Musical Making of Pyare Saheb

In the early years of the recording industry in India, male singers were generally reluctant to engage with the gramophone. For *gharānā* musicians in particular, there was some hesitation about the risk that sound recordings posed to the transmission of musical knowledge, their intellectual property, since they would have no say over the audiences and contexts for their disseminated recordings. However, there was also a larger question over the aesthetic connotations of the new media of performance, as well as the suggestion of vulgarity in a domain shaped by business interests and populated largely by *baijis*. Indeed, the new technology was dominated by the voices and repertoires of female performers, and it was noted by the industry specialist Will Gaisberg that women were quickly established as the favorites of audiences. As Amlan Das Gupta observed, "The only truly popular male artist he knew was Peara Saheb, and he had a voice like a woman's!"[104] Pyare Saheb is therefore remarkable in this period for two reasons: that he was one of the few male musicians of his time to enter the arena of mechanical reproduction, and that in his voice and musical choices he sang like a woman. With the additional background information provided by the lawsuit against him, these two facets of his career become more intelligible.

First, Pyare Saheb was unlike other professional musicians of his time, in that he came from an elite family with amateur interests in music, rather than being a professional *gharānā*. It is unlikely a coincidence that Pyare Saheb began to make these recordings only a year after the court case left him so economically vulnerable. Where other male artists may have harbored their reservations, Pyare Saheb saw an opportunity to relieve his financial worries, and without a *gharānā* musician's responsibilities to a collective identity he was free to act as he wished. Thus, the lawsuit provides a material explanation for Pyare Saheb's musical debut.

A striking omission from the court case, given the detailed exploration of Pyare Saheb's personal life, was that no court witness referred to his interests in music. That he was recording professionally a year later suggests that he had previously developed an advanced, active knowledge of music, yet had never performed openly. Previous attempts to account for his expertise have suggested that he only sang privately at Matiyaburj, studying under Wajid Ali himself and the *ṭhumrī* specialist Wazir Mirza Bala Qadar.[105] However, there is no solid contemporary evidence for this. In light of his relationship with Khas Mahal, there are two more plausible sites for Pyare Saheb's musical development.

The first is obviously Sarurbagh, since Pyare Saheb lived there for almost twenty years, much of which was spent in a close relationship with the musician, poet, and patron Khas Mahal, who enjoyed performances on a daily basis. The significance of this forum was neglected because of contemporary hesitations over the musical activities of respectable women, but also because Sarurbagh has been inaccurately conflated with Matiyaburj in popular memory. Moreover, since the musical activities here were for a *pardanishīn* audience (i.e., secluded women, their attendants, and their male relations), their relevance to public or male musicians has been neglected. However, there is clear evidence of Pyare Saheb's interactions with female singers in these circles. Besides his marriages to his cousin, Huzarara Begum,[106] and to Khas Mahal's great-granddaughter, Sarafrazo Jan, Pyare Saheb took several *mut'a* wives from among the *k̲h̲awāṣṣ* women of Sarurbagh: Kamman Jan (married c. 1896), who was formerly the *mut'a* wife of Khas Mahal's grandson, Chote Mirza;[107] Sarafrazo Jan, an in-house singer, who was also Khas Mahal's great-granddaughter (her mother and grandmother were both *mut'a* wives);[108] and Vilayati, referred to in the court case as a musician (*gāthīti*) in Khas Mahal's employ.[109]

Apart from the singers he married, Pyare Saheb also had connections to several other female musicians in the household:

> I remember Shaban, who was a musician, she was a slave girl or a servant girl, she was the daughter of one Nazir who had been a Mutahi wife of Wali Ahad, but who her father was I don't know. . . . I knew Daroga Hydri, she was a prostitute. She was a Mosaheb, attendant in Khasmahal's service. I did not dismiss her.[110]

While the matter at hand was Pyare Saheb's strategic infiltration of the household, and the language in his translated witness is colored by colonial terminology, there is clearly further evidence here of the floating and overlapping relationships between *k͟hawāṣṣ* women, their daughters, and elite men. Moreover, if we conjecture that "prostitute" in this context indicated a *ṯawā'if* turned *muṣāḥiba*, then evidently Pyare Saheb's acquaintance with female musicians at Sarurbagh would have been extensive, encompassing a variety of repertoires associated with both "domestic" and "public" women singers. Therefore there is abundant evidence that this male singer spent time and forged relationships with female performers. Since he came out of musical obscurity with a "light classical" repertoire associated with women's song, and a developed skill in falsetto, it would appear that the significant body of his training in music came from such women, be they his colleagues, employees, accomplices, wives or lovers.

This is not to suggest that Pyare Saheb had no interactions with male musicians. However, those too would most likely have been outside of Matiyaburj proper. Following Khas Mahal's death in 1894, Pyare Saheb began spending months at a time in a house at 10 Paddapukur Road in the Bhawanipur suburb of Calcutta.[111] In the years following Wajid Ali's death, Bhawanipur had become one of the city's leading forums for high-caliber musicians. The renowned music lover and patron Kesabcandra Mitra (1822–1901) lived on Paddapukur Road itself, where he invited Calcutta's leading resident and visiting musicians to perform, and would accompany several of them on the *mṛdaṅg*.[112] Kesabcandra Mitra was a crucial figure in the shaping of colonial Hindustani music, since he was from an elite background but took up musical practice and disciples, retained musicians from Matiyaburj, and set up a local music association, the Bhawanipur Sangit Sammilani (see chapter 6).[113] It seems very likely that it was through Kesabcandra's recitals that Pyare Saheb consolidated his relationship with the Pathuriaghat Tagores, since shortly after his legal proceedings he entered their service as a resident artist, which was his affiliation at the time of his first recordings.[114]

It thus appears that although Pyare Saheb was at a loss in material terms following his court case with Khas Mahal's family, he was in a prime position to become a musical celebrity. Having engaged intimately with women's music through his infiltration of Sarurbagh, and having later begun to develop his expertise in male gatherings (including with Ali Muhammad Khan),[115] he had positioned himself within a short period of time as a well-connected singer. But he was still in a financially volatile position. It was then that, like a deus ex machina, the global commercial recording industry arrived in Calcutta. Pyare Saheb exploited this new, uncertain possibility to the full at a time when other male musicians were more skeptical, and thus he launched an incredibly successful career. In time he became famous nationwide as the falsetto exponent of *ghazal* and *dādrā*, and would later be presented with gold medals by the rulers of Hyderabad, Mysore, Kashmir, and Bhopal.[116] Apart from his own performances,[117] Pyare Saheb hosted other celebrated musicians in his new home in Banaras in the first decades of the twentieth century,[118] and encouraged his son, Jani Saheb, to study the harmonium with Mirza Saheb (c. 1875–1937), himself a grandson of Wajid Ali.[119] With the occasional exception of Pyare Saheb's socializing with celebrity *baiji*s, the narrative threads of his success story present a public personality operating in a male-dominated world: a far cry from the nineteenth-century chapter of his life, which he spent cultivating his material influence and musical skills in a predominantly female domain.

Conclusion

This revisionist biography of Pyare Saheb has wider implications, since it indicates the unpredictable trajectories followed by even well-known musicians in this period. When elite men were studying music with a view to public performance, they engaged *gharānā ustād*s and frequented *ṭawā'if* salons as part of their training and development. However, the evidence from Sarurbagh restores the place of artistic aptitude and knowledge transmission closer to home, behind the *parda* of the *zanāna*, and mediated through the exploitative and sexual relationships between elite men and female dependents. To some extent, of course, Pyare Saheb was unusual, since his role in the recording industry, his idiosyncratic use of falsetto and feminine genres, and his providential solutions to his financial woes were particular to his case. In the larger context of Khas Mahal's relationship to Wajid Ali and the colonial regime, however, it is apparent that domestic music could play enabling and unsettling roles in both "domestic" and "public" domains. In the two decades when Pyare Saheb was the confidant of Khas Mahal, the queen had made several victories in her lifelong struggle for authority, financial freedom, and autonomy. The musical component to these debates was a mixed blessing to her cause, and it underlines the moral ambiguities surrounding musical knowledge in a respectable woman's hands. The historiographical silence regarding the musical contributions of both *pardanashīn* and their *k̲h̲awāṣṣ* attendants is the legacy of this ambiguity, despite facilitating the career of one of India's most celebrated male musicians.

6

Shared Tears: Court Music in the Networked Sphere

> The coffee shops of Calcutta are simply the low—the very low—music halls of London . . . a young girl from Benares performed before a number of rich Mahomedan merchants. She was a beautiful child—her age being but twelve or thirteen years—but there she sung, to be carried away by the first man who would pay the price of the spectacular who had brought her from up-country. The musicians who played to this girl's singing were Lucknow men. They were in appearance perfect types of the Indian mutineers depicted in home school books. This singing girl also ventured to display her accomplishments in English. I could not recognize the song she sang, but I caught the phrases "cheerily, merrily," "my Valentine," and "Oh! my darling."
>
> *TIMES OF INDIA*, 25 July 1889

> A Special Meeting of the Bengal Music School was held on Wednesday, the 9th instant, to do honor to Pundit Gopal Proshad Misser, a vocal musician of great celebrity. . . . Dr. Sourindro Mohun Tagore wound up the proceedings by presenting the musician with a Gold Medal and a Diploma of Merit, alluding, in grateful terms, to his indebtedness to the family of the Pundit for the musical education he had principally received from it. Several Native musicians were present, including some belonging to the staff of the Ex-King of Oudh.
>
> *INDIAN MIRROR*, 11 July 1879

These two newspaper extracts gesture to the interplay and tensions between musical cultures in nineteenth-century Calcutta. Both reports suggest that the older practice of importing musicians from Hindustan was alive and well, and they even identify the men involved as hailing from Lucknow. However, in the first report, a description of the nautch, the musicians are presented as immoral and potentially violent: a view informed both by a campaign against dancing girl entertainments, dating from at least 1837, and the hostility of the British toward Lucknow and its denizens following the Uprising.[1] The second report also recalls older associations with Lucknow in its invocation of the ex-king, Wajid Ali Shah; but here the musicians are a dignified ensemble, witnesses to a solemn celebration. Thus, the musician could be seen as either a pimp or an artist, and Lucknow itself as the site of either rebellion or connoisseurship.

Many histories of music have underlined the marginalization of Muslim musicians in processes of reform and modernization. In line with the imagery encapsulated in the first news report, scholars have noted how hereditary musicians were denounced and gradually written out of the colonial public sphere.[2] Instead, institutions, schools, and societies presented new options for a respectable, increasingly middle-class musical culture, as encapsulated in the meetings and medals of the second extract. However, the presence of the Awadhi musical vanguard in the heart of modern music's ceremonies suggests that reality was more complex. Rather than suggesting that musical patronage underwent a straightforward shift from the royal, courtly patronage of hereditary musicians to the middle-class domain of amateur performances and scholarship, this chapter will excavate the different kinds of mediatory connections forged between the Muslim musicians of Lucknow and the Hindu patrons of Bengal, augmented by the exile of Wajid Ali Shah.

Although there was a sustained attack on Muslims as inadequate or deviant custodians of musical culture, this was predominantly the preoccupation of a narrow circle of intellectuals. Ironically, outside their writings these same intellectuals continued to employ the older generation of *ustāds*, and continued with aspects of their performance practice that were deemed unthinkable in their written diatribes. There were also other arenas for music that were not oriented toward public taste or the larger questions of music's future trajectories. While these realms of listening and performance are more muted in the archive, they were extremely significant for the musical life of the city.

The Awadhi community at Matiyaburj was not confined to the site of the royal palace but gradually spread into a village-sized community, reaching up into the adjacent suburb of Khidirpur.[3] Elite migrants from Lucknow began to occupy an expanding portion of the southern city, as the king's relations grew in number and needed to be accommodated in their own apartments. Simultaneously, Wajid Ali became increasingly difficult in his old age and, as we saw in the last chapter, many relatives used their private resources or government aid to set up their own households. Gradually, numerous satellite properties of courtiers and royals branched off from the original core of the royal apartments. These provided venues for "high society" gatherings and musical entertainments that were only nominally related to the court proper.

Some of these gatherings were high-profile events. On 8 April 1872, for example, Amir Ali, the manager at Matiyaburj, hosted a music party in his house on South Kalinga Street with the High Court judge George Loch as his guest of honor. This particular gathering was a celebration of Loch's career in Calcutta, with the lieutenant-governor himself in attendance, as well as certain princes from Matiyaburj, members of the Mysore royal family, the maharaja of Vizianagram, the representative of Nepal, and Raja Kali Krishna Deb (1808–74) of Shobabajar, who presented Persian verses to Loch. Though pertaining to music and poetry rather than directly to politics, social gatherings at these properties were publicized events in colonial circles, a report of the evening in the *Englishman* even named the musicians involved: Kaukab Khan's father, Niamatullah Khan ("of Delhi"), performing on the *sarod* with an unnamed *tablā* player, followed by Ghulam Muhammad ("of the Panjab") on the *qānūn*.[4] Musicians crossed paths with potential patrons and high-status amateur musicians through these gatherings, so it is important to identify these satellite properties when plotting the landscape of colonial-era patronage.

To excavate these musical interactions, this chapter will focus on activities around elite or high-art music in Calcutta in the second half of the nineteenth century. The musicians in this chapter were evidently understood to be different from, and to have sometimes explicitly contrasted with, lower-class or street entertainers.[5] Aside from art musicians, this chapter will explore a group of patrons generally referred to as *bhadralok*, or the genteel class. This society had developed fairly recently, since it was composed largely of families from a "comprador" class of *zamīndārs* and middle-class agents who had benefited from business connections to the East India Company, or from the 1793 Permanent Settlement of Bengal. The term *bhadralok* applied to those Bengalis who were free from manual labour, and beyond that condition referred to three overlapping groups: an elite of propertied (*biṣaẏī*) and aristocratic (*abhijāta*) rajas and maharajas; middle-class (*madhyabitta*) professionals such as doctors, journalists, and lawyers; and the "poor but respectable" (*daridra athaca bhadro*), who were in some sense deemed culturally elevated from the body of the working classes (often disparagingly termed "low people," *choṭalok*).[6] The *bhadralok* therefore referred to a cultural identification, rather than a homogenous set of social prerequisites.[7] When the Calcutta press discussed the "Native elite," this evidently included Muslim gentry and aristocrats, but these communities were rarely considered *bhadralok*.[8]

Historians have cultivated an enormous literature on the *bhadralok*, which considers salient factors including family ritual, affiliation to social organizations such as *gotra* and *dal*, the transition between Mughal and colonial economies, mimicry of the West and Orientalism, and the tensions between traditionalism and modernity, as well as social mobility.[9] A major contention in cultural studies of the *bhadralok* is that "much of the nineteenth-century Bengali intellectual and political activity was directed toward erasing the hierarchical signification implied in the colonizer's view of public life."[10] The shape of elite Bengali culture reflected a conversation, often framed in English, between colonial power and knowledge and the colonized, who imitated, adopted, resisted, and translated the colonial.[11]

Examining the place of Hindustani music in *bhadralok* society demands a somewhat different conceptual frame. Histories of Bengali literature, for example, are often driven by the conflicting pulls toward the appropriation or mimicry of European styles on the one hand, and an indigenous impulse to assert a spiritual space untouched by colonialism on the other, albeit through a language that was reconceived and disciplined through European grammars and print technologies.[12] Music was different. While there was a steady undercurrent of regional Bengali performance cultures, until Rabindranath Tagore's innovations became fashionable, the *bhadralok* was primarily concerned with cultivating Hindustani art music, which had an older, precolonial presence in Bengal, but was nonetheless understood as coming from upper India. The most prestigious music was historically, not local. Therefore the *bhadralok*'s engagement with music was a negotiation with *another* Indian cultural sphere embedded in Mughal conventions, and later drawn into its own shifting sense of Bengali identity. Clearly, this related to a larger shift in consciousness driven by a colonial power dynamic. Calcutta had been the capital of British India since 1772 but, following 1857 and the fall of Delhi (and Lucknow), the preeminence of the city and its elite acquired a greater relevance and bearing to the rest of the subcontinent. This was not simply a conceptual shift, since in musical circles the number of celebrated artists in Calcutta dramatically began to increase, as the patronage landscape lost its two principal nodes.

This chapter begins with those musicians from Matiyaburj who found patronage beyond its boundaries, and then turns to the "public" face of Bengali musical society before considering the networks in Calcutta that prepared a middle ground between late Mughal and late colonial modes of participating in music.

Mobile Musicians

Given the scale of Wajid Ali Shah's investments in music at Matiyaburj, it is tempting to view the court as the ultimate forum of musical exchange between nawabi and *bhadralok* patronage. However, examining the personal histories of individual musicians indicates that they were not all devoted to the Lakhnavi court, and in some cases were picked up immediately by other patrons. As with other varieties of specialist court retainer, there was a professional expectation that musicians were mobile, and not tethered to any one location. Musicians habitually studied with masters from other cities, performed in seasonal fairs, and in some cases came from lineages associated with migrating mercenary armies.[13] It is also most likely that mobility increased in the period immediately following 1857, when Lucknow and Delhi were deleted from the patronage circuit. One example concerns the descendants of Modhu Khan, the *tablā* player of Lucknow, who were granted a substantial *koṭhī* by Wajid Ali around 1850 (hence the family becoming known as the Kothiwal *gharānā*). Despite their property there, Modhu's grandsons (the children of Gasita and Allah Bakhsh Khan) all left after 1857 and migrated to Kanpur, Patna, and Calcutta.[14] The turn of Hindustani musicians toward the exiled court in Calcutta was understandable in this context, but for most musicians Matiyaburj was not a final destination.

This section examines the career trajectories of these musicians to a level of detail that some readers might find unappealing. However, plotting this information is important for several reasons. Hindustani art music has been transmitted through the bodies and familial relationships of musicians, and tracing the lives, lineages, and networks of artists is integral to how musicians today position themselves within the musical landscape of north India. From a historical perspective, it is also crucial to credit the agency of individuals who were responsible for the circulation of music from Lucknow, rather than suggesting that disembodied styles autonomously spread without the mediation of specific musicians. In particular, looking at these microhistories reveals how expertise from Lucknow not only fed into the music scene in Calcutta but ultimately spread over a large area, including Rampur and Nepal. All that said, some readers might prefer to skim over the next few pages.

In chapter 4 I discussed the influence of Kaukab Khan (c. 1850–1919) on Sharar's representation of Matiyaburj. Kaukab's own family is representative of the migratory trend. Kaukab and Karamatullah Khan (1848–1933) were a celebrated pair and performed together at the Paris Exposition in 1900.[15] Kaukab had been based in Kathmandu with his father, Niamatullah Khan (c. 1816–1911), and left with him in 1903. He was then in western India for four years, and established in Calcutta by 1907, where he set up a school. Kaukab had married the daughter of Taj Khan, another vocalist of Matiyaburj who had also lived for some time in Nepal and left disciples in Bengal.[16] Karamatullah appears to have been based primarily in in Allahabad, but he moved to Calcutta in 1919 upon Kaukab's death, in order to take over the instruction of his students.

The brothers each wrote a musical treatise. These drew heavily upon the learning and insights of their father. Karamatullah's treatise consolidated Niamatullah's own thirty years of research, the highlight of which was Niamatullah's obtaining and translating a copy of an Arabic treatise, the *Kitāb al-Adwār* of al-Urmawi (d. 1294).[17] Niamatullah was an Afghan *sarod* player, and was employed in Matiyaburj for eleven years (providing the authority for Kaukab's account to Sharar),[18] but he was also connected to Kathmandu, Lucknow, and Bilgram (Bulandshahr), and to Delhi, where he died.[19] When he performed in Calcutta he was advertised as having come from Delhi.[20] His connection to Delhi was consolidated through his studying the *rabāb* with Basat Khan (c. 1800–c.1887), a Dihlavi *kalāwant* known for his expertise in *rabāb* and *dhrupad*.

Basat was the son of Miyan Chajju Khan, who according to the *Naghma-yi 'Andalīb* (1845)[21] was the son of the celebrated Delhi *kalāwant* Firoz Khan "Adarang." Along with his brothers Pyar Khan (d. 1857?) and Ja'far Khan, Basat was attached to the Lucknow court and was one of Wajid Ali's teachers.[22] However, his career after 1856 is uncertain. That year, he fled Lucknow for Bihar (Muradpur, Sahibganj), taking with him a hastily made copy of several Persian music treatises;[23] in later years he lamented the books and manuscripts destroyed in the course of the Uprising.[24] According to Dilipkumar Mukhopadhyay, Basat worked for the courts of Bihar and Banaras until about 1866, when he came to Matiyaburj, and became involved in a music festival in Calcutta in 1867.[25] He also stayed with the Pal Chaudhuris of Ranaghat (Nadia),[26] and had some connection to Hara Kumar Tagore (1798–1858) of Pathuriaghat and his son the musicologist S. M. Tagore (see below). He then left Bengal for Gaya, taking his sons with him, and died in Tikari in 1887.[27]

A quite different chronology is suggested in Kaukab and Karamatullah's treatises, in which they discuss the career of their father and his training with Basat. The brothers suggest that Niamatullah left Calcutta for Nepal in either 1865 (according to Kaukab) or c. 1872 (according to Karamatullah), when, according to them, Basat died.[28] There is partial evidence for both of these dates. Basat had written a letter of support for a Bengali music treatise patronized by S. M. Tagore, the *Saṅgītasāra*. This letter was published in 1869, but it was dated 1863, while a cosignatory, Basat's disciple Qasim Ali Khan, signed it in 1867.[29] This may suggest that Basat Khan had died prior to 1867, as otherwise one might expect him to have written at the same time as Qasim Ali. Supporting Karamatullah's dating is the aforementioned newspaper reference to Niamatullah performing in Calcutta in 1872, which makes no reference to his visiting from Nepal. Future research may shed further light upon the entangled chronologies of Niamatullah and his *ustād*; at present it cannot be said with certainty whether Basat died in 1867, 1872, or 1887.

Nonetheless, Basat's presence in Bengal had a longer legacy. Miner argues that Basat's migration introduced the *sursiṅgār*, the invention of his brother, Pyar Khan, to Bengal.[30] Basat's two sons, Ali Muhammad (c. 1824–98) and Muhammad Ali Khan, prolonged the family's connection to the region. Ali

Muhammad had a reputation for his expertise in *sursiṅgār*, and allegedly Wazir Khan of Rampur came to visit him for instruction.[31] In Calcutta he taught *dhrupad* to Tara Prasad Ghosh, who said that he always visited the *ustād* with gifts of sweetmeats and opium. Ali Muhammad died in Banaras. His brother, Muhammad Ali, was a singer and the last *rabābiya* of the family, working in Bengal and then Gidhaur, Banaras, and finally Lucknow.[32] Apart from Niamatullah, Basat was *ustād* to Qasim Ali Khan (d. 1890?), who had accompanied him to Calcutta.[33] Thereafter he found patrons among the aristocrats of rural and eastern Bengal, including Rajendra Narayan of Bhawal,[34] Bircandra Manikya of Tripura (r. 1862–96), and Panchakot at the Kasipur court. He is also known to have left disciples in Nepal.[35] Taken collectively, the family and disciples of Basat Khan indicate the circulation of expertise between multiple centers spread through Calcutta, Bengal, Bihar, the North-East, and Nepal, rather than just at Matiyaburj.

Families of *tablā* players also established roots in Calcutta. The founder of the Lucknow *tablā gharānā*, Bakhshu Khan (himself son of Hussain Khan, and grandson of Sudhar Khan of the Delhi *gharānā*), had a celebrated grandson, Muhammad (alias Mammad) Khan (d. 1879).[36] It is likely that Muhammad also went to Calcutta, since he has been associated with the nearby court of Nadajol (Midnapur).[37] However, by the 1870s he was in Lucknow again, since Sharar related an anecdote of a Maratha singer journeying there purely to sing with him.[38] Muhammad enjoyed other honors, including a verse dedicated to him by the poet Muhammad Askari "Sakin":

> *Tare par se jhaṛne lage sharar na taṛap to bulbul azbas*
> *Jalegā qazas jalegā qazas jalegā qazas jalegā qazas*
>
> Kept far from you, the nightingale begins to tremble
> Not from sparks, but from its fevered anguish
> The birdcage will burn, the birdcage will burn,
> The birdcage will burn, the birdcage will burn.[39]

While the family maintained its footing in Lucknow, two of Muhammad Khan's sons, Munne Khan (d. 1890) and Abid Husain (b. 1867), had many Bengali disciples.[40] Munne Khan had taught Ramprasanna Bandyopadhyay, who was also employed at Nadajol for a time, which might suggest that Munne was there with his father. Muhammad had two sisters, Motibibi and Chhotibibi ("Fat Miss" and "Little Miss"), who were also *tablā* players in the Lucknow court. Motibibi accompanied female singers and dancers, with the drums tied around her waist.[41] Chhotibibi married her brother's student, Chote Khan, Wajid Ali's handsome companion discussed in chapter 3.[42] The couple were employed at Matiyaburj with their son Babu Khan; from there,

Babu found employment in Rajabazar until his death in 1899, and left many Bengali students behind him.[43]

A Bengali musician's training rarely consisted of a single master-disciple relationship. To take one example, Nagendranath Bhattacharya (1856–1933) hailed from Ranaghat (Nadia), home to the Pal Chaudhuri family. He studied with Badal Khan and Ahmad Khan (see below), Bengali musicians such as Jadu Bhatta, and female vocalists including Srijan Bai and Imam Bandi, a famous *ṭappa* singer from Banaras who had also settled in Calcutta, as well as her son, Ramzan Khan.[44] Nagendranath's training in Bengal allowed him to master several Hindustani genres, and he went on to become a court musician in Nepal and Banaras.[45] Thus, although he is especially remembered as a proponent of the distinctively Bengali *ṭappa-k̲h̲ayāl*, his expertise in *ṭappa* had been cultivated by a songstress from Banaras, and his career lay within the circuits of Hindustani *ustād*s.

Many of the musicians employed at Matiyaburj who trained with *ustād*s there were Bengali, including Aghorenath Cakrabarti and Pramathanath Banerji. An insight into training at Matiyaburj is provided by Dilipkumar Mukhopadhyay's biographical sketch of Bamacaran (Shiromani) Bhattacharji. Bamacaran was to have a successful career as a *k̲h̲ayāl* singer, and studied with several Lakhnavi *ustād*s.[46] Bamacaran had grown up in upper India, dressed in a Hindustani style (pyjama and Panjabi), and kept a finely groomed beard; apparently no one would have guessed he was Bengali. He was based in Behala, in southwest Calcutta, where he began studying music with Ali Bakhsh around 1881, when he may have been in his early twenties. Ali Bakhsh of Gwalior had studied singing with Wajid Ali himself, and held a prominent position at Matiyaburj as an *ustād* to several of the female *jalsa*s. In later times he stayed on in Calcutta, in the Barabazar area, and was also the dance tutor of Malka Jan of Banaras.[47] Ali Bakhsh first brought Bamacaran into the *sabhā* at Matiyaburj in 1884.[48] Taj Khan was impressed by Bamacaran's voice and was surprised to discover that he was Bengali. He offered to teach Bamacaran, and Ali Bakhsh gladly passed his student on to him, since he considered Taj Khan to be the greatest *gunī* (expert) at Matiyaburj. Taj Khan's own style of *k̲h̲ayāl* was heavy in a manner reminiscent of *dhrupad*, with very strong *tān*s (melodic ornaments characterized by fast movements) and fast *gamak*s (curvaceous modulations between two to three notes). His career had begun in Lucknow and stayed in the west for some time, with a brief stint in Banaras. He arrived at Matiyaburj around 1880 and left after four or five years, apparently because he felt Wajid Ali was taking him for granted. His training of Bamacaran came to an abrupt end and, like Niamatullah Khan, he settled in Kathmandu. The experience of Bamacaran indicates how pedagogy at

Matiyaburj was not a uniform process but entailed different lengths of instruction with multiple *ustāds*, both established veterans and relative newcomers, inside and outside the court proper.

Some musicians passed from Hindustan to Bengal during the Matiyaburj period without any obvious connection to the court. Badal Khan (1833–1936) from Panipat settled in Calcutta in 1882 with the support of Dulichand Seth and Shyamlal Khetri. Badal was a *sāraṅgī* player and *tabliya* but also a vocalist, and he admired the Bengali form of *ṭappa* and *ṭap-khayāl*, which he thought a softer (since it avoided staccato) and sweeter alternative to the parent genres. He was also an admirer of Aghorenath Cakrabarti. He remained in Calcutta with his son Bachchu Khan, and had numerous Bengali disciples.[49]

Aside from the court's prestige and financial opportunities, the number of musicians and performances there naturally made it attractive to other collectives of musicians and appreciative patrons. I will now consider the two most significant collectives in the city: Pathuriaghat and Bhavanipur.

The Bengal Music School

In the summer of 1879, the scholar and music reformer Sourindro Mohan Tagore (1840–1914) played host to a number of musicians from northern India at the Bengal Music School, which he had established eight years earlier.[50] Tagore prepared prize-giving ceremonies for his guests: Vasudev Buwa Joshi (c. 1829–90), a *k̲h̲ayāl* artist from Gwalior then in his fifties,[51] came in June to be awarded with a silver medal and diploma, before the school's students and other musicians resident in Calcutta. In July, Tagore awarded a gold medal to Gopal Prasad Misra of Banaras before invited musicians from Matiyaburj. By 1879, Gopal Prasad was an elderly performer, yet he still sang a collection of *ālāp*s and *k̲h̲ayāl* compositions, along with his disciple Gopal Candra Cakravarty (1832–1903).[52] S. M. Tagore and his elder brother Jatindra Mohan Tagore (1831–1908) had a family connection to Gopal Prasad: they had been taught *sitār* along with their chief musician, Kshetramohan Goswami, by Gopal Prasad's brother, Lakshmi Narayan, who had died some time before 1879. Later, S. M. Tagore had personally sent Gopal Candra to Banaras to study with Gopal Prasad.[53] These events and the attention they garnered in the press celebrated and publicly affirmed three interrelated social circles: Bengali patrons of music, their closely defined court and school musicians, and musicians from north India. The Tagore brothers were especially adept at orchestrating these three circles.

S. M. Tagore claimed descent from Bhattanarayan, the legendary Brahman pandit who had "restored" Bengali civilization, and a line of learned musical connoisseurs.[54] In recent times the family had bought in auction estates from the *zamīndārs* of Dinajpur, Rajshahi, and Jessore.[55] Gopi Mohan Tagore built up the family's residences in Calcutta, at 65 and 66 Pathuriaghat Street, and the properties known today as 9 and 10 Prasanna Kumar Tagore Street.[56] He was part of the Mughal-oriented generation, and patronized the poet Kalidas Mukherjee, known as "Mirza" for his adoption of Hindustani dress. He also kept two *ustāds*, Sajju Khan and Lala Kewal Kishen, on monthly stipends.[57] His two sons, Prasanna Kumar Tagore and Hara Kumar (d. 1858, S. M. Tagore's father), were also personally invested in the arts; the former set up an amateur theater, and the latter studied singing, *sitār,* and *sūrbahar* (with Hassu Khan and potentially Basat Khan).[58]

Jatindra Mohan, Hara Kumar's eldest son, was celebrated in Calcutta for his philanthropy and public service.[59] His primary interest was in drama, and he produced plays at the Belgatchia theater, organizing for it a "native Orchestra" directed by Sourindro Mohan.[60] Though the brothers had a disagreement in 1885 and divided into two households, they were publicly reconciled in 1887 and continued to be considered together by the city's media.[61]

S. M. Tagore saw his interests in music as his own form of public service.[62] His training began at home, in Paturiaghat, and then from the age of nine at Hindu College. He began writing at the age of fifteen, with a work on European history and geography, a Bengali drama called *Muktābalī*, and a translation of the *Mālavikāgnimitra* of Kalidasa. His musical interests took hold at seventeen when he began studying the *śāstras*. In college he studied music from Tilakcandra Nyayabhusan, Laksmiprasad Misra of Banaras, and Kshetramohan Goswami. He was also interested in European instruments: Kshetramohan taught him the violin, and he employed a German tutor to teach him the pianoforte,[63] though the *sitār* was his preferred instrument.[64]

An article in the newspaper *The Hindu Patriot* from 14 February 1876, subsequently republished by S. M. Tagore himself, outlined in admiration his labors in

> not only resuscitating Hindu music, but also bringing it to the knowledge of the European public. . . . He has chosen for public benefit a line of occupation, in which he takes a special pleasure, and in which he has himself achieved a marked proficiency. The school of music, which he maintains at his sole expense, is training educated youths in Hindu music and diffusing among the educated classes generally a taste for it. . . . He has made Music the medium of a demonstration of loyalty to the Crown.[65]

This analysis of his career indicates several pertinent themes: revivalism; appeal to the British; altruism; self-promotion as a connoisseur; education;

cultivation of upper-class appreciation of music; and loyalism. In newspapers and in the introductions of musical works it was widely propounded that respectable and educated Bengalis knew nothing of music, particularly the art music of Hindustan. In 1873 at a gathering of the Bengal Music School, H. Woodrow, director of public instruction at La Martiniere College, noted:

> A few years back . . . one of his native friends (a very learned man) had told him that "he would sooner see his son dead at his feet than allow him to learn music." Now, what a healthy change has taken place in the hearts of the natives! Little did he think that he would live to see the day when the Bengalis would get over their prejudices, and begin to set to learning this branch of the Fine Arts in right earnest.[66]

Woodrow's anecdote conflated two crucial binaries that determined the respectability of music: knowledge and practice, public and private. There was no prejudice in polite Bengali society toward knowledge of Hindustani music in the early nineteenth century; indeed, it was a mark of (late Mughal, and hence cosmopolitan) sophistication. In 1881 it was said of Babu Matilal Seal (1792–1854): "He was a true Hindu, and had a good taste in music, engineering, and architecture."[67] Music was not remotely reprehensible in this context, but was regarded as a connoisseur's science. Throughout Lokenath Ghosh's *The Modern History of the Indian Chiefs, Rajas, Zamindars &c.*, the "Debretts" of colonial Bengal, there are references to Calcutta's elite residents being respected and informed patrons of music.[68] However, practicing music was more problematic, as it would be humiliating to be mistaken for a professional musician. Yet this was only a concern in the context of public performance. In private, the *bhadralok* might study either vocal or instrumental music without censure, and might potentially perform for family and friends. Individuals educated and employed through colonial structures were known for their private musical pursuits. Parvati Caran Sirkar (1811–43), educated at Hindu College and the Europhile headmaster of the Dacca School, "was fond of music from his early years and took a special delight in playing on the *sitara*."[69] A public musical profile was, however, out of the question.

The Tagore brothers rejected the Mughal distinctions between theory and practice, and between public and private studies in music, particularly through the institution of musical academies that specifically targeted students from respectable families. The new colonial hinterland posed new possibilities for the "Native gentleman": if the rulers were interested in music, their subjects, perhaps, would follow. S. M. Tagore targeted European curiosity in his innovative attempts to make it more socially acceptable for elite men to perform publicly. Aside from appealing to British tastes for the classical

("The Aryan race, like unto demi-gods, flourished ages prior to the time of Homer")[70] and racial theory ("Hindu music abounds in feeling and imagination; but for bolder passions, we must look where a colder climate develops a stronger race."),[71] Tagore made Hindustani music a vehicle for native loyalty. His music schools served as an arena of politicizing and hence enabling music in an elite yet public setting.

Tagore founded the Bengal Music School, "the first of its kind in India," on 3 August 1871.[72] It cannot be overstated how revolutionary this institution was for Hindustani music. Until then the highest (*uccāṅga*, etc.) music was an elite music, with an appointed *sitār* player or singer being called upon to perform for a defined enjoyer. The school represented a rupture with this world in two senses. First, the intimate setting of the private chamber, *khānā*, canopy, or *ćāṅdnī* (white cloth spread over the carpet) was replaced by an institution, a public schoolroom, that represented an entirely different set of social expectations and connotations; and second, the performers in the school's concerts were not hereditary musicians, but came from the "respectable" classes of Calcutta, and by paying for classes were both patrons and performers.[73] While there was a longer precedent for upper-class amateur performers of music,[74] from Wajid Ali to Tagore's own father, they had purposely limited their exposure as active musicians to the intimate realm. One generation on, the school was eroding that sensitivity.

From nineteen pupils over two classes in 1871, the Bengal Music School gradually grew, and by July 1875 sixty students were enrolled: two classes of vocal music, two of *sitār*, one of *mṛdaṅg*, and one of violin.[75] Classes were held in the Normal School on Chitpore Road.[76] In 1876, S. M. Tagore had installed a music teacher there, along with gifts of a table harmonium and tuning forks.[77] Tagore added more musicians to his staff, and by 1877 there were two vocal instructors, one Hindustani and one Bengali, and five instrumentalists.[78] Over the 1870s the key musicians associated with the school were Kshetramohan Goswami (1813–93), Kaliprasanna Bandyopadhyay (1842–1900), Ahmad Khan (see below), Udaycand Goswami, Ganga Bistoo (Bishnu?) Cakravarty, and Kalipada Mukhopadhyay.[79] As discussed in chapter 2, Kshetramohan had studied with Ramsankar Bhattacarya of Bishnupur, and then around 1847 moved to Calcutta, where he found employment at Pathuriaghat.[80] He also studied with Lakshmi Narayan of Banaras, and then became Tagore's teacher and directed the school's curriculum.[81] He made many of Tagore's schemes a reality, including his orchestral ensemble. These experiments had begun with the "Belgatchia Amateur Band" at the staging of Michael Madhusudan Dutt's *Ratnābalī* at the Belgatchia theater in July 1858.[82] A poor child actor, Kaliprasanna Bandyopadhyay, was performing the female lead role, and the Tagore brothers made him Kshetramohan's pupil. Kaliprasanna and Kshetramohan played particularly central roles in Tagore's later initiatives.

Tagore set up several other institutions, such as the Bengal Academy of Music (established in 1881), and arranged for music pedagogy elsewhere, including classes in theory and Vedic chanting at Sanskrit College, and for a music teacher to attend the A.U.A. Hindu Girls' School from 1877.[83] In August 1876, the *Hindoo Patriot* commented on "the introduction of similar institutions in some of the Mofussil towns."[84] These included schools in Connaghur and Shibpore (by 1874), and later, also with Tagore's support, the Bishnupur Saṅgīt Vidyālay (1883).[85]

The Bengal Music School was at the center of Tagore's network, and it provided him with a platform to publicize his own achievements and values. Several students followed him into the realm of musical publishing. Sarada Prasada Ghosh, who was awarded a silver medal for singing in January 1874, later edited a new publication of the Sanskrit treatise *Saṅgītaratnākara* (1879) and wrote his own short English treatise, *The Music of Hindustan* (1879).[86] The loudest of Tagore's disciples was Lokenath Ghosh, one of the school's first *sitār* students, who became the honorary secretary and registrar.[87] Fresh from his schooling, Lokenath published *Music's Appeal to India: An Original, Instructive and Interesting Story (Complete) Agreeable to the Taste of Both Young and Old* (1873). This was a more vitriolic work than Tagore's own writings, and it suggested that Muslim rule in India was responsible for the degeneration of the intellectual basis of music. Narrated by "Music" herself, the work described how musical science had abandoned India and fled to the court of Elizabeth I, returned with the British subordination of the Muslims in India, and most recently had begun "to live on the premises of the Calcutta Normal School, where I had access through the unwearied exertions of my most faithful devotees Professor Khetter Mohan Goswami and Raja S. M. Tagore."[88]

Lokenath was extremely conservative in his tastes, and he railed against the popular lyricist Nidhu Babu, and the Muslim exponents of music:

> These songs are voluptuous and have no connection to religion and morality. These songs are in a manner worthless, as they impress on the minds with vicious thoughts and immoral ideas. They are only loved by that class of men and women who have neither regard for their personal honour nor that of their country. The above class of men and women consist of dancing girls and Mohammedan Ustads. The Ustads and dancing girls together with several other of the most vicious character are spreading evil and committing the most atrocious crimes in this country.[89]

Lakshmi Subramanian has explored the venom against Muslims in this passage in detail,[90] and though it has been related to Tagore by association, I would suggest that this was more antagonistic than Tagore's own views. Lokenath's communalism was embedded in a larger diatribe against other musicians "of the most vicious character," including Nidhu Babu, a Hindu. While this went beyond Tagore's more restrained appraisal of music in Muslim hands, it was nonetheless in the spirit of his larger respectability campaign: music should be pious and moral, and should show due regard to the singer's personal honor and that of his nation.

Although Tagore and his followers were keen to cast their work as authentic Hindustani or "Hindu" music, in reality they were presenting something their guests had not seen before.[91] A new repertoire was another way to distance the respectable Bengali performers from their professional Hindustani and lower-status counterparts. The incorporation of Western instruments (especially violins and harmoniums), songs dedicated to European rulers and rendered in staff notation,[92] and renditions of the national anthem were also a way to garner support from the city's influential British population.

Abandoning the conventions of the *meḥfil*, concerts at the school prioritized variety. To take one example, there were multiple entertainments following a prize-giving ceremony on 9 August 1876. The instruments themselves were displayed as amusements: an elderly student who accompanied the others on *manjīra* "was very obliging and walked up to the ladies at the request of a gentleman and showed them his marvellous powers."[93] The students performed pieces arranged by Tagore and Kshetramohan, including one set to the tune of the famous *ghazal* "Tāza ba Tāza." The latter was an extremely famous composition and was established in the repertoire of dancing girls (in theory this should have unsettled the vitriolic Lokenath Ghosh, who was also present). The audience was bombarded by different musicians on different instruments:

> The playing of the "kanoon" with "sitars" and "mochanga" accompaniment, and the playing on the "nyastaranga" with "esrar" accompaniment, by Baboos Modun Mohun Barman, Baikanta Nath Basu, and Kally Prosunno Banerjee were very much appreciated, especially the blowing of two trumpets by applying them to the veins on the sides of the throat, and imparting by respiration a sound, not quite melodious, through them sufficiently strong and loud to keep up with an air played by an amateur on a string instrument.

The journalist stressed that the musician he heard was an "amateur." This was a very different enterprise from the customary nautch or *meḥfil*. The combination of instruments was unusual too: the *morcaṅg*, a plucked idiophone,

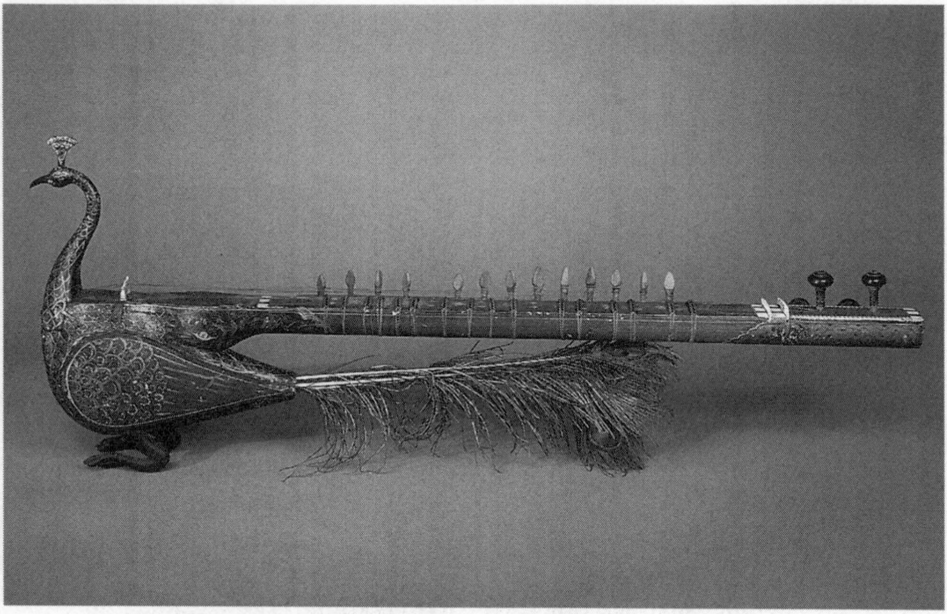

FIGURE 6.1. *Mayūrī* gifted by Tagore. © Metropolitan Museum of Art, New York.

does not typically accompany the *qānūn* or *sitār*, and seems to have been included to intrigue the audience rather than for its aesthetic appropriateness. Likewise, the *esrār* (*esrāj*) was, in Tagore's own words, "a very recent instrument."[94] Indeed, there is a theory that it had some connection to Matiyaburj and was taken to Gaya by none other than Basat Khan.[95]

Despite asserting Hindu music's antiquity, Tagore evidently took a particular interest in new and "revived" instruments. In the Crosby Brown Collection of instruments—dating from 1889, now at the Metropolitan Museum of Art, New York—is a *mayūrī* gifted by Tagore (figure 6.1).[96] This is a highly decorated and somewhat eccentric piece: it combines aspects of the *sitār* and *sārangī*, and its lower *tumbā* is distinctively shaped, painted, and decorated with feathers to look like a peacock (*mayūr*). This instrument, better known by the Persian word for "peacock," *ṯā'ūs*, was a recent invention; at that time, by Tagore's reckoning, it was approximately forty years old.[97] The *nyastaraṅga* was frequently noted by visitors and guests due to its peculiar playing technique, and Kaliprasanna Bandyopadhyay became quite renowned for his performances (figure 6.2).[98] While his name was reported in many travelogues and newspapers, a question lingered over the appropriateness of the *nyastaraṅga* in this particular setting, and some were of the opinion that "it

FIGURE 6.2. Kaliprasanna Bandyopadhyay with *nyastaraṅga*. National Anthropological Archives, Smithsonian Institution (NAA INV.04596100).

was, in fact, an eccentricity quite out of place in a school of music, and more suitable for a professional mountebank than for a scientific musician."[99]

Tagore arranged these instruments into new ensembles. On the occasion of the visit of the prince of Wales to India, Tagore arranged his associate instrumentalists into the model of a Western band or orchestra.[100] A fete was held by the "leading natives of Bengal" at the Belgatchia Villa on 26 December 1875. Descriptions of the decorations (fiery torches and *pandal*-like temporary structures) were complimentary, but the British guests were less impressed by the music. The band took center stage, since as soon as the prince entered,

> native minstrels, stationed in pavilions, played the national anthem. . . . The music which the bandsmen cajole from tin whistles, tom-toms, and zithers like scooped-out cucumbers, can claim no kinship with those strains of which Milton speaks, sweet enough to create a soul beneath the ribs of death. The chords are fluty, and the airs abrupt and chaotic. . . . Whatever, therefore, may be thought of the poetic character of the hymn of welcome [written by Tagore himself], a Bengali version of which was chanted as the Prince stepped along the carpeted passage to the dais, the musical accompaniment could command no English sympathy or admiration.[101]

J. Drew Gay, the correspondent for London's *Daily Telegraph*, was particularly dismissive: he complained about the "constant, droning sound" from the band's rehearsals, and compared their performance to the deafening fog signals he had encountered at the Baroda train station.[102] Although Drew Gay was unfamiliar with Hindustani music, he was nonetheless conscious that Tagore's musicians were amateurs, which to his mind entailed enthusiastic incompetence: "I think I might be chary of criticism thus far; the professionals are bearable, but alas for those who have to listen to the four amateurs . . . we pardon the noise the amateurs make for the sake of the words they sing. They should have very loyal hearts. Their lungs are undoubtedly powerful, though nature forgot to give them any vocal ability."[103]

Even the more sympathetic listeners were not sufficiently acquainted with Indian music to know that it was entirely novel for instrumentalists to form a band or to play the national anthem. Instead, they were keen to document the unfamiliar shapes of instruments, rather than the music itself, which they found "monotonous, mostly minor, the singing nasal."[104] Kaliprasanna Bandyopadhyay (described as "a Baboo, whose garb strongly reminds one of Cardinal Richelieu") was more popular with his *nyastaraṅga*, though some of the impressed correspondents erroneously confused the instrument's name for the musician's own: "We were obliged to let Nasataranga depart with a more solid claim than ever to the prestige of being the cleverest blower of a pipe in all India."[105] He was followed by Gopal Candra Cakravarty, "a bright-eyed, slim-looking artist" known to the correspondents by the "sweet name of Chuckerbutty,"[106] of whom Drew Gay gave another scathing review: "I hope I shall never hear Chuckerbutty sing any more. To attempt to describe his 'music' is impossible. He appears to have shut his mouth off from all communication with the nose, and to be shouting from the pit of his stomach. Enough, Chuckerbutty, the Prince longs to be delivered from thee."[107]

The band started up again: "the big Indian fiddles, zithers, horns, and cymbals, joined together in the execution of that passionate love melody which is supposed to have the power of tickling the sternest parent into smiles, and known as Taza Bataza Nuba Nu." Incredibly, given Tagore and Lokenath Ghosh's distaste for and uncompromising rejection of the nautch, at this point "dancing girls, in a cloud of green and gold drapery," appeared and began to dance to the tune, though it was now the early hours and the prince left their performance early to go into the villa for supper (figure 6.3).

While the British contingent accepted the entertainments as evidence of native loyalty and hospitality, the Belgatchia fete represents an unfortunate juxtaposition of cultures. Tagore's amateur musicians may well have performed poorly, but since their audience was a tour party fresh from London, there was little hope that their efforts would be recognized for what they were. Tagore's band and showcase of instruments was a startlingly new concept, cannily packaged as a representative traditional entertainment.

The performance of nautch girls alongside Tagore's band, most likely to their accompaniment, is remarkable for three reasons. First, Lokenath had written with bile against dancing girls and their accompanying *ustāds* only two years earlier, yet here his colleagues (he is not named in the reports, but he was almost certainly present) were assuming the latter role themselves. This must serve as a caution in our readings of vitriolic works to note discrepancies between rhetoric and practice; even the loudest proponents of moral reform in music could in reality perpetuate the older styles, the objects of their scorn. Second, by playing for the accompaniment of dancing girls, these "respectable" Babu amateurs were inadvertently taking on the connotations of the pimp. For at least the past forty years, propaganda in Calcutta had associated nautch girls with prostitution.[108] While the patronage of the nautch continued apace across the nineteenth century, the connotations of a procurer became fixed to the dancing girl's accompanist, and became something of a stereotype.[109] It is possible that these respectable babus viewed a revised version of the very famous "Tāza ba Tāza" tune, played with entirely different and radically modern instrumentation, adequately distant from the original nautch song to avoid social censure, even when nautch girls were

DANCE OF NAUTCH GIRLS BEFORE THE PRINCE OF WALES AT THE NATIVE ENTERTAINMENT, CALCUTTA
FROM A SKETCH BY ONE OF OUR SPECIAL ARTISTS

FIGURE 6.3. Dance of nautch girls before the prince of Wales. *The Graphic*, 29 January 1876. © Mary Evans Picture Library.

present. Finally, the inclusion of this tune and the classic entertainment of the dancing girl in an otherwise new repertoire and ensemble was itself a liminal moment for Hindustani performance culture, where the old and new worlds were brought together in an unfamiliar duet. "Tāza ba Tāza" was an entirely appropriate choice for the connection between them, since by that time this Persian *ghazal* had been widely circulated across continents, modulating in form and arrangement, and had acquired an international and sometimes even diplomatic function.[110]

Another area of innovation in performance that enjoyed a more positive reception was Tagore's *Tableaux Vivants*. These were staged dramatic spectacles with songs and instrumental music. He devised at least three sets: one on the subject of music itself, from 1874; another on empire, from 1877; and a third on the ten divine *avatārs* of Visnu, around 1880. The first set began with a series based on six principal *rāgas*, then introduced Bharat, the iconic sage associated with musical learning.[111] This was followed by a monologue from Music personified, and then by the goddess Saraswati, seated upon a throne of instruments, to whom students at the school sang a hymn.[112] In between acts there were instrumental interludes, and an interlocutor, Udaycand Goswami, provided a discourse on each *rāga* as it appeared onstage. These performances were well received by Indian and European audiences, though it is noteworthy that one Bengali newspaper was critical of the musical content, and suggested, "It would certainly have been more enhanced if some professional musician's services had been entertained."[113] The second set of *Tableaux* were representations of "the eastern subjects of Her Majesty, the various nations appearing in their own costumes, and offering a tribute of their respective country-products to the British Crown.[114] One correspondent was very impressed by this "entirely new description of native performance, which is certainly preferable to the unchanging *nautch*."[115]

The warm reception of these experiments led Tagore to publish a detailed guide to producing the *Tableaux Vivants* in 1880, based on his latest creation on the ten *avatārs* of Visnu.[116] Tagore declared that his tableaux were wholly Indian and entirely novel ("in which everything is national and nothing borrowed"), and that they spoke to the ancient lore of Hindu civilization.[117] Despite using a French name for the genre and a magic lantern in his staging, Tagore insisted that his presentation was an updated form of *mūrtti*, one of sixteen varieties of *deśī nātya* in ancient Sanskrit theory that drew heavily upon Aryan principles of stage management.[118]

While Tagore insisted that he was both a trailblazing pioneer and a loyal son of an ancient Sanskrit civilization, his music practices bear striking similarities to the innovations developed by his neighbor in Calcutta, Wajid Ali Shah. First, the very notion of the Bengal Music School and a system of pedagogy where students learned together from an *ustād* in assigned classes had been presaged by the *parīkḫāna*. It might be argued that the *parīkḫāna* was not an open institution, since it was primarily dedicated to Wajid Ali's wives—but the same could be said of the rather selective demographic of the Bengal Music School, whose pupils were far fewer in number than the hundreds of *shāgirds* in Matiyaburj. Second, Tagore's many enterprises were dependent on the notion that someone from the patron class had the right to perform himself, in public, without social recrimination or stigma: the possibility of the respectable amateur. Wajid Ali and his companions were early advocates of this principle, and courted controversy through their music making. Third, certain "innovations" at Paturiaghat evidently drew on experimental work at Matiyaburj. Aside from individual connections (as with Basat Khan and the *esrār*), the *Tableaux Vivants* must surely have taken some inspiration from the musical theater being staged contemporaneously in Matiyaburj under Wajid Ali's direction, from *naql* enactments of *rāgamālā*s to the Yogi Mela pantomimes. Finally, and most crucially, Tagore relied heavily on musicians from Matiyaburj, who brought their experience of the *parīḵẖāna* as a center of theatrical training to the Bengal Music School. In the following section I will consider precisely who these men were, and how they cemented the ties between Matiyaburj, in the south of the city, and Tagore Castle, in the north.

Between Nawab and *Bhadralok*

Although the musicians of Matiyaburj did not feature prominently in his histories of "Hindu music," S. M. Tagore had many connections with them. Basat Khan was a correspondent of the Bengal Music School, as seen in his recommendation of Kshetramohan Goswami's musical scholarship (above). Likewise, Tagore published a Hindustani letter of support for Kshetramohan by Maula Bakhsh of Baroda and Kaliprasanna Bandyopadhyay, signed by many musicians familiar to Wajid Ali Shah: Ahmad Khan, Ali Jan, Muhammad Khan, Taj Khan, Haidar Khan, Ghulam Muhammad, Niamatullah Khan, Ghulam Hussain Khan, Janun Khan, Aiyaz Ali Khan, Inayat Hussain Khan, and Ahsan Ali Khan.

Of these, Ahmad Khan *ḵẖayālī* was particularly influential. Wajid Ali named him as one of his own disciples.[119] Karam Imam tells us that Ahmad Khan was the son of Shakkar Qawwal of Lucknow, and brother of Muhammad Khan (potentially the same "Muhammad Khan" in the list of signatories). Ahmad Khan's *ḵẖayāl* was characterized by his outstanding knowledge of *rāga*, his *śuddha asthāyī*, and his *ṭappa*.[120] At Matiyaburj, Ahmad Khan taught the ladies of the Nur Manzil (established c. 1870) with Qayam Khan *raqqāṣ*. Wajid Ali was very pleased with this pair, since their students were "so skilled in *dhrupad*, *ḵẖayāl*, *caturaṅg*, *tarānā*, *ālāp*, and *arthabhāv* that they make you weep. Truthfully, their two teachers performed a true service and discipleship to me."[121] Just as Wajid Ali was compiling this report for *Banī* (1877), Ahmad Khan began to become involved with the Bengal School of

Music, and was most likely the Hindustani vocal master mentioned in 1877.[122] *The Statesman* provided a rich description of Ahmad Khan's performance at the school on 9 August 1876:

> The vocal music by Professor Ahmud Khan did not appear to have been much appreciated. According to the programme, the two parts sung by him were termed "Kheal" [*k̲h̲ayāl*] species and "Terana" [*tarānā*] species. The singer, an old man, played upon no instrument. His sons played the accompaniment on setars. The old man seemed to be one "of all motions," as he kept his hands moving most dexterously during the whole time he was exercising his lungs. A lady was anxious to know what the movement or the motions of the hands indicated. The gentleman, to whom the question was put, innocently replied that the performer wished to show that there were ups and downs in a man's life.[123]

The *Bombay Times* gave a briefer but more positive evaluation: "The vocal execution and expressive gesticulation of Professor Ahmud Khan were beyond all praise, and were greeted with enthusiastic applause."[124] Ahmad Khan later took on several influential Bengali students, including Benimadhab Adhikari ("Beni Ostad") and Amritalal Datta, who were both connected to Swami Vivekananda.[125]

Ahmad Khan's connection to Tagore prepared the ground for further relationships between the hereditary musicians of Lucknow and the new musical families of Calcutta. Ahmad's nephew, Murad Ali Khan, the son of Muhammad Khan, had many Bengali disciples, including Haraprasad Bandyopadhyay (1830–98). Haraprasad was a product of the burgeoning Bengal Music School community. He is remembered as being adept in the *vīṇā* and *sitār*, and he studied with Maula Bakhsh of Baroda during his time at Pathuriaghat, but was also competent in Western music. Murad Ali Khan almost certainly taught him *dhrupad* (Ahmad Khan was a *k̲h̲ayāl* specialist, but his brother Muhammad and his sons specialized in *dhrupad*),[126] which Haraprasad also studied from Ganganarayan Chattopadhyay (c. 1807–74) and the Misra family of Betia. There is also a suggestion that he may have studied *k̲h̲ayāl* and *ṭappa* from Saraswati Bai (1894–1974), the "first Brahman woman to sing on the concert stage."[127] Haraprasad's education in music and his subsequent career are in some sense representative of larger developments in Hindustani music: cultivated in high society, trained through a Bengal Music School community, and taking *ta'līm* from a Lakhnavi *ustād*, an older generation of Bengali *dhrupad* artist, and the Misras of Hindustan.

Sajjad Muhammad Khan was not as deeply involved in the workings of the Bengal Music School as Ahmad Khan, but he may have been among the anonymous "staff of the Ex-King of Oudh" who attended the school's ceremonies.[128] He was from another family of Lakhnavi musicians who migrated to Matiyaburj, and was later patronized by the Tagores.[129] He was an instrumentalist specializing in the left-hand technique (*kṛntan*), the *dhrupad* style of *sūrbahār*, and the *Purab baj* style of *sitār*.[130] Besides Tagore, Sajjad Muhammad had several important disciples, both Bengali and Hindustani. He gave instruction in the *sūrbahār* and *rabāb* to Gopal Candra Cakravarty, and their interaction developed into a *k̲h̲ayāl baj*.[131] He also taught the *sūrsiṅgār* to Kaukab Khan, thus contributing to the Delhi-oriented lineage of Basat Khan. Such was Sajjad Muhammad's reputation that there are several unverifiable traditions about musicians taking inspiration from him, including Bamacaran Bandyopadhyay.[132]

The presence of court musicians gave the Bengal Music School a sense of authenticity. The Tagore brothers were patrons in the established manner as much as advocates of a new culture, and they attracted a number of guest musicians. Asghar Ali Khan (1842–1912, son of Husain Ali and grandson of Ghulam Ali *rabābia* of Gwalior), was the court musician of Darbhanga. He performed alongside Ahmad Khan and the school's students in the autumn of 1876, on the *sarod* and *surchayun*, an experimental *sitār-sarod* hybrid developed by his father or uncle.[133] It is said that he characteristically played the *sarod* to sound like a flute.[134]

Tagore's pioneering work to bring musical culture into an elite Bengali domain with a Sanskritic past was dependent upon the precedents and expertise of the musicians from Matiyaburj. However, this was not the only form of interaction between the Lakhnavi musicians and their Bengali patrons. While the Bengal Music School enjoyed public attention, there was also an undercurrent of bemusement or distaste over its new ventures. In the following section I will turn to the more traditional patrons in Calcutta.

The "Networked" Sphere

A short distance from the Tagore residences were the Ghosh family houses at 46 and 47 Pathuriaghat Street. The descendants of Khelat Chandra Ghosh (1827–78) were major patrons of Hindustani musicians, and later of the All Bengal Music Conference, established in 1934. From the early twentieth century, Bhupendra Krishna Ghosh (1886–1941) commissioned portraits of all the musicians who passed through their house.[135] These portraits document the family's close association with individual artists. This fascination with celebrity musicians entered Bengali literature: nineteenth-century memoirs and biographical texts valued intimacy, a circle of familiarity, and grades of appreciation and connoisseurship.[136] These qualities are evidence of a persistent *meḥfil* culture that focused on intimately socializing around gifted artists and individuals, rather than the Bengal Music School and other institutions' emphasis on the public staging and dissemination of music.[137] The language of the musical memoir thus testifies to the persistence of smaller, elite gatherings, such as the *sabhā*, *majlis*, *baiṭhakkhānā*, and *jalsa*.

The *meḥfil*-oriented patrons were not opposed to Tagore and Bengal Music School culture, but they also offered an important alternative mode of musical appreciation. Since most musical scholarship for this period focuses on new developments, prioritizing reformist or nascent nationalist voices, these more conventional patrons have been overlooked even though their listening culture outlived that of their more radical contemporaries. They represent a transitional moment in which a relatively newly formed colonial elite society appropriated certain older Mughal cultural codes and modified others.

This elite listening culture is well attested to in Bengali memoir literature. Mukundadeb Mukhopadhyay[138] structured his recollections around sketches of interesting characters he had encountered in his lifetime, including the singer Nathu Khan, originally of Delhi.[139] Identifying the historical person of Nathu Khan in this account is not easy. Mukundadeb related him particularly to Bengali drummers, so it might be assumed that this is the Dilhavi *tablā* player of that name (1872–1940),[140] except that Mukundadeb described Nathu as a singer, and gave him memories of the Delhi court prior to 1857, fifteen years before the *tablā* player Nathu was born. However, asking different questions of these sources sheds light on the social history of Calcutta's listening culture.

Mukundadeb first met Nathu Khan at the Sarkar household in Bahubazar (Bowbazar).[141] This *bāṛī* (household) regularly hosted traveling musicians and was frequented by a number of appreciative listeners, including the Sanskrit scholars Nilmani Mukhopadhyay Nyayalankar (professor at Presidency and then at Sanskrit College) and Narasingha Candra Vidyalankar, both of whom were entranced by the *ustād*'s perfect Sanskrit pronunciation. Nathu Khan claimed that in the Delhi *darbār* he had sung in the three court languages: Persian, Sanskrit, and Urdu. However, Mukundadeb noted that by the time he met Nathu, the musician had transferred his career to Calcutta and was increasingly singing in Bengali.[142] On that particular occasion, Ramlal Datta of Bhadrakali, a Bengali gentleman who had studied singing, was also in attendance and exclaimed that Nathu was a true *nāyak*—to which Nathu humbly replied in Bengali that he merely sang *bhajan* ("*bhajan kari*").

Mukundadeb's account of this society of listeners and connoisseurs represented an interlinked series of elite, unpublicized spaces which served as the infrastructure for an informally organized community. This was very different from the listening scenes in Maharashtra and Madras described by Bakhle and Subramanian, who emphasize the role of formal associations, societies, and committees for musical patronage and appreciation.[143] This is an important distinction because the rise of formal, corporate bodies of listeners has been taken as evidence of music's dependency upon a public sphere, itself a driving force behind musical reform and consensus on taste. This in turn has drawn music into debates on education and the place of women in society. The evidence from Calcutta, however, suggests that despite the loud presence of the Bengal Music School and other public engagements with music in the printed archive, it was a more conservative elite "networked" sphere, instead of a public sphere, that was the platform for "serious" music making.

Based at the Sarkar house, Nathu Khan circulated between the mansions of his regular listeners, who took turns to convene new *meḥfil*s.[144] In Nilmani Nyayalankar's house, Mukundadeb saw Jatindra Mohan Tagore, Srinath Das (who brought along his own singer, Kalinath Bandyopadhyay), Romescandra Mitra, and Kesabcandra Mitra, all of whom Mukundadeb called *biśeṣajña* (specialist, discerning) in music.[145] Kesabcandra Mitra and several other amateur musicians accompanied Nathu Khan in performance and took *taʿlīm* from him.[146] After some time, Nathu Khan would relocate to live with another host but continue performing across multiple households.[147] Aside from the listeners and patrons, these gatherings were the nodes of contact in a network of musicians who were both Hindustani, including Ramzan Khan and Murad Ali Khan, and Bengali, including Jayakaran Misra and Aghorenath Cakrabarti. Aghorenath apparently cried when he heard Nathu Khan sing, saying that Nathu Khan had accomplished a fusion of vocal technique, learning, and devotion that he had not heard before, even in the likes of Jadu Bhatta, Rasul Bakhsh, Ali Bakhsh, Taj Khan, Farid Khan, and so on. Mukundadeb's memoir is typical of Bengali writers from the networked sphere in that his prose ripples through circles of listeners and musicians who had public profiles but convened behind closed doors. One named individual recalls the names of his peers, or other masters he has heard, indicating larger branches of hospitality, music making, and cultivation.

While Tagore was being celebrated for reclaiming the respectability of music, within the "networked" sphere many middle- to upper-class gentlemen were studying music through *ustād*s and other Bengalis in their orbit. A particularly significant cluster of expertise formed to the south of the city, in Bhavanipur; this is adjacent to Khiddurpur, and much closer to Matiyaburj than to the *bāṛī*s of north Calcutta. Here I shall briefly consider three individuals from this cluster, since their interactions with the court indicate the various forms of Matiyaburj's infiltration of the *bhadralok* "networked" sphere.

Jadab Krishna Basu (1848–1926) never became a very famous musician, but when he died of cancer aged seventy-eight he was mourned as the "venerable music professor of Bhavanipur" (*Bhavānipurer śraddheýa saṅgīta adhyāpak*).[148] His obituary commented on his early passion for music: his family was originally from Gobindpur and had him enrolled for a conventional middle-class education. Ensnared by the "seductive power of music," however, he neglected his studies, and during school hours would "listen with an engrossed mind to musical soirees in the house of the nawab of Matiyaburj," where he forged close connections with the *ustāds* there. It is noteworthy that in 1926, Wajid Ali's court was referred to as a *bāṛī*, which situated it as a node in the networked sphere of Calcutta's households. This is further evidence of Wajid Ali's resituating himself in his new terrain rather than remaining aloof in his shadow: Lucknow. By sitting at Matiyaburj, Jadab Krishna acquired an immersive training in high art music (*uccāṅga saṅgīt*), and when he performed in other *bāṛīs* his superior knowledge was acknowledged by other *ustāds*. His musical career is recorded little elsewhere, but in a photograph that accompanied his obituary he is represented with a *sarod* (figure 6.4). His obituary situated him as an interlocutor between Bengali society and prestigious Hindustani artistry. He had lamented how his countrymen had taken the nuances of music for granted and had lost their respect (*āsthā hārāiýā*) for *uccāṅga saṅgīt*. While they thought a little skill would suffice, he had devoted his entire life to music, and he ultimately set up his own association—the Bhavanipur Saṅgīt Sammilanī, a music school—and wrote a guide for his students.[149] While Jadab Krishna has largely been forgotten, his career drew together the nawabi court, the networked sphere of Calcutta *bāṛīs*, and later associations. This serves as a reminder that there was no strict distinction between *bāṛī* culture and the more public enterprises of the likes of Tagore. However, the Bhavanipur Saṅgīt Sammilanī had a much smaller profile than the very corporate Bengal Music School, and may be better understood as an extension of the networked community of music appreciation, rather than a purposive initiative to remodel musical culture.

Jadab Krishna's partner in establishing the Sammilanī was Kesabcandra Mitra (1822–1901), born to a wealthy local family in Bhavanipur based on Paddapukur Road. Kesabcandra Mitra fused together the functions of a patron—employing musicians from Matiyaburj, like Murad Ali Khan—and performer, himself becoming a celebrated *mṛdaṅg* player and accompanying Murad Ali, Jadu Bhatta, and Kshetramohan Goswami at times in performance.[150] His *guru-bhāī* was another gentleman musician, Murari Mohan

FIGURE 6.4. Jadab Krishna Basu. From *Saṅgīta Bijñān Prabeśikā* 3, no. 4 (1926): 209. Courtesy of the School of Cultural Texts and Records, Jadavpur University, Kolkata.

Gupta (c. 1824–1904), born to a family of physicians and trained as a mathematics professor before he retired early to pursue his musical interests.[151] He specialized in the *mṛdaṅg* and wrote two works of instrumental instruction: the *Mṛdaṅg Prabeśikā* ("Entry into the *Mṛdaṅg*," 1887) and *Saṅgīta Prabeśikā* ("Entry into Music," c. 1889–91). Kesabcandra and Murari Mohan taught many students together in the latter's private residence.[152] Together they indicate that the networked sphere was not merely one of appreciation, but also a forum for pedagogy that drew together multiple generations of Hindustani masters, their students who took on disciples of their own, and new recruits from Bengali families.

Finally, Kishorilal Mukhopadhyay provides an insight into what the expectations of the Bengali "amateur" musician were, and how those expectations influenced the forms of teaching that the older generation of Lakhnavi *ustāds* were willing to impart. Kishorilal was a *kulin* Brahman by birth and an attorney by training, but due to ill health he spent intermittent periods away from his practice, during which time he would study singing with Murad Ali Khan, whom he took into his home. Kishorilal also attended events at the Bengal Music School in the late 1870s, but he was not actively involved in its administration or a member of the school's committee.[153] He was more seriously related to the Bhavanipur circle, and kept a house in Tamluk, Midnapur, eighty-four kilometers from Calcutta, which became a satellite node of the networked sphere. One of his sons, Jadugopal Mukhopadhyay (1886–1976), an eminent revolutionary, described the gatherings that assembled there. Apart from Murad Ali Khan, Ali Bakhsh and other musicians with Matiyaburj connections attended, including Tasadduq Hussain Khan (1879–1940?), the nephew of Taj Khan, who had studied with him in Nepal.[154] Tasadduq Hussain, whose career was later propelled by All India Radio, was reliant upon this network when he came to Bengal. Both he and Kishorilal taught Surendranath Majumdar (1838–98) of Bhagalpur, a deputy magistrate and a well-known singer in his own right.[155] Other Bengali musicians developed their skills in this house, including Kishorilal's *guru-bhāī* Jadunath Ray (c. 1820–?), who was little-known in Calcutta, but who became the court musician (*sabhāgāẏak*) of Mayurbhanj, Odisha.[156] Thus there were varieties of engagement with musical training through this network, both amateur and professional.

Kishorilal himself began his training as an interested amateur, like Kesabcandra Mitra; but he increasingly developed a financial incentive to his practice. During his recess from his legal practice he performed professionally at the courts of local rajas, traveling to them by bullock cart. Murad Ali allegedly distinguished between the professional training he gave to Kishorilal and the "training of a critic" he provided to Kishorilal's other friends, which was designed "so that when good musicians come you will know enough to support them and they will be able to remain good musicians."[157] Therefore, though this period saw many musicians from respectable Bengali families acquire practical training in music, the *ustād*s nonetheless maintained the older dichotomy between the knowledge of the practitioner and that of the connoisseur-patron. The *ustād* could offer both, but reserved the intimate knowledge of the art for his poorer and hence professional disciples. When Kishorilal's health was restored and he returned to practicing law, he continued to sing in the courts of rajas during his three-month vacations, but no longer charged for his performances.[158]

This section has placed the musical public sphere orchestrated by the Tagore brothers into a larger perspective, and has suggested that there were alternative listening cultures adjacent to them in north Calcutta, but also to the south and in the countryside, which were more influential for the transmission of Hindustani music in Bengal. These have been conceived of in terms of a networked sphere—that is, one which was neither wholly private or wholly public, but which instead required a point of access or a personal introduction to unlock, and which operated through interconnected circles of musical professionals and enthusiasts playing host to each other in their own residences. This culture did not seek to monopolize musical culture, reform it, or craft its public presence; rather, it served as an informal infrastructure for listening, learning and sustaining the tradition. An examination of individuals in these circles indicates that there were internally recognized gradations of participation in music: the older, nonpractical connoisseur patron worked alongside the nonprofessional musician and the amateur turned professional. Significantly, it seems that *ustād*s from Matiyaburj held significant positions in this sphere and disseminated their knowledge of "high" (*uccaṅga*) music to different degrees, according to the professional status of their disciples or clients. In the following section I will turn to the figure of Murad Ali Khan, Kishorilal's own teacher, in order to discuss how Bengalis who were engaged in this network perceived their *ustād*s and understood their own position in the cultural history of Hindustan.

The Weeping Wizard: Murad Ali Khan

Paradoxically, an obstacle to critically reconstructing the careers of nineteenth-century musicians is the abundance of source material. In Urdu and Persian literature, *taẕkira*s and music treatises offer summary (and sometimes judgmental) accounts of noted artists, either to document the performances that specific authors enjoyed, to construct a cultural profile for a particular place, or to invoke the authority of practitioners in support of a new work's account of musical theory.[159] In Bengali literature, Hindustani musicians appeared as celebrity figures in "light" literature for cultured readers. Raking these works for "authentic" details of historical figures proves problematic, since the authors often had literary priorities that permitted the confusion of details and the romanticizing of oral memory. Approaching musical memoirs as a genre, however, sheds light on the character of the Hindustani musician in literary modes of nostalgia and historical consciousness, regionalism, and exoticism. To explore these forms of representation, this section will consider Murad Ali Khan as an example of the elusive yet well-attested musician.

In the late nineteenth century there were at least three noted Hindustani musicians named Murad Ali Khan. One was the *rabābia* and *sarodiya* Murad Ali Khan of Darbhanga, son of Ghulam Ali Khan of Rewa and brother to

Nanhe Khan.[160] Another Murad Ali was a *darbārī* musician of Hyderabad under Nizam Mir Muhammad Ali Khan (r. 1868–1911), who died in 1915. He was a singer trained in *dhrupad, horī* and *dhamar*, and is now associated with the Agra *gharānā*.[161] However, the earlier references in this chapter point to a third Murad Ali Khan: a singer associated with Lucknow, Delhi, Calcutta, and rural Bengal.

Twentieth-century Bengali music scholars have recorded the memory of a *dhrupad* artist from Hindustan who taught a large number of Bengali pupils, many of whom have already been mentioned: Aghorenath Cakrabarti, Haraprasad Bandyopadhayay, Jadunath Ray (court singer of Mayurbhanj), Asutosh Ray, Ramdas Goswami (1823–92), Pramathanath Bandyopadhyay, and Gopal Candra Cakravarty.[162] Murad Ali Khan is thought to have been a musician at Matiyaburj, where he introduced several Bengali artists, including his accompanist Kesabcandra Mitra and his disciples Aghorenath and Pramathanath, who sang there in their own right.[163] Outside Matiyaburj, Murad Ali Khan found support from the family of Hemcandra Datta of Majilpur, Kishorilal Mukhopadhyay, and Abinash Ghosh of Goabagan, in whose house Murad Ali died. The overall impression, then, is of a *dhrupadiya* from Lucknow who came first to Matiyaburj and then to the houses of Calcutta's elite, where he developed a large circle of students.

Can such a figure be identified outside of twentieth-century Bengali sources? A possible candidate is found in the *Ma'dan al-mūsīqī*. Karam Imam mentioned one Murad Ali Khan who was from a family of *k̲h̲ayāl* singers and was the grandson of Shakkar Qawwal of Lucknow. His uncle, Ahmad Khan (see above), and father, Muhammad Khan, were celebrated singers (unlike, in Imam's opinion, the other *ḍhāṛis* of Lucknow).[164] Muhammad had a successful career in the south and wore his hair in a southern-style topknot. He died in Rewa, where he had been employed on a salary of one thousand rupees per month.[165] Murad Ali Khan was the youngest of Muhammad's four sons, and according to Imam sang *k̲h̲ayāl* and *ṭappa* in the "Lucknow style." He himself had one son, Suleman, who became a disciple of a relative, Rajab Ali. The previous sources do not make any mention of Suleman, who perhaps did not cross over to Bengal; they focus on Murad Ali teaching Bengalis *dhrupad*. Imam's emphasis on *k̲h̲ayāl* and *ṭappa* would stress Murad Ali's specializing in contemporary Lakhnavi styles, but that is not to say he was not also proficient in *dhrupad*. It is therefore plausible, though not conclusive, that the Murad Ali Khan known to Karam Imam was the same singer who had a successful career in Bengal.

The fullest description of Murad Ali Khan comes from the family of Kishorilal Mukhopadhyay. Two of Kishorilal's sons became well-known figures:

Jadugopal Mukhopadhyay was imprisoned for his revolutionary activities, but his younger brother Dhan Gopal Mukerji (1890–1936), avoided a similar fate by emigrating first to Japan and then to the United States, where he became a well-regarded litterateur.[166] Murad Ali evidently made a profound impression on the brothers as children, since they both mentioned him in their memoirs. Dhan Gopal's characterization, in particular, provides a rare insight into the relationships forged between north Indian Muslim musicians and their Bengali patrons-cum-disciples.

Mukerji described his impressions of "that white-haired, white-bearded, and white-clad old man telling his beads of amber"[167] in two works: a largely autobiographical piece, *Caste and Outcast* (1923), and a discussion of nationalist politics, *My Brother's Face* (1924). Writing for an American readership largely unfamiliar with India, Mukerji wrote to inform but also enchant his audience. This had a significant impact on his writing style and his redaction of the historical kernels of his own life story. Murad Ali's musical skill was depicted in tandem with his charismatic presence in the Mukhopadhyay homestead, where he was at once the family's teacher, spiritual master, and storyteller.

In Mukerji's accounts these roles converged through Murad Ali's singing: he would sit with Jadugopal at his bedtime, "a white wizard guiding a ship by the magic of his voice. Ah, what a voice! He was the only one left who could sing Dipak—the Fire and Thunder melody. His tones were deep and vibrant as a bull-frog's."[168] Since the family was Hindu, Mukerji explained, Murad Ali taught the boys "Vishnu hymns."[169] This might refer to *dhrupad*, or perhaps suggest that like Nathu Khan, Murad Ali had added Bengali *bhajan* to his repertoire. Anecdotes about Murad Ali reflect his integration into the family over their twelve years together: "He had a terrific way of opening his mouth when he sang, and we used to tell him that he almost swallowed the universe." Murad Ali taught the boys that *rāga*s were fashioned by God himself as a means to keep men righteous: "So He sang out the sun, and rolled out the thunder melody. (But this tune has been lost for two thousand years.) Thus music was created to bring man back to God."[170] In *My Brother's Face*, the *ustād* became a yogi-like figure, preaching harmony between Muslims and Hindus.

Although it is impossible to judge the authenticity of Murad Ali's reported words, it seems likely that his memory of the musician has been significantly romanticized, becoming the holy wizard of Mukerji's memoirs. However, the very fact that the Muslim musician was venerated and welcomed into the Brahman household was the basis for his extrapolation. Mukerji recalls that his mother would break the laws of their caste and cook meat for Murad Ali, since he "had become my father's spiritual adviser, and therefore whatever he ate was spiritual."[171] Given that Muslim *ustāds* had been taking on Brahman disciples in Bengal since at least the mid-eighteenth century, Mukerji's memoir offers a glimpse into the kinds of relationship that may have been forged through musical training.

Mukerji's account of how Murad Ali came to work for his father is extremely romantic, and very different from the version of his life I have already outlined. He notes that Murad Ali was eighteen years old in 1857, which would put his birth in about 1839, and would place him in his early sixties when Mukerji knew him as a child. In Mukerji's tale, Murad Ali was the former court musician of the emperor of Delhi, rather than the nawab of Lucknow. During the Uprising of 1857 he saw the emperor's son shot, and abandoned his patron out of fear. The emperor died shortly afterward, having in his last moments cried, "Where is Moradali to sing to me now? I have paid him all his life." The guilt-ridden musician composed a "Remorse Song," which he would sing every evening from then on:

> O my king, for your sake I go as a mendicant of song from door to door, but desolation greets me as a great shadow on either hand! The glories are gone and wild animals prowl through the palaces. But the wild animals that prowl through my heart, who can take them away?

Mukerji claimed that this "terrible cry of anguish" could still be heard in India.[172] Evidently, his intention was to supply his American readership with a tragic figure turned mendicant: perhaps he felt that the dying emperor (notably in India rather than Rangoon) was a more dramatic option than the less well-known Wajid Ali Shah.

Although the historicity of Mukerji's background for Murad Ali Khan is problematic, it nonetheless gestures to how, at the turn of the twentieth century, the Hindustani *darbārī* musician became a motif and was reframed in writings by Bengalis. Mukerji was not alone in his representation of the weeping musician. The value of this figure becomes pronounced when read alongside the work of Dilipkumar Mukhopadhyay, who wrote extremely widely on Hindustani and Bengali music history, including the contributions of Wajid Ali Shah.[173] Mukhopadhyay was of the view that Murad Ali was indeed from Lucknow and in the service of the nawab when he first came to Calcutta.[174] In one of his more popular publications on musical biography, *Bhārater Saṅgīta Guṇī* ("India's Musical Talents," part 2), Mukhopadhyay crafted a number of detailed portraits. However, one of these was less convincing than the others: that of one Murad Khan. Although this Murad was not equated with Murad Ali, his portrayal is strikingly similar to Mukerji's account.

Dilipkumar Mukhopadhyay's essay on Murad Khan followed a "historical" episode in the life of Jagadindranath Ray, maharaja of Natore (1868–1926), famous in later life for his career in cricket and his editorship of the journal *Mānasī*. Jagadindranath had studied *pakhāwaj* in Natore, and became increasingly interested in music. When he completed his college studies in 1889, he ventured west for a tour of India. He had heard of a famous singer from the Delhi court, and he made it a priority to locate him in Old Delhi, where he had recently retired. While the essay (titled "Dillīr śeṣ darbārī," "Delhi's Last Court Musician")[175] was nominally about this singer, much of the story relates to Jagadindranath's frustrations in finding the elusive Murad Khan, since no one remembered his name. When he eventually finds the wizened singer in a back room in a back alley of the old city, Murad expresses his devotion to the long-dead emperor, saying that he had lost heart to sing ever again and had been wandering with his grief for twenty-seven years. However, moved by Jagadindranath's having made the long journey from Bengal to visit him, he adorns himself once more with his treasured *darbār pāgṛi,* dusts off his *tambūrā*, and begins to sing for his Bengali guest, who accompanies the *ustād* himself on a similarly dusty *pakhāwaj*. The two part as friends, but when Jagadindranath returns a week later for a second visit, he is informed that Murad died the previous day.

The entire episode is melodramatic. Murad's bereavement, his courage to sing again, and his sudden death render him a tragic figure. Compared to the other essays in the volume, the historical content of Murad's career appears insubstantial: the essay draws only from Jagadindranath's account, and is more concerned with the young Bengali than with the old Hindustani artist. The emphasis lies with the educated, musically adept noble (the royal house of Natore is described at length). It was Jagadindranath, rather than the denizens of Delhi, who remembered the legacy of Murad Khan, and he alone resurrected the *ustād*'s musical genius. In Murad's own words (relayed in the Bengali text): "You have come from the country of Bengal (*Bāṅglā muluka*) to hear my singing? But here in Delhi no man comes near me!"[176] The essay therefore looks back nostalgically to the lost lore of musicians who served the emperors and established the Bengalis as the sole caretakers of—and thus heirs to—elite Hindustani music.

Other Bengali authors included the trope of the nostalgic Hindustani musician in their works. My earlier discussion of Kishorilal Mukhopadhyay drew substantially on the revolutionary Jadugopal's memoir, which included Tasadduq Hussain's reminiscences about life and music in Nepal, and the migrations of his uncle, Taj Khan. In Mukundadeb Mukhopadhyay's account of Nathu Khan, Aghorenath Cakrabarti cries when he hears Nathu sing. Nathu himself weeps during his own recital, but also when he discusses his past career in Delhi and utters the name of Bahadur Shah.[177] When he later performs at the house of Ganeshcandra Candra, his host asks him how best to honor (*khātir*) him. Nathu replies, "I did not come for honor; music is my livelihood, I came for money. Ganesh Babu, what honor would you give me? I used to sit before the emperor of Delhi, the *vazīr* himself used to place the hookah pipe into my hand. Is there any other 'honor' after that?"[178]

Read individually, the portraits of musicians by these authors sometimes appear more romantic than historically accurate. Collectively, however, they indicate that the Bengali elites who listened to and studied with Hindustani *ustād*s, often assimilating them into their families, began to reflect on the cultural transition these men had navigated over the nineteenth century. The musician who wept at the name of the emperor became a recurring image. While it is quite possible that this was based on authentic observations, this trope had two cultural implications. First, it elevated the mystique of the musician as an artist who was saturated with emotion as he performed. That the music maker was not merely a technician of sound, or a mechanical servant of his patron, may have lent prestige to the art at a time when the elites were engaging with music themselves to increasingly professional standards. In other words, if the musician was an aesthete, he became a worthy aspiration for the Bengali enthusiast. Second, the relationship between the musician and the lost world of the Hindustani court was crucial. This can be seen as a literary expression of the Bengalis' fascination with exalted *uccāṅga* music, which they saw as stemming from the ancien régime of the Mughal Empire. Evoking nostalgia and mourning for a land and culture outside Bengal made it possible for the Bengali elite writer to render himself the inheritor and custodian of the Mughal legacy by appropriating the repertoires and experiences of the Hindustani *ustād*. This was perhaps an expression of nationalist discontent; it should be remembered that both of Kishorilal's sons were heavily involved in revolutionary activities. Their writings suggest that the *ustād* became the poetic embodiment of the lost world of non-British India, and that his tears and musical laments expressed a political outrage through sound and affect.

Conclusion

In 1896, S. M. Tagore commented on the current state of music in north India and drew attention to one Babu Mahesh Candra Sarkar, a Bengali amateur musician who had become one "of the best *Setár*-players of Benares of the modern day."[179] Tagore was especially keen to underline the "progress" made in (and for) Hindustani music by Bengali gentlemen who were not from older musical families themselves but had mastered the science of music through rigorous training. To Tagore, the notion of a Bengali becoming a celebrated doyen in the Hindustani heartlands must have been extremely appealing. This chapter has provided a context for Tagore's enterprises and accounted for the rise of public careers among elite amateur musicians. For Jadugopal Mukhopadhyay, who was personally invested in revolution rather than revolutionary musicology, there was a simple explanation: "In 1856 the English put the nawab of Lucknow under house arrest in Matiyaburj near Calcutta. One hundred and ten male and female musicians came with him. As a result, the propagation and popularity of high art music [*uccāṅga saṅgīter pracār o pracalan*] increased in Calcutta and Bengal."[180] Though Tagore and Jadugopal Mukhopadhyay were contemporaries and from similar social circles in Calcutta, their views of recent events in culture were strikingly different in emphasis. For Tagore, music was rooted in Bengal and was radiating outward as a beacon to guide the future of Hindustani music. To Jadugopal, Hindustani music had migrated into Bengal with the Hindustanis, and the region was gradually awakening to its possibilities. This disparity may be explained in part through reflection on the place of Matiyaburj in the narratives of Bengali self-construction, the negotiation between Mughal and colonial conventions, and the differentiated spheres of Calcutta society.

The longer significance of Wajid Ali's exile in Calcutta for Hindustani music did not lie in the person of the nawab alone, or even in his own experiments with performance, but rather in the entourage of musicians that accompanied him from upper India. This chapter began with an assessment of the court's position in ongoing circuits of movement over the subcontinent, and noted that not all of the musicians from Lucknow remained in Bengal; some continued onward to Bihar, Nepal, and Rampur.[181] The migrating careers of these musicians indicate that courtly patronage continued apace, despite the fall of Delhi and the exile of the Lucknow *darbār*. At the same time, the Bengal Music School established a new setting for music, with an emphasis on the public and institutional rather than the elite and intimate. However, such enterprises were embedded in developments driven forward by Wajid Ali Shah, particularly his own school of music at Matiyaburj, his staging of musical theater, and the nawabi acceptance of the nonprofessional performer of music. While Tagore was not as much of a pioneer as he would have his readers believe, he nonetheless translated the principles of the nawab's court into a less controversial form—certainly one that was appealing to the British administration. Taken together, the nawab and the *bhadralok* musicologist reflect the period's fascination with new forms, ensembles, and courses for music's trajectory, rather than merely perpetuating or glorifying what had come before.

This chapter has traced other realms of exchange between the Lakhnavis and Bengalis in the houses of north Calcutta, the networks of Bhavanipur, and the family residences in rural districts, mapping the larger informal geography of patronage in which Matiyaburj was a crucial node. This "networked" sphere was not driven by a modernizing strategy or invested in a project of public transformation, but was motivated by enthusiasts, patrons, amateur performers, and new kinds of professional Bengali musician. Bengali accounts of this sphere foregrounded the *bhadralok* as the last witnesses of Mughal Hindustan, permitting the Bengali to share in the traumas of, and nostalgia for, a courtly world that was not originally their own.

Conclusion

How far did colonialism transform north Indian art music? In the period between empires—one Mughal, one British—did the political landscape bleed into the aesthetic imaginary of music, dance, and poetry? The answer varies enormously across different nineteenth-century sources. On the one hand, the British authorities were routinely criticized for their willful neglect of the musical arts. This was seen as a prejudiced disengagement from Indian sensibilities, as well as the neglect of the authorities' responsibility as rulers to provide patronage to performing artists. This might suggest that the effects of colonialism were unintended consequences arising from neglect, rather than from active policies. We might also view the emergence of new communities of patrons—some adopting an older aristocratic mantle, some forming self-consciously modern and public bodies—as a response to this neglect, one that allowed the curation of music to remain in the hands of Indians rather than being co-opted into colonial agendas. However, it would be difficult to reconcile this line of argument with the struggles faced by certain artist communities over the colonial period and the institutional violence directed toward them—promoted by both colonial authorities and Indian interest groups—including the morality and policing campaigns, in the case of courtesans, or the branding of itinerant singers as "criminal tribes." Even in the case of elite male artists, who were less impacted by these policies, it is apparent that musical forms—lyrics, performance practices, instruments—evolved over this period, in line with new cultural preferences and technological possibilities.

However, the question remains whether these transitions were propelled directly by colonial rule, or unfolded according to their own momentum against the landscape of colonial rule? North Indian art music was not a static entity before the ascent of British control in the subcontinent, so its continuing evolution over the nineteenth century should hardly come as a surprise. At the same time, scholarship on Urdu nostalgia cautions us against uncritically accepting the narrative of a flourishing Mughal culture on the eve of 1857. Rather than imagining a chasm between two empires, then, do we need to look for subtler forms of transition in the social history of music?

Most histories of colonial-era music have been captivated by explicitly colonial productions: texts in English, musicologists in dialogue with Orientalists or British readers, and new ensembles, technologies, or notation systems overtly influenced by their European counterparts. However, while this conversation with colonialism was significant, its actors and priorities were but one small part of a much larger musical ecology. When we cast a wider net and consider neglected sources from the late eighteenth century onward and across different languages, it becomes increasingly evident that there was far more to musical culture in the late Mughal and early colonial periods than has previously been assumed.

One critical obstacle to a nuanced interpretation of how elite music was affected by the colonial encounter has been our limited sense of musical society immediately prior to the Raj. By starting earlier, before the era of high colonialism in the late nineteenth century, we can begin to fathom the depths of early-modern conversations on the nature of music and the role it had to play in conversations about the self, cosmology, and politics. Focusing on the shifting landscape of patronage in Bengal from the eighteenth century onward, I have followed some of these conversations in different settings and considered the cultural connotations of north Indian art music in "provincial" Bengal and Murshidabad. Music was deeply entangled in the multiple vernacular cultures that flowed and flowered in Mughal Bengal; while most histories of the region's music are reliant on sources in Sanskrit and Bengali, sources like the Persian *Ḥayy al-Arwāḥ* offer a more rounded picture of transregional intellectual engagements with music, and provide evidence of the pervasive interregional social and cultural connections between Bengal and the Hindustani heartlands in the eighteenth century. My analysis of these sources has underlined two broader themes. First, owing to the normative circulation of musicians between Hindustani and Bengali subimperial courts, elite music from upper India was considered superior to that of any local genre or musician. Bengalis certainly studied north Indian art music, but with few exceptions Bengali musicians were underrated by their local patrons, who preferred to employ "authentic" Hindustani *ustād*s. Second, the theoretical basis of elite music—in its broadest sense as pertaining to *rāga* and *tāla*, or in the more elite sense of identifying with particular canonical texts—was used extremely widely across Indian society, from *vaiṣṇava* temple priests to populist Muslim writers. This versatility of musical knowledge and its signifiers in different kinds of text indicates the nonsectarian range of applications for Hindustani music, even outside Hindustan itself.

I explored the connections between regions further by highlighting the significance of the career and exile of the seminal patron, performer, and intellectual Wajid Ali Shah. While far more is known about the last nawab of Awadh than about Bengali patrons, I have also presented a revisionist view of how Wajid Ali should be understood in terms of the culture he patronized and his contributions to the performing arts. To this day, many accounts of the king denounce or apologize for his decadence, having digested the damning reports penned by colonial officials of the debauched aesthete, which paved the way for annexation. I have put the language of decadence into a longer history of British debate over the proper place of leisure and pleasure, and analyzed how music in particular became entangled in the condemnation of nawabi rule. Acknowledging and then setting aside the colonial archive, and returning to the nawab's own substantial writings in Persian and Urdu, I have proposed several new considerations for interpreting the "decadence" of the nawabs as an aesthetic style, rather than imposing an Eurocentric concept of conspicuous consumption or immorality. These considerations include the poetic virtue of vulnerability, an appreciation of musical affect and the sensorium in relation to exerting power over others, music as the facilitator of social companionship, the appeal of fantasy and magic in the royal court, and the legitimation of nawabi rule by appealing to the musical legacies of other Muslim rulers. This analysis casts light on the inner culture of the nawabi court and the specifically Lakhnavi appreciation of musical aesthetics.

This revisionist history of Wajid Ali Shah extends to his exile in Calcutta, the history of which has only very recently been brought to the attention of English readers, and which has never been studied in detail in terms of its invaluable significance to the performing arts. Aside from documenting the activities of the court through English, Urdu, and Bengali sources, my reconstruction of Matiyaburj has four key implications for the larger field of South Asian cultural history. First, I have questioned the depiction of the court as represented by Abdul Halim Sharar, who until now has been widely accepted as a firsthand witness and authority on the "lost" world of Lucknow. I have stressed how Sharar's account of music and dance was substantially shaped by his two informants, Kaukab Khan and Binda Din Kathak, who had their own agendas shaped by twentieth-century considerations, and gave a misleading account of the nawab and his patronage.

By extension, I have demonstrated that Sharar required the courtly culture of Lucknow to have been terminated, along with its political existence, in

1856–57. While this was a crucial rhetoric device, it resulted in Matiyaburj being misconstrued as a haunting monument to a dead civilization. Supported by colonial accounts of an isolated eccentric, it has long been thought that Wajid Ali Shah did not engage with his new Bengali environment. However, his engagements with local music and dance cultures, including experiments with Bengali lyrics, refute this notion. The Matiyaburj years saw enormous innovations in the performing arts, and engagements with music-loving denizens of the colonial metropolis.

Engaging closely with Wajid Ali's actual practices nuances the established association between the nawab, *ṭhumrī*, and what later became Kathak dance. Wajid Ali had much wider interests; his senior wife, Khas Mahal, surpassed him in the writing of lyrics; and he innovated dance gestures as components of different developing genres, including *naql* and *rahas*. These additional sides to his musical career challenge the narrow view of his contributions as frivolous—yet another legacy of Sharar's representation.

Finally, my discussion of *naql* and the school for performing *mut'a* wives undermines the notion of nawabi music as an established or homogenous style of courtly entertainment that was then reformed or rejected by the colonial harbingers of musical modernity. The nawab himself was a pioneer and innovator, investing himself and his family in diverse practices from *dhrupad* to slapstick comedy. That these different strands of the performing arts were given an equal footing in their textual documentation (if anything, with a slight preference for the new) disrupts the dichotomies between "traditional" and "modern," "high" and "low," "elite" and "popular." While I have focused specifically upon the nawab's writings, it is hoped that this will provide new conceptual possibilities for scholars working on other authors, composers, and genres from the same period. Rather than viewing agents, ideas, or objects as pertaining *either* to Mughal *or* to colonial musical culture, we must view colonial-era practices in their own terms, and in conversation with multiple preexisting conventions and referents, as well as with their political hinterland.

In the final chapters of this book, I have considered the contributions that a court might make to wider culture. Rather than viewing royal courts in terms of the symbols and rituals surrounding the single male protagonist (in this case the nawab) in a single palace compound, we must also consider satellite households, dependents and retainers, and, perhaps most crucially, court women. While we have a growing sense of the histories of courtesans on the one hand, and middle-class women's education and mores on the other, by considering the cultural importance of "respectable" royal women and their domestic attendants we can begin to take seriously the formative role played by domestic and *zanāna* musicians in the careers of male musicians, especially those from elite backgrounds who began to perform professionally for the first time. My revisionist biography of the celebrity singer Pyare Saheb and my study of the musical achievements of his patron, Queen Khas Mahal, gestures to worlds of women's work with music that historians have not yet acknowledged.

Just as Pyare Saheb, a "modern" gramophone artist of Calcutta, actually emerged from the exiled court of Lucknow, similarly the middle-class music scene of the colonial capital was deeply infiltrated by nawabi musical culture. I have argued that the "innovations" of S. M. Tagore and the Bengal Music School, which have been privileged in earlier works of scholarship as a reflection of the colonial encounter, were in fact minority (albeit well-documented and highly publicized) practices. By returning to Tagore's activities with a new understanding of developments at Matiyaburj, I have also argued that this *bhadralok* musicologist was deeply indebted to his nawabi neighbor, who had foreshadowed many of these "modern" and "colonial" innovations, and had introduced the expert body of Awadhi musicians who shaped many of the *bhadralok* projects. Following the paths traveled by these musicians from the exiled court into Calcutta, and beyond into rural Bengal and Nepal, I have suggested that, rather than narrowing our gaze to the self-proclaimed "public" face of music in the city, we must consider a "networked sphere" of patrons and artists situated between "public" and "private." The major actors in this sphere did not seek to represent music to the colonial rulers, or to reform its character; but they were nonetheless crucial to the transmission and preservation of connoisseurship in Hindustani music and, in the end, substantially more important than the reformers.

The "networked sphere" was realized through the personal relationships between Awadhi musicians and their Bengali patrons and disciples. By reading Urdu accounts of musicians alongside Bengali memoirs of domestic performances, I have explored the affective relationships between enthusiasts and professionals across regional, linguistic, religious and class boundaries. Despite the romanticism of Bengali accounts of this listening society, however, these networks did not constitute a utopian or democratic space. Late Mughal hierarchies between professionals and amateurs were retained. Even as amateur musicians from socially esteemed backgrounds began to perform more publicly, their *ustād*s continued to distinguish between the training of the critic and that of the professional musician. By examining nostalgia and tropes of weeping in Bengali accounts of this society, I have argued that the Bengalis who closely engaged with the musicians from Mughal Delhi and nawabi Lucknow were fascinated by the end of the royal courts of Hindustan, and the displacement of their Hindustani associates. Crucially, within these meditations on loss was a clear sense of the transference of responsibility: the refugees from the ancien régime were represented in Bengali musical memoirs as taking solace in their Bengali caretakers, who in turn now saw themselves as the new custodians and inheritors of the elite arts of the vanquished Mughals, with the burden of ensuring the arts' survival for posterity.

Looking across this long timeline and the various formulations of musical knowledge and experiments with practice that proliferated in Bengal over this period, it is striking how Bengalis grew in confidence as custodians of the arts of Hindustan. Given that at the beginning of the nineteenth century, Bengali patrons still favored "authentic" musicians and musical works from north India, this longer history charts a great transition in self-recognition, such that by the end of the century Bengalis were taking command of the history, theory, and practice of elite art music. While the cultivation of regional identity in colonial Bengal has been discussed at length in other branches of cultural history, this is most often framed in terms of Calcutta's relationship to London and empire.[1] By contrast, when it comes to music it is more pertinent to consider a longer conversation between Bengal and other regions of South Asia, especially upper India: works of scholarship, patterns in patronage, and new forms of performance speak to a renegotiation of authority and cultural prestige within the vernacular communities of the subcontinent. Though such renegotiations were undoubtedly influenced by the politics and social transformations wrought by colonialism—the annexation, the destruction of Delhi, the choice of Calcutta as capital, and colonial language politics being the most obvious factors—they cannot be seen purely in terms of a conversation between colonizer and colonized. By moving beyond English-language works, restoring colonial-era musicology to its longer history, and acknowledging the changing connotations of region and language, we can nuance and expand the remit of the history of north Indian art music.

Acknowledgments

When I began researching South Asian cultural history, I never expected that I would end up writing a book on music. However, history led me to historical literature, which put me in touch with communities of singers who perform this literature today, and who opened my ears to the importance of sound and affect: the mediation of sounding, communicating bodies, and ultimately music. I am grateful to everyone, named here and unnamed, who inspired and helped me in the writing of this book.

The core of this book is based on research I carried out at King's College London, generously supported by the European Research Council as part of the collaborative project "Musical Transitions to European Colonialism in the Eastern Indian Ocean." I am enormously grateful to the principal investigator of this project, Katherine Butler Schofield, for guiding me through this process with limitless enthusiasm and support. Katherine and the rest of the team opened new worlds to me, and I would like to thank Jim Sykes, Jim Kippen, Allyn Miner, and Margaret Walker for helping me take my first steps. I developed this material further at the University of Oxford, supported by a Leverhulme Early Career Fellowship, and at SOAS University of London until it was ready for publication. Many thanks to Mary Al-Sayed, my anonymous reviewers, Fabiola Enríquez, Renaldo Migaldi, and everyone at the University of Chicago Press for making this book a reality.

Without my languages this would be a very different work, and I owe an enormous debt of gratitude to my teachers, especially Imre Bangha, Kalpana Pant, Aishwarj Kumar, Protima Dutt, and Hasna Hena Khala.

Between London and Oxford, I've taken inspiration from some wonderful friends and colleagues, including Francesca Orsini, Roy Fischel, Polly O'Hanlon, Richard Widdess, Anna Morcom, Francis Robinson, Samia Khatun,

Angela Impey, Rachel Harris, Lucy Durán, Ilana Webster-Kogen, Nick Gray, and Saeid Kordmafi, as well as my students at SOAS. I am also very grateful for advice and encouragement from the scholars I have met along the way, including (and in no particular order): Allison Busch, Makoto Kitada, Carla Petievich, Frances Pritchett, Monika Horstmann, Margrit Pernau, Kathryn Hansen, Gavin Flood, Jessica Frazier, Indrani Chatterjee, Jack Hawley, Davesh Soneji, Robert Skelton, David Irving, Julia Byl, Amlan Das Gupta, Lakshmi Subramanian, Jon Barlow, Vidya Rao, Lalita du Perron, Regula Qureshi, Rosie Llewellyn-Jones, Anindita Ghosh, Françoise Nalini Delvoye, Danuta Stasik, Richard Wolf, Tyler Williams, Thibaut d'Hubert, and Tiziana Leucci. I would also like to thank my friends and colleagues whom I have met through the international Brajbhasha and Early Hindi workshop series: too many to mention here, alas! I spoke about this project at an early stage with Kumkum Chatterjee, who was very encouraging and had some extremely helpful advice. I am grateful to Kalyan Chatterjee for making Kumkum Di's papers available. I am also thankful to Muhammad Ahmedullah and members of the Brick Lane Circle for their encouragement at various stages of my research.

I would like to thank Ustad Wajahat Khan for taking me on as his student in sitar and *k̲h̲ayāl*. While I have stumbled over the intricacies of *rāga*, he has given me a crucial insight into the life of Hindustani music and its practitioners that has been invaluable to this historical project.

I am extremely thankful to all the libraries and archives in India, the United Kingdom, and the United States that gave me permission to consult their collections. I owe a huge debt of gratitude to the directors and staff of the following institutions for their help, who are unfortunately too many to list individually: the National Archives of India, New Delhi; Sangeet Natak Akademi, New Delhi; Indira Gandhi National Centre for the Arts, New Delhi; the Uttar Pradesh State Archives, Lucknow; the West Bengal State Archives, Kolkata; Asiatic Society of Bengal, Kolkata; Indian National Library, Kolkata; Ramakrishna Mission, Kolkata; Bangiya Sahitya Parishad, Kolkata; School of Cultural Texts and Records, Jadavpur University; Centre for Studies in Social Sciences Calcutta Archive, Kolkata; Khuda Bakhsh Oriental Public Library, Patna; Salar Jung Museum Library, Hyderabad; Houghton and Widener Libraries, Harvard University; Butler Library, Columbia University; Van Pelt Library, University of Pennsylvania; the British Library, London; the Bodleian Library, Oxford; Cambridge University Library; the Victoria and Albert Museum, London; Maughan Library, King's College London; and SOAS University of London. Many of the texts I used in this project were made available to me through the collaborative efforts of the "Musical Transitions" team, and I would like to thank the European Research Council, Katherine Schofield, and David Lunn for coordinating these resources. I am also extremely grateful to Angela Waplington for all her help on the project.

Beyond the archives, I acquired key insights and guidance from local experts and the descendants of some of the figures in this study. In Kolkata, I am especially grateful to Jayantanath Ghosh, Mita Nag, Soumitra Das, Shahanshah Mirza, and Devajit Bandyopadhyay. In Bishnupur, I received excellent advice from Debabrata Singha Thakur and Pradip Kumar Singha. I learned a great deal in Lucknow from the late Ram Advani and Saleem Kidwai. I am especially grateful to Dr S. A. Sadiq for sharing his family archive, which proved invaluable for my study of his ancestor, Khas Mahal. I owe so much to my friend and colleague Jayesh Khandelwal in Vrindavan, who inspired my first interest in the study of music.

I have been extremely fortunate to have met such kind and generous people during my research trips in India. I am especially grateful to my host family in Kolkata: *jeṭhu-jeṭhimā* Partha Pratim and Agamani Gupta, Abhijit Gupta, and Sanjukta Ghosh. Thank you *so* much! For cake and concerts, thanks to Moushumi Bhowmik. Thanks to Lara Choksey for accompanying me to Murshidabad, and to Sagnik Atarthi for coming with me to Bishnupur. Siyaram Tivari was very kind when I landed unexpected upon his doorstep in Patna. Durga Dutta and his family were extremely generous when they welcomed me to Biborda.

The British Library is home to many fascinating people, and I am so glad that my being there led me to meet with the late Firdous Ali, who encouraged me to pursue my explorations of Urdu sources. I am especially grateful for his insights into the world of poets and courtesans hidden in the stacks and volumes of this labyrinthine institution, and for the example of his relentless zeal.

I am grateful to all my friends who have listened to me talk about this work as it has grown, especially Jenny McCallum, Adil Johan, Fabio Morabito, Tamara Turner, Raja Iskandar, Yvonne Liao, Tahnia Ahmed, Megan Robb, Chloe Alaghband-Zadeh, Razak Khan, Salma Siddique, Jessica Barker, Julie Vig, Piotr Borek, Biljana Zrnic, Christine Marrewa-Karowski, Nadia Cattoni, Aleksandra Turek, Paul Wordsworth, Sahba Shayani, Luigi Prada, Imaobong Umoren, and Jack Clift.

Layli Uddin has been my "reading buddy" for a very long time, and has been a sounding board, proofreader, critic, cake connoisseur, and valued friend throughout. The journey would not have been the same without her. Friendships come and go, but time spent in the library lasts forever. In a good way.

Richard has endured me talking about my research with formidable levels of patience and forbearance. The same might be true of Katya and Jujubee—but since they're cats, this is harder to say with any certainty.

Finally, I would like to thank my family for their support in my interests, however obscure. Thanks to my sister, Rowena, for her boundless enthusiasm. This book is dedicated to my parents: to my mother, for her constant encouragement and practical advice, which made this all a reality; and to my father, for his impractical fascination with arcane details (especially genealogies), which unquestionably inspired me in this work.

Bibliography

Primary Sources

ARCHIVAL RECORDS

India Office Records, London (IOR).
West Bengal State Archives (WBSA).
National Archives of India (NAI).
Selections from the Vernacular Newspapers Published in Punjab, North-Western Provinces and Oudh, Uttar Pradesh State Archives (SVNPP).

NEWSPAPERS AND PERIODICALS

Ākẖbār-i Dār-ul-Salṯānat
Amrita Bazar Patrika
Bombay Chronicle
Bombay Times and Journal of Commerce
Calcutta Review
Daily Telegraph
Dublin University Magazine
Illustrated London News
Manchester Guardian
Timaru Herald
Times of India
Urdu Guide

BENGALI BOOKS AND MANUSCRIPTS

Anon. "Jādabkṛṣṇa Basu." *Saṅgīta Bijñān Prabeśikā* 3, no. 4 (1926): 208.

Anon. "Saṅgītācārjýa Kālīprasanna Bidýābinoda Mahāśaýer Jībanī." *Saṅgīta Bijñān Prabeśikā* 2, no. 6 (1925): 284–89.

Anon. "Śaurīndramohan Ṭhakur." *Saṅgīta Bijñan Prabeśika* 2, no. 11 (1925): 527–30.

Bandyopadhyay, Brajendranath, and Sajanikanta Das, eds. *Bhāratacandra-Granthābali*. Kolkata: Bangiya Sahitya Parishat, 1943.

Bandyopadhyay, Gopesvar. *Bahubhāṣā Gīta*. Calcutta: Lekhaka, 1940.

Bandyopadhyaya, Ramesh Chandra. *Dwitiýa Dillī Biṣṇupur* Calcutta: Vasumati Sahitya Mandira, 1942.

Banerjee, Ramprasânna. *Saṅgīta Mañjari*. Calcutta: Kuntalin Press, 1935.

Das, Jayakrishna. "Madanamohanabandanā." Unpublished manuscript. Asiatic Society of Bengal, c. 1784. Ac. 4988.

Das, Radhamohan Sen. *Saṅgītataraṅga*. Calcutta: Bangala Press, 1818.

Das, Radhamohan Sen, and Harimohan Mukhopadhyay. *Saṅgītataraṅga*. Third edition. Calcutta: Bangabasi Steam Mission Press, 1903.

Ghosh, Aghoracandra. *Saṅgītasāgar*. Calcutta: Panchanan Ghosh, 1889.

Goswami, Kshetramohan. *Saṅgītasāra*. Calcutta: Prakrit Press, 1869.

Lahiri, Durgadas. *Bāṅgālīr Gān*. Calcutta: Bangabasi-Ilektro-Mesin Press, 1905.

Mallik, Jagannath Prasad Basu. *Saṅgītarasamādhurī*. Calcutta: Brajmohan Cakrabarti, 1844.

Mukhopadhyay, Jadugopal. *Biplabī Jībaner Smṛti*. Kolkata: Indian Associated Publishing, 1956.

Mukhopadhyay, Kalipada. *Bahulīn Tattva*. Calcutta: Prakrit Press, 1874.

Mukhopadhyay, Mukundadeb. *Āmār Dekhā Lok*. Calcutta: Bhudeb Publishing House, 1922.

Nisacar. *Samāj-Kucitra*. Calcutta: Notun Balmiki Press, 1865.

Rajasimha, Maharaja, and Kamal Krishna Simha. *Rāga-mālā O Saṅkṣipta Manasā Pāñcālī*. Calcutta: Bharatmihir Press, 1891.

Ray, Kartikeyacandra. *Deoýān Kārtikeýa Candra Rāýer Ātma-jīban Carita*. Calcutta: Indian Associated Publishing, 1956.

Sharma, Nanda Lal. *Saṅgīta Sūtra*. Calcutta: Bidyaratna Press, 1870.

Tagore, Jatindra Mohan. *Welcome Song*. Calcutta: n.p., 1876.

HINDI BOOKS

Lal, Lallu. *Sabhābilāsa*. Lucknow, India: Muṃśī Navalakiśora, 1882.

Kuvar, Bibi Ratna. *Premratna*. Banaras, India: Sultan-i-Hind, Banaras, 1863.

PERSIAN BOOKS AND MANUSCRIPTS

Borah, M. I., trans.. *Bahāristān-i-Ghaybī*. Gauhati, India: Government of Assam, 1936.

Khan, Tabataba'i Gholam-Hoseyn. *A Translation of the Seir Mutaqherin; or, View of Modern Times*. Calcutta: James White, 1789.

Rogers, Alexander, and Henry Beveridge, trans. *The Tūzuk-i-Jahāngīrī; or, Memoirs of Jahāngīr*. London: Royal Asiatic Society, 1909-14.

Salim, Ghulam Hussain. *Riyazu-s-Salatin*. Calcutta: Baptist Mission Press, 1902.

Shah, Wajid Ali. "Ṣaut al-Mubārak." Unpublished manuscript. British Library, London.

Ziauddin. "Ḥayy al-Arwāḥ." Unpublished manuscript. Persian 346, John Rylands Library, University of Manchester.

URDU BOOKS AND MANUSCRIPTS

Afsos, Sher Ali. *Araish-i Maḥfil*. Calcutta: Matb'ah Jal-ul-tin, 1903.

Bari, Maulvi Abdul. *Taẕkirat-ul-Ḵẖavātīn*. Lucknow, India: Nawal Kishor, 1930(?).

Faqir, Saiyid Muhammad Husain. *Al-durr al-manẓud fi radd-i bid'āt al-Maulūd*. Delhi: Matba-i Quddusi, 1891.

Hasan, Muhammad, Rais. *Ziya-yi Akhtar*. Cawnpore, India: Naval Kishor, 1878.
Imam, Hakim Muhammad Karam. *Ma'dan al-mūsīqī*. Lucknow, India: Hindustani Press, 1925.
Jan, Mir Yar Ali. *Musaddas-i Benazīr*. Rampur, India: State Press, 1950.
Khan, Muhammad Mardan Ali. *Ghunca-yi Rāg*. Lucknow, India: Naval Kishor, 1863.
Khan, Sadiq Ali. *Sarmāya-yi 'Ishrat: Mu'arrif Qānun-i Mūsiqī*. Delhi: Matba'-i Faiz Alam, 1884.
Raihani, Sayyid Muhammad Sajjad Husain. *Sawāniḥ-yi Shāh-i Avadh*. Meerut, India: Matba-yi Toti-yi Hind, 1887.
Mahal, Khas. *Masnavī-i-'Ālam*. Calcutta: Runaq Bakhsh, 1866.
Nassakh, Abdul Ghafur Khan. *Sakhan-i Shu'arā*. Lucknow, India: Naval Kishor, 1874.
Ranj, Muhammad Fasihuddin. *Bahāristān-i-Nāz*. Merut, India: Dar-ul-'Alum, 1869.
Shah, Wajid Ali. *Banī*. Calcutta: Matba'-i Sultani, 1987.
———. *Banī*. Hindi trans. by Roshan Taqi and Krishna Mohan Saxena. Lucknow, India: Sangeet Natak Academi, 1987.
———. *Dulhan*. Calcutta: Matba'-i Sultani, 1868.
———. "Nāju." Unpublished MS 4, acc. no. 476, Salar Jung Museum Library, Hyderabad.
———. *Nāju*. Calcutta: Matba'-i Sultani, 1869.
———. *Nāju*. Hindi trans. by Yogesh Pravin. Lucknow: Uttar Pradesh Sangit Natak Akademi, 1989.
Shah, Wajid Ali, and A. A. Khan. *Masnavī Huzn-i Akhtar: Vājid 'Alī Shāh kī āp bītī*. Lucknow, India: Vajid 'Ali Shah Akademi, 1981.
Shah, Wajid Ali, and Tehseen Sarwari. *Parīkhāna*. Karachi: n.p., 1958.
Sharar, Abdul Halim. *Hindustān men mashraqī tamaddun kā ākhirī namūnah: Yan'ī guzashtah-yi Lakhna'ū*. New Delhi: Maktabah-yi Jami'ah.
———. *Jān-i 'Ālam: Wājid 'Ālī Shāh ke Matiyāburj ke ḥālāt*. Lahore, India: Idara-yi Furgh-i Urdu, 1951.
———. *Lucknow: The Last Phase of an Oriental Culture*. English trans. by E. S. Harcourt and Fakhir Hussain. London: Paul Elek, 1975.

BOOKS AND MANUSCRIPTS IN ENGLISH AND EUROPEAN LANGUAGES

Anon. "The Administration of Oudh: First Report, to March 1859, Ordered by the House of Commons to Be Printed; 1859." *Calcutta Review* 68 (1860): 218–39.
Anon. *An Exposition in English and Hindustani of the Evil Tendency of Naches*. Calcutta: Baptist Mission Press, 1837.
Anon. *Nawab Nuzhutuddowla Abbas Hossain Khan versus Mirza Kurratulain and Others*. Official record of court proceedings, High Court of Calcutta, 1903.
Anon. "Oude, as a Kingdom." *Dublin University Magazine* 49, no. 289 (1857): 112–28.
Anon. *The Tagores of Calcutta*. Calcutta: Indian Mirror Office, 1880.
Anon. "The Territorial Aristocracy of Bengal: No. I, The Burdwan Raj." *Calcutta Review* 54, no. 108 (1872); 171–94.
Anon. "The Territorial Aristocracy of Bengal: No. II, The Nadiyá Ráj." *Calcutta Review* 55, no. 109 (1872): 85–118.
Anon. "Village Sketches in Oudh III: Echoes of the Mutiny." *Fraser's Magazine for Town and Country* 77 (1868): 242–58.
Alla, Taeb. *Lives of Maha Raja Apurva Krishna Bahadur, Poet Laureate to His Imperial Majesty of Delhi, and Member of the Hambury Academy, etc., his Father and Grandfather*. Calcutta: Catholic Orphan Press, 1847.

Arnold, Edwin. "The City of Palaces and Madras." *Times of India*, 23 March 1886.

Ascoli, F. D. *Early Revenue History of Bengal and the Fifth Report, 1812*. Oxford, UK: Clarendon Press, 1917.

Broughton, Thomas D. *Letters from a Mahratta Camp during the Year 1809*. Westminster, UK: Archibald Constable, 1892.

Conder, Josiah. *The Modern Traveller: A Popular Description, Geographical, Historical, and Topographical of the Various Countries of the Globe*. London: James Duncan, 1828.

Corbet, Mary Elizabeth. *A Pleasure Trip to India, during the Visit of H.R.H. the Prince of Wales*. London, W. H. Allen, 1880.

Dilke, Charles Wentworth. *Greater Britain: A Record of Travel in English-Speaking Countries during 1866 and 1867*. New York: Harper and Brothers, 1869.

Dufferin and Ava, Marchioness of. *Our Viceregal Life in India: Selections from My Journal 1884–1888*. London: John Murray, 1890.

Fayrer, J. *Notes of the Visits to India of Their Royal Highnesses the Prince of Wales and Duke of Edinburgh 1870–1875–6*. London: Kerby and Endean, 1879.

Furrell, James W. *The Tagore Family: A Memoir*. Calcutta: Thacker, Spink and Co., 1892.

Gay, J. Drew. *The Prince of Wales in India; or, From Pall Mall to the Punjab*. New York: R. Worthington, 1877.

Ghosh, Lokenath. *The Modern History of the Indian Chiefs, Rajas, Zamindars &c.* Part II. Calcutta: J. N. Ghose, 1881.

Ghosh, Sarada Prasada. *The Music of Hindustan*. Calcutta: Thos. S. Smith, 1879.

Grierson, G. A. *The Modern Vernacular Literature of Hindustan*. Calcutta: Asiatic Society, 1889.

Holwell, J. Z. *Interesting Historical Events Relating to the Provinces of Bengal and the Empire of Indostan* London: 1766.

Hunter, W. W. *The Annals of Rural Bengal*. New York: Leypoldt and Holt, 1868.

Long, James. *A Descriptive Catalogue of Bengali Works*. Calcutta: Sanders, Cones and Co., 1855.

Martin, Montgomery. "The History, Antiquities, Topography, and Statistics of Eastern India." *Monthly Review* 1, no. 4 (1838): 469–86.

Mukerji, Dhan Gopal. *Caste and Outcast*. Stanford, CA: Stanford University Press, 2002.

———. *My Brother's Face*. New York: E. P. Dutton, 1924.

Norton, Sara, and M. A. DeWolfe Howe. *Letters of Charles Eliot Norton*. Boston and New York: Houghton Mifflin, 1913.

Palmer, E. H. "Native Princes." *Allen's Indian Mail*, 25 March 1872, p. 292.

Prime, E. D. G. *Around the World: Sketches of Travel through Many Lands and over Many Seas*. New York: Harper and Brothers, 1872.

Sahibjee, Shettjee. "A Day with My Indian Cousins: III. The Nabob: The Man of Tears." *Times of India*, 30 September 1882.

Sleeman, W. H. *A Journey through the Kingdom of Oude in 1849–1850. London:* Richard Bentley, 1858.

Sprenger, Aloys. *A Catalogue of the Arabic, Persian and Hindu'sta'ny Manuscripts, of the Libraries of the King of Oudh*. Calcutta: Baptist Mission Press, 1854.

———. *Report of the Researches into the Muhammadan Libraries of Lucknow*. Calcutta: Office of the Superintendent of Government Printing 1896.

Tagore, Sourindro Mohan. *A Brief Account of the Tagore Family*. Calcutta: I. C. Bose, 1868.

———. *Public Opinion and Official Communications, about the Bengal Music School and Its President*, Calcutta: Panchanun Mookerjee, 1876.

———. *Six Principal Rágas, with a Brief View of Hindu Music*. Calcutta: Calcutta Central Press, 1877.

———. *The Ten Principal Avatars of the Hindus, with a Short History of Each Incarnation and Directions for the Representation of the Murtis as Tableaux Vivants*. Calcutta: Stanhope Press, 1880.

———. *Universal History of Music: Compiled from Diverse Sources, Together with Various Original Notes on Hindu Music*. Calcutta: N. G. Goswamy, 1896.

Wheeler, George. *India in 1875–76: The Visit of the Prince of Wales*. London: Chapman and Hall, 1876.

Wyman, Frederick F. *From Calcutta to the Snowy Range: Being the Narrative of Trip through the Upper Provinces of India to the Himalayas Containing an Account of Monghyr, Benares, Allahabad, Cawnpore, Lucknow, Agra, Delhi and Shimla*. London: Tinsley Brothers, 1866.

Secondary Sources: Articles, Books, and Dissertations

Anon. *Chairman's Choice, Great Memories: Peara Saheb, Ustad Majooddin Khan*. Cassette recording and liner notes, RPG and HMV, 1994.

Anon. "Gramophone Celebrities: 6." *Record News: Annual Magazine of Society of Indian Record Collectors (SIRC)*, 2006, pp. 14–15.

Ahmad, Muhammad Taqi. *Vājid ʿAlī Shāh: āḵẖirī tājdār-i Avadh*. Lucknow, India: Markaz-i Adab-i Urdu, 1975.

Ahmad, Safi. *Two Kings of Awadh, Muhammad Ali Shah and Amjad Ali Shah (1837–1847)*. Aligarh, India: P. C. Dwadash Shreni & Co., 1971.

———. *Vājid ʿAlī Shāh aur Shāh-i Jinn: Ek nādir maḵẖṭuṭah kī raushnī meṉ*. Luckow: Markaz-i Adab-i Urdu, 1984.

Ahmed, Aziz. "The British Museum Mirzanama and the Seventeenth Century Mirza in India.' " *Iran: Journal of the British Institute of Persian Studies* 13 (1975): 99–110.

Alaghband-Zadeh, Chloë. "Analysing Thumrī." Unpublished doctoral thesis, SOAS, University of London, 2013.

Al Faruqi, Lois Ibsen. "Music, Musicians and Muslim Law." *Asian Music* 17, no. 1 (1985): 3–36.

Alam, Muzaffar. *The Languages of Political Islam: India, 1200–1800*. Chicago: University of Chicago Press, 2004.

Ali, Daud. *Courtly Culture and Political Life in Early Medieval India*. Cambridge, UK: Cambridge University Press, 2004.

Ali, Muhammad Shaik Rahat, and Narahar Shambhurav Bhave. *Ṭhumrī-saṅgraha*. Baroda, India: Kachupura, 1949.

André, Naomi. *Voicing Gender: Castrati, Ttravesty, and the Second Woman in Early-Nineteenth-Century Italian Opera*. Bloomington: Indiana University Press, 2006.

Ansari, K. Humayun. "The Muslim World in British Historical Imaginations: 'Re-Thinking Orientalism'?" *British Journal of Middle Eastern Studies* 38, no. 1 (2011): 73–93.

Ansari, Tahir Hussain. "The Cultural and Literary Contribution of Nawab Wajid Ali Shah." *International Journal of English Language, Literature and Humanities* 2, no. 3 (2014): 181–89.

Archambault, Hannah L. "Becoming Mughal in the Nineteenth Century: The Case of the Bhopal Princely State." *South Asia: Journal of South Asian Studies* 36, no. 4 (2013): 479–95.

Asaduddin, M. "The West in the Nineteenth-Century Imagination: Some Reflections on the Transition from a Persianate Knowledge System to the Template of Urdu and English." *Annual of Urdu Studies* 18 (2003): 45–65.

Azad, Muhammad Husain. *Āb-e Hayāt: Shaping the Canon of Urdu Poetry*. Translated by Frances Pritchett and Shamsur Rahman Faruqi. Oxford, UK, and New Delhi: Oxford University Press, 2001.

Azhar, Mirza Ali. *King Wajid Ali Shah of Awadh*. Karachi: Royal Book Co., 1982.

Bakhle, Janaki. *Two Men and Music: Nationalism in the Making of an Indian Classical Tradition*. Ranikhet, India: Permanent Black, 2005.

Bandyopadhyay, Devajit. *Beśyāsaṅgīt, Bāījisaṅgīt*. Kolkata: Subarnarekha, 2001.

Banerjee, Brajendra Nath. *Begams of Bengal Mainly Based on State Records*. Calcutta: S. K. Mitra, 1942.

Banerjee, Jayasri. "The Theoretical Problematic of Bengali Music." *Journal of the Indian Musicological Society* 17, no. 1 (1986): 1–11.

Banerjee, Sumanta. "Marginalisation of Women's Popular Culture in Nineteenth Century Bengal." In K. Sangari and S. Vaid, eds., *Recasting Women: Essays in Indian Colonial History*, 127–79. New Brunswick, NJ: Rutgers University Press, 1989.

———. *The Parlour and the Streets: Elite and Popular Culture in Nineteenth-Century Calcutta*. Calcutta: Seagull Books, 1989.

Barlow, Jon. "The Sarod: Instrument Analysis." in A. Das Gupta, ed., *Music and Modernity: North Indian Classical Music in an Age of Reproduction*, 124–55. Kolkata: Thema, 2007.

———. "The Sarod: Its Forms and Voices." In A. Das Gupta, ed., *Music and Modernity: North Indian Classical Music in an Age of Mechanical Reproduction*, 89–123. Kolkata: Thema, 2007.

Barry, John. *Calcutta 1940*. Calcutta: Central Press, 1940.

Basu, Sharmadip. "Tuning Modernity: Musical Knowledge and Subjectivities in Colonial India, c. 1780s–c.1900." Unpublished doctoral thesis, Syracuse University, 2011.

Batabyal, Rakesh. "Who the 'Bhadralok' Was." *Economic and Political Weekly* 40, no. 35 (2005): 3834–36.

Bayly, C. A. *Empire and Information: Intelligence Gathering and Social Communication in India, 1780–1870*. Cambridge, UK: Cambridge University Press, 1996.

———. *Origins of Nationality in South Asia: Patriotism and Ethical Government in the Making of Modern India*. Delhi: Oxford University Press, 1998.

———. *Recovering Liberties: Indian Thought in the Age of Liberalism and Empire*. Cambridge, UK: Cambridge University Press, 2012.

Behl, Aditya. "Poet of the Bazaars: Nazir Akbarabadi, 1735–1830." In K. Hansen and D. Lelyveld, eds., *A Wilderness of Possibilities: Urdu Studies in Transnational Perspective*, 192–222. Delhi: Oxford University Press, 2005.

Benjamin, Walter. *Illuminations*. New York: Harcourt, Brace and World, 1968.

Bhatia, Varuni. "Images of Nabadwip: Place, Evidence, and Inspiration." In A Murphy, ed., *Time, History and the Religious Imaginary in South Asia*, 167–85. Abingdon, UK: Routledge, 2011.

Bhattacharya, Tithi. *The Sentinels of Culture: Class, Education, and the Colonial Intellectual in Bengal (1848–85)*. New Delhi: Oxford University Press, 2005.

Bhatnagar, G. D. *Awadh under Wājid 'Ali Shāh*. Varanasi, India: Bharatiya Vidya Prakashan, 1968.

Bhatt, Ravi. *The Life and Times of the Nawabs of Lucknow*. Delhi: Rupa, 2006.

Bhattacharya, Rimli. "The Nautee in 'the Second City of the Empire." *Indian Economic and Social History Review* 40, no. 2 (2003): 191–235.

Blanning, Tim. *The Triumph of Music: The Rise of Composers, Musicians and their Art*. Cambridge, MA: Harvard University Press.

Bor, Joep. *The Voice of the Sarangi: An Illustrated History of Bowing in India.* Bombay: National Centre for the Performing Arts, 1986–87.

Born, Georgina. "On Musical Mediation: Ontology, Technology and Creativity." *Twentieth-Century Music* 2, no. 1 (2005): 7–36.

Bose, Neilesh. *Recasting the Region: Language, Culture, and Islam in Colonial Bengal.* New Delhi: Oxford University Press, 2014.

Bredi, Daniela. "Nostalgia in the Re-Construction of Muslim Identity in the Aftermath of 1857 and the Myth of Delhi." *Cracow Indological Studies* 11 (2009): 137–56.

Brown, Katherine Ruth Butler. "Did Aurangzeb Ban Music? Questions for the Historiography of his Reign." *Modern Asian Studies*, 41, no. 1 (2007): 77–120.

———. "Hindustani Music in the Time of Aurangzeb." Unpublished doctoral thesis, School of Oriental and African Studies, University of London, 2003.

———. "If Music Be the Food of Love: Masculinity and Eroticism in the Mughal *Mehfil*." In F. Orsini, ed., *Love in South Asia: A Cultural History*, 61–83. Cambridge, UK: Cambridge University Press.

———. "The Libertine and the Spectacle: Masculinities and the *Bhand* Tamasha in 18C Delhi." Unpublished paper presented at the annual conference of the Society for Ethnomusicology, Hawaii, 2006.

———. "The Social Liminality of Musicians: Case Studies from Mughal India and Beyond." *Twentieth-Century Music* 3, no. 1 (2007): 13–49.

Calkins, Philip B. "The Formation of a Regionally Oriented Ruling Group in Bengal, 1700–1740." *Journal of Asian Studies* 29, no. 4 (1970): 799–806.

———. "The Role of Murshidabad as a Regional and Subregional Centre in Bengal." In *Studies in Bengali Literature, History, and Society*, 1–13. New York: Learning Resources in International Studies, 1974.

Capwell, Charles. "The Interpretation of History and the Foundations of Authority in the Vishnupur Gharana of Bengal." In S. Blum, P. V. Bohlman, and D. M. Neuman, eds., *Ethnomusicology and Modern Music History*, 59–102. Urbana: University of Illinois Press, 1986.

———. "Marginality and Musicology in Nineteenth-Century Calcutta: The Case of Sourindro Mohun Tagore." In B. Nettl and P. V. Bohlman, eds., *Comparative Musicology and Anthropology of Music: Essays on the History of Ethnomusicology*, 228–43. Chicago and London: University of Chicago Press, 1991.

———. "Musical Life in Nineteenth-Century Calcutta as a Component in the History of a Secondary Urban Center." *Asian Music* 18, no. 1 (1986): 139–63.

———. "Representing 'Hindu' Music to the Colonial and Native Elite of Calcutta." In J. Bor, F. Delvoye, J. Harvey, E. te Nijenhuis, eds., *Hindustani Music: Thirteenth to Twentieth Centuries*, Manohar, Delhi, 285–311. Delhi: Manohar, 2010.

———. "Sourindro Mohun Tagore and the National Anthem Project," *Ethnomusicology* 31, no. 3 (1987): 407–30.

Castro, Genoveva. "Wājid ʿAlī Shāh Plays Krishna's Stolen Flute: The Multiplicity of Voices in the King of Awadh's Dramatic Work." Unpublished doctoral dissertation, University of Washington, 2016.

Chakraborty, Shyamali. "To Sing or Not to Sing: In Search of One's Soul." *Think India Quarterly* 8, no. 2 (2005): 70–87.

Chakravarti, S. C. "Gopeshwar Banerjee." *Sangit Natak* 13:67–76.

Chakravorty, Pallabi. *Bells of Change: Kathak Dance, Women, and Modernity*. Kolkata: Seagull, 2008.

———. "Dancing into Modernity: Multiple Narratives of India's Kathak Dance." *Dance Research Journal* 38, no. 1-2 (2006): 115–36.

Chatterjee, Chhaya. *Śāstrīya Saṅgīta and Music Culture of Bengal through the Ages*. Delhi: Sharada, 1996.

Chatterjee, Indrani. "Alienation, Intimacy, and Gender: Problems for a History of Love in South Asia." In R. Vanita, ed., *Queering India: Same-Sex Love and Eroticism in Indian Culture and Society*, 61–76. London and New York: Routledge.

———. Introduction to *Unfamiliar Relations: Family and History in South Asia*, 3–45. New Brunswick, NJ: Rutgers University Press.

———. "Monastic Governmentality, Colonial Misogyny, and Postcolonial Amnesia in South Asia." *History of the Present* 3, no. 1 (2013): 57–98.

———. "Testing the Local against the Colonial Archive." *History Workshop Journal* 44 (1997): 215–24.

Chatterjee, Kumkum. "Cultural Flows and Cosmopolitanism in Mughal India: The Bishnupur Kingdom." *Indian Economic and Social History Review* 46, no. 2 (2009): 147–82.

———. *The Cultures of History in Early Modern India: Persianization and Mughal Culture in Bengal*. New Delhi: Oxford University Press, 2009.

Chatterjee, Partha. *The Black Hole of Empire: History of a Global Practice of Power*. Princeton, NJ: Princeton University Press, 2012.

———. *The Nation and Its Fragments*. Princeton, NJ: Princeton University Press, 1993.

———. *A Princely Impostor? The Strange and Universal History of the Kumar of Bhawal*. Princeton, NJ: Princeton University Press, 2002.

———. *Texts of Power: Emerging Disciplines in Colonial Bengal*, University of Minnesota Press, London.

Chattopadhyay, Swati. *Representing Calcutta: Modernity, Nationalism, and the Colonial Uncanny*. London: Routledge, 2006.

Chaudhuri, B. "Eastern India." In T. Raychaudhuri, I. Habib, and D. Kumar, eds., *The Cambridge Economic History of India*. Cambridge, UK: Cambridge University Press, 1983.

Clery, Emma J. *The Feminization Debate in Eighteenth-Century England: Literature, Commerce and Luxury*. London: Palgrave Macmillan, 2004.

Cohn, Bernard. "Representing Authority in Victorian India." In E. Hobsbawm and T. Ranger, eds., *The Invention of Tradition*, 165–210. Cambridge, UK: Cambridge University Press, 1983.

Curley, David L. *Poetry and History: Bengali Maṅgal-Kābya and Social Change in Precolonial Bengal*, New Delhi: Chronicle Books, 2008.

Dalmia, Vasudha. *The Nationalization of Hindu Traditions: Bhāratendu Hariśchandra and Nineteenth-Century Banaras*. Ranikhet, India: Permanent Black, 2010.

Dalrymple, William. *The Last Mughal: The Fall of a Dynasty: Delhi, 1857*. New York: Alfred A. Knopf, 2007.

Das, Neeta, and Rosie Llewellyn-Jones. *Murshidabad: Forgotten Capital of Bengal*. Mumbai: Marg Foundation, 2013.

Das Gupta, Amlan. "Women and Music: The Case of North India." In B. Ray, ed., *Women of India: Colonial and Post-Colonial Periods*, 454–84. New Delhi: Centre for Studies in Civilizations, 2005.

Dasgupta, Chittaranjan. *Bharater Śilpa-Sanskṛtira Paṭabhūmikāy Biṣṇupurer Mandira-Ṭerākoṭā*. Bishnupur, India: Srimati Sushama Dasgupta, 2000.

Dasgupta, Ratan. "Maharaja Krishnachandra: Religion, Caste and Polity in Eighteenth Century Bengal." *Indian Historical Review* 38, no. 2 (2011): 225–42.

Dasgupta, Samira, Rabiranjan Biswas, and Gautam Kumar Mallik. *Heritage Tourism: An Anthropological Journey to Bishnupur*. New Delhi: Mittal, 2009.

Devji, Faisal Fatehali. "Gender and the Politics of Space: The Movement for Women's Reform, 1857–1900." In S. Sarkar and T. Sarkar, eds., *Women and Social Reform in Modern India: A Reader*, 99–114. Ranikhet, India: Permanent Black, 2007.

Dimock, Edward C. *The Thief of Love: Bengali Tales from Court and Village*. Chicago: University of Chicago Press, 1963.

Diwan, Kumud. "Thumrinama: The Poorab-Ang Perspective." *Indian Horizons* 59, no. 1: 65–72.

D'Souza, Diana. "Gendered Ritual and the Shaping of Shi'ah Identity." In K. Pemberton and M. Nijhawan, eds., *Shared Idioms, Sacred Symbols, and the Articulation of Identities in South Asia*, 188–211. New York: Routledge, 2009.

Drake, Richard. "Decadence, Decadentism and Decadent Romanticism in Italy: Toward a Theory of Décadence." *Journal of Contemporary History* 17 (1982): 69–92.

Eaton, Richard Maxwell. *The Rise of Islam and the Bengal Frontier, 1204–1760*. Berkeley: University of California Press, 1993.

Elias, Norbert. *The Civilizing Process: The History of Manners and State Formation and Civilization* Oxford, UK: Blackwell, 1994.

Farrell, Gerry. "The Early Days of the Gramophone Industry in India: Historical, Social and Musical Perspectives." *British Journal of Ethnomusicology* 2: 31–53.

———. *Indian Music and the West*. Oxford, UK: Clarendon Press, 1997.

Faruqi, Shamsur Rahman. "Conventions of Love, Love of Conventions: Urdu Love Poetry in the Eighteenth Century." *Annual of Urdu Studies* 14 (1999): 3–32.

Firoze, M. "Calcutta: A Rendezvous of Persian Poets in the 19th Century." *Indo-Iranica* 43, no. 3–4 (1990): 77–88.

Fisher, Michael. "Women and the Feminine in the Court and High Culture of Awadh, 1772–1856." In G. R. G. Hambly, ed., *Women in the Medieval Islamic World: Power, Patronage and Piety*, 489–520. New York: St. Martin's Press, 1998.

Flatt, Emma J.. *The Courts of the Deccan Sultanates: Living Well in the Persian Cosmopolis*. Cambridge, UK: Cambridge University Press, 2019.

Forbes, Geraldine. *Women in Modern India*. Cambridge, UK: Cambridge University Press, 1996.

French, J. C. "The Land of Wrestlers (A Chapter in the Art of Bengal)." *Indian Arts and Letters* 1, no. 1 (1927): 15–29.

Fuess, Albrecht, and Jan-Peter Hartung. *Court Cultures in the Muslim World: Seventh to Nineteenth Centuries*. London: Routledge, 2011.

Gangopadhyay, Sunil. *Those Days*. Translated by Aruna Chakravarti. New Delhi: Penguin Books India, 1997.

Garg, Lakshminarayan. *Hamāre Saṅgīt Ratna*. Hathras, India: Sangeet Karyalaya, 1957.

Garrett, J. H. E. *Nadia (Bengal District Gazetteers)*. Calcutta: Bengal Secretariat Book Depot, 1910.

Ghosh, Anindita. *Power in Print: Popular Publishing and the Politics of Language and Culture in a Colonial Society, 1778–1905*. New Delhi: Oxford University Press, 2002.

———. "Revisiting the 'Bengal Renaissance': Literary Bengali and Low-Life Print in Colonial Calcutta." *Economic and Political Weekly* 37, 42 (2002): 4329–38.

———. "Singing in a New World: Street Songs and Urban Experience in Colonial Calcutta." *History Workshop Journal* 76, no. 1 (2013): 111–36.

Ghosh, Gautam. "Nobility or Utility? *Zamindars*, Businessmen, and *Bhadralok* as Curators of the Indian Nation in Satyajit Ray's *Jalsaghar* (*The Music Room*)." *Modern Asian Studies* 52, no. 2 (2018): 683–715.

Ghosh, Nikhil. *The Oxford Encyclopaedia of the Music of India*. New Delhi: Oxford University Press, 2011.

Ghosh, Pika. "Sojourns of a Peripatetic Deity." *RES: Anthropology and Aesthetics* 41 (2002): 104–26.

———. *Temple to Love: Architecture and Devotion in Seventeenth-Century Bengal*. Bloomington: Indiana University Press, 2005.

Ghuman, Nalini. *Resonances of the Raj: India in the English Musical Imagination, 1897–1947*. New York: Oxford University Press, 2014.

Gordon, Stewart. "Robes of Honour: A "Transactional" Kingly Ceremony." *Indian Economic Social History Review* 33, no. 3 (1996): 225–42.

Goswami, Prabhat Kumar. *Bhāratīya Saṅgīter Kathā*. Kolkata: n.p., 1975.

Goswamy, B. N. *Indian Costumes in the Collection of the Calico Museum of Textiles*. Ahmedabad, India: D. S. Mehta, 1993.

Green, Nile. *Bombay Islam: The Religious Economy of the West Indian Ocean, 1840–1915*. Cambridge, UK: Cambridge University Press, 2011.

Grimes, Jeffrey Michael. "The Geography of Hindustani Music: The Influence of Region and Regionalism on the North Indian Classical Tradition." Unpublished doctoral thesis, University of Texas at Austin, 2008.

Gowers, Emily. *Horace: Satires Book I*. Cambridge, UK: Cambridge University Press, 2012.

Gupta, Bunny, and Jaya Chalihia. "Chitpur." In S. Chaudhuri, ed., *Calcutta, the Living City: The Past*, 27–30. Kolkata: Oxford University Press, 1990.

———. "Exiles in Calcutta: The Descendants of Tipu Sultan." *India International Centre Quarterly* 18, no. 1 (1991): 181–88.

Gupta, Charu. *Sexuality, Obscenity, Community: Women, Muslims, and the Hindu Public in Colonial India* New York: Palgrave, 2002.

Gupta, Nagendranath. *Reflections and Reminiscences*. Bombay: Hind Kitabs, 1947.

Gupta, Narayani. *Delhi between Two Empires 1803–1931: Society, Government and Urban Growth*. New Delhi: Oxford University Press, 1981.

Haidar, Navina Najat. "The *Kitab-i Nauras*: Key to Bijapur's Golden Age." In N. N. Haidar and M. Sarkar, eds., *Sultans of the South: Arts of India's Deccan Courts, 1323–1687*, 26–43. New Haven, CT: Yale University Press, 2011.

Hakala, Walter. *Negotiating Languages: Urdu, Hindi, and the Definition of Modern South Asia*. New York: Columbia University Press, 2016.

Hambly, Gavin. "A Note on the Trade in Eunuchs in Mughal Bengal." *Journal of the American Oriental Society* 94, no. 1 (1974): 125–30.

Hamilton, James Sadler. *Sitar Music in Calcutta: An Ethnomusicological Study*. Delhi: Motilal Banarsidass, 1994.

Hansen, Waldemar. *The Peacock Throne: The Drama of Mogul India*. New York: Holt, Rinehart and Winston, 1972.

Harder, Hans. "The Modern Babu and the Metropolis: Reassessing Early Bengali Narrative Prose." In Stuart Blackburn and Vasudha Dalmia, eds., *India's Literary Histories: Essays on the Nineteenth Century*, 358–401. Delhi: Permanent Black, 2004.

Haq, Md. Enamul. *Muslim Bengali Literature*. Karachi: Pakistan Publications, 1957.

Hasan, Mushirul. *From Pluralism to Separatism: Qasbas in Colonial Awadh*. New Delhi: Oxford University Press, 2004.

Hatcher, Brian A. "Pandits at Work: The Modern Shastric Imaginary in Early Colonial Bengal." In M. S. Dodson and B. A. Hatcher, eds., *Trans-Colonial Modernities in South Asia*, 45–67. Abingdon, UK: Routledge, 2012.

Hay, Sidney. *Historic Lucknow*. Lucknow, India: Pioneer Press, 1939.

Head, Matthew. *Sovereign Feminine: Music and Gender in Eighteenth-Century Germany*. Berkeley: University of California Press, 2013.

Head, Raymond. "Corelli in Calcutta: Colonial Music-Making in India during the 17th and 18th Centuries." *Early Music* 13, no. 4 (1985): 548–53.

Herder, Hans. "The Modern Babu and the Metropolis: Reassessing Early Bengali Narrative Prose (1821–1862)." In S. H. Blackburn and V. Dalmia, eds., *India's Literary History: Essays on the Nineteenth Century* Delhi: Permanent Black, 2004.

Hilton, Matthew. "The Legacy of Luxury: Moralities of Consumption since the 18th Century." *Journal of Consumer Culture* 4, no. 1 (2004): 101–23.

Hussain, Mirza Jafar. *Qadīm Lakhna'ū kī āk̲h̲irī bahār*. New Delhi: Taraqqi-yi Urdu Biyuro, 1981.

Ikegame, Aya. *Princely India Re-Imagined: A Historical Anthropology of Mysore from 1799 to the Present*. Abingdon, UK: Routledge, 2013.

Jafri, Rais Ahmad. *Vājid 'Alī Shāh aur unka 'ahed*. Lahore, Pakistan: Kitab Manzil.

Kakorvi, Muhammad Azmat Ali. *Tavārīk̲h̲-i Mulk-i Avadh, bah Murraqa'-yi K̲h̲usravī*. Lucknow: Zaki Kakorvi, 1986.

Katz, Max. *Lineage of Loss: Counternarratives of North Indian Music*. Middletown, CT: Wesleyan University Press.

Kaviraj, Sudiptu. "Laughter and Subjectivity: The Self-Ironical Tradition in Bengali Literature." *Modern Asian Studies* 34, no. 2 (2000): 379–406.

———. "The Two Histories of Literary Culture in Bengal." In S. Pollock, ed., *Literary Cultures in History: Reconstructions from South Asia*, 503–66. Berkeley and Los Angeles: University of California Press, 2003.

———. 'Writing, Speaking, Being: Language and the Historical Formation of Identities in India." In A. Sarangi, ed., *Language and Politics in India*, 312–50. New Delhi: Oxford University Press, 2009.

Kazmi, Sayyid Manzzar Husain. *Vājid 'Alī Shāh: Unkī shā'irī aur mars̲iye*. Karachi: Shaukat Ali and Sons.

Khan, Mofakhkhar Hussain. *The Bengali Book: History of Printing and Bookmaking*. Dhaka: Bangla Academy Dhaka, 2001.

Khan, Razak. "Minority Pasts: The Other Histories of a 'Muslim Locality,' Rampur 1889–1949." Unpublished doctoral thesis, Freie Universität Berlin, 2014.

Kia, Mana. *Persianate Selves: Memories of Place and Origin before Nationalism*. Stanford, CA: Stanford University Press, 2020.

Kidwai, Saleem. "The Singing Ladies Find a Voice." *Seminar* 540 (2004): 48–54.

Kinnear, Michael S. *The Gramophone Company's First Indian Recordings 1899–1908*. Bombay: Popular Prakashan, 1994.

Kippen, James. "Mapping a Rhythmic Revolution through Eighteenth- and Nineteenth-Century Sources on Rhythm and Drumming in North India." In R. K. Wolf, S. Blum, and C. Hasty, eds., *Thought and Play in Musical Rhythm: Asian, African, and Euro-American Perspectives*, 253–72. New York: Oxford University Press, 2019.

———. *The Tabla of Lucknow: A Cultural Analysis of a Musical Tradition*. New Delhi: Manohar, 2005.

———. "Working with the Masters." In G. Barz and T. J. Cooley, eds., *Shadows in the Field: New Perspectives for Fieldwork in Ethnomusicology*, 125–40. New York: Oxford University Press, 2008.

Koch, Ebba. "The Mughal Emperor as Solomon, Majnun, and Orpheus, or the Album as a Think Tank for Allegory." *Muqarnas* 27 (2010): 277–311.

Koch, Lars-Christian. "Rabindrasangeet: Rabindranath Tagore's Musical Legacy." In R. S. Kumar, ed., *The Last Harvest: Paintings of Rabindranath Tagore*, 47–53. Ahmedabad, India: Mapin, 2010.

Kothari, Sunil. *Kathak: Indian Classical Dance Art*. New Delhi: Abhinav Publications, 1989.

Kozlowski, Gregory C. "Muslim Women and the Control of Property in North India." In S. Sarkar and T. Sarkar, eds., *Women and Social Reform in Modern India: A Reader*, 20–43. Ranikhet, India: Permanent Black, 1998.

———. "Private Lives and Public Piety: Women and the Practice of Islam in Mughal India." In G. R. G. Hambly, ed., *Women in the Medieval Islamic World: Power, Patronage, and Piety*, 469–88. New York: St. Martin's Press.

Kuczkiewicz-Fraś, Agnieszka. "The Beloved and the Lover: Love in Classical Urdu Ghazal." *Cracow Indological Studies* 12 (2010): 199–222.

Kumar, Ritu, and Cathy Muscat. *Costumes and Textiles of Royal India*. London: Christie's Books, 1999.

Kumari, Meena. "Contribution of Nawabs to the Classical Music." In R. Taqui, ed., *Images of Lucknow*, 133–36. Lucknow, India: New Royal Book Co., 2005.

Lal, Ruby. *Coming of Age in Nineteenth-Century India: The Girl-Child and the Art of Playfulness*. Cambridge, UK: Cambridge University Press, 2013.

———. *Domesticity and Power in the Early Mughal World*, Cambridge, UK: Cambridge University Press, 2005.

———. "Historicizing the Harem: The Challenge of a Princess's Memoir." *Feminist Studies* 30, no. 3 (2004): 590–616.

Lal, Vinay. "Masculinity and Femininity in *The Chess Players*: Sexual Moves, Colonial Manoeuvres, and an Indian Game." *Manushi: A Journal of Women and Society* 92–93 (1996): 41–50.

Lehmann, Nicole Manon. "Sama und die, Schönheit' im Kathak: Nordindischer Tanz und seine ihn konstituierenden Konzepte am Beispiel der Lucknow-gharānā." Doctoral dissertation, Universität zu Köln, 2008.

Lelyveld, David. "Upon the Subdominant: Administering Music on All-India Radio." *Social Text* 39 (1994): 111–27.

Lethbridge, Roper. *The Golden Book of India*. Delhi: Aakar Books, 2005 (first published 1893).

Llewellyn-Jones, Rosie. *A Fatal Friendship: The Nawabs, the British, and the City of Lucknow*. Delhi: Oxford University Press, 1985.

———. "Introduction: 'The City' on the Bhagirathi" and "The Nawabs and Their Changing Fortunes." In N. Das and R. Llewellyn-Jones, eds., *Murshidabad: Forgotten Capital of Bengal*, 12–13 and 18–27. Mumbai: Marg Foundation, 2013.

———. *The Last King in India: Wajid Ali Shah* London: C. Hurst, 2014.

———. *A Man of the Enlightenment in Eighteenth-Century India: The Letters of Claude Martin 1766–1800*. Delhi: Permanent Black, 2003.

———. *A Very Ingenious Man: Claude Martin in Early Colonial India*. Oxford, UK: Oxford University Press, 1992.

Losty, J. P. "Eighteenth-Century Mughal Paintings from the Swinton Collection." *Burlington Magazine* 159, no. 1375 (2013): 789–99 and figure 29.

———. "Murshidabad Painting 1750–1820." In N. Das and R. Llewellyn-Jones, eds., *Murshidabad: Forgotten Capital of Bengal*, 82–105. Mumbai: Marg Foundation, 2013.

Malik, Jamal. *Islam in South Asia: A Short History*. Leiden, Netherlands: Brill, 2008.

Mallik, Abhaya Pada. *History of Bishnupur-Raj (An Ancient Kingdom of West Bengal)*. Calcutta: Kuntaline Press, 1921.

Mani, Lata. *Contentious Traditions: The Debate on Sati in Colonial India*. Berkeley: University of California Press, 1998.

Manuel, Peter. "The Evolution of Modern Thumrī." *Ethnomusicology* 30, no. 3 (1986): 470–90.

———. "Music in Lucknow's Gilded Age." In S. Markel and T. B. Gude, eds., *India's Fabled City: the Art of Courtly Lucknow*, 243–49. London: Prestel, 2010.

———. "Music, the Media, and Communal Relations in North India, Past and Present." In D. Ludden, ed., *Making India Hindu*. Bombay: Oxford University Press, 1996.

———. "The Popularization and Transformation of the Light-Classical Urdu Ghazal-Song." In A. Appadurai, F. J. Korom, and M. A. Mills, eds., *Gender, Genre, and Power in South Asian Expressive Traditions*, 347–61. Philadelphia: University of Pennsylvania Press, 1991.

———. *Ṭhumrī in Historical and Stylistic Perspectives*. Delhi: Motilal Banarsidass, 1989.

Markovits, Claude, Jacques Pouchepadass, and Sanjay Subrahmanyam, eds. *Society and Circulation: Mobile People and Itinerant Cultures in South Asia, 1750–1950*. London: Anthem Press, 2006.

Marshall, Peter. "Masters and Banians in Eighteenth-Century Calcutta." In B. B. King and M. N. Pearson, eds., *The Age of Partnership: Europeans in Asia before Dominion*, 191–214. Honolulu: University Press of Hawaii, 1979.

McCutchion, David. *Brick Temples of Bengal: From the Archives of David McCutchion*. Edited by George Michell. Princeton, NJ: Princeton University Press, 1983.

———. *The Temples of Bankura District*. Calcutta: Writers Workshop, 1972.

McDermott, Rachel Fell. *Mother of My Heart, Daughter of My Dreams: Kālī and Umā in the Devotional Poetry of Bengal*. New York: Oxford University Press, 2001.

McGuire, John. *The Making of a Colonial Mind: A Quantitative Study of the Bhadralok in Calcutta, 1857–1885*. Canberra: Australian National University, 1983.

McLane, John R. *Land and Local Kingship in Eighteenth-Century Bengal*. Cambridge, UK: Cambridge University Press, 1993.

McNeil, Adrian. "Making Modernity Audible: *Sarodiyas* and the Early Recording Industry." *South Asia: Journal of South Asian Studies* 27, no. 3 (2004): 315–37.

Metcalf, Barbara D. "Islam and Power in Colonial India: The Making and Unmaking of a Muslim Princess." *American Historical Review* 116, no. 1 (2011): 1–30.

Metcalf, T. R. "Landlords without Land: The U. P. Zamindars Today." *Pacific Affairs* 40, no. 1-2 (1967): 5–18.

Michaels, Axel, and Christoph Wulf, eds. *Exploring the Senses: South Asian and European Perspectives on Rituals and Performativity*. New Delhi: Routledge India, 2014.

Minault, Gail. *Secluded Scholars: Women's Education and Muslim Social Reform in Colonial India*. New Delhi: Oxford University Press, 1998.

Miner, Allyn. "Raga in the Early Sixteenth Century." In F. Orsini and K. B. Schofield, eds., *Tellings and Texts: Music, Literature and Performance in North India*, 385–406. Cambridge, UK: Open Book Publishers, 2015.

——— "The Scandalous Ghulam Raza.' Paper presented at the Annual Conference on South Asia, Madison, WI, 16 October 2013.

———. *Sitar and Sarod in the 18th and 19th Centuries*. Delhi: Motilal Banarsidass, 1997.

Mirza, Kaukab Qadr Sajjad Ali. *Vājid ʿAlī Shāh kī adabī aur saqāfatī k͟hidmāt*. New Delhi: Taraqqi-yi Urdu Biyuro, 1995.

Misra, Susheela. *Musical Heritage of Lucknow*. New Delhi: Harman, 1991.

Mitchell, Lisa. "Literary Production at the Edge of Empire: The Crisis of Patronage in Southern India under Colonial Rule." In S. Agha and E. Kolsky, eds., *Fringes of Empire: People, Places, and Spaces in Colonial India*, 236–56. New Delhi: Oxford University Press, 2009.

Mitra, Rajyeshwar. "Music in Old Calcutta." In S. Chaudhuri, ed., *Calcutta: The Living City; Vol. 1: The Past*, 179–85. Calcutta: Oxford University Press, 1990.

Morcom, Anna. *Illicit Worlds of Indian Dance: Cultures of Exclusion*. Oxford, UK: Oxford University Press, 2013.

Mourad, Kenizé. *Dans la ville d'or et d'argent*. Paris: Robert Laffont, Paris, 2010.

Mukherjee, S. N. "Class, Caste, and Politics in Calcutta, 1815–38." In E. Leach and S. N. Mukherjee, eds., *Elites in South Asia*, 33–78. London: Cambridge University Press.

Mukhopadhyay, Dilipkumar. *Aẏodhyar Nabāb Oẏājid Ālī Śāh*. Kolkata: Shankha Prakashan, 1984.

———. *Bāṅgālīra rāga saṅgīta carcā*. Kolkata: Firma KLM, 1976.

———. *Bhārater Saṅgīt Guṇī*, Pt. 1. Kolkata: A. Mukherji, 1977.

———. *Bhārater Saṅgīt Guṇī*, Pt. 2. Kolkata: A. Mukherji, 1980.

———. *Biṣṇupur Gharānā*. Calcutta: Buklyaht, 1963.

Mukhopadhyay, Kumarprasad. *Maẏhphil*. Kolkata: Dey's Publishing, 2001.

Nag, Monilal. "Vishnupur: The Famous Gharana of Bengal." *Indian Musicological Society Journal* 4, no. 1 (1973): 46–47.

Naim, C. M. "Ghalib's Delhi: A Shamelessly Revisionist Look at Two Popular Metphors." *Annual of Urdu Studies* 18 (2003): 3–24.

———. "Individualism within Conformity: A Brief History of *Waz'dārī* in Delhi and Lucknow." *Indian Economic and Social History Review* 48, no. 1 (2011): 35–53.

———. "Interrogating 'The East,' 'Culture,' and 'Loss' in Abdul Halim Sharar's *Guzashta Lakhna'u*." In A. Patel and K. Leonard, eds., *Indo-Muslim Cultures in Transition*, 189–204. Leiden, Netherlands: Brill, 2012.

———. *Urdu Texts and Contexts: The Selected Essays of C. M. Naim*. Delhi: Permanent Black, 2004.

Nandy, Ashis. *The Intimate Enemy: Loss and Recovery of Self under Colonialism*. New Delhi: Oxford University Press, 1983.

———. *Return from Exile*. New Delhi: Oxford University Press, 1998.

Neuman, Daniel M. *The Life of Music in North India: The Organization of an Artistic Tradition*. Chicago: University of Chicago Press, 1990.

Neuman, Daniel, Shubha Chaudhuri, and Komal Kothari. *Bards, Ballads and Boundaries: An Ethnographic Atlas of Musical Traditions in West Rajasthan*. Calcutta: Seagull Books, 2006.

Nijenhuis, Emmie Te. *Musicological Literature*. Wiesbaden, Germany: Otto Harrassowitz, 1977.

Nijenhuis, Emmie te, and Françoise "'Nalini'" Delvoye. "'Sanskrit and Indo-Persian Literature on Music." In J. Bor, F. N. Delvoye, J. Harvey, and E. te Nijenhuis, eds., *Hindustani Music: Thirteenth to Twentieth Centuries*, 35–64. New Delhi: Manohar, 2010.

O'Hanlon, Rosalind. "Kingdom, Household and Body: History, Gender and Imperial Service under Akbar." *Modern Asian Studies* 41, no. 5 (2007): 889–923.

———. "Manliness and Imperial Service in Mughal North India." *Journal of the Economic and Social History of the Orient* 42, no. 1 (1999): 47–93.

Oldenburg, Veena Talwar. *The Making of Colonial Lucknow, 1856–1877*. Princeton, NJ: Princeton University Press, 1984.

Orsini, Francesca. "How to Do Multilingual Literary History? Lessons from Fifteenth- and Sixteenth-Century North India." *Indian Economic and Social History Review* 49, no. 2 (2012): 225–46.

———. "What Did They Mean by 'Public'? Language, Literature and the Politics of Nationalism." *Economic and Political Weekly* 34, no. 7 (1999): 409–16.

Parker, Kunal M. " 'A Corporation of Superior Prostitutes': Anglo-Indian Legal Conceptions of Temple Dancing Girls, 1800–1914." *Modern Asian Studies* 32, no. 3 (1998): 559–633.

Peterson, Indira Viswanathan. "King Serfoji II of Thanjavur and European Music." *Journal of the Music Academy Madras* 84 (2013): 57–71.

Perkins, Christopher Ryan. "Partitioning History: The Creation of an *Islāmī Pablik* in Late Colonial India, c.1880–1920." Unpublished doctoral thesis, University of Pennsylvania, 2011.

Pernau, Margrit. *Ashraf into Middle Classes: Muslims in Nineteenth-Century Delhi*. New Delhi: Oxford University Press, 2013.

———. "The Delhi Urdu Akhbar: Between Persian Akhbarat and English Newspapers." *Annual of Urdu Studies* 18 (2002): 1–27.

———. *Emotions and Modernity in Colonial India: From Balance to Fervor*. New Delhi: Oxford University Press, 2019.

———. "India in the Victorian Age: Victorian India?" In M. Hewitt, ed., *The Victorian World*, 639–55. London: Routledge, 2012.

Pernau, Margrit, and Yunus Jaffrey. *Information and the Public Sphere: Persian Newsletters from Mughal Delhi*. New Delhi: Oxford University Press, 2009.

Perron, Lalita du. *Hindi Poetry in a Musical Genre: Ṭhumrī Lyrics*. Abingdon, UK: Routledge, 2007.

Petievich, Carla. *Assembly of Rivals: Delhi, Lucknow and the Urdu Ghazal*. New Delhi: Manohar, 1992.

———. *When Men Speak as Women: Vocal Masquerade in Indo-Muslim Poetry*. New Delhi: Oxford University Press, 2007.

Pinault, David. *Horse of Karbala: Muslim Devotional Life in India*. Basingstoke, UK: Palgrave, 2001.

Pinto, Rochelle. *Between Empires: Print and Politics in Goa*. New Delhi: Oxford University Press, 2007.

Platts, John T. *A Dictionary of Urdū, Classical Hindī, and English*. London: W. H. Allen, 1884.

Pritchett, Frances W. " 'The Chess Players': From Premchand to Satyajit Ray." *Journal of South Asian Literature* 21, no. 2 (1986): 65–78.

———. *Nets of Awareness: Urdu Poetry and Its Critics*. Berkeley and Los Angeles: University of California Press, 1994.

Qureshi, M. Aslam. *Wajid Ali Shah's Theatrical Genius*. Lahore, Pakistan: Vanguard Books, 1987.

Qureshi, Regula Burckhardt. "The Indian Sarangi: Sound of Affect, Site of Contest." *Yearbook for Traditional Music* 29 (1997): 1–38.

———. "Islamic Music in an Indian Environment: The Shi'a Majlis." *Ethnomusicology* 25, no. 1 (1981): 41–71.

———. "A Mine of Music History from Nineteenth-Century Lucknow." In J. Bor, F. Delvoye, J. Harvey, and E. te Nijenhuis, eds., *Hindustani Music: Thirteenth to Twentieth Centuries*, 221–38. Delhi: Manohar, 2010.

———. "Whose Music? Sources and Contexts in Indic Musicology." In B. Nettl and P. Bohlman, eds., *Comparative Musicology and Anthropology of Music: Essays on the History of Ethnomusicology*, 152–68. London: University of Chicago Press, 1991.

Rahman, M. Raisur. "Beyond Centre-Periphery: Qasbahs and Muslim Life in South Asia." *South Asian History and Culture* 5, no. 2 (2014): 163–78.

Raihani, Sayyid Muhammad Sajjad Husain. *Sawāniḥ-yi Shāh-i Avadh*. Meerut, India: Matba-yi Toti-yi Hind, 1887.

Ramusack, Barbara N. *The Indian Princes and Their States*. Cambridge, UK: Cambridge University Press, 2007.

Ranade, Ashok. "The Musical Evolution of the Gazal." *National Centre for the Performing Arts Quarterly Journal* 3, no. 1 (1974): 23–25.

Ranjan, Rajendra. "Brajbhāṣā-kāvya aur saṅgīt." *Sangita* 35 (1969): 40–49.

Ray, Satyajit. "My Wajid Ali Is Not 'Effete and Effeminate.'" *Illustrated Weekly of India*, 31 December 1978, pp. 49–51.

Ray, Sukumar. *Music of Eastern India: Vocal Music in Bengali, Oriya, Assamese and Manipuri with Special Emphasis on Bengali*. Kolkata: Firma KLM, 1985.

———. "Phases of Music of Bengal in the 19th Century: Dhrupad." *Journal of the Indian Musicological Society* 2 (1980): 9–13.

Raychaudhuri, Tapan. *Bengal under Akbar and Jahangir: An Introductory Study in Social History*. Delhi: Munshiram Manoharlal, 1966.

Richards, John F. *The Mughal Empire*. Cambridge UK: Cambridge University Press, 1995.

Rizavi, Syed Masud Hasan. "On 'Urdu Drama Aur Stage.'" *Indian Literature* 3, no. 1 (1959–60): 138–40.

Rizvi, Masud Hasan. *Sulṭān-i 'ālam Wājid 'Alī Shāh: Ek tārīḵẖī muraqqa'*. Lucknow, India: All India Mir Academy, 1977.

———. *Urdū ḍrāmā aur istej*. Lucknow, India: Kitab Ghar, 1957.

Rizvi, Saiyid Athar Abbas. *A Socio-Intellectual History of the Isnā 'Asharī Shī'īs in India*. New Delhi: Munshiram Manoharlal, 1986.

Robb, Megan. *Print and the Urdu Public: Muslims, Newspapers and Urban Life in Colonial India*. New York: Oxford University Press, 2021.

Robb, Peter. *Useful Friendship: Europeans and Indians in Early Calcutta*. New Delhi: Oxford University Press, 2014.

Robinson, Andrew. *Satyajit Ray: The Inner Eye*. London: André Deutsch, 1989.

Robinson, Francis. *Islam and Muslim History in South Asia*. Delhi: Oxford University Press, 2000.

———. "Islamic Reform and Modernities in South Asia." *Modern Asian Studies* 42, no. 2-3 (2008): 259–81.

———. "Technology and Religious Change: Islam and the Impact of Print." *Modern Asian Studies* 27, no. 1 (1993): 229–51.

Rosse, Michael David. "The Movement for the Revitalization of 'Hindu' Music in Northern India, 1860–1930: The Role of Associations and Institutions." Unpublished doctoral thesis, University of Pennsylvania, 1995.

Roy, Swarup. *The Observant Owl: Hootum's Vignettes of Nineteenth-Century Calcutta: Kaliprasanna Sinha's Hootum Pyanchar Naksha*. Kolkata: Black Kite, 2008.

Ruffle, Karen G. *Gender, Sainthood, and Everyday Practice in South Asian Shi'ism*. Chapel Hill: University of North Carolina Press, 2011.

Russell, Ralph, and Khurshidul Islam. *Ghalib 1797–1869: Life and Letters*. New Delhi: Oxford University Press, 1994.

———. "The Satirical Verse of Akbar Ilāhābādī (1846–1921)." *Modern Asian Studies* 8, no. 1 (1974): 1–58.

Sachdeva, Shweta. "In Search of the *Tawa'if* in History: Courtesans, Nautch Girls and Celebrity Entertainers in India (1720s-1920s)." Unpublished doctoral thesis, School of Oriental and African Studies, University of London, 2008.

Saha, Prabhat Kumar. *Some Aspects of Malla Rule in Bishnupur [1590–1806 AD]*, Calcutta: Ratnabali, 1995.

Sahaya, Sitala, and Sripati Sahaya. *Vājid Alī Śāh*. Ray Bareli, India: Shivgarh, 1935.

Said, Edward. *Culture and Imperialism*. London: Chatto and Windus, 1993.

———. *Reflections on Exile and Other Literary and Cultural Essays*. London: Granta Books, 2000.

Salomon, Carol. "The Cosmogonic Riddles of Lalan Fakir." In A. Appadurai, F. J. Korom, and M. A. Mills, eds., *Gender, Genre, and Power in South Asian Expressive Traditions*, 267–304. Philadelphia: University of Philadelphia Press, 1991.

Samiuddin, Abida. *Encyclopaedic Dictionary of Urdu Literature*. New Delhi: Global Vision, 2007.

Santha, K. S. *Begums of Awadh*. Varanasi, India: Bharati Prakashan, 1980.

Sanyal, Amiya Nath. "Music and Song." In Atulchandra Gupta, ed., *Studies in the Bengal Renaissance*, 306–18. Jadavpur, India: National Council of Education, 1958.

Sanyal, Ritwik, and Richard Widdess. *Dhrupad: Tradition and Performance in Indian Music*. Aldershot, UK: Ashgate, 2004.

Sarkar, Jadunath. *Bengal Nawabs*. Kolkata: Asiatic Society, 1985.

Sarkar, Tanika. *Hindu Wife, Hindu Nation: Community, Religion, and Cultural Nationalism*. Bloomington: Indiana University Press, 2001.

Sartori, Andrew. *Bengal in Global Concept History: Culturalism in the Age of Capital*. Chicago: University of Chicago Press, 2008.

———. "Emancipation as Heteronomy: The Crisis of Liberalism in Later Nineteenth-Century Bengal." *Journal of Historical Sociology* 17, no. 1 (2004): 56–86.

Sassatelli, Roberta. "Self and Body." In F. Trentmann, ed., *The Oxford Handbook of the History of Consumption*, 633–52. Oxford, UK: Oxford University Press, 2012.

Schaefer, R. Murray. *The Soundscape: Our Sonic Environment and the Tuning of the World*. Rochester, VT: Destiny Book, 1993.

Schofield, Katherine Butler. "Chief Musicians to the Mughal Emperors: The Delhi *Kalāwant Birāderī*." In ITC Sangeet Research Academy (Kolkata), ed., *Dhrupad, Its Future: Proceedings of the ITC-SRA (West) Seminar*. Mumbai: ITC-SRA, 2013.

———. "The Courtesan Tale: Female Musicians and Dancers in Mughal Historical Chronicles, c. 1556–1748." *Gender & History* 24, no. 1 (2012): 150–71.

———. "Emotions in Indian Music History: Anxiety in Late Mughal Hindustan." *South Asian History and Culture* 12, no. 2-3 (2021): 182–205.

———. *Music and Musicians in Late Mughal India, 1748–1858: Histories of the Ephemeral*. Cambridge, UK: Cambridge University Press, 2022.

Sharma, Amal Das. *Musicians of India Past and Present: Gharanas of Hindustani Music and Genealogies*. Calcutta: Naya Prokash, 1993.

Shukla, Shatrughna. *Ṭhumrī kī utpatti, vikāsa, aur śailiyā*. Delhi: Delhi University Press, 1983.

Silver, Brian. "The *Adab* of Musicians." In B. D. Metcalf, ed., *Moral Conduct and Authority: The Place of* Adab *in South Asian Islam*, 315–29. London: University of California Press, 1984.

Sinh, Ranbir. *Wajid Ali Shah: The Tragic King*. Jaipur, India: Publication Scheme Jaipur, 2002.

Sinha, Pradip. *Calcutta in Urban History*. Calcutta: Firma KLM, 1978.

Skelton, Robert. "Murshidabad Painting." *Marg* 10, no. 1 (1956): 10–22.

Sreenivasan, Ramya. "Drudges, Dancing Girls, Concubines: Female Slaves in Rajput Polity, 1500–1850." In I. Chatterjee and R. M. Eaton, eds., *Slavery and South Asian History*, 136–61. Bloomington: Indiana University Press, 2006.

Sripantha. *Meṭiẏāburujer Nabāb*. Kolkata: Ananda, 1990.

Stark, James A. *Bel Canto: A History of Vocal Pedagogy*. Toronto: University of Toronto Press, 1999.

Stark, Ulrike. *An Empire of Books: The Nawal Kishore Press and the Diffusion of the Printed Word in Colonial India*. Delhi: Permanent Black, 2007.

———. "Knowledge in Context: Raja Shivaprasad as Hybrid Intellectual and People's Educator." In M. S. Dodson and B. A. Hatcher, eds., *Trans-Colonial Modernities in South Asia*, 68–91. Abingdon, UK: Routledge, 2012.

Subrahmanyam, Sanjay. *Courtly Encounters: Translating Courtliness and Violence in Early Modern Eurasia*. Cambridge, MA: Harvard University Press, 2012.

Subrahmanyam, Sanjay, and Muzaffar Alam. *Writing the Mughal World: Studies on Culture and Politics*. New York: University Press Scholarship Online, 2015.

Subramanian, Lakshmi———. "Faith and the Musician: 'Ustads' in Modern India." *Economic and Political Weekly* 41, no. 45 (2006): 4648–50.

———. *From the Tanjore Court to the Madras Music Academy: A Social History of Music in South India*. New Delhi: Oxford University Press, 2006.

———. "The Master, Muse and the Nation: The New Cultural Project and the Reification of Colonial Modernity in India." *South Asia: Journal of South Asian Studies* 23, no. 2 (2000): 1–32.

Sundar, Pushpa. *Patrons and Philistines: Arts and the State in British India, 1773–1947*. Delhi: Oxford University Press, 1995.

Suvorova, Anna A. *Masnavi: A Study of Urdu Romance*. Oxford, UK: Oxford University Press, 2000.

Tagore, Pramantha. "Music and the Emerging City: A Study of Centres of Musical Patronage in North Calcutta (1800–1950)." Unpublished paper presented at the Department of English, Jadavpur University, 26 June 2013.

Taj, Afroz. *The Court of Indar and the Rebirth of North Indian Drama*. New Delhi: Anjuman Taraqqi Urdu, 2007.

Tapadar, Anil. *Kolkātār Chota Lakhnau*. Kolkata: Subarnarekha, 2002.

Taylor, Woodman. "Penetrating Gazes: The Poetics of Sight and Visual Display in Popular Indian Cinema." *Contributions to Indian Sociology* 36 (2002): 297–322.

Taylor, Joanne. *The Forgotten Palaces of Calcutta*. New Delhi: Niyogi Books, 2006.

Tlili, Sarra. *Animals in the Qur'an*. New York: Cambridge University Press, 2012.

Trivedi, Madhu. *The Emergence of the Hindustani Tradition: Music, Dance and Drama in North India, 13th to 19th Centuries*. Gurgaon, India: Three Essays Collective, 2012.

———. "Hindustani Music and Dance: An Examination of Some Texts in the Indo-Persian Tradition." In M. Alam, F. N. Delvoye, and M. Gaborieau, eds., *The Making of Indo-Persian Culture: Indian and French Studies*, 281–306. New Delhi: Manohar, 2000.

———. *The Making of the Awadh Culture*. Delhi: Primus, 2010.

Turner, James. *The Liberal Education of Charles Eliot Norton*. Baltimore: Johns Hopkins University Press, 1999.

Turnovsky, Geoffrey. *The Literary Market: Authorship and Modernity in the Old Regime*. Philadelphia: University of Pennsylvania Press, 2010.

Van der Linden, Bob. *Music and Empire in Britain and India: Identity, Internationalism, and Cross-Cultural Communication*. New York: Palgrave Macmillan, 2013.

Vanita, Ruth. *Gender, Sex, and the City: Urdu Rekhti Poetry in India, 1780–1870*. New York: Palgrave Macmillan, 2012.

Varadpande, M. L. *History of Indian Theatre: Loka Ranga, Panorama of Indian Folk Theatre*. New Delhi: Abhinav, 1992.

Varma, Bhagavaticaran. *Patana*. Lucknow, India: Ganga Pustakamala Karyalaya, 1965 (1929).

Vidyarthi, Govind. "Melody through the Centuries." *Sangeet Natak Akademi Bulletin* 11-12 (1959-60): 6–14, 13–26, 33, 49–58.

Wade, Bonnie C. *Imaging Sound: An Ethnomusicological Study of Music, Art, and Culture in Mughal India*. Chicago: University of Chicago Press, 1998.

Wali, Abdul, trans. *Sorrows of Akhtar: An Autobiographical Account of the Deposition and Imprisonment of the Sultan-i-'Ālam Wājid Ali Shah, the Last King of Oudh*. Calcutta: Baptist Mission Press, 1926.

Walker, Margaret E. *India's* Kathak *Dance in Historical Perspective*. Farnham, UK: Ashgate, 2014.

———. "The 'Nautch' Reclaimed: Women's Performance Practice in Nineteenth-Century North India." *South Asia: Journal of South Asian Studies* 37, no. 4 (2014): 551–67.

Walthall, Anne. *Servants of the Dynasty: Palace Women in World History*. Berkeley: University of California Press, 2008.

Weidman, Amanda. "Gender and the Politics of Voice: Colonial Modernity and Classical Music in South India." *Cultural Anthropology* 18, no. 2 (2003): 194–232.

White, Daniel E. *From Little London to Little Bengal: Religion, Print, and Modernity in Early British India, 1793–1835*. Baltimore: John Hopkins University Press, 2013.

Widdess, Richard. *The Rāgas of Early Indian Music: Modes, Melodies and Musical Notations from the Gupta Period to c. 1250*. Oxford, UK: Clarendon Press, 1995.

Williams, Richard David. "Music, Lyrics, and the Bengali Book: Hindustani Musicology in Calcutta, 1818–1905." *Music & Letters* 97, no. 3 (2016): 465–95.

———. "Reflecting in the Vernacular: Translation and Transmission in Seventeenth- and Eighteenth-Century North India." *Comparative Studies of South Asia, Africa and the Middle East* 39, no. 1 (2019): 96–110.

———. "Songs between Cities: Listening to Courtesans in Colonial North India." *Journal of the Royal Asiatic Society* 27, no. 4 (2017): 591–610.

Woodfield, Ian. *Music of the Raj: A Social and Economic History of Music in Late Eighteenth Century Anglo-Indian Society*. Oxford, UK: Oxford University Press, 2000.

Wright, O. "A Preliminary Version of the *Kitāb al-Adwār*." *Bulletin of the School of Oriental and African Studies* 58, no. 3 (1995): 455–78.

Zbavitel, Dušan. *Bengali Literature*. Wiesbaden, Germany: Otto Harassowitz, 1976.

Zon, Bennett. *Evolution and Victorian Musical Culture*. Cambridge, UK: Cambridge University Press, 2017.

Notes

Note on Transliteration

1. John T. Platts, *A Dictionary of Urdū, Classical Hindī, and English* (London: W. H. Allen, 1884).

Introduction

1. Shettjee Sahibjee, "A Day with My Indian Cousins, III. The Nabob: The Man of Tears," *Times of India*, 30 September, 1882 (originally published in *Vanity Fair*).

2. Nanda Lal Sharma, *Saṅgīta Sūtra* (Calcutta: Bidyaratna Press, 1870) 22. My translation.

3. For example, Margaret E. Walker, *India's Kathak Dance in Historical Perspective* (Farnham, UK: Ashgate, 2014); Janaki Bakhle, *Two Men and Music: Nationalism in the Making of an Indian Classical Tradition* (Ranikhet, India: Permanent Black, 2005); Lakshmi Subramanian, "The Master, Muse and the Nation: The New Cultural Project and the Reification of Colonial Modernity in India," *South Asia: Journal of South Asian Studies* 23, no. 2: 1–32; Shweta Sachdeva, "In Search of the Tawa'if in History: Courtesans, Nautch Girls and Celebrity Entertainers in India (1720s–1920s)," unpublished doctoral thesis, School of Oriental and African Studies, University of London; Regula Burckhart Qureshi, "The Indian Sarangi: Sound of Affect, Site of Contest," *Yearbook for Traditional Music* 29 (1997): 1–38; Saleem Kidwai, "The Singing Ladies Find a Voice," *Seminar* 540 (2004): 48–54.

4. For example, Charles Capwell, "Marginality and Musicology in Nineteenth-Century Calcutta: The Case of Sourindro Mohun Tagore," in B. Nettl and P. V. Bohlman, eds., *Comparative Musicology and Anthropology of Music: Essays on the History of Ethnomusicology* (Chicago and London: University of Chicago Press, 1991), 228–43; "Representing "Hindu" Music to the Colonial and Native Elite of Calcutta," in J. Bor, F. Delvoye, J. Harvey, and E. te Nijenhuis, eds., *Hindustani Music: Thirteenth to Twentieth Centuries* (Delhi: Manohar, 2010), 285–311; Gerry Farrell, *Indian Music and the West* (Oxford, UK: Clarendon Press, 1997).

5. Cf. Pinto's critique of the historiography of nineteenth-century Goan elite society in Rochelle Pinto, *Between Empires: Print and Politics in Goa* (New Delhi: Oxford University Press, 2007), 1–34.

6. Francis Robinson, "Islamic Reform and Modernities in South Asia," *Modern Asian Studies* 42, no. 2-3 (2008): 259–81; "Islam and the Impact of Print in South Asia," in F. Robinson, *Islam and Muslim History in South Asia* (Delhi: Oxford University Press, 2000), 66–104.

7. Brian Hatcher, "Pandits at Work: The Modern Shastric Imaginary in Early Colonial Bengal," in M. S. Dodson and B. A. Harcher, eds., *Trans-Colonial Modernities in South Asia* (Abingdon, UK: Routledge, 2012), 45–67; Vasudha Dalmia, *The Nationalization of Hindu Traditions: Bhāratendu Hariśchandra and Nineteenth-Century Banaras* (Ranikhet, India: Permanent Black, 2010).

8. Durgadas Lahiri, *Bāṅgālīr Gān* (Calcutta: Bangabasi-Ilektro-Mesin Press, 1905), 1003.

9. I borrow this phrase from Turnovsky's revisionist analysis of modern authorship in French literature: Geoffrey Turnovsky, *The Literary Market: Authorship and Modernity in the Old Regime* Philadelphia: University of Pennsylvania Press, 2010), 4.

10. Peter Manuel, "Music in Lucknow's Gilded Age," in S. Markel and T. B. Gude, *India's Fabled City: The Art of Courtly Lucknow* (London: Prestel, 2010), 246; Pallabi Chakravorty, *Bells of Change: Kathak Dance, Women, and Modernity* (Kolkata: Seagull, 2008), 29.

11. Partha Chatterjee, *The Black Hole of Empire: History of a Global Practice of Power* (Princeton, NJ: Princeton University Press, 2012); Rosie Llewellyn-Jones, *The Last King in India: Wajid Ali Shah* (London: C. Hurst, 2014).

12. For a summary history of nawabi Awadh, see Madhu Trivedi, *The Making of the Awadh Culture* (Delhi: Primus Books, 2010). On Europeans in Awadh, see Rosie Llwellyn-Jones, *A Fatal Friendship: The Nawabs, the British, and the City of Lucknow* (Delhi: Oxford University Press, 1985).

13. I draw upon Georgina Born's adoption of assemblage theory developed by Gilles Deleuze and Pierre Bourdieu. See Georgina Born, "On Musical Mediation: Ontology, Technology and Creativity," *Twentieth-Century Music* 2, no. 1 (2005): 7–36.

14. Regula Burckhardt Qureshi, "Whose Music? Sources and Contexts in Indic Musicology," in Nettl and Bohlman, *Comparative*, 152–68.

15. Capwell, "Marginality," 298.

16. E.g., Bennett Zon, *Evolution and Victorian Musical Culture* (Cambridge, MA: Cambridge University Press, 2017), 96–114.

17. Farrell, *Indian*; Lakshmi Subramanian, *From the Tanjore Court to the Madras Music Academy: A Social History of Music in South India* (New Delhi, Oxford University Press, 2006); Sharmadip Basu, "Tuning Modernity: Musical Knowledge and Subjectivities in Colonial India, c.1780s–c.1900.," unpublished doctoral thesis, Syracuse University, 2011; Michael David Rosse, "The Movement for the Revitalization of 'Hindu' Music in Northern India, 1860–1930: The Role of Associations and Institutions," unpublished doctoral thesis, University of Pennsylvania, 1995.

18. Farrell, *Indian*, 65–71.

19. Farrell, *Indian*, 54; cf. 76.

20. Bakhle, *Two*, ix, 3–6.

21. Kumkum Chatterjee, *The Cultures of History in Early Modern India: Persianization and Mughal Culture in Bengal* (New Delhi: Oxford University Press, 2009); "Cultural Flows and Cosmopolitanism in Mughal India: The Bishnupur Kingdom," *Indian Economic and Social History Review* 46, no. 2 (2009): 147–82.

22. For a comprehensive description of this reconfiguration, see Walker, *India's Kathak*.

23. Katherine Butler Brown, "If Music Be the Food of Love: Masculinity and Eroticism in the Mughal *Mehfil*," in F. Orsini, *Love in South Asia: A Cultural History* (Cambridge, UK: Cambridge University Press, 2006), 61–83; Katherine Butler Brown, "The Social Liminality of Musicians: Case Studies from Mughal India and Beyond," *Twentieth-Century Music* 3, no. 1 (2007): 13–49; Emma J. Flatt, *The Courts of the Deccan Sultanates: Living Well in the Persian Cosmopolis* (Cambridge, UK: Cambridge University Press, 2019), 109–14.

24. Rosalind O'Hanlon, Manliness and Imperial Service in Mughal North India," *Journal of the Economic and Social History of the Orient* 42, no. 1 (1999): 47–93; Carla Petievich, *When Men Speak as Women: Vocal Masquerade in Indo-Muslim Poetry* (New Delhi: Oxford University Press, 2007); Brown, "If Music."

25. E.g., Peter Robb, *Useful Friendship: Europeans and Indians in Early Calcutta* (New Delhi: Oxford University Press, 2014); Margrit Pernau, *Emotions and Modernity in Colonial India: From Balance to Fervor* (New Delhi: Oxford University Press, 2019).

26. Axel Michaels and Christoph Wulf, *Exploring the Senses: South Asian and European Perspectives on Rituals and Performativity* (New Delhi: Routledge India, 2014).

27. The term "musicology" may be considered problematic by scholars of Western art music in a pre-twentieth-century context. However, since I am referring to a different culture, I follow the example of other Indologists in using the term to refer to indigenous musical scholarship.

28. Arabic and Persian treatises on West Asian music also date back to the first millennium, but the first known Persian works specifically on Indian music were written in the fourteenth century CE.

29. See especially Richard Widdess, *The Rāgas of Early Indian Music: Modes, Melodies, and Musical Notations from the Gupta Period to c.1250* (Oxford, UK: Clarendon Press, 1995); Emmie te Nijenhuis, *Musicological Literature* (Wiesbaden, Germany: Otto Harrassowitz, 1977); Emmie te Nijenhuis and Françoise "Nalini" Delvoye, "Sanskrit and Indo-Persian Literature on Music," in Bor, *Hindustani*, pp. 35–64; Katherine Ruth Butler Brown, "Hindustani Music in the Time of Aurangzeb," unpublished doctoral thesis, School of Oriental and African Studies, University of London, pp. 27–80.

30. Exceptions include Allyn Miner, *Sitar and Sarod in the 18th and 19th Centuries* (Delhi: Motilal Banarsidass, 1997); Madhu Trivedi, "Hindustani Music and Dance: An Examination of Some Texts in the Indo-Persian Tradition," in M. Alam, F. N. Delvoye, and Gaborieau, eds., *The Making of Indo-Persian Culture: Indian and French Studies* (New Delhi: Manohar, 2000), 281–306; and Madhu Trivedi, *The Emergence of the Hindustani Tradition: Music, Dance and Drama in North India, 13th to 19th Centuries* (Gurgaon, India: Three Essays Collective, 2012).

31. Farrell, *Indian*; Bakhle, *Two*; Basu, "Tuning."

32. Richard David Williams, "Music, Lyrics, and the Bengali Book: Hindustani Musicology in Calcutta, 1818–1905," *Music & Letters* 97, no. 3: 465–95.

33. "Garlands of *rāgas*"—that is, verses and paintings on the theme of the visual abstraction of the melodic modes basic to musical composition, arranged according to recognizable (though flexible) taxonomic systems (*mat*).

34. Specifically, I have consulted records in the West Bengal State Archives, the Uttar Pradesh State Archives, the National Archives of India, and the India Office, London.

35. Daniel M. Neuman, *The Life of Music in North India: The Organization of an Artistic Tradition* (London: University of Chicago Press, 1990); James Kippen, *The Tabla of Lucknow: A Cultural Analysis of a Musical Tradition* (New Delhi: Manohar, 2005); Brian Silver, "The *Adab* of Musicians," in B. D. Metcalf, ed., *Moral Conduct and Authority: The Place of* Adab *in South Asian Islam* (London: University of California Press, 1984), 315–29.

36. Katherine Butler Schofield, "Chief Musicians to the Mughal Emperors: The Delhi *Kalāwant Birāderī*," in ITC Sangeet Research Academy (Kolkata), ed., *Dhrupad, Its Future: Proceedings of the ITC-SRA (West) Seminar* (Mumbai: ITC-SRA, 2013).

37. Richard David Williams, "Songs between Cities: Listening to Courtesans in Colonial North India," *Journal of the Royal Asiatic Society* 27, no. 4 (2017): 591–610, here 598.

38. Neuman first suggested that the *gharānā* was limited to aeteliers of instrumentalists, but Kippen has since discussed *tablā* and other accompanist *gharānās*. Kippen, *Tabla*, 63–65. It is unclear when the term *gharānā* was first used for communities of musicians; certainly by 1863 it was a recognized term, since it appeared without further explanation in the Urdu treatise *Ghunca-yi Rāg* in connection to dancers in Lucknow. See Muhammad Mardan Ali Khan, *Ghunca-yi Rāg* (Lucknow, India: Naval Kishor, 1863), 123–25.

39. Katherine Butler Schofield, *Music and Musicians in Late Mughal India, 1748–1858: Histories of the Ephemeral* (Cambridge, UK: Cambridge University Press, 2022); Max Katz, *Lineage of Loss: Counternarratives of North Indian Music* (Middletown, CT: Wesleyan University Press, 2017).

40. Bakhle, *Two*, 37.

41. James Kippen, "Working with the Masters," in G. Barz and T. J. Cooley, eds., *Shadows in the Field: New Perspectives for Fieldwork in Ethnomusicology* (New York: Oxford University Press, 2008), 125–40.

42. On the historiography of "invisible" women, see Indrani Chatterjee, "Testing the Local against the Colonial Archive," *History Workshop Journal* 44 (1997): 215–24.

43. Indrani Chatterjee, "Monastic Governmentality, Colonial Misogyny, and Postcolonial Amnesia in South Asia," *History of the Present* 3, no. 1 (2013): 57–98.

44. Robinson, *Islam*, 51–51 and 66–104; Jamal Malik, *Islam in South Asia: A Short History* (Leiden, Netherlands: Brill, 2008), 78, 148.

45. Nile Green, *Bombay Islam: The Religious Economy of the West Indian Ocean, 1840–1915* (Cambridge, UK: Cambridge University Press, 2011).

46. Francis Robinson, "Technology and Religious Change: Islam and the Impact of Print," *Modern Asian Studies* 27, no. 1 (1993): 229–51.

47. Barbara N. Ramusack, *The Indian Princes and Their States* (Cambridge, UK: Cambridge University Press, 2007), 141. The debate on the duration and extent of courtly patronage is summarized in Lalita du Perron, *Hindi Poetry in a Musical Genre: Ṭhumrī Lyrics* (Abingdon, UK: Routledge, 2007), 62–63.

48. Green, *Bombay*; Margrit Pernau and Yunus Jaffrey, *Information and the Public Sphere: Persian Newsletters from Mughal Delhi* (New Delhi: Oxford University Press, 2009), 11; Francesca Orsini, "What Did They Mean by 'Public'? Language, Literature and the Politics of Nationalism," *Economic and Political Weekly*, 34, no. 7 (1999): 409–16; Margrit Pernau, *Ashraf into Middle Classes: Muslims in Nineteenth-Century Delhi* (New Delhi: Oxford University Press, 2013).

49. Anindita Ghosh, "Revisiting the "Bengal Renaissance': Literary Bengali and Low-Life Print in Colonial Calcutta," *Economic and Political Weekly* 37, no. 42 (2002): 4329–38; Ulrike Stark, *An Empire of Books: The Nawal Kishore Press and the Diffusion of the Printed Word in Colonial India* (New Delhi: Orient Blackswan, 2008)16; Bunny Gupta and Jaya Chalihia, "Chitpur," in S. Chaudhuri, ed., *Calcutta, the Living City: The Past* (Kolkata: Oxford University Press, 1990), 29.

50. Pernau, *Information*, 31; Margrit Pernau, "The Delhi Urdu Akhbar: Between Persian Akhbarat and English Newspapers," *Annual of Urdu Studies* 18 (2002): 1–27.

51. Margrit Pernau, "India in the Victorian Age. Victorian India?," in M. Hewitt, ed., *The Victorian World* (London: Routledge, 2012), 647.

52. Partha Chatterjee, *Texts of Power: Emerging Disciplines in Colonial Bengal* (Minneapolis: University of Minnesota Press, 1995); Sumanta Banerjee, "Marginalisation of Women's Popular Culture in Nineteenth Century Bengal," in K. Sangari and S. Vaid, eds., *Recasting Women:*

Essays in Indian Colonial History (New Brunswick, NJ: Rutgers University Press, 1990), 127–79; *The Parlour and the Streets: Elite and Popular Culture in Nineteenth Century Calcutta* (Calcutta: Seagull Books, 1989); Pushpa Sundar, *Patrons and Philistines: Arts and the State in British India, 1773–1947* (Delhi: Oxford University Press, 1995); David Lelyveld, "Upon the Subdominant: Administering Music on All-India Radio," *Social Text* 39 (1994): 111–27. For Indian music influencing British music, see Ian Woodfield, *Music of the Raj: A Social and Economic History of Music in Late Eighteenth Century Anglo-Indian Society* (Oxford, UK: Oxford University Press, 2000); Nalini Ghuman, *Resonances of the Raj: India in the English Musical Imagination, 1897–1947* (New York: Oxford University Press, 2014).

53. Peter Manuel, *Thumri in Historical and Stylistic Perspectives* (Delhi: Motilal Banarasidass, 1990); Perron, *Hindi Poetry*; Joep Bor, *The Voice of the Sarangi: An Illustrated History of Bowing in India* (Bombay: National Centre for the Performing Arts, 1987).

54. See, for example, Indira Viswanathan Peterson, "King Serfoji II of Thanjavur and European Music," *Journal of the Music Academy Madras* 84 (2013): 57–71.

55. Edward Said, *Culture and Imperialism* (London: Chatto and Windus, 1993), 15.

56. E.g., Capwell, "Marginality."

57. Bob Van der Linden, *Music and Empire in Britain and India: Identity, Internationalism, and Cross-Cultural Communication* (New York: Palgrave Macmillan, 2013).

58. For the relationships between knowledge production, colonial power, and nationalism, see Partha Chatterjee, *The Nation and Its Fragments* (Princeton, NJ: Princeton University Press, 1993).

59. Lisa Mitchell, "Literary Production at the Edge of Empire: The Crisis of Patronage in Southern India under Colonial Rule," in S. Agha and E. Kolsky, eds., *Fringes of Empire: People, Places, and Spaces in Colonial India* (New Delhi: Oxford University Press, 2009), 236–56.

60. See Williams, "Music, Lyrics, and the Bengali Book."

61. Said, *Culture*, 217.

62. Cf. Claude Markovits, Jacques Pouchepadass, and Sanjay Subrahmanyam, *Society and Circulation: Mobile People and Itinerant Cultures in South Asia, 1750–1950* (London: Anthem Press, 2006).

63. Muzaffar Alam. *The Languages of Political Islam: India, 1200–1800* (Chicago: University of Chicago Press, 2004); Francesca Orsini, "How to Do Multilingual Literary History? Lessons from Fifteenth- and Sixteenth-Century North India," *Indian Economic and Social History Review* 49, no. 2 (2012): 225–46.

64. M. Asaduddin, "The West in the Nineteenth-Century Imagination: Some Reflections on the Transition from a Persianate Knowledge System to the Template of Urdu and English," *Annual of Urdu Studies* 18 (2003): 45–65.

65. Sudiptu Kaviraj, "Writing, Speaking, Being: Language and the Historical Formation of Identities in India," in A. Sarangi, ed., *Language and Politics in India* (New Delhi: Oxford University Press, 2009), 319f12.

66. C. A. Bayly, *Empire and Information: Intelligence Gathering and Social Communication in India, 1780–1870* (Cambridge, UK: Cambridge University Press, 1996).

67. Lars-Christian Koch, "Rabindrasangeet: Rabindranath Tagore's Musical Legacy," in R. S. Kumar, ed., *The Last Harvest: Paintings of Rabindranath Tagore* (Ahmedabad, India: Mapin, 2012), 47–53.

68. My translation of Urdu text from Ralph Russell and Khurshidul Islam, "The Satirical Verse of Akbar Ilāhābādī (1846–1921)," *Modern Asian Studies* 8, no. 1 (1974): 9.

69. William Dalrymple, *The Last Mughal: The Fall of a Dynasty: Delhi, 1857* (New York: Alfred A. Knopf, 2007); Vena Talwar Oldenburg, *The Making of Colonial Lucknow, 1856–1877* (Princeton, NJ: Princeton University Press, 1984).

70. Sadiq Ali Khan. *Sarmāya-yi ᶜIshrat: Muᶜarrif Qānun-i Mūsiqī* (Delhi: Matbaᶜ-i Faiz Alam, 1884 [1874–75]).

71. Narayani Gupta, *Delhi between Two Empires 1803–1931: Society, Government and Urban Growth* (New Delhi: Oxford University Press, 1981), 30–54.

72. Mushirul Hasan, *From Pluralism to Separatism: Qasbas in Colonial Awadh* (New Delhi: Oxford University Press, 2004) 17. See also Oldenburg, *Making*, 181–260; Megan Robb, *Print and the Urdu Public: Muslims, Newspapers and Urban Life in Colonial India* (New York: Oxford University Press, 2021); M. Raisur Rahman, "Beyond Centre-Periphery: Qasbahs and Muslim Life in South Asia," *South Asian History and Culture* 5, no. 2 (2014): 163–78.

73. M. Raisur Rahman, *Locale, Everyday Islam, and Modernity: Qasbah Towns and Muslim Life in Colonial India* (New Delhi: Oxford University Press, 2015).

74. Hannah L.Archambault, "Becoming Mughal in the Nineteenth Century: The Case of the Bhopal Princely State," *South Asia: Journal of South Asian Studies* 36, no. 4 (2013): 479–95; Razak Khan, "Minority Pasts: The Other Histories of a 'Muslim Locality,' Rampur 1889–1949," unpublished doctoral thesis, Freie Universität Berlin, 2014.

75. Abdul Halim Sharar, *Hindustān men mashraqī tamaddun kā ākhirī namūnah: Yancī guzashtah-yi Lakhna'ū* (New Delhi: Maktabah-yi Jamicah, 1971). English translation by E. S. Harcourt and Fakhir Hussain, *Lucknow: The Last Phase of an Oriental Culture* (London: Paul Elek, 1975).

76. Eve Tignol, "Nostalgia and the City: Urdu *Shahr Āshob* Poetry in the Aftermath of 1857," *Journal of the Royal Asiatic Society* 27, no. 4 (2017): 559–73.

77. Williams, "Songs."

78. On the Persianate model, see Mana Kia, *Persianate Selves: Memories of Place and Origin before Nationalism* (Stanford, CA: Stanford University Press, 2020); Flatt, *Courts of the Deccan*.

79. Norbert Elias, *The Civilizing Process: The History of Manners and State Formation and Civilization* (Oxford, UK: Blackwell, 1994); Anne Walthall, *Servants of the Dynasty: Palace Women in World History* (Berkeley: University of California Press, 2008); Albrecht Fuess and Jan-Peter Hartung, *Court Cultures in the Muslim World: Seventh to Nineteenth Centuries* (London: Routledge, 2011).

80. T. R. Metcalf, "Landlords without Land: The U. P. Zamindars Today," *Pacific Affairs* 40, no. 1-2 (1967): 5–18; Aya Ikegame, *Princely India Re-Imagined: A Historical Anthropology of Mysore from 1799 to the Present* (Abingdon, UK: Routledge, 2013).

Chapter 1

1. Maharaja Rajasimha and Kamal Krishna Simha, *Rāga-mālā O Saṅkṣipta Manasā Pāñcālī* (Calcutta: Bharatmihir Press, 1891), 1.

2. Rajasimha and Simha, *Rāga-mālā*, 1.

3. Allyn Miner, "Raga in the Early Sixteenth Century," in F. Orsini and K. B. Schofield, eds., *Tellings and Texts: Music, Literature and Performance in North India* (Cambridge, UK: Open Book Publishers, 2015), 385–406; Richard David Williams, "Reflecting in the Vernacular: Translation and Transmission in Seventeenth- and Eighteenth-Century North India," *Comparative Studies of South Asia, Africa and the Middle East* 39, no. 1 (2019): 96–110.

4. Jaysari Banerjee, "The Theoretical Problematic of Bengali Music," *Journal of the Indian Musicological Society* 17, no. 1 (1986): 1–11.

5. Sartori, *Bengal*, 1–6.

6. Sartori, *Bengal*, 8.

7. See for example, Anindita Ghosh, *Power in Print: Popular Publishing and the Politics of Language and Culture in a Colonial Society, 1778–1905* (New Delhi: Oxford University Press, 2006), and "Singing in a New World: Street Songs and Urban Experience in Colonial Calcutta," *History Workshop Journal* 76, no. 1 (2013): 111–36; Banerjee, *Parlour*; Neilesh Bose, *Recasting the Region: Language, Culture, and Islam in Colonial Bengal* (New Delhi: Oxford University Press, 2014).

8. David Collection, Copenhagen, Inv. no. D 28/1994. Murshidabad(?), 1760–70. Similar productions from Murshidabad include an illustrated copy of the *Dastur-i-Himmat*, now in the Chester Beatty Library.

9. Bonnie Wade, *Imaging Sound: An Ethnomusicological Study of Music, Art, and Culture in Mughal India* (Chicago: University of Chicago Press, 1998), 63–64, 75–84.

10. Brajendranath Bandyopadhyay and Sajanikanta Das, *Bhāratacandra-Granthābali*, part 2 (Kolkata: Bangiya Sahitya Parishat, 1943), 7; my translation. See also Edward C. Dimock, *The Thief of Love: Bengali Tales from Court and Village* (Chicago: University of Chicago Press, 1963), 32.

11. *Shehnāi* is a conical shawm. *Kāḍā* (similar to *ḍhak*) and *ḍhol* are large cylindrical or barrel-shaped drums. The *naubat* is an ensemble of drums, trumpets and oboes deployed to signal authority and royal presence. *Jhāñjha* are cymbals.

12. R. Murray Schaefer, *The Soundscape: Our Sonic Environment and the Tuning of the World* (Rochester, VT: Destiny Books, 1993).

13. Bandyopadhyay, *Bhāratacandra*, 130.

14. Rosie Llewellyn-Jones, "Introduction: 'The City' on the Bhagirathi" and "The Nawabs and Their Changing Fortunes," in N. Das and R. Llewellyn-Jones, eds., *Murshidabad: Forgotten Capital of Bengal* (Mumbai: Marg Foundation), 12–13, 18–27.

15. Tapan Raychaudhuri, *Bengal under Akbar and Jahangir: An Introductory Study in Social History* (Delhi: Munshiram Manoharlal, 1966), 49–53.

16. Md. Enamul Haq, *Muslim Bengali Literature* (Karachi: Pakistan Publications, 1957), 97.

17. The eunuchs of Bengal were especially prized, particularly those from the *sarkārs* of Ghoraghat and Sylhet; Alexander Rogers and Henry Beveridge, *The Tūzuk-i-Jahāngīrī; or, Memoirs of Jahāngīr*, vol. 1 (London: Royal Asiatic Society, 1909–14), 150; Gavin Hambly, "A Note on the Trade in Eunuchs in Mughal Bengal," *Journal of the American Oriental Society* 94, no. 1 (1974): 125–30.

18. Raychaudhuri, *Bengal*, 53–54.

19. Chaya Chatterjee, *Śāstrīya Saṅgīta and Music Culture of Bengal through the Ages* (Delhi: Sharada, 1996), 343.

20. John F. Richards, *The Mughal Empire* (Cambridge, UK: Cambridge University Press, 1995), 107–9.

21. M. I. Borah, *Bahāristān-i-Ghaybī*, vol. 2 (Gauhati, India: Government of Assam, 1936), 484; cf. 512–13, 686.

22. Borah, *Bahāristān-i-Ghaybī*, vol. 1, 96; cf. 130.

23. Ghulam Hussain Salim and Abdus Salim, *Riyazu-s-Salatin* (Calcutta: Baptist Mission Press, 1902), 347.

24. Salim and Salim, *Riyazu-s-Salatin*, 18.

25. Salim and Salim, *Riyazu-s-Salatin*, 257, 260.

26. Chatterjee, *Cultures*, 222; Rosalind O'Hanlon, "Kingdom, Household and Body: History, Gender and Imperial Service under Akbar," *Modern Asian Studies* 41, no. 5 (2007): 889–923.

27. Chatterjee, *Cultures*, 148.

28. Philip B. Calkins, "The Formation of a Regionally Oriented Ruling Group in Bengal, 1700–1740," *Journal of Asian Studies* 29, no. 4 (1970): 799–806.

29. Philip B. Calkins, *Studies in Bengali Literature, History, and Society: The Role of Murshidabad as a Regional and Subregional Centre in Bengal* (New York: Learning Resources in International Studies, 1974).

30. Robert Skelton, "Murshidabad Painting," *Marg* 10, no. 1 (1956): 10–22; J. P. Losty, "Murshidabad Painting 1750–1820," in Das and Llewellyn-Jones, *Murshidabad*, 82–105.

31. Jadunath Sarkar, *Bengal Nawabs* (Kolkata: Asiatic Society, 1985), 122.

32. Tabataba'i Gholam-Hoseyn Khan, *A Translation of the Seir Mutaqherin'; or, View of Modern Times* (Calcutta: James White, 1789), 689.

33. Sarkar, *Bengal Nawabs*, 110.

34. NMS IL.2013.8.4. See J. P. Losty, "Eighteenth-Century Mughal Paintings from the Swinton Collection," *Burlington Magazine* 159, no. 1375 (2017): 789–99, figure 29.

35. Ziauddin, "Ḥayy al-Arwāḥ," unpublished and undated MS, John Rylands Library University of Manchester, Persian 346. I am grateful to Katherine Butler Schofield for directing me to this text, and to Parmis Mozafari for a draft translation. See Katherine Butler Schofield, "Emotions in Indian Music History: Anxiety in Late Mughal Hindustan," *South Asian History and Culture* 12, no. 2–3 (2021): 182–205.

36. Aloys Sprenger, *A Catalogue of the Arabic, Persian and Hindu'sta'ny Manuscripts, of the Libraries of the King of Oudh* (Calcutta: Baptist Mission Press, 1854), 265.

37. Ziauddin, *Ḥayy*, f.55b.

38. Ziauddin, *Ḥayy*, f.62.

39. Ziauddin, *Ḥayy*, ff.51, 58b, 60b–61.

40. Brajendra Nath Banerjee, *Begams of Bengal Mainly Based on State Records* (Calcutta: S. K. Mitra, 1942), 40–42.

41. Llewellyn-Jones, "Murshidabad's," p. 43.

42. Translated in Walter Hakala, *Negotiating Languages: Urdu, Hindi, and the Definition of Modern South Asia* (New York: Columbia University Press, 2016), 100.

43. John R. McLane, *Land and Local Kingship in Eighteenth-Century Bengal* (Cambridge, UK: Cambridge University Press, 1993), 6.

44. Calkins, "Formation," 802.

45. Rachel Fell McDermott, *Mother of My Heart, Daughter of My Dreams: Kālī and Umā in the Devotional Poetry of Bengal* (New York: Oxford University Press, 2001).

46. McDermott, *Mother,* 89. For the royal family of Burdwan, see Anon., "The Territorial Aristocracy of Bengal: No. I, The Burdwan Raj.," *Calcutta Review* 54, no. 108 (1872): 171–94. Tejascandra was originally from Kotli, Lahore, and Mahtabchandra's two wives had families in Pattiala and Oudh; p. 172.

47. Basu, "Tuning," 276. *Ḵhayāl* did not become entrenched in Bengali music as successfully as *dhrupad* or *ṭappa*. Dilipkumar Mukhopadhyay, *Bāṅgālīra rāga saṅgīta carcā* (Kolkata: Firma KLM, 1976), 258.

48. Aghoracandra Ghosh, *Saṅgītasāgar* (Calcutta: Panchanan Ghosh, 1889), 589–93.

49. Ghosh, *Saṅgītasāgar*, 594.

50. Mahtabchandra composed and published *rāga* songs. Chatterjee, *Śāstrīya*, 226–27.

51. Mukhopadhyay, *Bāṅgālīra*, 66.

52. For *k̲hayāl* in Bengal, see Mukhopadhyay, *Bāṅgālīra*, 65–82, 258–286; Chatterjee, *Śāstrīya*, 358–61; Jeffrey Michael Grimes, "The Geography of Hindustani Music: The Influence of Region and Regionalism on The North Indian Classical Tradition," unpublished doctoral thesis, University of Texas at Austin, 2008, 164–93.

53. David L. Curley, *Poetry and History: Bengali Maṅgal-Kābya and Social Change in Precolonial Bengal* (New Delhi: Chronicle Books, 2008), 198–223. For the historiography of Nadia, see Varuni Bhatia, "Images of Nabadwip: Place, Evidence, and Inspiration," in A Murphy, ed., *Time, History and the Religious Imaginary in South Asia* (Abingdon, UK: Routledge, 2011), 167–85.

54. Anon., "The Territorial Aristocracy of Bengal: No. II, The Nadiyá Ráj," *Calcutta Review* 55, no. 109 (1872): 97–98. Cf. Ratan Dasgupta, "Maharaja Krishnachandra: Religion, Caste and Polity in Eighteenth Century Bengal," *Indian Historical Review*, 38, no. 2 (2011): 225–42.

55. Anon., "The Territorial Aristocracy of Bengal," 110.

56. Bandyopadhyay, *Bhāratacandra*, 21.

57. Mukhopadhyay, *Bāṅgālīra*, 173–74. It should be noted that some fifty-four songs are found in a musical portion of the *Annadamaṅgal*, with *rāga* and *tāla* prescriptions. The vocabulary of the *Saraswatī Bandanā* also suggests developed musical training.

58. Chatterjee refers to a Visram Khan at Bikrampur (Dacca district) in the court of Raja Rajballabha, along with a Kalandar Khan and Abu Baras, Chatterjee, *Śāstrīya*, 343.

59. "Nadiyá," 114.

60. Mukhopadhyay, *Bāṅgālīra*, 176–77, 197.

61. Mukhopadhyay, *Bāṅgālīra*, 175.

62. Report in *Tatvabodhinī Patrikā*, as discussed in Mukhopadhyay, *Bāṅgālīra*, 177.

63. Chatterjee, *Śāstrīya*, 343.

64. Mukhopadhyay, *Bāṅgālīra*, 227–28.

65. J. H. E. Garrett, *Nadia (Bengal District Gazetteers)* (Calcutta: Bengal Secretariat Book Depot, 1910), 162.

66. Mukhopadhyay, *Bāṅgālīra*, 259. Kartakeyacandra's autobiography was published as Kartikeyacandra Ray, *Deoẏān Kārtikeẏa Candra Rāẏer Ātma-jīban carita* (Calcutta: Indian Associated Publishing, 1956).

67. Ratan Dasgupta, "Maharaja Krishnachandra: Religion, Caste and Polity in Eighteenth Century Bengal," *Indian Historical Review* 38, no. 2 (2011): 228.

68. Jsiah Conder, *The Modern Traveller: A Popular Description, Geographical, Historical, and Topographical of the Various Countries of the Globe*, vol. 3 (London: James Duncan, 1828), 119–20.

69. Chatterjee, "Cultural Flows"; Pika Ghosh, *Temple to Love: Architecture and Devotion in Seventeenth-Century Bengal* (Bloomington: Indiana University Press, 2005); Abhaya Pada Mallik, *History of Bishnupur-Raj: An Ancient Kingdom of West Bengal* (Calcutta: Kuntaline Press, 1921).

70. David McCutchion, *Brick Temples of Bengal: From the Archives of David McCutchion*, edited by George Michell (Princeton, NJ: Princeton University Press, 1983), 155–56. See also David McCutchion, *The Temples of Bankura District* (Calcutta: Writers Workshop, 1972).

71. McCutchion used this term referring to the nine small shrines on its upper level (McCutchion, *Brick Temples*); Pika Ghosh understands it to mean "new bejewelled," referring to its decoration.

72. Sridhar temple, Bishnupur. See Ghosh, *Temple to Love*, 42, 219n13; McCutchion, *Temples of Bankura District*, 28; McCutchion, *Brick Temples*, 118–20, 137–38, 149, 151–52, 157, 162, and plates 424–29.

73. Alangiri Raghunatha temple (1810), Banpas Shiva temple in Raypara, Ghurisa Gopala-Lakshmi temple, Bhattamati Ratneshvara temple, and Mankar Deuleshvara temple. For details on these see McCutchion, *Brick Temples*.

74. Chatterjee, *Śāstrīya*, 248.

75. J. C. French, "The Land of Wrestlers: A Chapter in the Art of Bengal," *Indian Arts and Letters* 1, no. 1 (1927): 15–16; W. W. Hunter, *The Annals of Rural Bengal* (New York: Leypoldt and Holt, 1868), 439–46; Chatterjee, "Cultural," 159; Ghosh, *Temple*, 18.

76. Skelton, "Murshidabad," 19.

77. Ghosh further argued that Islamic designs, particularly Sultanate-period mosques, inspired the temples' congregational spaces: Ghosh, *Temple*, 65–94.

78. Chatterjee, "Cultural," 160.

79. Ghosh, *Temple*, 18.

80. J. Z. Holwell, *Interesting Historical Events Relating to the Provinces of Bengal and the Empire of Indostan*, part 1 (London:1766), 197–99; Abbé Raynal cited in French, "Land," 17; cf. Salim, *Riyazu*, 257.

81. Samira Dasgupta, Rabiranjan Biswas, and Gautam Kumar Mallik, *Heritage Tourism: An Anthropological Journey to Bishnupur* (New Delhi: Mittal, 2009), 26.

82. Katherine Butler Brown, "Did Aurangzeb Ban Music? Questions for the Historiography of his Reign," *Modern Asian Studies* 41, no. 1 (2007): 77–120.

83. Mallik, *History of Bishnupur-Raj*, 46–47.

84. A local legend relates how Raghunath II fell in love with a Muslim dancer in his retinue, Lalbai, and built her a pavilion, Nutun Mahal. She was ultimately drowned in the Lalbandh tank, and Raghunath was murdered by his queen. See Prabhat Kumar Saha, *Some Aspects of Malla Rule in Bishnupur [1590–1806 A.D.]* (Calcutta: Ratnabali, 1995), 300; Mallik, *History of Bishnupur-Raj*, 47–49. For parallels in Mughal cautionary tales, see Katherine Butler Schofield, "The Courtesan Tale: Female Musicians and Dancers in Mughal Historical Chronicles, c. 1556–1748," *Gender & History* 24, no. 1 (2012): 150–71.

85. Mallik, *History of Bishnupur-Raj*, 111.

86. Song 183 in Ramprasanna Banerjee, *Saṅgīta Mañjari* (Calcutta: Kuntalin Press, 1935), 469.

87. Dilipkumar Mukhopadhyay, *Biṣṇupur Gharānā* (Calcutta: Buklyaht, 1963); Amal Das Sharma, *Musicians of India Past and Present: Gharanas of Hindustani Music and Genealogies* (Calcutta: Naya Prokash, 1993), 212; Charles Capwell, "The Interpretation of History and the Foundations of Authority in the Vishnupur Gharana of Bengal," in S. Blum, P. V. Bohlman, and D. M. Neuman, eds., *Ethnomusicology and Modern Music History* (Champaign: University of Illinois Press, 1991), 59–102.

88. Sharma, *Musicians*, 212. Examples include using *komal nishad* for Behag and Basant, and *abaroha* in Bhairav; *teevra madhyam* does not appear in the rendering of Ramkali or Purabi, while *suddha dhaivata* appears in Purabi. Cf. S. C. Chakravarti, "Gopeshwar Banerjee," *Sangit Natak* 13 (1969): 67–76; James Sadler Hamilton, *Sitar Music in Calcutta: An Ethnomusicological Study* (Delhi: Motilal Banarsidass, 1994) 29, 206.

89. Especially under Bir Hambir (a contemporary of Akbar), Gopal Singha (r. 1712–48), and Chaitanya Singha (r. 1748–1801). Saha, *Aspects*, 290.

90. Local *kīrtan* shares the same *rāgas* as *dhrupad*, and follows the same guidelines on hours of performance, accompanying instruments, and four-part structure. Saha, *Aspects*, 292–99.

91. The extensive collection of the Jogesh Chandra Roy Bidyanidhi Purakriti Bhaban in Bishnupur is currently inaccessible to scholars.

92. Jayakrishna Das, "Madanamohanabandanā," unpublished MS, Asiatic Society of Bengal, ac. 4988, c. 1784.

93. Dasgupta identified a manuscript in Bishnupur which contained Narottama Thakur's *kīrtan* lyrics (MS no. 4668). I was unable to consult this MS owing to the inaccessibility of the archive upon my visit. Chittaranjan Dasgupta, *Bharater Śilpa-Saṅskṛtira Paṭabhūmikāy Biṣṇupurer Mandira-Ṭerākoṭā* (Bishnupur, India: Srimati Sushama Dasgupta, 2000), 187.

94. McLane, *Land*, 145.

95. Pika Ghosh, "Sojourns of a Peripatetic Deity," *RES: Anthropology and Aesthetics* 41 (2002): 104–26; McLane, *Land*, 215–16.

96. Hunter, *Annals*, 78f.

97. Likewise, Nadia, Rajshahi, and Cossijurah. F. D. Ascoli, *Early Revenue History of Bengal and the Fifth Report, 1812* (Oxford, UK: Clarendon Press, 1917), 214.

98. McLane, *Land*, 213.

99. McLane, *Land*, 295–97.

100. Mallik, *History*, 73.

101. Mallik, *History*, 72, 72n13.

102. Sharma, *Musicians*, 211–13.

103. Chatterjee, *Śāstrīya*, 214; Miner, *Sitar*, 149.

104. Pradap Kumar Singha, a Bishnupur historian, suggests that musicians found patronage from centers including Raipur (Bankura district), Kasipur (Panchakot), Narajol (Midnapur), Mahisadal, Tripura, Coochbehar, Durapur, and Rupnarayanpur. Personal communication, October 2012.

105. Other disciples include Ambika Charan Banerji, Gadadhar Das Gupta, Haradhan Chakravorty, Ishwar Chandra Sarkar, and Kartik Chandra Sarkar.

106. For *khaṇḍār bānī*, see Ritwik Sanyal and Richard Widdess, *Dhrupad: Tradition and Performance in Indian Music* (Aldershot, UK: Ashgate, 2004), 80–86.

107. Sukumar Ray, "Phases of Music of Bengal in the 19th Century: Dhrupad," *Journal of the Indian Musicological Society* 2 (1980): 7.

108. Mukhopadhyay, *Bāṅgālīra*, 235–57. Karunamoyee taught in Bardhaman Girls High School, was herself a *sitār* and *pakhāvaj* player, and would accompany Ramapati. See Shyamali Chakraborty, "To Sing or Not to Sing: In Search of One's Soul," *Think India Quarterly* 8, no. 2 (2005): 77.

109. Under Maharaja Bir Chandra Manikya (r. 1862–96).

110. Three further disciples of Ramsankar are noteworthy: Ramkalpa Mukherjee; Nafar Chandra Nag, the great-grandfather of Gokul Chandra Nag, the leading twentieth-century proponent of Bishnupur *gharānā*; and Keshav Chandra Chakravorty, employed by Taraknath Pramanik in Calcutta.

111. Sourindro Mohan Tagore, *Universal History of Music: Compiled from Diverse Sources, Together with Various Original Notes on Hindu Music* (Calcutta; N. G. Goswamy, 1896), 84; Ramesh Chandra Bandyopadhyaya, *Dwitiẏa Dillī Biṣṇupur* (Calcutta: 1942).

112. Dasgupta, *Heritage*, 110. Later the Ramsaran Sangeet Mahavidyalaya.

Chapter 2

1. See, for example, Rajyeshwar Mitra, "Music in Old Calcutta," in S. Chaudhuri, ed., *Calcutta: The Living City Vol. 1: The Past* (Calcutta: Oxford University Press, 1990), 179–85; Banerjee, *Parlour*; Rimli Bhattacharya, "The Nautee in 'the Second City of the Empire,'" *Indian Economic*

and Social History Review 40, no. 2 (2003): 191–235; Amiya Nath Sanyal, "Music and Song," in Atulchandra Gupta, ed., *Studies in the Bengal Renaissance* (Jadavpur, India: National Council of Education, 1958), 306–18.

2. Pradip Sinha, *Calcutta in Urban History* (Calcutta: Firma KLM, 1978), 39–40.

3. Ralph Russell and Khurshidul Islam, *Ghalib 1797–1869: Life and Letters* (New Delhi: Oxford University Press, 1994), 49–50.

4. M. Firoze, "Calcutta: A Rendezvous of Persian Poets in the 19th Century," *Indo-Iranica* 43, no. 3–4 (1990): 77–88.

5. Significant urban patrons included the Tagores of Jorasanko and Pathuriaghat, Sobhabazar (Raja Nabakrishna), Paikpara (Sinha family), Maszidbari (Guha family), Simulia (Ashutosh Deb, and Kailas Bose's concert hall), Entally (Debs), the Malliks of Sindurpatti, Bowbazar (Matilal), Dewanbari of Hidaram Banerjee Lane, Harakutir of Pathuriaghat, the House of Taraknath Pramanik, Mahishadal Bhavan of Wellesly, the House of the Chakraborty family of Thantharia, Bhawanipur (Kesab Mitra), and many others. See Ray, "Phases," 13.

6. Sanjay Subrahmanyam and Muzaffar Alam, *Writing the Mughal World: Studies on Culture and Politics* (New York: University Press Scholarship Online, 2015), 401–5.

7. Sher Ali Afos, *Araish-i Maḥfil* (Calcutta: Matb'ah Jal-ul-tin, 1903), 123–24.

8. On Radhamohan's connection to Fort William, see Williams, "Music, Lyrics," 468–70.

9. Williams, "Music, Lyrics," 468–70.

10. The first edition was published by the *Bāṅgālā* Press of Haracandra Ray (operated 1817–25). Radhamohan published *Bidvanmoda-taraṅgiṇī* ("River of Scholastic Zeal") in 1826 from the same press. Mofakhkhar Hussain Khan, *The Bengali Book: History of Printing and Bookmaking*, vol. 2 (Dhaka: Bangla Academy, 2001), 73, 77.

11. Radhamohan Sen Das and Harimohan Mukhopadhyay, *Saṅgītataraṅga*, 3rd ed. (Calcutta: Bangabasi Steam Mission Press, 1903).

12. Schofield, *Music and Musicians.*

13. Lallu Lal, *Sabhābilāsa*, 6th ed. (Luckow, India: Muṃśī Navalakiśora, 1882).

14. Radhamohan Sen Das, *Saṅgītataraṅga* (Calcutta: Bangala Press, 1818), 5.

15. Williams, "Music, Lyrics," 470–74.

16. Jagannath Prasad Basu Mallik, *Saṅgītarasamādhurī* (Calcutta: Brajmohan Cakrabarti, 1844), viii.

17. Peter Manuel, "Music, the Media, and Communal Relations in North India, Past and Present," in D. Ludden, ed., *Making India Hindu* (Bombay: Oxford University Press, 1996), 119–39; Lakshmi Subramanian, "Faith and the Musician: "Ustads" in Modern India," *Economic and Political Weekly* 41, no. 45 (2006): 4648–50.

18. James Turner, *The Liberal Education of Charles Eliot Norton* (Baltimore: Johns Hopkins University Press, 1999), 72–74.

19. See Bayly, *Empire and Information*, 198.

20. Norton to Louisa Norton (Calcutta, October 22, 1849). Sara Norton and M. A. DeWolfe Howe, *Letters of Charles Eliot Norton* (Boston and New York: Houghton Mifflin, 1913), 47.

21. Bunny Gupta and Jaya Chaliha, "Exiles in Calcutta: The Descendants of Tipu Sultan," *India International Centre Quarterly* 18, no. 1 (1991): 181–88.

22. Ghulam Muhammad Sultan, *Kārnāmah-i Ḥaydarī* (Calcutta: Baptist Mission, 1848).

23. Gupta and Chaliha, "Exiles," 183–84.

24. This building later became the Tollygunge High English School. See John Barry, *Calcutta 1940* (Calcutta: Central Press, 1940), 166.

25. Norton, *Letters*, 41.

26. Taeb Alla, *Lives of Maha Raja Apurva Krishna Bahadur, Poet Laureate to His Imperial Majesty of Delhi, and Member of the Hambury Academy, etc., his Father and Grandfather* (Calcutta: Catholic Orphan Press, 1847), 9–10.

27. Alla, *Lives*, 9–10.

28. Alla, *Lives*, 9–10.

29. *Friend of India*, May 3, 1849, p. 277.

30. Norton, *Letters*, 43.

31. Haradhan Dutt, *Dutt Family of Wellington Square* (Calcutta: Haradhan Dutt, 1995), 38; Norton, *Letters*, 43–46.

32. Norton, *Letters*, 37.

33. Norton, *Letters*, 37.

34. Norton, *Letters*, 45–47.

35. Norton, *Letters*, 50–53.

36. Norton, *Letters*, 53. *Abhinaya* entails communicating the dimensions of a lyric through gestures of the hands and expressions of the face.

37. James Long, *A Descriptive Catalogue of Bengali Works* (Calcutta: Sanders, Cones and Co., 1855), 73–74.

38. Mallik, *Saṅgītarasamādhurī*, ii.

39. Mallik, *Saṅgītarasamādhurī*, iv.

40. Sanyal, "Music," 312.

41. Sukumar Ray, *Music of Eastern India: Vocal Music in Bengali, Oriya, Assamese and Manipuri with Special Emphasis on Bengali* (Kolkata: Firma KLM, 1985), 89; Mitra, "Music," 181–82; Mukhopadhyay, *Bāṅgālīra*, 1–39.

42. Dušan Zbavitel, *Bengali Literature* (Wiesbaden, Germany: Otto Harassowitz, 1976), 206–7; Mukhopadhyay, *Bāṅgālīra*, 40–64.

43. Hindustani musicians continued teaching Hindustani *ṭappa*, including Ahmed Khan, Imam Bandi, and her son Ramjan Khan. See Sanyal, "Music," 311.

44. For parallels in Europe, see Tim Blanning, *The Triumph of Music: The Rise of Composers, Musicians and their Art* (Cambridge, MA: Harvard University Press, 2008).

45. Hans Harder, "The Modern Babu and the Metropolis: Reassessing Early Bengali Narrative Prose," in Stuart Blackburn and Vasudha Dalmia, eds., *India's Literary Histories: Essays on the Nineteenth Century* (Delhi: Permanent Black, 2004), 358–401.

46. Nisacar, *Samāj-Kucitra* (Calcutta: Notun Balmiki Press, 1865), 29–31.

47. Raymond Head, "Corelli in Calcutta: Colonial Music-Making in India during the 17th and 18th Centuries," *Early Music* 13, no. 4 (1985): 548–53.

Chapter 3

1. Carla Petievich, *Assembly of Rivals: Delhi, Lucknow and the Urdu Ghazal* (New Delhi: Manohar, 1992), ix.

2. Manuel, *Ṭhumrī*, 66–67.

3. Petievich, *Assembly*; Frances W. Pritchett, *Nets of Awareness: Urdu Poetry and Its Critics* (Berkeley and Los Angeles: University of California Press, 1994), 169–84; Aditya Behl, "Poet of the Bazaars: Nazir Akbarabadi, 1735–1830," in K. Hansen, and D. Lelyveld, eds., *A Wilderness of Possibilities: Urdu Studies in Transnational Perspective* (Delhi: Oxford University Press 2005), 192–222.

4. Charu Gupta, *Sexuality, Obscenity, Community: Women, Muslims, and the Hindu Public in Colonial India* (New York: Palgrave, 2002).

5. Abdul Wali, *Sorrows of Akhtar: An Autobiographical Account of the Deposition and Imprisonment of the Sultan-i-cĀlam Wājid Ali Shah, the Last King of Oudh* (Calcutta: Baptist Mission Press, 1926), 4; Ravi Bhatt, *The Life and Times of the Nawabs of Lucknow* (Delhi: Rupa, 2006), 57–58.

6. For details see Llewellyn-Jones, *Last King*, 11–48.

7. Sripantha, *Meṭiẏāburujer Nabāb* (Kolkata: Ananda, 1990), 81–82.

8. Swarup Roy, *The Observant Owl: Hootum's Vignettes of Nineteenth-Century Calcutta: Kaliprasanna Sinha's Hootum Pyanchar Naksha* (Kolkata: Black Kite, 2008). See Herder, "Modern Babu."

9. Roy, *Observant*, 90.

10. A number of Urdu (or English-Urdu bilingual) newspapers were printed and circulated in Calcutta, including *The Urdu Guide*, *Ākhbār-i Dār-ul-Salṭānat*, and *Muzhar-ul-Ajāib*. Wajid Ali wrote at least one article (on the meaning of Muharram) which was printed in *Ākhbār-i Dār-ul-Salṭānat* in 1881.

11. *Amrita Bazar Patrika*, 14 September 1882, pp. 5–6; 29 September 1887, pp. 4–5.

12. "The Late King of Oudh," reprinted in *Timaru Herald* 46, no. 4186 (1888): 3.

13. Nagendranath Gupta, *Reflections and Reminiscences* (Bombay: Hind Kitabs, 1947), 33–35.

14. *Kaleid Ummed*, 2 January 1869, *SVNPP* 1869, p. 19.

15. Gupta, *Reflections*, 40–41.

16. WBSA poll file 30L, proc B 216–220, August 1882.

17. WBSA genl proc 92–101, February 1862.

18. Llewellyn-Jones, *Last King*, 232.

19. Llewellyn-Jones, *Last King*, 198.

20. WBSA judl proc 309–13, March 1861, p. 227.

21. NAI Foreign Department, pol. A. February 1862, nos. 71–76.

22. K. Humayun Ansari, "The Muslim World in British Historical Imaginations: "Rethinking Orientalism"?," *British Journal of Middle Eastern Studies* 38, no. 1 (2011): 73–93. For the concept of nawabi decadence in Rampur see Khan, "Minority."

23. Charles Wentworth Dilke, *Greater Britain: A Record of Travel in English Speaking Countries During 1866 and 1867* (New York: Harper and Brothers, 1869), 403. The same was said of his "indolent" and "flabby" architecture in Lucknow, Llewellyn-Jones, *Last King*, 56.

24. Frederick F. Wyman, *From Calcutta to the Snowy Range: Being the Narrative of Trip through the Upper Provinces of India to the Himalayas Containing an Account of Monghyr, Benares, Allahabad, Cawnpore, Lucknow, Agra, Delhi and Shimla* (London: Tinsley Brothers, 1866), 140.

25. Wyman, *From Calcutta*, 143.

26. Wyman, *From Calcutta*, 140–41.

27. Dilke, *Greater*, 403.

28. Ashis Nandy, *The Intimate Enemy: Loss and Recovery of Self under Colonialism* (New Delhi: Oxford University Press, 1983), 15–16.

29. Dilke, *Greater*, 403.

30. Wyman, *From Calcutta*, 142.

31. E.g., Anon., "Village Sketches in Oudh III: Echoes of the Mutiny," *Fraser's Magazine for Town and Country* 77 (1868): 254.

32. Wyman, *From Calcutta*, 143.

33. Dilke, *Greater*, 404.

34. E. H. Palmer, "Native Princes," *Allen's Indian Mail*, 25 March 1872, p. 292. Palmer (1840–82) was a Cambridge academic and professor of Arabic (1871–81).

35. See also Anon., "The Administration of Oudh: First Report, to March 1859, Ordered by the House of Commons to be Printed; 1859." *Calcutta Review* 68 (1860): 220, 223–24, 229.

36. Palmer, "Native," 292.

37. E. D. G. Prime, *Around the World: Sketches of Travel through Many Lands and over Many Seas* (New York: Harper and Brothers, 1872), 205.

38. J. Drew Gay, *The Prince of Wales in India; or, From Pall Mall to the Punjaub* (New York: R. Worthington, 1877), 195.

39. Edwin Arnold, "The City of Palaces and Madras," *Times of India*, 23 March 1886.

40. Matthew Hilton, "The Legacy of Luxury: Moralities of Consumption since the 18th Century," *Journal of Consumer Culture* 4, no. 1 (2004): 101–23.

41. Sanjay Subrahmanyam, *Courtly Encounters: Translating Courtliness and Violence in Early Modern Eurasia* (Cambridge, MA: Harvard University Press, 2012).

42. Matthew Head, *Sovereign Feminine: Music and Gender in Eighteenth-Century Germany* (Berkeley: University of California Press, 2013), 31.

43. Adam Smith (1776) had polarized the whimsical nobility and the moral merchants; see Roberta Sassatelli, "Self and Body," in Trentmann, *Handbook*, 633–52, here p. 635.

44. Head, *Sovereign*, 31.

45. Emma J. Clery, *The Feminization Debate in Eighteenth-Century England: Literature, Commerce and Luxury* (London: Palgrave Macmillan, 2004), 6.

46. Sassatelli, "Self," 635.

47. Llewellyn-Jones, *Last King*, 69.

48. IOR Political and Foreign Consultations 11 December 1847, no. 156.

49. IOR Political and Foreign Consultations 11 December 1847, no. 191; Llewellyn-Jones, *Last King*, 73–75.

50. "Oudh," *Times of India*, 3 September 1851.

51. "Oudh," *Times of India*, 3 September 1851.

52. Anon., "Oude, as a Kingdom," *Dublin University Magazine* 49, no. 289 (1857): 112–28.

53. Anon., "Oude, as a Kingdom," 115; here citing an earlier description from 1852.

54. Anon., "Oude, as a Kingdom," 115.

55. Anon., "Oude, as a Kingdom," 116.

56. Claims that the king played female characters continued, including Sidney Hay, *Historic Lucknow* (Lucknow, India: Pioneer Press, 1939), 54; and recently, Anna A. Suvorova, *Masnavi: A Study of Urdu Romance* (Oxford, UK: Oxford University Press, 2000), 187.

57. W. H. Sleeman, *A Journey through the Kingdom of Oude in 1849–1850*, vol. 1 (London: Richard Bentley, 1858), lxxi.

58. Emily Gowers, *Horace: Satires Book I* (Cambridge, UK: Cambridge University Press, 2012), 90.

59. Brown, "Hindustani," 118–76.

60. Mirza Ali Azhar, *King Wajid Ali Shah of Awadh* (Karachi: Royal Book Co., 1982), 194.

61. E.g., IOR Political and Foreign Consultations, 11 December 1847.

62. An illustrated manuscript of the *'Ishqnāma* is preserved in Windsor Castle Library. Quotations are from a modern Urdu paraphrase of the original. See Wajid Ali Shah and Tehseen Sarwari, *Parīk͟hāna* (Karachi: n.p., 1958), 25.

63. Shah, *Parīkẖāna*, 38ff.

64. Shah, *Parīkẖāna*, 35–36.

65. Hakim Muhammad Karam Imam, *Ma'dan al-mūsīqī* (Lucknow, India: Hindustani Press, 1925; partial English trans. 1959–60); Govind Vidyarthi, "Ma'dan al-mūsīqī ('Melody through the Centuries')," *Sangeet Natak Akademi Bulletin* 11–12: 18, 24. Wajid Ali included *dhrupad* compositions by Pyar Khan in his own compilations of lyrics; see chapter 4. For the history of the *birāderī*, see Schofield, "Chief Musicians."

66. Sharar, *Lucknow*, 137.

67. Shah, *Parīkẖāna*, 103.

68. Shah, *Parīkẖāna*, 48; cf. Miner, *Sitar*, 122; Imam, "Melody," 24.

69. Miner, *Sitar*, 122, 220–21.

70. Shah, *Parīkẖāna*, 48.

71. Shah, *Parīkẖāna*, 56.

72. Shah, *Parīkẖāna*, 62.

73. Sharar, *Lucknow*, 137–38.

74. Neuman, *Life*, 92–94.

75. The text describes society c. 1858, though the earliest known MS is dated 1869. For details relating to dating, see Regula Burckhardt Qureshi, "A Mine of Music History from Nineteenth-Century Lucknow," in Bor, *Hindustani*, 221–38.

76. Brown, "Hindustani," 169.

77. Shah, *Parīkẖāna*, 114–15.

78. Stewart Gordon, "Robes of Honour: A 'Transactional' Kingly Ceremony," *Indian Economic Social History Review* 33, no. 3 (1996): 225–42; C. A. Bayly, *Origins of Nationality in South Asia: Patriotism and Ethical Government in the Making of Modern India* (Delhi: Oxford University Press, 1998), 172–209; Richards, *Mughal*, 107.

79. Allyn Miner, "The Scandalous Ghulam Raza," unpublished paper presented at the Annual Conference on South Asia, Madison, WI, 16 October 2013.

80. Shah, *Parīkẖāna*, 57.

81. See Miner, "Scandalous."

82. *'Ishqnāma*. By a Lucknow artist, 1849–50. 24 × 16 cm. Royal Library, Windsor Castle, RCIN 1005035.

83. Shah, *Parīkẖāna*, 94.

84. G. D. Bhatnagar, *Awadh under Wājid 'Ali Shāh* (Varanasi, India: Bharatiya Vidya Prakashan, 1968), 48, 232.

85. Sleeman, *Journey*, I. lx–xi; Miner, *Sitar*, 114–17.

86. Miner, *Sitar*, 116, 122, 129.

87. Aziz Ahmed, "The British Museum Mirzanama and the Seventeenth Century Mirza in India," *Iran: Journal of the British Institute of Persian Studies* 13 (1975): 101.

88. Brown, "Hindustani," 135.

89. Shah, *Parīkẖāna*, 57.

90. Abdul Halim Sharar, *Jān-i 'Ālam: Wājid 'Ālī Shāh ke Matiyāburj ke ḥālāt* (Lahore, Pakistan: Idara-yi Furgh-i Urdu),1951, 67–68.

91. Brown, "Hindustani," 142.

92. Brown, "Hindustani," 172–73.

93. Brown, "Hindustani," 132.

94. Brown, "Hindustani," 145.

95. Imam, "Melody," 24.

96. Tagore, *Universal*, 76.

97. *Akhbār-i-Anjuman-i-Punjāb*, 8 December 1871. See SVNPP 4, 742.

98. Hindu rituals provided specific contexts for rulers to dance in. See Thomas D. Broughton, *Letters from a Mahratta Camp During the Year 1809* (Westminster, UK: Archibald Constable, 1892), 26.

99. SVNPP 4, 743.

100. Gupta, *Sexuality*; Pernau, *Ashraf*. For parallels in Bengal, see Banerjee, *Parlour*.

101. Montgomery Martin, "The History, Antiquities, Topography, and Statistics of Eastern India," *Monthly Review* 1, no. 4 (1838): 481.

102. Brown, "Hindustani," 127.

103. Shah, *Parīkḫāna*, 107–8.

104. Wajid Ali Shah, *Banī* (Calcutta: Matba'-i Sultani, 1877), 233–47. See also a Hindi transliteration, *Banī*, by Roshan Taqi and Krishna Mohan Saxena (Lucknow, India: Sangeet Natak Academi, 1987). All translations are from the 1877 original. For forms of social interaction in mushairas, see C. M. Naim, *Urdu Texts and Contexts: The Selected Essays of C.M. Naim* (Delhi: Permanent Black, 2004), 108–19.

105. Shah, *Banī*, 240–44.

106. On the social position of *ḍoms*, see Daniel Neuman, Shubha Chaudhuri, and Komal Kothari, *Bards, Ballads and Boundaries: An Ethnographic Atlas of Musical Traditions in West Rajasthan* (Calcutta: Seagull Books, 2006), 278–79.

107. Neuman, Chaudhuri, and Kothari, *Bards, Ballads and Boundaries*, 236–37. My thanks to Carla Petievich and Megan Robb for their thoughts on this passage.

108. For parallels in Mughal and medieval courtly cultures, see Brown, "If Music"; O'Hanlon, "Kingdom"; and Daud Ali, *Courtly Culture and Political Life in Early Medieval India* (Cambridge, UK: Cambridge University Press, 2004).

109. Brown, "Hindustani," 126; Indrani Chatterjee, "Alienation, Intimacy, and Gender: Problems for a History of Love in South Asia," in R. Vanita, ed., *Queering India: Same-Sex Love and Eroticism in Indian Culture and Society* (London and New York: Routledge, 2001), 65–66.

110. Shamsur Rahman Faruqi, "Conventions of Love, Love of Conventions: Urdu Love Poetry in the Eighteenth Century," *Annual of Urdu Studies* 14 (1999): 20, 24; Agnieska Kuczkiewicz-Fraś, "The Beloved and the Lover: Love in Classical Urdu Ghazal," *Cracow Indological Studies* 12 (2010): 199–222.

111. Petievich, *When Men*, 136.

112. This does not feature in the illustrations of the Royal Library '*Ishqnāma* (1849–50), or in certain other pre-1856 paintings.

113. Ritu Kumar and Cathy Muscat, *Costumes and Textiles of Royal India* (London: Christie's Books, 1999), 165.

114. As a Muslim, Wajid Ali only revealed his left nipple; Hindus customarily wore the *parda* opening to the right. See Platts, *Dictionary*, 97. Cf. B. N. Goswamy, *Indian Costumes in the Collection of the Calico Museum of Textiles* (Ahmedabad, India: D. S. Mehta, 1993), 28.

115. Kumar and Muscat, *Costumes and Textiles*, 165.

116. Seen on display in the National Gallery of Modern Art, New Delhi.

117. Muhammad Husain Azad, Frances Pritchett, and Shamsur Rahman Faruqi, *Āb-e ḥayāt: Shaping the Canon of Urdu Poetry* (Oxford, UK, and New Delhi: Oxford University Press), 301; see also 275–302. For a critique of the "Lucknow school" concept, see Petievich, *Assembly*.

118. Shah, *Banī*, 233.

119. According to Platts, *Dictionary*, 907, "*girebān-meṅ muṅh ḍālnā (apne)*"—literally, to cast one's face inside the collar—is "to look within oneself; to confess and be ashamed of (one's) faults."

120. Platts, *Dictionary*, 418. Cf. synonyms "*jaib-pāra*, adj. Having the collar rent; sad:—*jaib-ćākī*, s.f. heart-rending," 412.

121. For a discussion of the Lucknow *parīkẖāna*, see Sachdeva, "Search," 164–71; Llewellyn-Jones, *Last*, 127–63.

122. A tradition, based on Qur'an 21:79, that when the Prophet David sang his hymns of praise, the birds joined him when they heard his beautiful voice. See Sarra Tlili, *Animals in the Qur'an* (New York: Cambridge University Press, 2012), 171.

123. Shah, *Parīkẖāna*, 127–28.

124. Miner, *Sitar*, 29–30, 81–90. The most celebrated musicians in the court of Muhammad Shah were Firoz Khan "Adarang," Ni'amat Khan "Sadarang," and Anjha Baras Khan. See Schofield, "Chief."

125. Navina Najat Haidar, "The Kitab-i Nauras: Key to Bijapur's Golden Age," in N. N. Haidar and M. Sarkar, eds., *Sultans of the South: Arts of India's Deccan Courts, 1323–1687* (New Haven, CT: Yale University Press, 2011), 26–43.

126. Shah, *Parīkẖāna*, 128.

127. Llewellyn-Jones, *Last*, 51.

128. Mas'ud Hasan Rizvi, *Urdū ḍrāmā aur istej* (Lucknow, India: Kitab Ghar, 1957); Ranbir Sinh, *Wajid Ali Shah: The Tragic King* (Jaipur, India: Publication Scheme Jaipur, 2002), 97; Meena Kumari, "Contribution of Nawabs to the Classical Music," in R. Taqui, ed., *Images of Lucknow* (Lucknow, India: New Royal Book Co., 2005), 135.

129. Afroz Taj, *The Court of Indar and the Rebirth of North Indian Drama* (New Delhi: Anjuman Taraqqi Urdu, 2007), 26; Susheela Misra, *Musical Heritage of Lucknow* (New Delhi: Harman, 1991), 76. For a list compiled by Wajid Ali of his own works, see Shah, *Banī*, 240f.

130. Llewellyn-Jones, *Last*, 53–54.

131. Qureshi, *Wajid*, 140–41.

132. Llewellyn-Jones, *Last*, 53.

133. E.g., Bhatt, *Life*, 159.

134. Qur'an 21:82, 27:17, 39, 34:12–4, and 38:37–8.

135. Ebba Koch, "The Mughal Emperor as Solomon, Majnun, and Orpheus, or the Album as a Think Tank for Allegory," *Muqarnas* 27 (2010): 280.

136. Koch, "Mughal Emperor," 283.

137. Khan, *Ghunca*. The association of the nawab with jinns continued. See Ṣafi Aḥmad, *Vājid 'Alī Shāh aur Shāh-i Jinn: Ek nādir makẖṯuṯah kī raushnī meṉ* (Lucknow, India: Markaz-i Adab-i Urdu, 1984).

138. These drawings were not included in the second edition (1879).

139. Llewellyn-Jones, *Last*, 54–55; Taj, *Court*, 28.

140. Shah, *Parīkẖāna*, 109.

141. M. Aslam Qureshi, *Wajid Ali Shah's Theatrical Genius* (Lahore, Pakistan: Vanguard Books, 1987), 24–25.

142. Nusseem Jounpore, 13 July 1869, SVNPP vol. 2, p. 339.

143. The same phrase in Persian was inscribed in gold around the inside of Shah Jahan's Hall of Private Audience in Delhi. See Waldemar Hansen, *The Peacock Throne: The Drama of Mogul India* (New York: Holt, Rinehart and Winston, 1972), 180.

144. Richard Drake, "Decadence, Decadentism and Decadent Romanticism in Italy: Toward a Theory of Décadence," *Journal of Contemporary History* 17 (1982): 85.

Chapter 4

1. Edward Said, *Reflections on Exile and Other Literary and Cultural Essays* (London: Granta Books, 2000), 173.

2. WBSA, poll file 98, proc. 1–2 May 1879, p. 183.

3. Shah, *Banī*, 3.

4. Frances W. Pritchett, "'The Chess Players': From Premchand to Satyajit Ray," *Journal of South Asian Literature*, 21, no. 2 (1986): 65–78; Vinay Lal, "Masculinity and Femininity in *The Chess Players*: Sexual Moves, Colonial Manoeuvres, and an Indian Game," *Manushi: A Journal of Women and Society* 92–93 (1996): 41–50.

5. Satyajit Ray, "My Wajid Ali Is Not "Effete and Effeminate","" *Illustrated Weekly of India*, 31 December 1978, pp. 49–51; Andrew Robinson, *Satyajit Ray: The Inner Eye* (London: André Deutsch, 1989), 242–43; Ashis Nandy, *Return from Exile* (New Delhi: Oxford University Press, 1998), 209–16.

6. Novels include, in Urdu, Ahmad, *Vājid*. In Hindi, Sitala Sahaya and Sripati Sahaya, *Vājid Alī Śāh* (Ray Bareli: Shivgarh, 1935); and Bhagavaticaran Varma, *Patana* (Lucknow, India: Ganga Pustakamala Karyalaya, 1929). In French, Kenizé Mourad, *Dans la ville d'or et d'argent* (Paris : Robert Laffont, 2010).

7. Sripantha, *Metiýāburujer*; Dilipkumar Mukhopadhyay, *Aýodhýar Nabāb Oýājid Ālī Śāh* (Kolkata, 1984); Anil Tapadar, *Kolkātār Chota Lakhnau* (Kolkata: Subarnarekha, 2002).

8. Sayyid Muhammad Sajjad Husain Raihanị, *Sawāniḥ-yi Shāh-i Avadh* (Meerut, India: Matba-yi Toti-yi Hind, 1887); Muhammad Azmat Ali Kakorvi, *Tavārīḵẖ-i Mulk-i Avadh, bah Murraqaᶜ-yi Ḵẖusravī* (Lucknow, India: Zaki Kakorvi, 1986); Kaukab Qadr Sajjad Ali Mirza, *Vājid ʿAlī Shāh kī adabī aur saqāfatī ḵẖidmāt* (New Delhi: Taraqqi-yi Urdu Biyuro, 1995); Sayyid Masud Hasan Rizvi, *Sulṭan-i ʿālam Wājid ʿAlī Shāh: Ek tārīḵẖī muraqqaʿ* (Lucknow, India: All India Mir Academy, 1977); Rizvi, *Urdū*; Muhammad Rais Hasan, *Ziya-yi Aḵẖtar* (Cawnpore, India: Naval Kishor, 1878); Muhammad Taqi Ahmad, *Vājid ʿAlī Shāh: Āḵẖirī tājdār-i Avadh* (Lucknow, India: Markaz-i Adab-i Urdu, 1975), especially 123–25 for his contribution to the arts.

9. Sharar published these essays 1914–19 in his monthly journal, *Dil Gudāz*, reprinted as Sharar, *Hindustān*. All translations from Harcourt and Hussain.

10. C. M. Naim, "Interrogating 'The East,' 'Culture,' and 'Loss' in Abdul Halim Sharar's *Guzashta Lakhna'u*," in A. Patel and K. Leonard, eds., *Indo-Muslim Cultures in Transition* (Leiden, Netherlands: Brill, 2012), 189–204; Christopher Ryan Perkins, "Partitioning History: The Creation of an *Islāmī Pablik* in Late Colonial India, c. 1880–1920.," unpublished doctoral thesis, University of Pennsylvania, 2011; especially pp. 304–79.

11. The British Library, London. WD 4166.

12. Llewellyn-Jones, *Last*, 190.

13. E.g., Llewellyn-Jones, *Last*, 159, 255.

14. For his arrival, see Llewellyn-Jones, *Last*, 18, 117–18.

15. Sachdeva, "Search," 174–77.

16. Wajid Ali Shah and A. A. Khan, *Masnavī Ḥuzn-i Aḵẖtar: Vājid ʿAlī Shāh kī āp bītī* (Lucknow, India: Vajid ʿAli Shah Akadmi, 1981); Llewellyn-Jones, *Last*, 117–18, 124.

17. NAI Foreign, F.C., 2 September 1859, 170–72.

18. IOR/L/PS/6/549 Coll. 45/1. Cf. Llewellyn-Jones, 167–68.

19. Llewellyn-Jones, *Last*, 147, 200. Details of the buildings can be found in the reports on repairs: NAI Foreign, Political A, March 1875, 365–75.

20. Description from Amir Ali; see WBSA political file 98, proc. 1–12, May 1879, p. 191. For a general description see Sharar, *Lucknow*, 70f.

21. "Police Raid on a Gambling House," *Times of India*, 5 February 1885.

22. Mowbray Thomson, 15 July 1878: WBSA poll file 98, proc. 1–2, May 1879, p. 177; WBSA poll file 98, proc. 1–2, May 1879, p. 238.

23. Llewellyn-Jones, *Last*, 171.

24. IOR/L/PS/6/534 Coll. 2/19, June 1864–October 1864. Cf. WBSA, poll file 98, proc. 1–2, May 1879, p. 175.

25. *Mut'a* were temporary or "pleasure" marriages, as will be explained below. WBSA, poll file 98, proc. 1–2, May 1879, p. 201.

26. IOR/L/PS/6/549 coll. 45/1, September 1866–October 1866.

27. Wajid Ali Shah to Mowbray Thomson, 28 May 1878, WBSA, poll file 98, proc. 1–2, May 1879, p. 181. On the menagerie, see Llewellyn-Jones, *Last*, 211, 218–19.

28. Report by Mowbray Thomson and Amir Ali, WBSA, poll file 98, proc. 1–2, May 1879, pp. 190–91.

29. Llewellyn-Jones, *Last*, 205ff.

30. WBSA, poll file 98, proc. 1–2, May 1879, pp. 137–260.

31. Bakhle, *Two*, 23–29.

32. Gifting conventions for patrons are recorded in the Delhi *akḫbārāt*. See Pernau, *Information*.

33. IOR/L/PS/6/549, coll. 45/1, September 1866–October 1866.

34. Figures from *Banī*, discussed in Kumari, "Contribution," 135; Sachdeva, "Search," 178.

35. Sharar, *Lucknow*, 17.

36. Naim, "Interrogating," 189.

37. Sharar, *Lucknow*, 74.

38. Naim, "Interrogating," 193; Sharar, *Lucknow*, 193.

39. Naim, "Interrogating," 197–99.

40. Sharar, *Lucknow*, 193; cf. 47. See also Francis Robinson, untitled review, *Modern Asian Studies* 11, no. 2 (1977): 298–302.

41. Mirza Jafar Hussain, *Qadīm Lakhna'ū kī āḵḫirī bahār* (New Delhi: Taraqqi-yi Urdu Biyuro, 1981).

42. Naim, "Interrogating," 203.

43. On nostalgia in these essays, see Perkins, "Partitioning," 336–50. For parallels in Delhi, see C. M. Naim, "Ghalib's Delhi: A Shamelessly Revisionist Look at Two Popular Metphors," *Annual of Urdu Studies* 18 (2003): 3–24; Daniela Bredi, "Nostalgia in the Re-Construction of Muslim Identity in the Aftermath of 1857 and the Myth of Delhi," *Cracow Indological Studies* 11 (2009): 137–56; Pernau, *Emotions and Modernity*, 195–218.

44. Perkins, "Interrogating," 329–31.

45. Sharar, *Lucknow*, 101.

46. Pritchett, *Nets*; Bredi, "Nostalgia."

47. On the lost *darbār* rights of the poet Asadullah Khan, see NAI, Foreign, General B, June 1862, p. 81.

48. Firoze, "Calcutta"; Abida Samiuddin, *Encyclopaedic Dictionary of Urdu Literature* (New Delhi: Global Vision, 2007), 472. For Urdu poets circulating in Bengal, see Abdul Ghafur Khan Nassakh, *Sakhan-i Shuʿarā* (Lucknow, India: Naval Kishor, 1874).

49. Including Sayyid Muzaffar Ali Khan Asir (1800–1881), Mufti Amir Ahmad Amir Minai (1828–1900), and Sayyid Zamin Ali Jalal (1834–1909). See the endnotes in Sharar, *Lucknow*, 255–56.

50. Rizvi, *Sulṭān*, 126–27. This seems to be a different Sadiq Ali Khan from the author of *Sarmāya-yi ʿIshrat* (below).

51. Firoze, "Calcutta," 80.

52. Sharar, *Lucknow*, 137.

53. See Katz, *Lineage*.

54. Sharar, *Lucknow*, 137.

55. Sharar, *Lucknow*, 137–38.

56. Sharar, *Lucknow*, 138.

57. Katz, *Lineage*.

58. Wajid Ali Shah, "Ṣaut al-Mubārak," unpublished MS (c. 1852), British Library, London, 14835.e.1 p. 5; see also Rizvi, *Sulṭān*, 161–63.

59. "Preserving" in the sense that chapters on *sur*, *tāla*, and instruments are conventional subjects. Wajid Ali's approach to these topics was innovative: for *sur* he employed the unusual metaphor of a tree for the human body, with the rustling of branches and leaves as the sounding of notes. See Shah, *Ṣaut*, 10–11.

60. Kippen notes that Wajid Ali's treatment of *tāla* is quite distinctive. The nawab mixed old and new terms from Persian and Sanskrit, omitted "uncommon" *tāla*s he thought redundant, and also did not provide the *ṭheka*s for *tāla*s he had not personally practiced. See James Kippen, "Mapping a Rhythmic Revolution through Eighteenth- and Nineteenth-Century Sources on Rhythm and Drumming in North India," in R.K. Wolf, S. Blum, and C. Hasty, eds., *Thought and Play in Musical Rhythm: Asian, African, and Euro-American Perspectives* (New York: Oxford University Press, 2019), 253–72.

61. From the Urdu translation of the Persian original, see Rizvi, *Sulṭan*, 162.

62. The most thorough treatment of the nawab's writings to date is Mirza, *Vājid*.

63. Llewellyn-Jones, *Last*, 261–63.

64. A fraction of the Royal Libraries was catalogued before 1857. See Llewellyn-Jones, *Last*, 93–95; Sprenger, *Catalogue*; Aloys Sprenger, *Report of the Researches into the Muhammadan Libraries of Lucknow* (Calcutta: Office of the Superintendent of Govt. Print., 1896).

65. Shah, *Banī*, 243.

66. Wajid Ali Shah, *Nāju* (Calcutta: Matba'-i Sultani). I have also consulted a manuscript version, MS 4, acc. no. 476, Salar Jung Museum Library, Hyderabad; and a Hindi transliteration, Yogesh Pravin, trans., *Nājo* (Lucknow, India: Uttar Pradesh Sangit Natak Akademi, 1898). All quotations are from the printed text unless otherwise indicated.

67. Wajid Ali Shah, *Dulhan* (Calcutta: Matba'-i Sultani, 1873).

68. I have been unable to locate an extant copy of *Chanchal Nāzanīn*. According to Rizvi, it shares attributes with *Banī*, including Wajid Ali's lament over the conduct of his *mutʿa* wives. Rizvi also records mention of another text by the nawab, the *Risāla-i Mūsiqī* (Discourse on Music"), which Muzaffar Ali Amir called a tract on the "science of singing" (ʿ*ilm-i ghinā*); it is unclear whether this was a separate work or another text by a different name. See Rizvi, *Sulṭan*, 127–28.

69. Katz, *Lineage*.

70. Cited in Bakhle, *Two*, 109–12.

71. The *gat* is the building block of extended dance sequences, known in contemporary performance as *nikas* or *bhav*. See Margaret E. Walker, "The "Nautch" Reclaimed: Women's Performance Practice in Nineteenth-Century North India," *South Asia: Journal of South Asian Studies* 37, no. 4 (2014): 8.

72. Qureshi, "Mine."

73. For *tāl* in these works, see Kippen, "Mapping." The identity of the author of *Sarmāya*, Sadiq Ali Khan, is uncertain as there are at least two possible candidates: a *k̲h̲ayāl* vocalist (d. 1910?) with connections to Wajid Ali, or an instrumentalist based primarily in Betia and Banaras. See Manuel, *Ṭhumrī*, 68; Nikhil Ghosh, *The Oxford Encyclopaedia of the Music of India* (New Delhi: Oxford University Press, 2011), 909.

74. Walker, "Nautch," 9–14.

75. Though Mirza Raushan Zamir's much earlier *Tarjoma-yi Pārījātak* (1666) preserves Ahobala's substantial third chapter on dance. Brown, "Hindustani," 68–9.

76. I am grateful to Margaret Walker for indicating this to me.

77. "Pure classical" is Harcourt and Hussain's translation. The original reads *a'lā qism*, "superior order" of music.

78. Sharar, *Lucknow*, 137.

79. Sharar, *Lucknow*, 138.

80. Formal features associated with these terms include a greater emphasis on sentiment and lyric, flexibility of *rāga*, and less emphasis on *ālāp*. Manuel, "Music," 247.

81. Du Perron, *Hindi*, 2, 52, 59; Manuel, *Ṭhumrī*, 34ff.; Chloë Alaghband-Zadeh, "Analysing Thumrī," unpublished doctoral thesis, SOAS, University of London, 2013, pp. 112, 148; Peter Manuel, "The Popularization and Transformation of the Light-Classical Urdu *Ghazal*-Song," in A. Appadurai, F. J. Korom, and M. A. Mills, eds., *Gender, Genre, and Power in South Asian Expressive Traditions* (Philadelphia: University of Pennsylvania Press, 1991), 350; Kumud Diwan, "Thumrinama: The Poorab-Ang Perspective," *Indian Horizons* 59, no. 1 (2012): 65–72.

82. Translation from du Perron, *Hindi*, 160–61.

83. This verse was included in a Bengali fictional account of Wajid Ali's arrival in Calcutta. Sunil Gangopadhyay, *Those Days*, trans. Aruna Chakravarti (New Delhi: Penguin Books India, 1997), 359–65.

84. Shatrughna Shukla, *Ṭhumrī kī utpatti, vikāsa, aur śailiyā* (Delhi: Delhi University, 1983), 212–13; Manuel, *Ṭhumrī*, 20; du Perron, *Hindi*, 57; Katz, *Lineage*, 9–43. Shukla himself does not suggest that this song is Wajid Ali's own creation.

85. Faiyaz Khan performed the song at the Fourth All-India Music Conference in Lucknow, in January 1925. Katz, *Lineage*, 19.

86. This song entered the instrumental practice of Kaukab Khan's *gharānā* members, including *sarod* player Irfan Khan Saheb, who states that this has been the case since the song's composition in the nineteenth century. Katz, *Lineage*.

87. Sharar, *Lucknow*, 137.

88. There are two other candidates for the name *Kadar Piyā*. Manuel suggests a grandson of Navab Nasiruddin Haidar, and Pant (1973) suggests Wazir Mirza (1836–1902). See Manuel, *Ṭhumrī*, 68; du Perron, *Hindi*, 28.

89. Shah, *Nāju*, 2–3.

90. Identified by *tak̲h̲alluṣ* as Nasr, Jalal, Nizami, Rang, and Hans Malha.

91. Shah, *Nāju*, 199ff.

92. Shah, *Nāju*, 60–61.

93. Shah, *Nāju*, 25–26; see also a *sādrā* by Pyar Khan, 72–73.

94. "*Rāja Rāma niranjana hindu pati salṭān. . . .*" Shah, *Nāju*, 29; cf. 48–49.

95. Shah, *Nāju*, 44–45.

96. Shah, *Banī*, 318–19.

97. Sanyal, *Dhrupad*, 57; Trivedi, *Making of the Awadh*, 120. This view was documented by Willard in 1834.

98. Shah, *Banī*, 319.

99. Sharar, *Lucknow*, 136.

100. Sharar, *Jān*, 66.

101. *Jhumur* and *gad khemṭā* are both associated with Bengali *kīrtan*. The term *Jhumur* can also refer to a narrative drama, and the "light" *khemṭā tāl* is considered appropriate for *ṭhumrī*. Lyrics prescribed for *khemṭā* echo *ṭhumrī*s in subject matter. See Devajit Bandyopadhyay, *Beśyāsaṅgīt, Bāījisaṅgīt* (Kolkata: Subarnarekha, 2001).

102. See Katherine Butler Brown, "The Libertine and the Spectacle: Masculinities and the *Bhand* Tamasha in 18C Delhi," unpublished paper presented at the annual conference of the Society for Ethnomusicology, Hawaii, 2006.

103. Shah, *Banī*, 136–37. For a Hindi transliteration, see Roshan Taqi and Krishna Mohan Saxena, trans., *Banī* (Lucknow, India: Sangit Natak Akademi), 120–21. The final line of this verse is an amended (and most likely corrupted) reading of the earlier version in *Nāju*. Hence, the translation is only an approximation.

104. His menagerie of pigeons and zoo animals also indicates his love of meticulous collections.

105. Shah, *Nāju*, 263.

106. Shah *Nāju*, 260; Pravin, *Nājo*, 142. The Urdu MS and printed text have a number of peculiar spellings or scribal errors which are corrected by the Hindi editor of the 1989 Hindi edition. In the original, *parbash* in the first line is *parkash*, but this is less intelligible.

107. Pravin corrected this to the Bangla.

108. Shah, *Nāju*, 264; Pravin, *Nājo*, 144. Pravin rendered *bosho* in the first line as *posho*, but this is less intelligible.

109. Shah, *Nāju*, 261; Pravin, *Nājo*, 142. *Cunnī* in the Urdu originals has been rendered *cenī* by Pravin. This word is problematic, but may be read as an "Urdu-ized" form of the Bangla *cenī*.

110. Du Perron, *Hindi*.

111. See Sharma, *Saṅgīta*, 22. The "Lucknow *Ṭhumrī*" here is anonymous, but the author was identified as Wajid Ali Shah when it was reprinted in Lahiri, *Bāṅgālīr*, 1003. Cf. Gopesvar Bandyopadhyay, *Bahubhāṣā Gīta* (Calcutta: Lekhaka, 1940), 86.

112. See NAI Foreign; Political part A, September 1864, pp. 166–68.

113. Chatterjee, *Śāstrīya*, 213. Cf. Mitra, "Music," 183.

114. Dilipkumar Mukhopadhyay, *Bhārater Saṅgīt Guṇī*, part 2 (Kolkata: A. Mukherji, 1980), 30.

115. See Bhatt, *Life*, 209.

116. Joanne Taylor, *The Forgotten Palaces of Calcutta* (New Delhi: Niyogi Books, 2006), 59.

117. Sharma, *Musicians*, 217; Chatterjee, *Śāstrīya*, 213; Mitra, "Music," 183; Prabhat Kumar Goswami, *Bhāratīya Saṅgīter Kathā* (Kolkata: n.p., 1975), 226.

118. See the Preface in Pravin, *Nājo*, xvi. Mukhopadhyay also suggests that Tagore visited Matiyaburj: Mukhopadhyay, *Aýodhýar*, 166. The full text of the song is provided in an article on

Brajbhasha lyrics, in which the author notes that the composer of the lyric is unknown: Rajendra Ranjan, "Brajbhāṣā-kāvya aur saṅgīt," *Sangita* 35 (1969): 48.

119. V. Prem Kumari and Meena Kumari disagreed with Pravin's account of a dancing Wajid Ali Shah; see Kumari, "Contribution," 136.

120. Shah, *Banī*, 58.

121. Sharar, *Lucknow*, 141–42.

122. Sharar, *Lucknow*, 142. This account is retold by the descendants of Binda Din today. See Pallabi Chakravorty, "Dancing into Modernity: Multiple Narratives of India's Kathak Dance," *Dance Research Journal* 38, no. 1-2 (2006): 115–36.

123. Kumari, "Contribution," 136; Walker, *India's*, 100–104. From her exhaustive survey of Indian and colonial literary and visual archives, Walker maintains that there was no dance called Kathak prior to the twentieth century. In the nineteenth century there were communities of performing artists known as Kathaks, or by the surname Kathak, but they were not all dancers. See also Chakravorty, "Dancing." The only possible reference I have found to anyone from this family is to one "Binderpershad" (Binda Din Prasa?) who made a claim for a pearl bracelet belonging to the nawab. Unfortunately, the original file is currently missing: NAI Foreign, revenue A, April 1860, 33–37. The view that Wajid Ali was taught dance by Kathaks is extremely widespread; e.g., see Sunil Kothari, *Kathak: Indian Classical Dance Art* (New Delhi: Abhinav Publications, 1989), 24. Cf. Nicole Manon Lehmann, *Sama und die ‚Schönheit' im Kathak: Nordindischer Tanz und seine ihn konstituierenden Konzepte am Beispiel der Lucknow-gharānā*, published doctoral dissertation, Universität zu Köln, 2008, p. 162.

124. Imam, "Melody," 25.

125. Walker, *India's*.

126. Khan, *Ghunca*, 123, 125.

127. Khan, *Ghunca*, 127.

128. Cf. Imam, "Melody," 25.

129. Sharar, *Jān*, 67. Other authors seemed unaware that this was a controversial topic. Cf. Gupta, *Reflections*, 90.

130. Sharar, *Lucknow*, 138–39.

131. Platts, *Dictionary*, 1130; cf. Trivedi, "Hindustani," 297.

132. Imam, *Ma'dan*, 47.

133. Imam, *Ma'dan*, 49.

134. Some women were "expectant" *mut'a*, perhaps implying that they had yet to come of age. Shah, *Banī*, 321.

135. Platts, *Dictionary*, 595.

136. Shah, *Banī*, 309–10.

137. Shah, *Banī*, 319. According to the *Ghunca-yi Rāg*, danced *bhāv* was appropriate for the lyrics of *ghazal*, *ṭappa*, *ṭhumrī*, *dādrā*, and *khemṭa*, but not for *k͟hayāl*, *dhrupad*, *tarānā*, and *sargam*. See Khan, *Ghunca*, 125. It should be noted that by this time (1863), Bengali *khemṭa* was understood as a common song genre by Hindustani musicologists.

138. Shah, *Banī*, 311–12, 317.

139. Shah, *Banī*, 315, 316, 318, 320.

140. Shah, *Banī*, 322.

141. E.g., Imam, "Melody," 25.

142. See the cases of Dunni Khan in Sharar, *Jān*, 69; and of Taj Khan, who abandoned Matiyaburj for Nepal after being slighted:, Mukhopadhyay, *Bhārater*, 43.

143. Varadpande describes *naql* as a community rather than a genre, akin to *bhagat-baz*. See M. L. Varadpande, *History of Indian Theatre: Loka Ranga, Panorama of Indian Folk Theatre* (New Delhi: Abhinav, 1992), 139–49. However, *naql* is not a community; the term refers to a genre performed by the *naqqāl* (a common Persian equivalent to the *bhānḍ*), just as *qaul* is the genre performed by *qawwāls*.

144. Shah, *Banī*, 134.

145. Shah, *Banī*, 310.

146. Shah, *Banī*, 230–48.

147. Shah, *Banī*, 265.

148. Platts, *Dictionary*, 1120.

149. Walker, *India's*, 91. In a bilingual Hindustani-English anti-*nautch* pamphlet from 1837, *nāyika* is synonymous for "procuress." See Anon., *An Exposition in English and Hindustani of the Evil Tendency of Naches* (Calcutta: Baptist Mission Press, 1837).

150. Shah, *Banī*, 266.

151. Shah, *Banī*, 250.

152. Shah, *Banī*, 255–56.

153. C. M. Naim, "Individualism within Conformity: A Brief History of *Waz'dārī* in Delhi and Lucknow," *Indian Economic and Social History Review* 48, no. 1 (2011): 35–53. They were also known in south India and Bengal, see Ruth Vanita, *Gender, Sex, and the City: Urdu Rekhti Poetry in India, 1780–1870* (New York: Palgrave Macmillan, 2012), 176–77.

154. E.g., Sharar, *Jān*, 67.

155. Naim gives an example of a gentleman caught in public with an untied *angarkhā* string, who then made that his custom style (*waẓ'*). Other characters wore women's clothing or jewelry, or shaved half their face. Naim, "Individualism," 43, 45.

156. The most detailed studies of the *rahas* to date are Rizvi, *Urdū*, part 1, pp. 71–194, 212–24; and Qureshi, *Wajid*, 16–22, 30–38, 138–51. More recently, see Genoveva Castro, "Wājid 'Alī Shāh Plays Krishna's Stolen Flute: The Multiplicity of Voices in the King of Awadh's Dramatic Work," unpublished doctoral dissertation, University of Washington, 2016.

157. Platts, *Dictionary*, 609. Sharar wrote that *rahas* was a *vaiṣṇava* performance tradition developed in Braj, and conveyed to Lucknow by performers from Mathura who inspired the king. This has been rejected by other authors, who believe that Sharar is confusing *rāsalīlā* with *rahas*. Sharar, *Lucknow*, 64, 146.

158. Syed Masud Hasan Rizavi, (1959–1960). "On 'Urdu Drama Aur Stage,'" *Indian Literature* 3, no. 1 (1959–60): 138–40; Taj, *Court*; Kathryn Hansen, *Grounds for Play: The "Nauṭaṅkī" Theatre of North India* (Berkeley: University of California Press, 1992), 75–76.

159. Shah, *Banī*, 310.

160. Sinh, *Wajid*, 90–103.

161. Trivedi, *Making*, 115–17.

162. Shah, *Banī*, 310.

163. Sharar, *Lucknow*, 64.

164. Kumari, "Contribution," 135.

165. Sinh, *Wajid*, 99.

166. Qureshi, *Wajid*, 32. For Ifrit in *qiṣṣā* and *dāstān* see Pritchett, *Marvelous*.

167. Shah, *Banī*, 320.

168. Ascertaining the full size of Wajid Ali's family is difficult: apart from his three *nikāḥ* (contractual, highest status) wives, he married hundreds of women. The *mut'a* ("pleasure")

marriages were fixed-term contracts. Should a *mut'a* wife become pregnant, she would be elevated to an intermediate rank (*mahal*). Some *mut'a* contracts were set for fifty years, while others were brief, and Wajid Ali occasionally divorced and remarried the same women. In 1879 the British government counted one living *nikāḥ* wife, and "about" 262 *mut'a*. See WBSA, poll file 98, proc. 1–12, May 1879, p. 211; cf. Llewellyn-Jones, *Last*, 127, 144.

169. Sharar, *Lucknow*, 71.

170. E.g., Tanika Sarkar, *Hindu Wife, Hindu Nation: Community, Religion, and Cultural Nationalism* (Bloomington: Indiana University Press, 2001); Geraldine Forbes, *Women in Modern India* (Cambridge, UK: Cambridge University Press, 2001), 10–63; Gail Minault, *Secluded Scholars: Women's Education and Muslim Social Reform in Colonial India* (New Delhi: Oxford University Press, 1998); Lata Mani, *Contentious Traditions: The Debate on Sati in Colonial India* Berkeley: University of California Press, 1998); Ruby Lal, *Coming of Age in Nineteenth-Century India: The Girl-Child and the Art of Playfulness* (Cambridge, UK: Cambridge University Press, 2013).

171. E.g. SVNPP vol. 13 (1880), p. 410; vol. 17 (1884), p. 251; and vol. 20 (1887), pp. 142–43.

172. On the reform of women among "service gentry," see Faisal Fatehali Devji, "Gender and the Politics of Space: The Movement for Women's Reform, 1857–1900," in S. Sarkar and T. Sarkar, eds., *Women and Social Reform in Modern India: A Reader* (Ranikhet, India: Permanent Black, 2007), 99–114.

173. Shah, *Banī*, 308ff.

174. *Ustāds* were called *mugannī*, implying singer and musician. Named *mugannī*s include Inayat Husain Khan, Ali Bakhsh, Taj Khan, Ghulam Husain Khan, Pir Khan, Faisal Imam, Haidar Khan, Ghulam Muhammad *qanūn-nivāz*, and Ahmad Khan.

175. Shah, *Banī*, 332.

176. Shah, *Banī*, 319.

177. Shah, *Banī*, 312.

178. Shah, *Banī*, 312–13.

179. Shah, *Banī*, 365ff. Cf. Sachdeva, "Search," 181–83.

180. Sharar, *Lucknow*, 71.

181. NAI, Foreign, Political A, January 1862, p. 194.

182. WBSA political file 98, proc. 1–12, May 1879, p. 171. Wajid Ali treated his older wives particularly poorly, commenting, "The women are old and ugly, and can bear no more children; they are no use to me" (p. 231).

183. IOR, file I A, May 1887, pp. 232–37.

184. IOR, file S I, May 1889, pp. 37–44.

185. IOR, file S I, May 1889, pp. 37–44.

186. Banerjee, *Dangerous*, 65–69. English church ministers petitioned the government to reinstate portions of the C.D.A., but were rejected: see WBSA police file 189, proc. 10–14, November 1887, p. 153.

187. Maulvi Abdul Bari, *Taẕkirat-ul-Ḵhavātīn* (Lucknow, India: Nawal Kishor, 1930), 25–26; Vanita, *Gender*, 6. For *rekhtī* poetry, see Petievich, *When*.

188. On the implications of colonial attitudes to "public women," see Anna Morcom, *Illicit Worlds of Indian Dance: Cultures of Exclusion* (Oxford, UK: Oxford University Press, 2013).

189. Lois Ibsen al Faruqi, "Music, Musicians and Muslim Law," *Asian Music* 17, no. 1 (1985): 3–36.

190. K. S. Santha, *Begums of Awadh* (Varanasi, India: Bharati Prakashan, 1980), 210; Sharar, *Lucknow*, 71.

191. Sharar, *Lucknow*, 74.

192. IOR internal branch "A" proceedings, file I A, October 1887, no. 340.

193. Llewellyn-Jones, *Last*, 244.

194. Sayyid Manzzar Husain Kazmi, *Vājid ʿAlī Shāh: Unkī shāʾirī aur marṣiye* (Karachi: Shaukat Ali and Sons, 1991).

195. Wajid Ali had Baqir's *Bahar-al-anwár* (an encyclopaedia of Shiʿa history) printed in the mid-1830s; see Sprenger, *Report*, 5. He also wrote a history of the Prophet's family, see Tahir Hussain Ansari, "The Cultural and Literary Contribution of Nawab Wajid Ali Shah," *International Journal of English Language, Literature and Humanities* 2, no. 3 (2014): 181–89.

196. *Āḵḥbār-i Dār-ul-Salṯānat*, 20 September 1881, p. 15.

197. Including Kamaluddin (d. 1881–82), a specialist on Ibn Sina, who lectured in Calcutta. See Saiyid Athar Abbas Rizvi, *A Socio-Intellectual History of the Isnā ʿAsharī Shīʿīs in India* (New Delhi: Munshiram Manoharlal, 1986), 243.

198. Justin Jones, *Shiʿa Islam in Colonial India: Religion, Community and Sectarianism* (New York: Cambridge University Press, 2012), 46; Rizvi, *Socio-Intellectual*, 147, 158–59.

199. Rizvi, *Socio-Intellectual*, 147.

200. Saiyid Muhammad Husain Faqir, *Al-durr al-manẓud fi radd-i bidʿāt al-Maulūd* (Delhi: Matba-i Quddusi, 1891).

201. Other forms of sonic representation of his power, including the twenty-one-gun salute, had been denied him. For Wajid Ali's complaint, see WBSA political File 98, proc. 1–12, May 1879, p. 186. Cf. Llewellyn-Jones, 246–47. This slight was discussed in the press, e.g., in *The Bombay Times and Journal of Commerce*, 11 June 1856.

202. IOR file I A, October 1887, 339–50; Llewellyn-Jones, *Last*, 257.

203. IOR file I A, October 1887, 339–50.

204. Llewellyn-Jones, *Last*, 261–63.

205. Llewellyn-Jones, *Last*, 202, 215.

Chapter 5

1. Amlan Das Gupta, "Women and Music: The Case of North India," in B. Ray, ed., *Women of India: Colonial and Post-Colonial Periods* (New Delhi: Centre for Studies in Civilizations, 2005), 454–84.

2. Sachdeva, "In Search of the *Tawa'if*."

3. E.g., the illustrated verse depicting Ali Jan of the male (*mardān*) *ṯawāʾif*, perhaps from the mid-1860s, in Mir Yar Ali Jan Sahib's (1810–86) *Musaddas-i Benazīr*.

4. Sachdeva, "In Search of the *Tawa'if*," 91 and 103. See also Schofield, "The Courtesan Tale"; Morcom, *Illicit Worlds*.

5. Gupta, *Sexuality*.

6. Muhammad Fasihuddin Ranj, *Bahāristān-i-Nāz* (Meerut, India: Dar-ul-ʿAlum, 1869), 45.

7. M. A. Bari, *Taẕkirat-ul-ḵḥawātīn* (Lucknow, India: Naval Kishor, 1930?), 117 and 133–34. For more on these anthologies, see Williams, "Songs."

8. Bibi Ratna Kuvar, *Premratna* (Banaras, India: Sultan-i-Hind, 1863), i–ii.

9. Ulrike Stark, "Knowledge in Context: Raja Shivaprasad as Hybrid Intellectual and People's Educator," in M. S. Dodson and B. A. Hatcher, eds., *Trans-Colonial Modernities in South Asia* (Abingdon, UK: Routledge, 2012), 68–91.

10. G. A. Grierson, *The Modern Vernacular Literature of Hindustan* (Calcutta: Asiatic Society, 1889), 99.

11. Cf. Minault, *Secluded*, 24; C. M. Naim, *Urdu Texts and Contexts: The Selected Essays* (Delhi: Permanent Black, 2004), 202–24.

12. Cf. Ruby Lal, *Domesticity and Power in the Early Mughal World* (Cambridge, UK: Cambridge University Press, 2005).

13. Devji, "Gender"; Minault, *Secluded*; Barbara Metcalf, "Islam and Power in Colonial India: The Making and Unmaking of a Muslim Princess," *American Historical Review* 116, no. 1 (2011): 1–30; Archambault, "Becoming."

14. Manuel, *Ṭhumrī*, 74–75.

15. Shah, *Parīk͟hāna*, 21.

16. Much of the information in this chapter is taken from the official reports of the 1903 court case *Nawab Nuzhutuddowla Abbas Hossain Khan versus Mirza Kurratulain and Others* (henceforth *Khan versus Kurratulain*), brought before the High Court of Calcutta, kept in the possession of Khas Mahal's living descendants. I am grateful to Dr. S. A. Sadiq for sharing these documents with me. Here, see p. 924.

17. See Rosie Llewellyn-Jones, *A Very Ingenious Man: Claude Martin in Early Colonial India* (Oxford, UK: Oxford University Press, 1992).

18. Rosie Llewellyn-Jones, *A Man of the Enlightenment in Eighteenth-century India: The Letters of Claude Martin 1766–1800* (Delhi: Permanent Black, 2003), 162fn31; Khas Mahal discussed this ancestry herself in a letter to the British Agent, dated 24 September 1883; *Khan versus Kurratulain*, p. 351.

19. Santha, *Begums*, 209; Sachdeva, "Search," 165; Azhar, *King*, vol. 2, p. 38.

20. Shah, *Parīkhāna*, 21.

21. Khas Mahal introduced a number of women, including Suleiman Pari, Ajaib Khanum (Ajaib Pari), Sukh Badan Wali (Wajeer Pari), Shah Buksh *K͟hawāṣṣs*, Altaf Buksh *K͟hawāṣṣs*, Nur Afshan Pari, and Bilkis Pari. See Santha, *Begums*, 211.

22. Shah, *Parīkhāna*, 83–84.

23. Santha, *Begums*, 212. To impede this alleged plot, Janab-i-Alia married Wajid Ali to a daughter of Ali Naqi Khan, Nawab Akhtar Mahal (Raunaq Ara Begum) in June 1851. See Bhatt, *Life*, 61; Sleeman, *Journey*, vol. 1, pp. lxxiii–lxxiv.

24. Wali, *Sorrows*, 10.

25. For the genealogy of Wajid Ali Shah, see Christopher Buyers, *The Royal Ark*, www.royalark.net/India4/oudh15.htm, accessed 5 November 2013.

26. *Khan versus Kurratulain*, 165.

27. NAI foreign, political, 27 November 1858, nos. 503–16; foreign, political, 27 May 1858, nos. 503–6.

28. Santha, *Begums*, 214–16.

29. Letter from Nawab Khas Mahal Begum to Sir J. L. M. Lawrence, 30 June, 1864, see IOR/L/PS/6/534, coll 2/19, June–Oct 1864. Cf. NAI foreign, political A, November 1864, nos. 269–70.

30. See Al Faruqi, "Music"; David Pinault, *Horse of Karbala: Muslim Devotional Life in India* (Basingstoke, UK: Palgrave, 2001); Regula Qureshi, "Islamic Music in an Indian Environment: The Shi'a Majlis," *Ethnomusicology* 25, no. 1 (1981): 41–71.

31. Sharar, *Lucknow*, 139, 149. For female orators (*zakira*), see Diana D'Souza, "Gendered Ritual and the Shaping of Shi'ah Identity," in K. Pemberton and M. Nijhawan, eds. *Shared Idioms, Sacred Symbols, and the Articulation of Identities in South Asia* (New York: Routledge, 2009), 198–201.

32. IOR/L/PS/6/534, coll. 2/19, June–October 1864. For patronage by queens, see Gregory C. Kozlowski, "Private Lives and Public Piety: Women and the Practice of Islam in Mughal India,"

in G. R. G. Hambly, ed., *Women in the Medieval Islamic World: Power, Patronage, and Piety* (New York: St. Martin's Press, 1998), 469–88.

33. Gregory C. Kozlowski, "Muslim Women and the Control of Property in North India," in Sarkar and Sarkar, *Women*, p. 22.

34. IOR/L/PS/6/534, coll. 2/19, June–October 1864.

35. Cf. Chatterjee, *Gender*; Michael Fisher, "Women and the Feminine in the Court and High Culture of Awadh, 1772–1856," in Hambly, *Women*, 489–520.

36. WBSA, political, file 98, proc. 1–2, May 1879, p. 161. Hakim Muhammad Masih was Khas Mahal's principal agent; *Khan versus Kurratulain*, p. 551.

37. Shah, *Parīk̲h̲āna*, 65–66.

38. Shah, *Nājo*. Khas Mahal's *ṭhumrī*s are also available in twentieth-century anthologies, including Muhammad Shaik Rahat Ali and Narahar Shambhurav Bhave, *Ṭhumrī-saṅgraha*, vol. 2 (Baroda, India: Kachupura, 1949), 33.

39. Shah, *Nāju*, 25; Pravin, *Nājo*, 12. The *nasta'līq* orthography differs from Brajbhasha conventional forms. In particular, Khas Mahal aspirated unexpected consonants, such as *lambo-dh-are* as opposed to *lambo-d-are*, and chose nonaspirated forms in unlikely places, as in *bi-ga-no* rather than *bi-gha-no*.

40. Shah, *Nāju*, 76–77; cf. Pravin, *Nājo*, 37.

41. Parvati has a musical role, especially relating to Rāg Dipak; see Brown, "Hindustani," 65, 187n17.

42. Shah, *Nāju*, 71; Pravin, *Nājo*, 34.

43. In Shi'a Islam *Panj-tan*, "The Five" are the Prophet, Fatimah al-Zahra, Ali, Hasan, and Husain. According to the *ḥadīth* of the People of the Cloak (*ahl-e kisā'*), these five comprise the *ahl-e bait*, the immediate family of the Prophet. Karen G. Ruffle, *Gender, Sainthood, and Everyday Practice in South Asian Shi'ism* (Chapel Hill: University of North Carolina Press, 2011), 53.

44. For other instances of *avatār* expressing Islamic concepts, see Eaton, *Rise*, 289–90; Carol Salomon, "The Cosmogonic Riddles of Lalan Fakir," in A. Appadurai, F. J. Korom, and M. A. Mills, eds., *Gender, Genre, and Power in South Asian Expressive Traditions* (Philadelphia: University of Philadelphia Press, 1991), 294.

45. Shah, *Nāju*, 79–81, 138–43.

46. Bari, *Taẓkirat*, 120.

47. *Khan versus Kurratulain*, pp. 761–62; cf. p. 349. Her cousin, Jahandar Mirza, commented that the *Diwān* compositions were mostly "love poems."

48. Vanita, *Gender*, 6. A collection of Khas Mahal's *ghazal*s is known as *Bayāẓ-i 'Ishq* ("Diary of Love"); see Bhatt, *Life*, 139.

49. Khas Mahal, *Masnavī-i-'Ālam* (Calcutta: Runaq Bakhsh, 1866). The only extant copy I have traced is incomplete.

50. Mahal, *Masnavī-i-'Ālam*, 101–13, 124f. (*ghazal*); also 113–24 (*ṭhumrī*).

51. *Khan versus Kurratulain*, pp. 77, 761. Khas Mahal did not know English.

52. *Khan versus Kurratulain*, pp. 761–762, 803.

53. Thursday is commonly associated with remembering the dead. Qureshi, *Islamic*, 45.

54. *Khan versus Kurratulain*, p. 803. Pyare Saheb's witness.

55. *Khan versus Kurratulain*, p. 915.

56. In later years, Wajid Ali attempted to prevent Khas Mahal from selling her properties. Wajid Ali Shah to Secretary to the Government of India, 28 September 1886. IOR/R/1/1/782, file I A March 1887, nos. 238–41.

57. WBSA, political 15C, proc. B, 94–98, March 1883.

58. Letters from Wajid Ali Shah, 28 September 1886, and C. Macaulay, 14 January 1887, both IOR/R/1/1/782, file I A, May 1887, nos. 238–41.

59. Cf. *parda* protocols in Bhopal. See Metcalf, "Islam."

60. For Rajput parallels, see Ramya Sreenivasan, "Drudges, Dancing Girls, Concubines: Female Slaves in Rajput Polity, 1500–1850," in I. Chatterjee and R. M. Eaton, eds., *Slavery and South Asian History* (Bloomington: Indiana University Press, 2006), 143–44.

61. For categories of female performer, see Schofield, "Courtesan"; Morcom, *Illicit*, 32–41. For domestic women in political historiography, see Indrani Chatterjee, introduction to *Unfamiliar Relations: Family and History in South Asia* (New Brunswick, NJ: Rutgers University Press, 2004), 3–45.

62. The following information is taken from the testimonies of *k̲h̲awāṣṣ* women throughout *Khan versus Kurratulain.*

63. Cf. Ruby Lal, "Historicizing the Harem: The Challenge of a Princess's Memoir," *Feminist Studies* 30, no. 3 (2004): 591.

64. *Khan versus Kurratulain*, p. 234.

65. *Khan versus Kurratulain*, p. 254.

66. For *ḥarams* in early nineteenth-century Lucknow, see Safi Ahmad, *Two Kings of Awadh, Muhammad Ali Shah and Amjad Ali Shah (1837–1847)* (Aligarh, India: P. C. Dwadash Shreni & Co., 1971), 91–94.

67. *Khan versus Kurratulain*, pp. 76, 255, 237, 251.

68. *Khan versus Kurratulain*, p. 1042.

69. *Khan versus Kurratulain*, p. 555.

70. Auction handbill, *Khan versus Kurratulain*, p. 1041.

71. Wade, *Imaging*, pp. 72–101.

72. *Khan versus Kurratulain*, p. 231. For *naẕr* as a graded "act of incorporation" see Bernard Cohn, "Representing Authority in Victorian India," in E. Hobsbawm and T. Ranger, eds., *The Invention of Tradition* (Cambridge, UK: Cambridge University Press, 1983), 168–69. For its poetic connotations, see Woodman Taylor, "Penetrating Gazes: The Poetics of Sight and Visual Display in Popular Indian Cinema," *Contributions to Indian Sociology* 36 (2002): 303–4.

73. *Khan versus Kurratulain*, pp. 243–45.

74. Walter Benjamin, *Illuminations* (New York: Harcourt, Brace and World, 1968).

75. Recordings began in India in 1899, but the commercial industry only advanced from 1902. See Gerry Farrell, "The Early Days of the Gramophone Industry in India: Historical, Social and Musical Perspectives," *British Journal of Ethnomusicology* 2 (1993): 31–53; Adrian McNeil, "Making Modernity Audible: *Sarodiya*s and the Early Recording Industry," *South Asia: Journal of South Asian Studies* 27, no. 3 (20040: 315–37; Das Gupta, "Women and Music"; Sachdeva, "Search," 286–92.

76. Sachdeva, "Search," 239–58, 299–305.

77. This set forms part of the Parimal Ray Collection, Centre for Studies in Social Sciences, Calcutta.

78. Advertisements in the *Bombay Chronicle*, 24 June 1921; 10 March 1923; 24 January 1924. He also gave concerts in Baliwala's Grand Theatre on 27 June 1921 and in Bandra at the Cinema de Luxe on 11 March 1923. I am grateful to Kathryn Hansen for drawing my attention to these announcements.

79. Peter Manuel, "The Evolution of Modern Thumrī," *Ethnomusicology* 30, no. 3 (1986): 479.

80. Michael Kinnear, *The Gramophone Company's First Indian Recordings 1899–1908* (Bombay: Popular Prakashan, 1994), 27–28, 36.

81. Kinnear, *Gramophone*, 104, 134–35, 176–77, 178, 222, 241–42, 265.

82. Manuel, "Evolution," p. 489f10. Further analysis of Pyare Saheb's recordings may improve our understanding of his voice culture. While earlier scholars have always considered him "falsetto," there are other possibilities, such as a "mixed voice" (*voce mista*). See James A. Stark, *Bel Canto: A History of Vocal Pedagogy* (Toronto: University of Toronto Press, 1999), 86–87; Naomi André, *Voicing Gender: Castrati, Travesty, and the Second Woman in Early-Nineteenth-Century Italian Opera* (Bloomington: Indiana University Press, 2006), 43–44.

83. Ashok Ranade, "The Musical Evolution of the Gazal," *National Centre for the Performing Arts Quarterly Journal* 3, no. 1 (1974): 23–25.

84. Liner notes accompanying cassette recording (1994). *Chairman's Choice, Great Memories: Peara Saheb, Ustad Majooddin Khan*, RPG and HMV. A biography of Pyare Saheb in Anon., "Gramophone Celebrities—6," *The Record News: Annual Magazine of Society of Indian Record Collectors (SIRC)*, 2006, pp. 14–15, suggests that his father was a musician in Wajid Ali Shah's employ, and that he also studied *kathak*. I have found no evidence for this, and according to Pyare Saheb's own witness his father was not a professional musician.

85. Date of birth calculated from *Khan versus Kurratulain*, p. 764. His family history was widely discussed in this lawsuit. See, e.g., pp. 80, 675–76.

86. *Khan versus Kurratulain*, p. 794.

87. *Khan versus Kurratulain*, pp. 76, 343.

88. *Khan versus Kurratulain*, p. 343.

89. *Khan versus Kurratulain*, p. 767.

90. *Khan versus Kurratulain*, p. 255.

91. *Khan versus Kurratulain*, p. 551.

92. *Khan versus Kurratulain*, pp. 71, 98.

93. *Khan versus Kurratulain*, p. 76.

94. *Khan versus Kurratulain*, pp. 76, 207, 213.

95. *Khan versus Kurratulain*, p. 343.

96. Khas Mahal was also a guardian of Pyare Saheb's mother.

97. *Khan versus Kurratulain*, p. 220.

98. *Khan versus Kurratulain*, p. 74.

99. *Khan versus Kurratulain*, pp. 214–15.

100. *Khan versus Kurratulain*, pp. 75, 357.

101. According to the document, Khas Mahal had never recognized their mother as her legal daughter-in-law. *Khan versus Kurratulain*, pp. 91, 601.

102. *Khan versus Kurratulain*, pp. 96, 608.

103. *Khan versus Kurratulain* p. 610.

104. Das Gupta, "Women," 468.

105. Ghosh, *Oxford Encyclopaedia*, 835.

106. The daughter of his maternal aunt, Gulshan Ara Begum, and Mirza Kamer Kader. They later had a disagreement and informally separated, and Huzarara moved to Lucknow. Their only daughter died before 1900.

107. *Khan versus Kurratulain*, pp. 216, 232, 819.

108. Sarafrazo Jan was the daughter of Bara Mirza, Chote Mirza's brother. She later quarreled with Pyare Saheb and removed to Chandernagore. *Khan versus Kurratulain*, pp. 790, 819.

109. *Khan versus Kurratulain*, p. 245.

110. *Khan versus Kurratulain*, p. 782.

111. *Khan versus Kurratulain*, pp. 76, 101.

112. Sharma, *Musicians*, 275; Ghosh, *Oxford Encyclopaedia*, 540.

113. Ghosh, *Oxford Encyclopaedia*, 540.

114. Lakshminarayan Garg, *Hamāre Saṅgīt Ratna*, part 1 (Hathras, India: Sangeet Karyalaya), 213; Kinnear, *Gramophone Company*, 28.

115. Sharma, *Musicians*, 65.

116. Garg, *Hamāre*, 213.

117. For Pyare Saheb's later career, see "Gramaphone Celebrities: 6," 14–15.

118. According to one anecdote, Pyare Saheb hosted a *meḥfil* in his house in Banaras, attended by Rehmat Khan of Gwalior (1852–1922), Kallan Khan of Agra (d. 1925), Channa Khan *sāraṅgiya*, Bade Maina, Husna Bai, Suggan Bai, Vidyadhari Bai, Janghi Khan the harmonium player, and Bundu Khan *sāraṅgiya*. It was at this gathering that Pyare Saheb "discovered" Maujuddin Khan, the son of the *sitar* player Ghulam Hasan. See *Chairman's Choice*.

119. Ghosh, *Oxford Encyclopaedia*, 672; Sharma, *Musicians*, 138.

Chapter 6

1. See Sachedva, "Search," 326–31; Anon., *Exposition*; Kunal M. Parker, "'A Corporation of Superior Prostitutes': Anglo-Indian Legal Conceptions of Temple Dancing Girls, 1800–1914," *Modern Asian Studies* 32, no. 3 (1998): 559–633; Williams, "Songs between Cities."

2. Barlow, "Music," 1786; Bakhle, *Two*; Subrahmanian, "Faith"; Farrell, *Indian*; Das Gupta, "Women."

3. See, for example, NAI foreign, political A, February 1862, pp. 71–76; IOR file I A, October 1887, 339–50.

4. *The Englishman*, 10 April 1872; reprinted in *Times of India*, 13 April 1872.

5. According to the Bengal License Act of 1879, the latter orders of performer were listed with other trades including "Stamp-vendors. Photographers. Dancers. Actors. Snake-charmers. Musicians. Singers. Jugglers. Planters." See *Amrita Bazar Patrika*, 17 July 1879. For street music, see Banerjee, *Parlour*.

6. Swati Chattopadhyay, *Representing Calcutta: Modernity, Nationalism, and the Colonial Uncanny* (London: Routledge, 2006), 138–39.

7. Tithi Bhattacharya, *The Sentinels of Culture: Class, Education, and the Colonial Intellectual in Bengal (1848–85)* (New Delhi: Oxford University Press, 2005).

8. E.g., *The Times of India*, 2 December 1885, p. 3.

9. John McGuire, *The Making of a Colonial Mind: A Quantitative Study of the Bhadralok in Calcutta, 1857–1885* (Canberra: Australian National University, 1983); Peter Marshall, "Masters and Banians in Eighteenth-Century Calcutta," in B. B. King and M. N. Pearson, eds., *The Age of Partnership: Europeans in Asia before Dominion* (Honolulu: University Press of Hawaii, 1979), 191–14; S. N. Mukherjee, "Class, Caste, and Politics in Calcutta, 1815–38," in E. Leach and S. M. Mukherjee, eds., *Elites in South Asia* (London: Cambridge University Press, 1970), 33–78; Sinha, *Calcutta*.

10. Chattopadhyay, *Representing*, 138.

11. Chatterjee, *Texts*; Andrew Sartori, "Emancipation as Heteronomy: The Crisis of Liberalism in Later Nineteenth-Century Bengal," *Journal of Historical Sociology* 17, no. 1 (2004), 56–86;

Sudiptu Kaviraj, "Laughter and Subjectivity: The Self-Ironical Tradition in Bengali Literature," *Modern Asian Studies* 34, no. 2 (2000): 379–406; Rakesh Batabyal, "Who the 'Bhadralok' Was," *Economic and Political Weekly* 40, no. 35 (2005): 3834–36.

12. Chatterjee, *Nation*; Sudipta Kaviraj, "The Two Histories of Literary Culture in Bengal," in S. Pollock, ed., *Literary Cultures in History: Reconstructions from South Asia* (Berkeley and Los Angeles: University of California Press, 2003), 503–66.

13. Jon Barlow, "The Sarod: Instrument Analysis," in A. Das Gupta, ed., *Music and Modernity: North Indian Classical Music in an Age of Reproduction* (Kolkata: Thema, 2007), 124–55.

14. Kippen, *Tabla*, 69–82.

15. Sharar, *Lucknow*, 135. Suggestions of other dates are summarized in Jon Barlow, "The Sarod: Its Forms and Voices," in Das Gupta, *Music*, 89–123. The year 1900 has recently been identified as the most likely date by David Lunn and Max Katz; personal communication, June 2014. This family lineage is the focus of Katz, *Lineage of Loss*.

16. Miner, *Sitar*, 154; Mitra, "Music," 182; Chatterjee, *Śāstrīya*, 212, 253. The family's connection to Bengal continued into the twentieth century with the *sitār* player Waliullah Khan, Niamatullah's grandson. Miner, *Sitar*, 153.

17. See O. Wright, "A Preliminary Version of the *Kitāb al-Adwār*," *Bulletin of the School of Oriental and African Studies* 58, no. 3 (195): 455–78.

18. Sharar, *Lucknow*, 137.

19. Rais Ahmad Jafri, *Vājid ʿAlī Shāh aur unka ʿahed* (Lahore, Pakistan: Kitab Manzil, 1958), 149; McNeil, "Making," 320.

20. *The Englishman*, 10 April 1872; reprinted in *The Times of India*, 13 April 1872. See chapter 5.

21. By Muhammad Riza bin Abul Kasim Tabataba, a comprehensive treatise on the arts of poetry written for Wajid Ali Shah. British Library, or. 1811, f. 211b.

22. Sharar, *Lucknow*, 138.

23. The *Shams al-aswāt*, the *Usūl al-Naghmat-i Āṣafī*, and the *Saṅgīt Sarswati*. I am grateful to Max Katz and Katherine Schofield for their thoughts on this MS.

24. See Basat Khan's prefatory letter in Kshetramohan Goswami, *Saṅgītasāra* (Calcutta: Prakrit Press, 1869).

25. Dilipkumar Mukhopadhyay, *Bhārater Saṅgīt Guṇī*, part 1 (Kolkata: A. Mukherji, 1977), 61–66, 92–93.

26. On this family, see B. Chaudhuri, "Eastern India," in T. Raychaudhuri, I. Habib, and D. Kumar, *The Cambridge Economic History of India*, vol. 2 (Cambridge, UK: Cambridge University Press, 1983), 113.

27. Mukhopadhyay, *Bhārater*, part 1, 61.

28. Max Katz, private communication, September 2014.

29. Goswami, *Saṅgītasāra*.

30. Miner, *Sitar*, 119. Karam Imam believed Basat had invented the instrument himself.

31. Ghosh, *Oxford*, 38.

32. Miner, *Sitar*, 150.

33. Miner, *Sitar*, 140, 149–150.

34. Miner, *Sitar*, 140. For the Bhawal family, see Roper Lethbridge, *The Golden Book of India* (Delhi: Aakar Books, 2005 [1893]), 436; and Partha Chatterjee, *A Princely Impostor? The Strange and Universal History of the Kumar of Bhawal* (Princeton, NJ: Princeton University Press, 2002).

35. Miner, *Sitar*, 150.

36. Kippen, *Tabla*, 73–74.

37. Chatterjee, *Śāstrīya*, 278.

38. Sharar, *Lucknow*, 139.

39. Cited in Jafri, *Vājid*, 149.

40. Chatterjee, *Śāstrīya*, 285–87; Kippen, *Tabla*, 74.

41. Ghosh, *Oxford*, 687.

42. Goswami, *Bhāratīya*, 226; Chatterjee, *Śāstrīya*, 212.

43. Chatterjee, *Śāstrīya*, 212, 278.

44. Chatterjee, *Śāstrīya*, 213; Sharma, *Musicians*, 239.

45. Sharma, *Musicians* 103.

46. There is a suggestion that he studied *sitār* with Basat Khan, perhaps at Ranaghat. Chatterjee, *Śāstrīya*, 213; Sharma, *Musicians*, 217.

47. Chatterjee, *Śāstrīya*, 211; Sachdeva, "Search," 221.

48. Mukhopadhyay, *Bhārater*, part 2, 37.

49. Chatterjee, *Śāstrīya*, 212; Sanyal, "Music," 311; Sharma, *Musicians*, 97.

50. Charles Capwell, "Sourindro Mohun Tagore and the National Anthem Project," *Ethnomusicology* 31, no. 3 (1987): 407–30.

51. Wade, *Khyāl*, 41; Sharma, *Musicians*, 82.

52. See Sharma, *Musicians*, 46, 216; Sourindro Mohan Tagore, *Public Opinion and Official Communications, about the Bengal Music School and Its President* (Calcutta: Panchanun Mookerjee, 1876), supplement, 261–62.

53. Chatterjee, *Śāstrīya*, 254.

54. Sourindro Mohan Tagore, *A Brief Account of the Tagore Family* (Calcutta: I. C. Bose, 1868), 11; Anon., "Śaurīndramohan Ṭhakur," *Saṅgīta Bijñan Prabeśika* 2, no. 11 (1925): 527–30.

55. Anon., *The Tagores of Calcutta* (Calcutta: Indian Mirror Office, 1880), 6.

56. Pramantha Tagore, "Music and the Emerging City: A Study of Centres of Musical Patronage in North Calcutta (1800–1950)," unpublished paper presented at the Department of English, Jadavpur University, 26 June 2013, p. 14.

57. On Gopi Mohan: James W. Furrell, *The Tagore Family: A Memoir* (Calcutta: Thacker, Spink and Co., 1892), 69–72.

58. Furrell, *Tagore*, 81, 128. Cf. Tagore, "Music," 14.

59. He was twice appointed to the Bengal Legislative Council, and to the Viceroy's Legistlative Council. Anon., "Tagores," 5–13.

60. Lokenath Ghosh, *The Modern History of the Indian Chiefs, Rajas, Zamindars &c.* part 2 (Calcutta: J. N. Ghose, 1881), 172.

61. *Amrita Bazar Patrika*, 22 September, 1887, p. 1; *The Times of India*, 5 October 1885, p. 5; McGuire, *Making*, 24.

62. On Tagore's musicological writings, see Williams, "Music, Lyrics."

63. Furrell, *Tagore*, 173ff.

64. Anon., "Tagores," 23.

65. Tagore, *Public*, 29.

66. Tagore, *Public*, 3.

67. Ghosh, *Modern*, 50.

68. Ghosh, *Modern*, 56–59, 63, 142.

69. Ghosh, *Modern*, 259.

70. Tagore, *Public*, 46.

71. Tagore, *Public*, 279.

72. Tagore, *Universal*, 87.

73. Cf. Bakhle, *Two*, 62–82; Capwell, "Musical."

74. Cf. Vidyarthi, "Melody," 20–21.

75. Tagore, *Public*, 37.

76. Tagore, *Public*, 7.

77. Tagore, *Opinion*, 52.

78. Tagore, *Public*, supplement, 162.

79. Author of *Bahulīn Tattva* (Calcutta: Prakrit Press, 1874).

80. Lokenath Ghosh attempted to elevate Kshetramohan's family by including him in *The Modern History*, 329–330.

81. On his contributions to musical scholarship, see Williams, "Music, Lyrics."

82. See Saha, *Aspects*, 304–5; Capwell, "Musical," 144.

83. Tagore, *Universal*, 88; Tagore, *Public*, supplement, 47.

84. Tagore, *Public*, 40.

85. Tagore, *Public*, 9; Dasgupta, *Heritage*, 110 (later the Ramsaran Sangita Mahavidyalaya).

86. Sarada Prasada Ghosh, *The Music of Hindustan* (Calcutta: Thos. S. Smith, 1879). Originally published in the *Calcutta Review*.

87. Tagore, *Public*, 2–4; supplement, 261.

88. Cited in Subramanian, *Tanjore*, 66.

89. Ghosh, *Music's*, 20. See also Subramanian, "Master," 15.

90. Subramanian, "Master," 14–16; *Tanjore*, 65–67.

91. For a typical Tagorean entertainment, see Marchioness of Dufferin and Ava, *Our Viceregal Life in India: Selections from My Journal 1884–1888* (London: John Murray, 1890), 275–77.

92. E.g., Tagore's *Fifty Stanzas in Sanskrit, in honor of H.R.H. the Prince of Wales*, written to commemorate the Prince's 1875 tour: Tagore, *Public*, 28, 41. J. M. Tagore published a Bangla song for the same occasion: Jatindra Mohan Tagore, *Welcome Song* (Calcutta: n.p., 1876).

93. As reported in *The Statesman*, 11 August 1876. Tagore, *Public*, 36–39.

94. Cited in Miner, *Sitar*, 58.

95. Miner, *Sitar*, 59.

96. Accession no. 89.4.163.

97. Cf. Karam Imam in Miner, *Sitar*, 57–58; Khan, *Sarmāya-yi 'Ishrat*, 278.

98. Capwell, "Musical," 145–47; Anon., "Saṅgītācārjẏa Kālīprasanna Bidẏābinoda Mahāśaẏer Jībanī," *Saṅgīta Bijñān Prabeśikā* 2, no. 6 (1925), 284–89.

99. Tagore, *Public*, 45.

100. Tagore, "Music," p. 18.

101. George Wheeler, *India in 1875–76: The Visit of the Prince of Wales* (London: Chapman and Hall, 1876), 199. Cf. J. Fayrer, *Notes of the Visits to India of Their Royal Highnesses the Prince of Wales and Duke of Edinburgh 1870–1875–6* (London: Kerby and Endean, 1879), 73.

102. Gay, *Prince*, 205–6.

103. Gay, *Prince*, 206.

104. Mary Elizabeth Corbet, *A Pleasure Trip to India, During the Visit of H.R.H. the Prince of Wales* (London: W. H. Allen, 1880), 52.

105. Wheeler, *India*, 200.

106. Wheeler, *India*, 200.

107. Gay, *Prince*, 204–7.

108. Anon., *An Exposition*.

109. Farrell, "Early," 37.

110. When the Shah of Persia visited London in 1873, he was entertained at Covent Garden with a rendition of *Tāza ba Tāza*; reported in Calcutta's *Urdu Guide*, 28 June 1873, p. 399.

111. See also Sourindo Mohan Tagore, *Six Principal Rágas, with a brief view of Hindu Music* (Calcutta: Calcutta Central Press, 1877).

112. Tagore, *Public*, 4–9.

113. *Halishahar Pattrica*, 30 January 1874; Tagore, *Public*, 5.

114. Tagore, *Public*, supplement, 24–26.

115. February 1877; Tagore, *Public*, 46–47.

116. Sourindro Mohan Tagore, *The Ten Principal Avatars of the Hindus, with a Short History of Each Incarnation and Directions for the Representation of the Murtis as Tableaux Vivants* (Calcutta: Stanhope Press, 1880).

117. Tagore, *Ten Principal Avatars*, i.

118. Tagore, *Ten Principal Avatars*, 1–7.

119. Shah, *Banī*, 319.

120. Vidyarthi, "Melody," 19; Mukhopadhyay, *Aýodhýar*, 168.

121. Shah, *Banī*, 319.

122. Tagore, *Public*, supplement, 162.

123. *The Statesman*, 11 August 1876; Tagore, *Public*, 38.

124. Tagore, *Public*, 45.

125. Goswami, *Bhāratīya*, 226; Chatterjee, *Śāstrīya*, 212.

126. Vidyarthi, "Melody," p. 19.

127. Ray, *Music*, 92. Cf. Amanda Weidman, "Gender and the Politics of Voice: Colonial Modernity and Classical Music in South India," *Cultural Anthropology* 18, no. 2 (2003): 204.

128. See Miner, *Sitar*, 151; Jafri, *Vājid*, 150.

129. Mukhopadhyay, *Aýodhýar*, 169; Monilal Nag, "Vishnupur: The Famous Gharana of Bengal," *Indian Musicological Society Journal* 4, no. 1 (1973): 46–47.

130. Miner, *Sitar*, 151.

131. Gopal Candra Cakravarty went on to teach Ramprasanna Bandyopadhyay, *guru* to Gokul Nag. Interview with Mita Nag, 6 September 2012.

132. Mukhopadhyay, *Bhārater*, part 2, 169.

133. Tagore, *Public*, 44; Miner, *Sitar*, 154.

134. Sharma, *Musicians*, 90–92.

135. Tagore, "Music," 4–7; Soumitra Das, "Pictures of Silent Music," *Telegraph, Calcutta: Metro*, 30 April 2004. I am grateful to Bhupendra Krishna Ghosh's son, Jayantanath Babu.

136. This kind of literature continues apace; e.g., Kumarprasad Mukhopadhyay, *Maýhphil*, (Kolkata: Dey's Publishing, 2001).

137. See also Gautam Ghosh, "Nobility or Utility? *Zamindars*, Businessmen, and *Bhadralok* as Curators of the Indian Nation in Satyajit Ray's *Jalsaghar (The Music Room)*," *Modern Asian Studies* 52, no. 2 (2018): 683–715.

138. The son of the educationist Bhudev Mukhopadhyay (1827–94). See C. A. Bayly, *Recovering Liberties: Indian Thought in the Age of Liberalism and Empire*, Cambridge, UK: Cambridge University Press, 2012), 162.

139. Mukundadeb Mukhopadhyay, *Āmār Dekhā Lok* (Calcutta: Bhudeb Publishing House, 1922), 168–77.

140. Sharma, *Musicians*, 279, 280; Chatterjee, *Śāstrīya*, 211, 280.

141. Most likely home to the descendants of Radhamohan Sarkar, a music lover of the 1830s. Banerjee, *Parlour*, 103.

142. Mukhopadhyay, *Āmār*, 169–70.

143. Bakhle, *Two*, 62–82.

144. For other patron households, see Chatterjee, *Śāstrīya*, 206–11.

145. Mukhopadhyay, *Āmār*, 172.

146. Mukhopadhyay, *Āmār*, 175; Chatterjee, *Śāstrīya*, 211, 280.

147. Mukhopadhyay, *Āmār*, 176.

148. Anon., "Jādabkṛṣṇa Basu," *Saṅgīta Bijñān Prabeśikā* 3, no. 4 (1926): 208.

149. Titled *Saṅgītadarpaṇa*. I have been unable to locate a copy.

150. Ghosh, *Modern*, 409; Ghosh, *Oxford*, 540. The *Oxford Encylopaedia* claims that Kesabcandra had studied *pakhāvaj* in the lineage of Lala Bhagwan Singh (Bhagwandas) of the Punjab (466–67), through Lala Harikishan and Lala Kevalkishan. who made their careers in Calcutta, and their Bengali disciples Ramcandra and Nimai Cakravarti (p. 697). Cf. Chatterjee, *Śāstrīya*, 281.

151. Chatterjee, *Śāstrīya*, 281–81; Ghosh, *Oxford*, 697–98.

152. Chatterjee, *Śāstrīya*, 281–84.

153. Tagore, *Public*, supplement, 261.

154. Jadugopal Mukhopadhyay, *Biplabī Jībaner Smṛti* (Kolkata: Indian Associated Publishers, 1363/1956), 155–56.

155. Ibid. Mukhopadhyay, *Biplabī Jībaner Smṛti*, 155–56; cf. Sharma, *Musicians*, 236, 242.

156. Chatterjee, *Śāstrīya*, 211; Ray, *Music*, 92.

157. Dhan Gopal Mukerji, *Caste and Outcast* (Stanford, CA: Stanford University Press, 2002), 57.

158. Mukerji, *Caste and Outcast*, 59.

159. E.g., Khan, *Sarmāya-yi 'Ishrat*, 4–5.

160. Hamilton, *Sitar*, 107–9. Murad Ali is also associated with Rampur and has been credited with the invention of the *sarod*. See Miner, *Sitar*, 135, 139, 209–10.

161. Ghosh, *Oxford*, 696.

162. Ray, *Music*, 92; Chatterjee, *Śāstrīya*, 211–12; Mukhopadhyay, *Aẏodhyar*, 166–67.

163. Mitra, "Music," 182–83; Sanyal "Music," 311; Chatterjee, *Śāstrīya*, 213.

164. He was distinguished for his *tāns*, *palta*, *tehrīr*, and *zamzama* techniques.

165. Vidyarthi, "Melody," 19.

166. See Gordon H. Chang's introduction in Mukerji, *Caste*, 1–40.

167. Dhan Gopal Mukerji, *My Brother's Face* (New York: E. P. Dutton, 1924), 130.

168. Mukerji, *Brother's*, 130. The decline in use of *rāga* Dipak is testified in other texts, including the *Maᶜdan-ul Mūsīqī*. See Vidyarthi, "Melody," 51.

169. Mukerji, *Caste*, 57.

170. Mukerji, *Caste*, 58.

171. Mukerji, *Caste*, 57.

172. Mukerji, *Caste*, 58.

173. Mukhopadhyay, *Aẏodhyar*.

174. Mukhopadhyay, *Aẏodhyar*, 166–67; *Bhārater*, part 2, 45.

175. Mukhopadhyay, *Bhārater*, part 2, 15–27.

176. Mukhopadhyay, *Bhārater*, part 2, 22.

177. Mukhopadhyay, *Āmār*, 171.

178. Mukhopadhyay, *Āmār*, 175.

179. Tagore, *Universal*, 60.

180. Mukhopadhyay, *Biplabī*, 155.

181. Musicians circulating in Rampur were documented in Mīr Yar Ali Jan, *Musaddas-i Benazīr* (Rampur, India: State Press, 1950).

Conclusion

1. For a recent example, see Daniel E. White, *From Little London to Little Bengal: Religion, Print, and Modernity in Early British India, 1793–1835* (Baltimore: John Hopkins University Press, 2013).

Index

Page numbers in italics refer to figures.